Psychology E

Personality and Individual Differences

Terence Butler
Southampton Solent University

Laura Scurlock-Evans
University of Worcester

Series editor:
Dominic Upton
University of Worcester

PEARSON

Harlow, England • London • New York • Boston • San Francisco • Toronto • Sydney
Auckland • Singapore • Hong Kong • Tokyo • Seoul • Taipei • New Delhi
Cape Town • São Paulo • Mexico City • Madrid • Amsterdam • Munich • Paris • Milan

PEARSON EDUCATION LIMITED
Edinburgh Gate
Harlow CM20 2JE
United Kingdom
Tel: +44 (0)1279 623623
Web: www.pearson.com/uk

First published 2013 (print and electronic)

ISBN: 978-0-273-73515-1 (print)
        978-0-273-73718-6 (PDF)
        978-1-4479-1599-7 (eText)

British Library Cataloguing-in-Publication Data
A catalogue record for the print edition is available from the British Library

Library of Congress Cataloging-in-Publication Data
Butler, Terence, 1950-
    Personality and individual differences / Terence Butler, Laura Scurlock-Evans.
        p. cm. -- (Psychology express)
    Includes bibliographical references and index.
    ISBN 978-0-273-73515-1 (pbk.)
    1. Personality. 2. Individual differences. I. Scurlock-Evans, Laura. II. Title.
    BF698.B883 2013
    155.2--dc23
                                2012030142

10 9 8 7 6 5 4 3 2 1
17 16 15 14 13

Print edition typeset in 9.5/12.5 Avenir LT Pro 45 Book by 3
Print edition printed and bound in Malaysia (CTP-VP)

NOTE THAT ANY PAGE CROSS REFERENCES REFER TO THE PRINT EDITION

Contents

The PsychologyExpress series

→ UNDERSTAND QUICKLY
→ REVISE EFFECTIVELY
→ TAKE EXAMS WITH CONFIDENCE

'All of the revision material I need in one place – a must for psychology undergrads.'
Andrea Franklin, Psychology student at Anglia Ruskin University

'Very useful, straight to the point and provides guidance to the student, while helping them to develop independent learning.'
Lindsay Pitcher, Psychology student at Anglia Ruskin University

'Engaging, interesting, comprehensive … it helps to guide understanding and boosts confidence.'
Megan Munro, Forensic Psychology student at Leeds Trinity University College

'Very useful … bridges the gap between Statistics textbooks and Statistics workbooks.'
Chris Lynch, Psychology student at the University of Chester

'The answer guidelines are brilliant, I wish I had had it last year.'
Tony Whalley, Psychology student at the University of Chester

'I definitely would (buy a revision guide) as I like the structure, the assessment advice and practice questions and would feel more confident knowing exactly what to revise and having something to refer to.'
Steff Copestake, Psychology student at the University of Chester

'The clarity is absolutely first rate … These chapters will be an excellent revision guide for students as well as providing a good opportunity for novel forms of assessment in and out of class.'
Dr Deaglan Page, Queen's University, Belfast

'Do you think they will help students when revising/working towards assessment? Unreservedly, yes.'
Dr Mike Cox, Newcastle University

'The revision guide should be very helpful to students preparing for their exams.'
Dr Kun Guo, University of Lincoln

'A brilliant revision guide, very helpful for students of all levels.'
Svetoslav Georgiev, Psychology student at Anglia Ruskin University

Introduction

Not only is psychology one of the fastest-growing subjects to study at university worldwide, it is also one of the most exciting and relevant subjects. Over the past decade the scope, breadth and importance of psychology have developed considerably. Important research work from as far afield as the UK, Europe, the USA and Australia has demonstrated the exacting research base of the topic and how this can be applied to all manner of everyday issues and concerns. Being a student of psychology is an exciting experience – the study of mind and behaviour is a fascinating journey of discovery. Studying psychology at the degree level brings with it new experiences, new skills and knowledge. As the Quality Assurance Agency (QAA) has stressed:

> psychology is distinctive in the rich and diverse range of attributes it develops – skills which are associated with the humanities (e.g. critical thinking and essay writing) and the sciences (hypotheses-testing and numeracy).

> (QAA, 2010, p. 5)

Recent evidence suggests that employers appreciate these skills and knowledge of psychology graduates, but in order to reach this pinnacle you need to develop your skills, further your knowledge and most of all successfully complete your degree to your maximum ability. The skills, knowledge and opportunities that you gain during your psychology degree will give you an edge in the employment field. The QAA stresses the high level of employment skills developed during a psychology degree:

> due to the wide range of generic skills, and the rigour with which they are taught, training in psychology is widely accepted as providing an excellent preparation for many careers. In addition to subject skills and knowledge, graduates also develop skills in communication, numeracy, teamwork, critical thinking, computing, independent learning and many others, all of which are highly valued by employers.

> (QAA, 2010, p. 2)

This book is part of the comprehensive new series, Psychology Express, which helps you achieve these aspirations. It is not a replacement for every single text, journal article, presentation and abstract you will read and review during the course of your degree programme. It is in no way a replacement for your lectures, seminars or additional reading. A top-rated assessment answer is likely to include considerable additional information and wider reading – and you are directed to some of these in this text. This revision guide is a conductor: directing you through the maze of your degree by providing an overview of your course, helping you formulate your ideas, and directing your reading.

Each book within Psychology Express presents a summary coverage of the key concepts, theories and research in the field, within an explicit framework of revision. The focus throughout all of the books in the series will be on how you should approach and consider your topics in relation to assessment and exams. Various features have been included to help you build up your skills and knowledge, ready for your assessments. More detail of the features can be found in the guided tour for this book on page viii.

By reading and engaging with this book, you will develop your skills and knowledge base and in this way you should excel in your studies and your associated assessments.

Psychology Express: Personality and Individual Differences is divided into 11 chapters and your course has probably been divided up into similar sections. However, we, the series authors and editor, must stress a key point: do not let the purchase, reading and engagement with the material in this text restrict your reading or your thinking. In psychology, you need to be aware of the wider literature and how it interrelates, and how authors and thinkers have criticised and developed the arguments of others. So even if an essay asks you about one particular topic, you need to draw on similar issues raised in other areas of psychology. There are, of course, some similar themes that run throughout the material covered in this text, but you can learn from the other areas of psychology covered in the other texts in this series as well as from material presented elsewhere.

We hope you enjoy this text and the others in the Psychology Express series, which cover the complete knowledge base of psychology:

- *Biological Psychology* (Emma Preece): covering the biological basis of behaviour, hormones and behaviour, sociobiology and evolutionary psychology and so on.
- *Cognitive Psychology* (Jonathan Catling and Jonathan Ling): including key material on perception, learning, memory, thinking and language.
- *Developmental Psychology* (Penney Upton): from pre-natal development through to old age, the development of individuals is considered. Childhood, adolescence and lifespan development are all presented.
- *Personality and Individual Differences* (Terence Butler and Laura Scurlock-Evans): normal and abnormal personality, psychological testing, intelligence, emotion and motivation are all covered in this book.
- *Social Psychology* (Jenny Mercer and Debbie Clayton): a critical perspective on social psychology is presented and includes attributions, attitudes and group relations (including close relationships).
- *Statistics in Psychology* (Catherine Steele, Holly Andrews and Dominic Upton): an overview of data analysis related to psychology is presented along with why we need statistics in psychology. Descriptive and inferential statistics, and both parametric and non-parametric analysis, are included.
- *Research Methods for Psychology* (Steve Jones and Mark Forshaw): research design, experimental methods, discussion of qualitative and quantitative methods and ethics are all presented in this text.

- *Conceptual and Historical Issues in Psychology* (Brian M. Hughes): the foundations of psychology and its development from a mere interest into a scientific discipline. The key conceptual issues of current-day psychology are also presented.

This book, and the other companion volumes in this series, should cover all your study needs (there will also be further guidance on the website). It will, obviously, need to be supplemented with further reading and this text directs you towards suitable sources. Hopefully, quite a bit of what you read here you will already have come across and the text will act as a jolt and to set your mind at rest – you do know the material in depth. Overall, we hope that you find this book useful and informative as a guide for both your study now and in your future as a successful psychology graduate.

Revision note

- Use evidence based on your reading, not on anecdotes or your 'common sense'.
- Show the examiner you know your material in depth – use your additional reading wisely.
- Remember to draw on a number of different sources: there is rarely one 'correct' answer to any psychological problem.
- Base your conclusions on research-based evidence.

Before you begin, you can use the **study plan** available on the companion website at **www.pearsoned.co.uk/psychologyexpress** to assess how well you know the material in this book and identify the areas where you may want to focus your revision.

Guided tour

→ **Understand key concepts quickly**

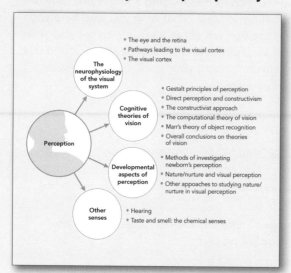

Start to plan your revision using the **Topic maps**.

Grasp **Key terms** quickly using the handy definitions. Use the flashcards online to test yourself.

Key terms

Algorithm: an algorithm is basically a method for solving a problem using a finite sequence of instructions.

In this way a problem space can be explored and hopefully the goal state will eventually be achieved. However, there are two main problems with the algorithm above – first, there is no mechanism for the algorithm to avoid getting into a loop where it either goes round in circles in the problem space, or simply

→ **Revise effectively**

How do schemas affect memory?

Scripts and schemas can lead to systematic biases in recall. Information congruent with a schema will be more likely to be recalled than incongruent information (Brewer & Treyens, 1981). However, highly distinctive information – like a skull in a shopping trolley – is more likely to be remembered than more commonplace items, the 'von Restorff' effect.

KEY STUDY

Remembering congruent and incongruent items

Brewer and Treyens (1981) asked participants to recall the contents of an office in which they waited. Congruent objects (e.g. chair) were better-remembered by participants than incongruent objects (e.g. skull). Many participants also reported seeing books – congruent objects – that had not been present in the room.

Schemas influence memory early on in life: Martin and Halverson (1983) found that children frequently changed the sex of the actor performing sex-inconsistent activities when recalling previously presented pictures.

Quickly remind yourself of the **Key studies** using the special boxes in the text.

Test your knowledge

The nature of attention

3.1 What are the three functions of attention?

3.2 What is the attentional spotlight?

3.3 Outline the zoom lens approach to visual attention.

3.4 Describe feature integration theory.

Answers to these questions can be found on the companion website at:
www.pearsoned.co.uk/psychologyexpress

Prepare for upcoming exams and tests using the **Test your knowledge** and **Sample question** features.

Compare your responses with the **Answer guidelines** in the text and on the website.

Answer guidelines

✳ *Sample question*   *Essay*

Is the multi-store model of memory the most appropriate way to view memory?

Approaching the question

This question requires a broad knowledge of memory theory. You'll need to give an overview of the model in question before going on to present limitations and alternatives.

Important points to include

Start with an overview of the multi-store model, specifying each element and briefly describing each. Next, evaluate the model, presenting some of the shortcomings. These include the type of information being presented, individual differences in recall ability and oversimplification. To do just this would only

→ **Make your answers stand out**

Use the **Critical focus** boxes to impress your examiner with your deep and critical understanding.

CRITICAL FOCUS

Schema theory

Schemas allow us to take shortcuts in interpreting information. However, these shortcuts can mean that we may disregard relevant information in favour of information that confirms our pre-existing beliefs. This means that schemas can contribute to stereotypes and mislead by making it hard to retain new information not conforming to established schemas.

Although schema theories provide a comprehensive framework to explain the structure and organisation of knowledge in long-term memory, several problems exist. First is that there is no real consensus on the properties of schemas. This has led to a range of theories being proposed including Bartlett's schemata (1932), Schank and Abelson's

Make your answer stand out

In addition to doing all outlined above, the best answers will also examine what is meant by attention, drawing on Chun and Wolfe's (2000) work which has argued that attention is multifaceted, consisting of separate processes and loci of selection. Answers may also place the theories in their historical context – for example Broadbent's work was shaped by the information-processing approach prominent in cognitive psychology at the time, while later conceptualisations such as Chun and Wolfe's are influenced by computational theory.

Go into the exam with confidence using the handy tips to **make your answer stand out**.

Guided tour of the companion website

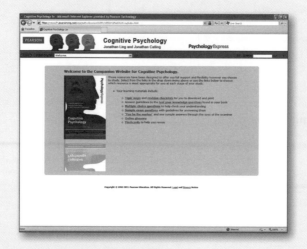

→ Understand key concepts quickly

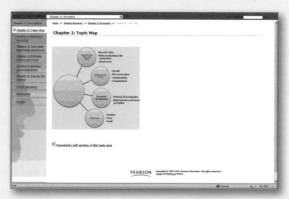

Printable versions of the **Topic maps** give an overview of the subject and help you plan your revision.

Test yourself on key definitions with the online **Flashcards**.

→ Revise effectively

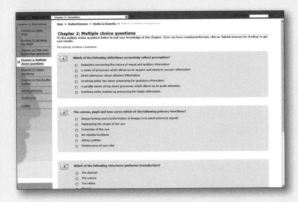

Check your understanding and practise for exams with the **Multiple choice questions**.

→ Make your answers stand out

Evaluate sample exam answers in the **You be the marker** exercises and understand how and why an examiner awards marks.

Put your skills into practice with the **Sample exam questions**, then check your answers with the guidelines.

All this and more can be found at
www.pearsoned.co.uk/psychologyexpress

Acknowledgements

Authors' acknowledgements

Terence Butler: I would like to thank Janey Webb and Neha Sharma of Pearson for ensuring communications and my co-author for her careful attention in key areas throughout the book.

Laura Scurlock-Evans: I would like to say a big thank you to my husband, Rhys Evans, for his unwavering support and patience whilst working on this project, and to my colleagues in Psychological Sciences for all their advice and encouragement. I would also like to thank the series editor, Professor Dominic Upton, for providing this wonderful opportunity to become involved with the series.

Series editor's acknowledgements

I am grateful to Janey Webb and Jane Lawes at Pearson Education for their assistance with this series. I would also like to thank Penney, Francesca, Rosie and Gabriel for their dedication to psychology.

Dominic Upton

Publisher's acknowledgements

Our thanks go to all reviewers who contributed to the development of this text, including students who participated in research and focus groups which helped to shape the series format:

Dr Andrew Cooper, Goldsmiths, University of London
Professor Simon Handley, University of Plymouth
Dr Paul Hutchings, Swansea Metropolitan University
Dr Joanne Lusher, London Metropolitan University
Dr Susan Rasmussen, University of Strathclyde
Dr Hilary Tait, Edinburgh Napier University

Student reviewer:
Andrea Franklin, student at Anglia Ruskin University

We are grateful to the following for permission to reproduce copyright material:

Figures

Figure 2.1 adapted from *The Biological Basis of Personality*, (Eysenck, H. 1967), Courtesy of Charles C. Thomas Publisher, Ltd., Springfield, Illinois.; Figures 8.2 and 8.3 adapted from The Cattell–Horn–Carroll Theory of Cognitive Abilities, 2nd ed., Guilford (McGrew, K. 2005), In D. Flanagan & P. Harrison (eds.), *Contemporary Intellectual Assessment: Theories Tests & Issues*; permission conveyed through Copyright Clearance Center, Inc.; Figure 8.6 adapted from *Human Cognitive Abilities* (Carroll, J. 1993), Courtesy of Cambridge University Press, USA.

Tables

Table 2.5 adapted from *Personality, Individual Differences and Intelligence*, 2nd ed., Pearson Education (Maltby, J., Day, L., & Macaskill, A. 2010) p. 167; Table 3.3 adapted from Genes, evolution, and personality, *Behavior Genetics*, 31, pp. 243–73 (Bouchard, T. & Loehlin, J. 2001), Republished with permission of Taylor & Francis Group LLC – Books, from *Development, Genetics, and Psychology*; permission conveyed through Copyright Clearance Center, Inc.; Table 7.1 adapted from Profiting from controversy: Lessons from the person–situation debate, *American Psychologist*, 43, pp. 23–34 (Kenrick, D. & Funder, D. 1988), APA, adapted with permission.; Table 9.3 after *Development, Genetics and Psychology*, Erlbaum (Plomin, R. 1986), Republished with permission of Taylor & Francis Group LLC – Books; permission conveyed through Copyright Clearance Center, Inc.

In some instances we have been unable to trace the owners of copyright material, and we would appreciate any information that would enable us to do so.

Introduction to individual differences and personality

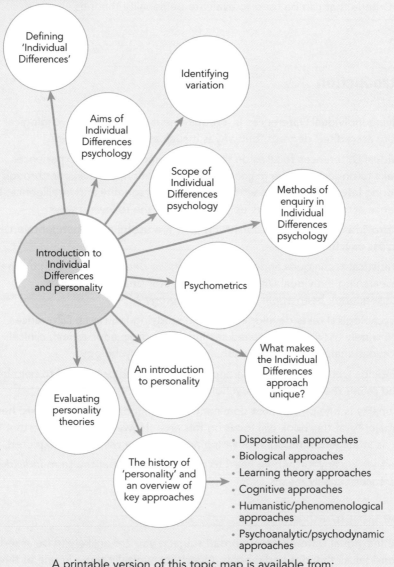

- Dispositional approaches
- Biological approaches
- Learning theory approaches
- Cognitive approaches
- Humanistic/phenomenological approaches
- Psychoanalytic/psychodynamic approaches

A printable version of this topic map is available from:
www.pearsoned.co.uk/psychologyexpress

→ *Revision checklist*

Essential points you should know:
- ❏ What the term 'Individual Differences' refers to
- ❏ The aims and scope of Individual Differences
- ❏ Methodology associated with Individual Differences
- ❏ What the term 'personality' refers to
- ❏ Why psychologists study Personality and Individual Differences
- ❏ Criteria that can be used to evaluate personality theories

Introduction

Studying Individual Differences is a requirement of all British Psychological Society accredited degrees, but why is it such an important topic?

Individual Differences focuses on the whole person and their experiences. It seeks to understand the major sources of variation in behaviour, through exploring **latent (hidden) constructs**, such as **personality** and intelligence. Its influence across psychology is demonstrated in the following ways:

1 It provides psychological constructs that are useful as 'dependent variables' across psychology.

2 Statistical techniques and methodology have been developed through researching Individual Differences (e.g. **factor analysis**) and have subsequently been applied across psychology.

3 Psychological tests developed through studying Individual Differences are widely used across applied settings, including: educational, clinical, occupational, counselling, health and forensic psychology.

4 Findings from Individual Differences research have been used to help inform and refine theories across psychology.

Personality is one of the most dominant topics in Individual Differences; hence the majority of this book will focus on this area. However, other important topics such as intelligence, mood, motivation and creativity will also be explored.

Before we go any further we need to define exactly what the term *Individual Differences* actually means.

Assessment advice

Since Individual Differences is a broad subject, you are unlikely to be asked to consider all theories and models. Questions typically come in one of three formats: an area of Individual Differences is specified (e.g. personality or intelligence), a particular theory is specified (e.g. Eysenck's **PEN model**) or *you* are given the opportunity to make your own selection. In the first two instances the question is likely to give you an insight into the debates and evidence which should be evaluated. In the latter case you will be assessed against the soundness of your choice of topic (and your coverage and evaluation of it) regarding the degree to which it allows you to address the assessment.

A problem-based learning question in this area would seek to explore your appreciation of the way in which a specific approach would be much more able to contribute to solving a problem than other approaches.

Sample question

Could you answer the question below? It is a typical essay question that could arise on this topic. Guidelines on answering the question are included at the end of this chapter, whilst a sample problem question and guidance on tackling it can be found on the companion website at **www.pearsoned.co.uk/psychologyexpress**.

 Sample question   *Essay*

Critically discuss the ways in which Individual Differences psychology has contributed to our understanding of human nature.

Defining 'Individual Differences'

The term 'Individual Differences' has come to mean various things, which can be confusing. For example, it is widely used to refer to both an *approach* to studying phenomena of interest, and the *phenomena* of interest themselves (Mahoney, 2011). Adding to the confusion is the fact that 'Individual Differences' is also used interchangeably with other related (but subtly different) terms (Lubinski, 2000), including:

- Differential psychology
- Personality psychology
- Intelligence

In this book 'Individual Differences psychology' will be used to refer to the field of study. Individual Differences psychology seeks to understand how we should best describe the ways in which people vary and how and why such variations in behaviour come about (Cooper, 2002, p. 1).

'Individual Differences' will denote the characteristics of interest to psychologists. These characteristics (e.g. personality, intelligence, 'likeability') can be conceptualised at different levels of detail, or **bandwidth**.

Aims of Individual Differences psychology

Cooper's (2002) definition highlights the core aims of Individual Differences psychology as identifying the general characteristics which can be used to predict similarities and differences in the way people think, feel and behave (Mahoney, 2011). These similarities and differences are referred to as **variation**.

There are two types of variation of interest to Individual Differences psychologists:

- **Inter-individual variation**: the ways in which people differ from each other;
- **Intra-individual variation**: the ways in which a person's own behaviour, thoughts and feelings can vary (e.g. seem out of character, or change across time or situations).

The aims of many Individual Differences theorists are to identify the *structure*, *determinants* (causes) and *processes* (Caprara & Cervone, 2000) underpinning inter- and intra-individual variability.

- Historically the focus has been on identifying the structure of Individual Differences, such as personality. This has led to the criticism that the field has become bogged down with the task of description, resulting in the proliferation of disparate taxonomies (classification systems).
- More recently, theorists have placed greater emphasis on explaining Individual Differences, to understand *how* and *why* similarities and differences exist.
- The challenge for contemporary theories of Individual Differences is to integrate these three aspects cohesively and comprehensively.

Identifying variation

Many Individual Differences constructs are latent (not directly observable), posing a problem for their identification and measurement. To resolve this issue theorists seek to identify *observable* features which are believed to reflect or indicate the presence of the latent variable. This represents the **accessibility debate**, which is highly contentious (Mahoney, 2011) for the following reasons:

- Do latent constructs actually exist or are they superficially imposed by theorists?
- Is it actually possible to identify and measure latent constructs?
- How can we assess the accuracy of our representations and measurements of latent constructs?

The accessibility debate is fundamental to the field of psychometrics (see Chapter 10).

It is important to recognise that the aims of Individual Differences psychologists may differ according to the approaches they adopt.

CRITICAL FOCUS

Nomothetic and Idiographic approaches to studying Individual Differences

The majority of Individual Differences theories, such as the personality theories of Cattell (1943; Cattell & Kline, 1976) and Eysenck (Eysenck & Eysenck, 1975, 1976) and the Intelligence theories of Spearman (1904) and Thurstone (1934, 1935, 1938), follow the **nomothetic approach**; they seek to identify personality characteristics which are universal. This approach typically involves making statistical comparisons across individuals and groups to identify how they differ on these characteristics. The nomothetic approach is also associated with making **norm group** comparisons. In the statistical sense, **norms** are numbers, values, levels or ranges that are representative of a group, which can be used as a basis for comparison with individual cases. This allows you to see where an individual's score falls in relation to the norm group (e.g. above or below average). This is similar to comparing the latitudinal and longitudinal coordinates of different cities in the world and looking at whether they lie above or below the equator.

The nomothetic approach has been criticised by some, such as Gordon Allport (1961), who argued that it has limited predictive value for how individuals will behave in specific situations. For this reason, some theorists adopt the **idiographic approach** to studying Individual Differences. This approach usually focuses on a single individual and builds up a detailed account of their life, or an event of interest. For example, Allport (1961) employed this approach to explore what makes individuals unique in terms of their personality. Theorists adopting this approach argue that it can provide a more meaningful and holistic understanding of human nature. However, the terms used to describe one individual are only appropriate to that specific individual, and should not be used to describe anyone else. This makes comparisons difficult, if not impossible.

Test your knowledge

1 How do the nomothetic and idiographic approaches to studying Individual Differences differ?

2 What are the key strengths and limitations of the nomothetic approach to Individual Differences?

3 What might the key strengths and limitations of the idiographic approach to Individual Differences be?

Scope of Individual Differences psychology

The scope of Individual Differences psychology is vast. To help appreciate the topics of interest in this field we will use Larsen & Buss' (2010) six **domains of**

knowledge. Larsen and Buss discussed these domains in relation to personality psychology, but they are relevant to all Individual Differences.

Table 1.1 **Six domains of knowledge**

Domain name	Core characteristics
Dispositional	• Cuts across all other domains because it emphasises that Individual Differences reside within the individual.
Biological	• Sees biological systems as the building blocks of all thoughts, feelings and behaviour. • Has strong ties with the dispositional approach.
Sociocultural	• Contrasts with the dispositional and biological approaches because it recognises the impact of social and cultural processes on the individual.
Cognitive-experiential	• Focuses on people's thoughts, information processing and subjective experiences and how these are organised.
Intrapsychic	• Primarily concerned with the unconscious and instinctual mechanisms underpinning individual differences. • Most commonly associated with the work of Freud, **neo-Freudians** and psychoanalysis.
Adjustment	• Concerned with the ways in which people are able to adapt and cope with different events and across the lifespan.

Source: Adapted from Larsen & Buss (2010).

Domains of knowledge refer to the boundaries of psychologists' knowledge, expertise and interests, and therefore represent the individual's 'specialism' (Larsen & Buss, 2010). Many psychologists operate within one or two domains and are therefore interested in a specific and limited set of aspects of human nature. Ultimately this means there are few theories which seek to account for *all* domains of knowledge, which limits our understanding of Individual Differences.

CRITICAL FOCUS

Micro-, grand and ultimate theories

Historically there have been shifts in the emphasis placed on the *scale* of Individual Differences theories:

- Until the mid-twentieth century emphasis was placed on **grand theories** (often referred to as 'schools of thought'), which aimed to understand the *whole person* (Engler, 2008). An example of a grand theory is Freud's psychoanalytic theory of personality, which seeks to understand the development, stability and mechanisms of personality.
- Since (roughly) the 1950s, **micro-theories** have gained prominence. Micro-theories are more fine-grained and narrow in focus. They seek to understand specific features of phenomena, such as aiming to explain 'conscientiousness', rather than personality as a whole.

- More recently there has been increasing speculation about whether an 'ultimate' theory of Individual Differences is possible. An ultimate theory would need to provide a comprehensive conceptual framework that unifies pre-existing grand theories and provides direction for future exploration. It would need to provide an explanation of the phenomenon at each level of the domains of knowledge.

Test your knowledge

1 Why might an ultimate theory of Individual Differences be difficult to develop?

2 How might a theory of Individual Differences that focuses on the biological and dispositional domains of knowledge differ from (and be similar to) a theory that focuses on the adjustment and sociocultural domains?

3 Why do you think there may have been historical shifts in the focus on types of theory (e.g. dispositional to sociocultural, and grand to micro-theory?

Further reading

Topic	Key reading
Critical discussion of the aims and scope of Individual Differences psychology	Chapter 1 (Individual Differences: aims, methods and ethics) in B. Mahoney, (2011). *Critical thinking in psychology: Personality and individual differences.* Exeter: Learning Matters.

Methods of enquiry in Individual Differences psychology

Historically, there have been shifts in the methodology associated with Individual Differences psychology. Early research (e.g. in radical behaviourism) was more strongly associated with experimental research conducted in laboratory settings:

- **True experiments** require the researcher to be able to manipulate some variables whilst holding all others constant (controlling them) and usually uses random group designs.

- True experiments are often seen as the 'gold standard' of research because if control is properly exercised (and the experiment is said to have **internal validity**) you can be more confident that any changes you record in your dependent variable(s) are due to the manipulations you made to your independent variable (Bryman & Cramer, 2011).

- That is, you can more legitimately make *causal inferences* about the relationship between the variables you are studying (Bryman & Cramer, 2011).

True experimental research has been criticised in relation to Individual Differences psychology because it often took place in artificial, sterile and unrealistic conditions (Lisney, 1989). This raises the question of whether research findings accurately reflect 'real life' (Lisney, 1989). For this reason later research attempted to take into account more **ecologically valid** settings. This, coupled with the difficulties associated with conducting true experiments in Individual Differences psychology, means that this field more frequently employs correlational and case study research designs.

- Problems arise because Individual Difference variables are usually confounded (tangled up with) with *person variables* (Robins, Fraley & Krueger, 2007). Person variables (also called participant variables) are characteristics which cannot be isolated or manipulated (e.g. a person's gender). So, when designing an experiment on *intelligence*, we are not able to exclude other person variables such as *motivation*. For this reason quasi-experimental methods and correlational designs tend to be adopted.

- Correlational research designs accompanied by statistical techniques such as **regression**, factor analysis and **structural equation modelling** are particularly useful tools for exploring the ways in which different variables *interact* to influence thinking, feeling and behaviour.

- **Correlational designs** tend to involve studying non-manipulated variables (Bryman & Cramer, 2011), and is common in personality and intelligence research.

- **Quasi-experiments** are similar to true experiments, but lack their rigorous control and frequently involve *non-equivalent* groups (Heppner, Wampold & Kivlighan, 2007). Basically, this means that you are not able to randomly assign people to groups, but must group people on some naturally occurring variable (e.g. gender). Researchers then use statistical techniques to try to compensate for this lack of physical control, and may then manipulate other variables to explore the interactions between variables.

Although quasi-experiments and correlational designs exert less control over the variables of interest, they may have greater **external validity** (Sizkmund & Babin, 2005).

KEY STUDY

Example of a quasi-experiment designed to examine the causal relationship between exposure to media violence and increase in violent behaviour

The links between violence in the media and acts of violence have long been of interest to psychologists. Much research on this topic has involved attempts to conduct true experiments, which usually take place in laboratory settings, such as Bandura's 'bashing bobo' study (Bandura, Ross & Ross, 1961) and Liebert and Baron's 'help or hurt' study (1972). Although these studies could exert a strong degree of experimental control (required for good internal validity and therefore the capacity to infer causality), they involved artificial scenarios. For this reason, some researchers, such as Leyens et al. (1975), have attempted to conduct quasi-experiments in the field. Leyens et al. (1975) observed the behaviour of individuals living in four cottages which were part of a minimum-security institution for adolescent boys in Belgium. Initially the researchers observed 'normal' behaviour in the cottages (a baseline) and identified two cottages in which more aggressive inmates lived and two cottages in which less aggressive inmates lived. Next, for a period of a week one cottage from each of the two groups (more versus less aggressive) were shown either violent films or neutral films. Following these movies the number of verbal and physical displays of aggression were observed by the researchers.

The results indicated that more aggressive acts were recorded after the violent, compared to the neutral films, and that this increase was more noticeable for the groups of participants who already displayed a greater tendency towards aggression than the other participants. These effects were also observed to continue through to a post-treatment week for the inmates who had displayed aggressive tendencies at baseline, but not the participants from the less aggressive group.

Test your knowledge

1   What other factors may have affected Leyens et al.'s study?
2   What ethical issues do you think this study may raise?

- **Case studies** feature prominently in Individual Differences psychology and allow you to explore a particular phenomenon and an individual's functioning as a whole (Robins, Fraley & Krueger, 2007). By studying individuals holistically across situations or across time, we are able to learn about their responses, experiences and behavioural outcomes.
- The case study methodology was championed by Gordon Allport, George Kelly and Sigmund Freud (amongst others) and has strong ties with the idiographic approach.

Appropriately chosen and implemented research designs help us to demonstrate the **validity** of our results and theory. It is important to ask questions of the suitability of the methods used in research, as this helps us identify areas for improvement that could have implications for the application, comprehensiveness and coherence of theories.

The technique of 'cross validation', which is particularly valued in Individual Differences psychology, involves examining multiple approaches to establishing validity. The different types of validity that we may need to consider depending on the designs we employ are outlined in Table 1.2 below. These concepts are also explored in Chapter 10 (Psychometrics).

Ensuring theories and measures are based on robust and accurate research is of both practical and ethical importance (see Chapter 10 for further discussion), because the findings of research and tools developed (e.g. measures of personality) are frequently used for important purposes, such as job selection and recruitment or therapeutic decisions.

Table 1.2 **Types of validity**

Types of validity	Explanation
Empirical validity	Does the evidence support the propositions?
Predictive validity	Occurs when a theory/concept is able to make satisfactory predictions of an outcome.
Criterion validity	The extent to which the outcomes of a theory/concept can be judged against some external measure.
Face validity	Does the theory/concept recognised have widespread recognition?
Construct validity	The theory is constructed such that it corresponds to the field in which it is to be employed.
Content validity	Is the content of the theory/concept applicable to the topic?
Convergent validity	Does the theory make satisfactory predictions of constructs which *should be related* to each other?
Discriminant validity	Does the theory make satisfactory predictions of constructs which *should not be related* to each other?

 Sample question   ***Problem-based learning***

You are asked to develop a piece of research to examine whether listening to music with 'violent' lyrics *causes* an increase in displays of aggressive behaviour in adolescent boys and girls. What information will you need (and where can this be found) in order to design this research effectively? What theoretical, methodological and ethical issues will you need to consider and how might you overcome them? See Chapters 10 and 11 for a discussion of ethical issues in Individual Differences research.

Psychometrics

Psychometrics is the field concerned with the *scientific measurement* of psychological phenomena (Individual Differences). This represents the predominant approach within Individual Differences psychology (Mahoney, 2011), and much of our knowledge of Individual Differences generated by this approach is used to help make important decisions in applied settings (see Chapters 10 and 11 for further discussion). This approach is controversial owing to the key assumptions which define it:

- *Scaling*: Individual Differences data can be reduced to numbers or quantities.
- *Error*: Data collection and scaling will involve some error (systematic and random), but this error can be dealt with sufficiently through experimental control and statistical control.

- *Statistical models*: statistical techniques can be used to develop models of Individual Differences.

Test your knowledge

1   What research methodologies are commonly associated with Individual Differences psychology?
2   Why is it important that research findings in Individual Differences psychology are accurate and valid?
3   What issues might researchers have to overcome when studying Individual Differences?

Further reading

Topic	Key reading
Overview of methodology	Revelle, W., Wilt, J. & Condon, D. (2011). Methodological advances in differential psychology. In T. Charmorro-Premuzic, S. Stumm & A. Furnham (eds), *Handbook of Individual Differences*, Chichester: Wiley-Blackwell, pp. 39–74.
	Lear, M. & Hoyle, R. (2009). Methods for the study of Individual Differences in social behaviour. In M. Lear & R. Hoyle, *Handbook of Individual Differences in social behaviour*. New York: Guilford Press.

What makes the Individual Differences approach unique?

Although theories and research in Individual Differences are concerned with similar topics to other branches of psychology (e.g. behaviour and cognition), it goes about studying them in a different way. Whereas most other fields start from the assumption that people are basically the same and therefore attempts to identify *universal laws of behaviour*, Individual Differences psychology seeks to identify what makes people *unique*, by identifying how people *differ* from one another (Cooper, 2002).

Individual Differences psychology is also broadly underpinned by several assumptions which, when combined, set it apart from other fields in psychology:

- *Enduring patterns*: people can be characterised by their 'typical' thoughts, feelings and behaviours (e.g. dispositions, personality), which are relatively stable. These enduring patterns can be used to infer similarities and differences between people or groups.
- *Scientifically measurable*: similarities and differences between people can be measured scientifically.

● **Aggregate data**: data collected from research can be aggregated in meaningful ways, although this has implications for the way it can be interpreted.

● *Consequences*: The way in which Individual Differences are studied, the format in which Individual Differences data are collected and used to develop theory and psychometric tests, has significant consequences for people. For example, theory, psychometric tests and therapy developed through the Individual Differences approach will impact on people in clinical, counselling, health, occupational, forensic and educational contexts.

● *Person–environment interaction*: recently there has been a recognition of the way that an individual's characteristics affect, and are affected by, environmental, situational and cultural factors. However, the Individual Differences approach assumes that these interactions have the potential to be understood through continuing scientific investigation.

Test your knowledge

1   In what ways is Individual Differences psychology different from other fields in psychology?

2   What are the key interests and concerns of Individual Difference psychologists?

3   What might the key contributions of Individual Differences psychology be to other fields in psychology?

Further reading

Topic	Key reading
Overview of Individual Differences	Chapter 1: Introducing Individual Differences – from everyday to psychological questions. In T. Chamorro-Premuzic (2011). *Personality and Individual Differences*, 2nd edn. Chichester: BPS Blackwell.
Overview of the history of Individual Differences	Revelle, W., Wilt, J. & Condon, D. (2011). Individual Differences and differential psychology: A brief history and prospect. In T. Chamorro-Premuzic, S. Stumm & A. Furnham (eds), *Handbook of Individual Differences*, Chichester: Wiley-Blackwell, pp. 3–38.

✳ Sample question   Problem-based learning

You have been asked to develop an intervention for anti-social behaviour in secondary schools in the UK. You need to provide a well-evidenced strategy to deal with the causes and development of anti-social behaviour, and will need to consider:

● which domains of knowledge you will need to examine and why;

● what areas of Individual Differences theory and research could be useful to examine and why;

● how you will evaluate and apply existing theory and research.

An introduction to personality

The term 'personality' is a familiar one; however, it has come to have many different meanings. For example, the media and academic writing tend to define the term 'personality' in very different ways (Chamorro-Premuzic, 2011). The way in which personality is defined in a theory will tell you something about a theorist's approaches to studying it. There are too many definitions to explore them all here, but the general definition used in this book is from Gordon Allport (1961), who pioneered the use of the term in psychology. He felt that personality was 'a dynamic organisation, inside the person, of psychophysical systems that create the person's characteristic patterns of behaviour, thoughts and feelings' (p. 11).

Although this is reasonably comprehensive, it should be noted that more contemporary definitions also include reference to the impact of 'the interaction of the individual with the environment ... a self-regulating system with the capacity to serve individual development and well being' (Caprara & Cervone, 2000, p. 11). This reflects a general shift in contemporary research from focusing on the individual exclusively to appreciating the impact of environmental, social and interpersonal relationship factors (i.e. the emergence of the interactionist debate).

The history of 'personality' and an overview of key approaches

The concept of personality is an ancient one (Mahoney, 2011), dating back to Greek philosophers such as Hippocrates and Galen. It has developed much since this time, but the idea of a person having a stable 'temperament' or 'disposition' still pervades contemporary theories.

Psychologists study personality because it helps us to:

● understand human nature;

● understand what motivates behaviour (particularly important for developing behavioural change interventions);

● understand how personality develops and changes across the lifespan;

● understand differences/similarities in people's experiences;

● measure and predict personality, e.g. assessing person–organisation fit in occupational selection and recruitment.

Shifts in paradigms across psychology (such as from behavioural to social-cognitive) have resulted in new insights and understandings of personality. However, the result is that there is no single approach to studying personality.

Key approaches discussed in this book include: dispositional (Chapter 2), biological (Chapter 3), learning theory approaches (Chapter 4), cognitive (Chapter 5), humanistic (Chapter 5) and psychoanalytic/psychodynamic (Chapter 6). Each approach has distinct characteristics owing to its underlying assumptions (although some do overlap), so you need to be aware of their unique strengths and limitations as well as those of the field in general.

These approaches will be examined in depth in the following chapters, but it is useful to know the broad timeline of the development of approaches and their general aims, as this shows you how the field of personality psychology has developed over time. It is important to recognise that personality theorists have been concerned with different domains of knowledge and have adopted significantly different perspectives. For example, trait theorists are most associated with the dispositional and biological domains, whereas psychoanalytic theorists are most associated with the intrapsychic and adjustment domains of knowledge.

Dispositional approaches

- Timeline: The dispositional approach dates back to ancient Greece, with the work of philosophers such as Galen. It has remained popular (particularly in the form of trait theory), although in the 1960s/1970s a serious challenge was posed to it in the form of the **situationist debate** (sparked mainly by Walter Mischel). The dispositional approach now appears more secure, with the inclusion of interactionist principles in the 1990s, through the work of individuals such as David Funder.

- Key trait theorists: Gordon Allport (1897–1967), Raymond Cattell (1905–1998), Hans Eysenck (1916–1997), Paul Costa, Robert McCrae, Gerard Saucier.

- It views personality as relatively stable and enduring characteristics within an individual (i.e. they 'take' these characteristics with them across their lifespan and across situations).

- It is strongly associated with **trait theory**, although type models are also popular and recently theories have developed which place greater emphasis on other forms of personality characteristics (e.g. values) and situational factors. Trait theories state that personality is comprised of distinct and observable 'types' such as introversion and extraversion.

- A number of trait-dispositional models of personality have strong evidential support and have demonstrated predictive value, for example, in understanding alcohol and drug abuse and in health and wellbeing promotion.

- Theorists such as Allport, Cattell, Eysenck and more recently Costa and McCrae have developed models that have promoted understanding of person variables as explanations of behaviour.

- Models tend to be based on behavioural observation, usually measured by means of self-report questionnaires.

- The current consensus of thinking about the trait-dispositional approach views the 'Big Five' model as the most successful predictor of behaviour. The model emerged as a 'consensus' from amongst competing models which seemed to measure very similar constructs (Funder, 2001).

- Dispositional theories cannot claim to encapsulate the totality of human personality (Funder, 2001). Funder (2001) also states that although any personality construct can be mapped on to the 'Big Five', it is not possible to derive the personality constructs from information presented in the five dimensions. Funder provides the example that, although the authoritarian personality can be described as high on 'conscientiousness' and low on 'agreeableness' and 'openness to experience', authoritarianism cannot be reduced to these dimensions as a summary of its total characterisation.

Biological approaches

- Timeline: The biological approach also dates back to ancient Greece, with the four 'humours' or temperaments, proposed by Hippocrates (460–370 BC) and Galen (AD 130–200). Research in this area is now blossoming at an exponential rate (Funder, 2001), with advances in technology allowing researchers to explore links between genes, hormones and activity in the brain, and behaviour.

- Key theorists: William Sheldon (1898–1977), Hans Eysenck (1916–1997), Jeffrey Gray (1934–2004), David Buss, Robert Plomin, Avshalom Caspi.

- Biological approaches to personality have strong links with the dispositional approach, which is best demonstrated by Eysenck's PEN model. Models such as this seek to identify the links between physiology and personality traits.

- This approach comprises three main stands: neurophysiological (e.g. Eysenck's PEN, Gray's BAS/BIS model), behavioural genetics (e.g. Bergeman et al., 1993) and evolutionary theories (e.g. Buss' (1991) theory of personality and adaptation), which are also known as sociobiological models (Wilson, 1975).

- Many early biological approaches, particularly neurophysiological models, borrowed heavily from the behaviourist principles of conditioning. In recent years greater emphasis has been placed on understanding genetic and evolutionary perspectives of personality, examining how concepts such as phenotypes and genotypes can shed light on variation in human nature.

- Behavioural genetics and evolutionary models are concerned with understanding the heritability of personality and how the concept of evolution can explain the basis of the five-factor model, how individual differences arise and how the concept of 'life history' relates to personality.

- This approach is most commonly associated with the twin-study methodology, which has revealed interesting and sometimes unexpected results (Chamorro-Premuzic, 2011).

- With advances in technology, it has been possible to examine the relationship between biological factors and personality in different ways, such as 'sociogenomic personality psychology' (Roberts & Jackson, 2008).

Learning theory approaches

- Timeline: Learning theory gained prominence in the early twentieth century in the form of radical behaviourism and later with social learning (or social-cognitive) theories from the 1960s onwards.
- Key theorists: Ivan Pavlov (1849–1936), John Watson (1878–1958), Burrhus Frederic (BF) Skinner (1904–1990), John Dollard (1900–1980), Neal Miller (1909–2002), Julian Rotter, Albert Bandura, Walter Mischel.
- The term 'learning theory approaches' is most commonly associated with the behaviourist paradigm which dominated psychology in the USA until the middle of the twentieth century.
- Behaviourism's lack of interest in internal mental processes resulted in the rise of social-cognitive and cognitive approaches. These later approaches increasingly recognised individuals' perceptual and subjective views as important aspects of personality.
- Social-cognitive approaches extended behaviourist models to include intervening cognitive variables and identified a number of useful concepts for understanding personality, such as Bandura's (1962) concept of vicarious learning (learning by observations of the learning of others).
- The interactivity of social-cognitive variables, such as those identified in Mischel's Cognitive Affective Personality System (CAPS; 1999) has been highlighted as a strength of this approach.
- The key limitation of the current research topics in social-cognitive theory is the lack of coherence, which has arisen from the number of mini-topics examined independently of each other by theorists in the field. In order for a fully formed theory to be developed, this disorganisation needs to be addressed.

Cognitive approaches

- Timeline: Cognitive approaches started to gain prominence in the 1960s and 1970s (alongside social learning theories, which are also known as social-cognitive theories), owing to dissatisfaction with behaviourist principles of excluding mental processes from theory and research. As well as having strong ties with social learning theories, this approach is also associated with the humanistic/phenomenological approach.
- Key theorists: Herman Witkin (1916–1979), Aneseth Petrie, George Kelly (1905–1967), Albert Ellis (1913–2007).
- It developed owing to an interest in how people perceive and process information differently from one another.

- Some cognitive personality theories, such as Kelly's (1955) personal construct theory, have strong ties with the humanistic approach. This is because they place emphasis on people's subjective experiences and cognitions and how these interacted to develop and impact on personality. George Kelly's personal construct psychology demonstrated the importance of seeing explanations in the world through the eyes of others and has constructed a method by which this can be systematically explored. This insight enables us to explain motivations and behaviour that lacked meaningful explanations from other theories.

Humanistic/phenomenological approaches

- Timeline: This approach was most influential in the 1950s–1970s, but declined in popularity until recently, with renewed interest in the phenomenological approach and increased appreciation of studying individual experiences through cross-cultural perspectives (Funder, 2001).
- Key theorists: Abraham Maslow (1908–1970), Carl Rogers (1902–1987) and George Kelly (1905–1967).
- Humanistic theories (also known as phenomenological theories) are concerned with individuality, as they are heavily influenced by the phenomenological philosophical position. This position argues that people's relationship with the world is based upon *subjective* perceptions, suggesting that no two people will experience the same event in the same way.

Psychoanalytic/psychodynamic approaches

- Timeline: These originated from the work of Sigmund Freud in the late nineteenth century and remained extremely influential until the mid-twentieth century. However, there has been a renewed interest in the approaches developed by Freud and neo-Freudians in the 1990s, through the work of individuals such as Drew Westen (1998).
- Key theorists: Sigmund Freud (1856–1939), Alfred Adler (1870–1937), Erik Erikson (1902–1994), Karen Horney (1885–1952), Carl Jung (1875–1961). Psychoanalytic theories, also referred to as psychodynamic (because they view personality as a result of the conflict between conscious and unconscious forces within an individual), developed primarily from the work of Sigmund Freud.
- Freud's theories developed from his years of clinical practice, using the therapeutic method he developed (psychoanalysis). They have been adapted and developed by theorists such as Erik Erikson and Karen Horney and continue to be popular today.
- The key criticism of psychodynamic theories is that they are not easily testable and therefore are not associated with mainstream approaches to the study of personality.

- Psychodynamic approaches continue to alert us to issues that the dominant theories are not always well equipped to address. In particular, psychodynamic theories continue to offer explanations for unconscious motivations and the recognition that these processes operate in parallel with conscious processes (Westen, 1998).

You can see that many theories cross over different fields, such as Eysenck's PEN model (dispositional and biological) and George Kelly's personal construct theory (cognitive and humanistic). It is important to recognise that none of the approaches fully captures the structures and processes within the person and our inability to synthesise understandings from the different approaches hinders efforts to develop a comprehensive and coherent understanding of personality. This is where many contemporary personality psychologists are calling for future efforts to be focused (McAdams & Pals, 2006).

Evaluating personality theories

A number of themes form the basis for the evaluation of personality theory. Table 1.3 summarises some of the key questions which can be used to examine how theories are similar and in what ways they are distinct. Keep these in mind when reading the following chapters.

Table 1.3 **Assumptions for distinguishing theories and determining commonalities**

Pole A	Pole B
Does the theory aim to be universal?	Does the theory aim to be only uniquely applied?
Is the emphasis essentially on environmental or genetic factors?	Does the theory suggest that personality is interactively determined?
Is there an assumption of minimal personal control (i.e. deterministic)?	Is there an assumption of free will?
Are people primarily viewed as proactive?	Are people primarily viewed as passive or responsive?
Does the theory make optimistic future projections?	Does the theory make negative future projections?

Maltby, Day and Macaskill (2010) propose a number of standards for evaluating the effectiveness of theories, as outlined in Table 1.4.

A further issue which should be considered is whether it *integrates* knowledge from across the six domains outlined in the table.

Table 1.4 **Criteria for evaluating personality theories**

Standard	Description
Description	Does the theory identify and direct you to the important issues?
Explanation	Does the theory provide a convincing explanation for why behaviour observed occurs?
Empirical validity	Does the theory generate testable predictions?
Testability	Does the theory allow for effective operationalisation of the concepts which need to be examined?
Comprehensiveness	Does the theory appear 'complete' and provide insights into a wide range of behaviours?
Parsimony	Does the theory appear simple, without being oversimplified? That is, is the smallest number of concepts included to *effectively* explain phenomena?
Heuristic value	Does the theory generate interest and research in the phenomena?
Applied value	Does the theory have *practical* value?

✱ Sample question   Essay

Critically compare and evaluate three different approaches to studying personality. Providing evidence from relevant theory and research, state which approach you feel provides the most comprehensive account of personality and why.

Test your knowledge

1   Produce a 'sequence' of the key approaches discussed in this chapter – how do you think they may have influenced each other?

2   Why might George Kelly's and Hans Eysenck's theories overlap different approaches?

3   What information could you use to examine and compare the effectiveness of the biological and psychoanalytic personality theories?

Further reading

Topic	Key reading
Overview of the history of personality	Funder, D. (2001). Personality, *Annual Review of Psychology, 52,* 197–221.
Overview of the study of personality	Chapters 1 (The domain of personality psychology) and 2 (Origins, history and progress) in G. Caprara & D. Cervone (2000). *Personality: Determinants, dynamics and potentials.* Cambridge: Cambridge University Press.

Chapter summary: putting it all together

→ Can you tick all the points from the revision checklist at the beginning of this chapter?

→ Attempt the sample question from the beginning of this chapter using the answer guidelines below.

→ Go to the companion website at **www.pearsoned.co.uk/psychologyexpress** to access more revision support online, including interactive quizzes, sample questions with answer guidelines, 'you be the marker' exercises, flashcards and podcasts you can download.

Answer guidelines

Guidelines on answering the sample questions presented at the start of the chapter are given below.

 Sample question   ***Essay***

Critically discuss the ways in which Individual Differences psychology has contributed to our understanding of human nature.

Approaching the question

The first step in this essay is to define what Individual Differences psychology is, what its aims are and how these differ from other fields in psychology. You should note that it explores many issues which are also of interest in other branches of psychology and explore the implications of this. You should state what aspects of Individual Differences psychology you are going to explore (e.g. impact of methodologies and applications of Individual Differences research) and return to this in your conclusion to demonstrate how you have address each of these topics.

Important points to include

The main topics to cover include the following:

● Explore how Individual Differences psychologists conceptualise 'human nature' and contrast them (such as Freud's negative view with Horney's positive view of human nature, and the focus of behaviourism on observable actions in comparison to the cognitivist focus on intervening mental processes).

● Consider research methodologies (e.g. research design, statistical techniques and the field of psychometrics – see Chapter 10 for further information) and explore how these have impacted on findings in Individual Differences psychology and across psychology in general.

● You may wish to examine the impact of psychometric tests, such as the personality questionnaires based on trait theories (see Chapter 2), on the measurement of personality across psychology and in applied settings (see Chapter 10).

- Explore how Individual Differences theory and research have contributed to the development of clinical and therapeutic applications, such as psychoanalytic, person-centred and cognitive approaches to treating psychological distress and disorder (e.g. see Chapters 5 and 6).
- Explore how Individual Differences theory and research have contributed to the development of selection and recruitment processes (see Chapter 11) in industry, and the implications of this.
- Controversies in Individual Differences psychology, such as the tautology of the concepts of **intelligence** and the **intelligence quotient** (IQ) and the concept of **personality disorder** (see Chapters 8, 9, 10 and 11) and how they have impacted on research and the ethics of the field.

Ensure that you examine the strengths and limitations of the Individual Differences approach to understanding human nature, such as the debate concerning 'scaling' techniques that are widely employed. Provide an indication of ways in which this could be mitigated and support with evidence from research.

> ### Make your answer stand out
>
> *Individual Differences psychology is a vast subject, so you need to avoid your essay turning into a one-dimensional list of topics areas. Highlight the immensity of the subject area and indicate that you will be focusing on a subset of these issues, with a sound justification of why you have chosen to explore the issues you have. It may help to focus on one area in Individual Differences psychology, such as personality, and provide examples of theory, practice and research from this field to highlight the issues you wish to examine (but recognise that there are other topics which are also important, such as intelligence and motivation).*
>
> *A strong essay will also examine the future potential contributions of Individual Differences psychology to developing our understanding of human nature, such as the advances in technology that are allowing us to examine the relationship between genetics and behaviour and the growing interest in evolutionary theories. You may wish to conclude by exploring the possibility of an ultimate theory of Individual Differences psychology, which could draw the disparate approaches (such as biological, learning theory, psychoanalytic and humanistic approaches) together.*

Notes

2

Dispositional approaches to personality

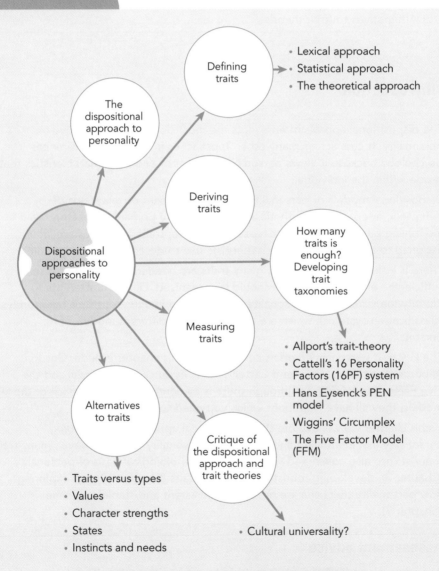

Defining traits
- Lexical approach
- Statistical approach
- The theoretical approach

The dispositional approach to personality

Deriving traits

Dispositional approaches to personality

How many traits is enough? Developing trait taxonomies

Measuring traits

- Allport's trait-theory
- Cattell's 16 Personality Factors (16PF) system
- Hans Eysenck's PEN model
- Wiggins' Circumplex
- The Five Factor Model (FFM)

Alternatives to traits

Critique of the dispositional approach and trait theories

- Traits versus types
- Values
- Character strengths
- States
- Instincts and needs

- Cultural universality?

A printable version of this topic map is available from:
www.pearsoned.co.uk/psychologyexpress

> **→ Revision checklist**
>
> *Essential points you should know:*
> - ❏ What the dispositional approach to personality is
> - ❏ What personality traits, trait taxonomies and types are
> - ❏ The lexial, statistical and theoretical approaches to deriving traits
> - ❏ Prominent trait taxonomies and their strengths and limitations
> - ❏ The strengths and limitations of the dispositional approach overall
> - ❏ Alternatives to 'trait theories'

Introduction

The dispositional approach represents the most dominant perspective on personality. It cuts across many other approaches in Individual Differences psychology because it views personality as a set of enduring characteristics that reside *within* the individual.

Dispositional models of personality typically represent observations of behaviour, adopt the nomothetic approach and are primarily concerned with identifying personality **traits** or **types**. In essence, traits and types are *labels* assigned to characteristics, which theorists use to describe how people differ.

There is little consensus on how many traits are needed to describe personality sufficiently, or how these traits should be organised. Different attempts to identify the structure of personality have resulted in numerous trait **taxonomies** (classification systems), which are associated with different models of personality.

The key trait personality models considered in this chapter include: Gordon Allport's trait theory, Raymond Cattell's 16PF, Eysenck's PEN model and the Five Factor Model (FFM). Although there is evidential support for each of these models, they all have limitations which you need to be aware of.

In this chapter we will explore the dispositional approach to *describing* personality (i.e. identifying and organising personality traits); however, many trait theorists are also concerned with exploring the *biological basis* of personality (Chapter 3), developing robust measures of traits (Chapter 10) and exploring how personality traits change or remain consistent and stable over time (Chapter 7).

Assessment advice

Assessments are likely to ask you either to explore the dispositional approach to personality in general, or to evaluate one trait theory in particular. So, when reading the question you need to consider whether your answer should focus on *breadth* or *depth* of topic.

To evaluate a specific trait model effectively you should consider its usefulness, research evidence, strengths and limitations. You should also be aware of other trait theories, which you can make comparisons with. The question may also provide you with the scope to compare dispositional trait theories with theories developed through other approaches (e.g. psychodynamic), in which case you need to carefully select theories which illuminate the important debates in the field. The danger is that you will become side-tracked with describing your chosen personality taxonomies at the price of evaluating them, so make sure you get this balance right.

For your answer to be strong you should demonstrate an understanding of the strengths and limitations of the methodology used in research, such as the method used to derive traits, and how this impacts on personality theory.

Sample question

Could you answer the question below? It is a typical essay question that could arise on this topic. Guidelines on answering the question are included at the end of this chapter, whilst a sample problem question and guidance on tackling it can be found on the companion website at **www.pearsoned.co.uk/psychologyexpress**

 Sample question   *Essay*

Critically discuss the extent to which the method(s) theorists use to identify traits impacts upon our understanding of personality.

The dispositional approach to personality

The dispositional approach views personality as the 'qualities that people carry around with them, that belong to them, that are somehow part of them' (Carver & Scheier, 1998). This view is underpinned by a number of assumptions:

- Personality is driven by *internal* factors.
- Personality can be inferred from people's behaviour.
- The *differences* between people's personalities can be described and measured.
- Personality is relatively stable across time.
- Personality is relatively stable across situations.

The dispositional approach can be contrasted with the *situational* approach.

- **Situationists** argue that instead of being internally driven, personality is constructed by *external* factors.
- Situational theorists suggest that personality should be viewed as a series of unrelated behaviours, or states, which arise from the *context* in which they occur (Mischel, 1968). Therefore, the core set of personality characteristics which dispositional theorists seek to identify does not actually exist!

CRITICAL FOCUS

Dispositional, situational and interactionist approaches

Some contemporary approaches, such as Funder's 'personality triad' (Funder, 2006, 2009; Sherman, Nave & Funder, 2010), seek to combine the dispositional and situational approaches in meaningful ways. Many 'dispositional' theorists and researchers now accept that behaviour is likely to be a product of both personality and situational factors. This position has come to be known as **interactionism**, or the **person–situation interaction approach**.

Test your knowledge

1   In what ways do the dispositional and situational approaches differ in how they view personality?
2   What aspects of the dispositional approach do you initially think could be problematic or controversial?

Further reading

Topic	Key reading
Person–situation interaction debate	Funder, D. (2006). Towards a resolution of the personality triad: Persons, situations, and behaviour. *Journal of Research in Personality*, *40(1)*, 21–34.
Person–situation debate	Fleeson, W. & Noftle, E. (2008). The end of the person–situation debate: An emerging synthesis in the answer to the consistency question. *Social and Personality Psychology Compass, 2(4)*, 1667–84.

Defining traits

In contemporary psychology, traits are usually considered to be the fundamental units of personality (Weiner & Craighead, 2010) and are seen as dimensions along which people can be rated 'according to the degree to which they manifest a particular characteristic' (p. 150; Burger, 2010). For example, a score of 8 along a trait dimension of 'conscientiousness' (on a scale of 1 to 10), would represent a high degree of conscientiousness. However, this view is not shared by everyone; numerous definitions of traits are available, which can be confusing

(Saucier & Goldberg, 1996). The definition adopted by a theorist will tell you something about the role they view traits as playing, and how they view the relationship between traits and behaviour.

The concept of 'traits' fulfils two key functions in personality research, which are usually viewed as mutually exclusive and suggest different relationships between traits and behaviour:

1 Traits as reflecting *internal causal properties* (Alston, 1975). This conceptualisation views traits as *independent* of external behaviour and therefore requires measures that are also independent of behaviour.

2 Traits as *descriptive summaries of characteristics* (Saucier & Goldberg, 2001). This approach makes no assumptions about internality or causality and refers only to *expressed behaviour*.

These two conceptualisations have divided theorists and shaped the way in which they seek to identify traits.

Deriving traits

Three main approaches to identifying traits are used in dispositional personality research:

1 **Lexical approach**

2 **Statistical approach**

3 **Theoretical approach**

Lexical approach

The lexical approach to identifying traits has shaped the work of many personality theorists, such as Allport, Cattell and Wiggins, and is based upon the **lexical hypothesis**. The lexical hypothesis originally developed from the work of Sir Francis Galton (1822–1911), who believed that the key to understanding personality lay in the language used to describe it (Galton, 1884). Galton argued that the most meaningful personality descriptors become encoded into language as *single words*.

Three key assumptions underpin the lexical hypothesis:

1 Personality descriptors that are used more frequently in language indicate more important characteristics (frequency; Hampson, 2000)

2 Personality descriptors with a greater number of synonyms reflect more important characteristics (synonym frequency; Saucier & Goldberg, 1996).

3 Personality descriptors with corresponding terms in many different languages indicate cross-culturally important characteristics (cross-cultural universality; Saucier & Goldberg, 1996).

Practical application of theory Applying the lexical hypothesis

In a fictional pilot study presented in Table 2.1 below, examining personality descriptors in the English language, it can be seen that 'conscientiousness' has 5 words associated with it (n_{ass} = 5) and has a rating of 10 for its frequency of use (n_{freq} = 10). 'Endeavour', however, has more words associated with it but a lower frequency of use (n_{ass} = 6; n_{freq} = 6). The total usage of words associated with 'conscientiousness' is given as 50 (N_{tot} = 50). Therefore, the descriptor 'conscientiousness' appears to be a more important descriptor of a personal characteristic than 'endeavour' and 'expeditious'.

Table 2.1 Results of a fictional pilot study on word frequency amongst associated words

Personality label	List of associated words	n_{ass}	n_{freq}	N_{tot}
Conscientious	Dutiful, fastidious, meticulous, observant, scrupulous	5	10	50
Endeavour	Act, attempt, effort, exertion, strive, try to	6	6	36
Expeditious	Active, fast, hasty, prompt	4	9	36

Theorists adopting the lexical approach therefore use dictionaries and similar resources to develop lists (or lexicons) of personality descriptors and using the above method are able to identify traits which appear most important to a particular culture.

Points to consider

- The lexical approach is a key generative method, or starting point, for identifying important individual differences (Ashton & Lee, 2005).

- It potentially provides vast numbers of trait descriptors (a seminal lexicon produced by Allport and Odbert in 1936 produced over 4500 personality descriptors). Although this makes data rich, the lexicons produced can be unwieldy and difficult to use in personality testing and research.

- It views language as the core tool for understanding personality. Although language as a social process must be important, this premise brings into question how accurately traits are portrayed in language, and what each personality descriptor's relationship is to every other personality descriptor in a language (Saucier & Goldberg, 1996).

- Traits and the theories they correspond to may be tied to the culture in which they are developed and therefore may not be generalisable to other cultures (Juni, 1996).

- Adjectives tend to be the only type of word from which personality descriptors are identified. However, personality is also conveyed by other types of word, e.g. nouns or verbs (Saucier and Goldberg, 1996).

- Terms with evaluative connotations tend to be deliberately excluded from lexicons, although they are likely to represent important concepts within a culture (Benet-Martínez & Waller, 2002). When evaluative terms have been included in research using the lexical approach, different personality trait dimensions have been identified from those which dominate personality theory (Benet-Martínez & Waller, 2002).

Statistical approach

The statistical approach to deriving traits was pioneered by Raymond Cattell, who wanted to identify traits *empirically*. To do this required a method of reducing down data produced by the lexical approach, such as Allport's list of 4500 personality descriptors. Cattell employed a range of techniques to achieve this, primarily using factor analysis.

Factor analysis is a statistical analysis technique that allows you to identify groups of terms (e.g. personality descriptors) from a large pool of items, that 'cluster' together. The large pool of terms will usually have been generated using the lexical approach and converted into personality-relevant sentences that large samples of people have then rated. For example, people will be asked to rate the extent to which they feel the sentence 'I enjoy meeting new people' applies to them on a scale of 1 to 7 (with 1 being Strongly disagree and 7 being Strongly agree). Clusters of terms appear because some items are similar to each other, but dissimilar to all other terms. These clusters of terms are taken to indicate an underlying construct (factor) which can be given a name (label) that 'sums up' the qualities of all the terms that comprise it. For example, if the terms 'punctual', 'hard working', 'works to a high standard' and 'thorough' were found to cluster together, they could be 'summed up' by the label 'conscientious'. This is how many theorists derive names for the personality traits in their taxonomies.

Factor analysis therefore provides a potential method for reducing down the data produced by the lexical approach, identifying the order of importance of traits, and a means of identifying the *structure* of personality (i.e. how traits are organised). It is an important concept to the whole field of Individual Differences psychology and particularly **psychometrics**.

Points to consider

- 'Reducing down' data may result in loss of detail and an 'averaging out' of all that makes individuals unique.
- Raymond Cattell and other theorists viewed this method as 'objective'. However, there are elements of subjectivity, such as when choosing what terms to enter into the analysis and choosing factor names.
- The data which form the basis of the statistical approach are usually collected via self-report measures (see Chapter 10). The relationship between self-reported behaviour and actual behaviour has historically identified discrepancies; this may impact on our understanding of personality.

The theoretical approach

Unlike the lexical and statistical approaches to deriving traits, which make no prior judgement about the relative importance of traits, the theoretical approach directs the research to which traits are *important* to identify. The theory also often indicates which traits are more important in relation to each other.

Points to consider

- The theoretical approach may provide a more coherent picture of personality traits.
- It can provide a clear justification for the inclusion and exclusion of traits.
- It may overlook important traits because the theory does not direct the researcher to them.
- This approach is heavily influenced by the strengths and limitations of the individual theories directing the derivation of traits.

Personality theorists often adopt a combination of approaches to identifying traits: for example, using the lexical approach or theoretical approaches to identify traits initially and using statistical techniques to reduce data down to manageable numbers of traits (Norman, 1963; Cattell & Kline, 1976; Goldberg, 1990).

 Sample question   *Problem-based learning*

You are a researcher working for a government department and your team has been asked to develop a new personality model aimed primarily at understanding risk-taking behaviour. Your task is to write a short brief outlining which method of identifying the important traits you need to include in your model; will you recommend using the lexical, theoretical or statistical approach (or a combination) to do this? What information will you need to provide? What issues will you need to consider and how will you overcome any issues in implementing your choice of method?

Test your knowledge

1. Can you briefly outline the strengths and limitations of the lexical, statistical and theoretical approaches to identifying traits?
2. In what circumstances would you use the lexical, statistical and theoretical approaches to indentifying traits?
3. How might you combine the three approaches effectively to identify personality traits?

Further reading	
Topic	*Key reading*
Overview of the personality trait concept	Part 1, section 1 (pp. 3–37). Matthews, G., Deary, I. & Whiteman, M. (2003). *Personality traits.* Cambridge: Cambridge University Press.
Critique of the lexical approach	Saucier, G. (2009). Recurrent personality dimensions in inclusive lexical studies: Indications for a big six structure, *Journal of Personality, 77(5),* 1577–614.
	Mollaret, P. (2009). Using common psychological terms to describe other people: From lexical hypothesis to polysemous conception, *Theory and Psychology, 19(3),* 315–44.
Overview of factor analysis	Chapter 17: Exploratory factor analysis. In A. Field (2009). *Discovering statistics using SPSS* (3rd edn). London: Sage.

How many traits is enough? Developing trait taxonomies

Historically there has been little agreement about the number or structure of traits required to sufficiently describe and explain personality (Kline, 2000). Many personality classifications have therefore developed, as researchers working from different approaches investigate the issue in different ways.

Personality classification systems are usually called trait taxonomies; as well as specifying the number of traits required, these taxonomies also specify the relative importance and bandwidth of the traits included, and how these traits should be organised or structured.

Allport's trait-theory

Gordon Allport was a strong supporter of the lexical approach to deriving traits and his work has since influenced many other theorists (e.g. Cattell).

KEY STUDY

Example of the lexical approach

In 1936 Allport and Odbert produced one of the largest lexical lists, with 18,000 words describing individual differences, of which 4500 described personality traits. This lexicon has subsequently been used by numerous theorists (such as Cattell) in their research and has therefore been influential in our understanding of personality.

Allport felt that the nomothetic approach to personality was only useful for uncovering **common personality traits** (1961), but an idiographic approach which examined *personal dispositions* could provide a more meaningful description and explanation of personality. This is because you can see how

31

traits *come together* to produce individual uniqueness. According to Allport's theory, personal disposition traits could be classified as either **cardinal**, **central** or **secondary** (Maltby, Day & Macaskill, 2010).

Table 2.2 **Allport's trait classifications**

Trait name	Description
Cardinal traits	A single trait that typically dominates an individual's personality and behaviour. These are viewed as a 'driving force' behind personality.
Central traits	The 5–10 traits (approximately) which best describe an individual's personality.
Secondary traits	These traits may only be observable in specific situations and refer to an individual's preferences, rather than the core constituents of their personality.

Allport felt that this approach to personality would provide a greater ability to predict how an *individual* would behave in given situations than relying only on common personality traits (Allport, 1961).

Points to consider

- Allport's theory recognises the complexity of personality and explores personality *holistically*.
- It potentially provides better means of predicting *individuals'* behaviour.
- It recognises the different bandwidth of traits in explaining and deriving human behaviour.
- It tends only to be able to study individuals one at a time to identify their personal dispositions and is therefore time and resource intensive.
- It is not conducive to making comparisons between people, as people must be described in terms that are unique to them.

Cattell's 16 Personality Factors (16PF) system

Cattell was a pioneer of the statistical approach to personality and developed one of the largest trait taxonomies in personality theory.

KEY STUDY

Example of the statistical approach

Cattell and Kline (1976) used Allport and Odbert's (1936) lexical list, and explored other personality assessment and psychiatric literature to develop a comprehensive list of traits, sufficient to explain all individual differences in personality. A team of raters reduced the initial 4500 trait names to 171, by removing all synonyms. The team of raters then assessed individuals on these traits, to see which were evident and which were not, and reduced the list to 36 trait names. From exploring the other literature noted above, 10 new trait names were added to the list, resulting in a final number of

46 traits. Cattell and Kline labelled these traits 'surface traits'. To examine how these surface traits clustered together, and therefore to identify the structure of personality, Cattell and Kline collected data on individuals' traits using a variety of techniques and sources, from large samples of people.

Data sources included:

- **L-data** – Life record data, such as educational qualifications.
- **Q-data** (also referred to as S-data) – data from personality questionnaires.
- **T-data** – data from standardised testing procedures (i.e. tests which could not be faked)

The data were analysed using factor analysis, and revealed 16 major clusters of surface traits, which Cattell called **primary factors**, or *source traits*.

Raymond Cattell described his 16 primary factors in terms of *scales* with positive and negative *poles*. These factors were also labelled in order of how good they were at explaining differences between people (see Table 2.3).

Table 2.3 Cattell's 16 Personality Factors

Factor	Positive pole	Negative pole
Factor A	Outgoing	Reserved
Factor B	More intelligent	Less intelligent
Factor C	Stable	Emotional
Factor E	Assertive	Humble
Factor F	Happy-go-lucky	Sober
Factor G	Conscientious	Expedient
Factor H	Venturesome	Shy
Factor I	Tender-minded	Tough-minded
Factor L	Suspicious	Trusting
Factor M	Imaginative	Practical
Factor N	Shrewd	Forthright
Factor O	Apprehensive (guilt prone)	Placid (assurance)
Factor Q_1	Experimenting	Conservative
Factor Q_2	Self-sufficient	Group–tied (adherence)
Factor Q_3	Controlled	Casual (discipline)
Factor Q_4	Tense	Relaxed (tension)

Factor Q is broken down into four because it is the least good predictor of behaviour.

Cattell found that several of the scales correlated moderately to highly with each other, and he was able to reduce the original taxonomy down to five *second-order* factors (see Table 2. 4)

Table 2.4 **Cattell's second-order factors**

Extraversion versus Introversion
High Anxiety versus Low Anxiety
Tough Poise versus Emotionality
Independence versus Subduedness
High Control versus Low Control

Cattell's taxonomy is one of the most dominant personality taxonomies and is also one of the largest in the field. The 16 Personality Factor system forms the basis of a questionnaire (widely used in recruitment and selection) called the 16PF (Cattell, Eber & Tatsuoka, 1970). A massively revised version of the questionnaire was published in 1994 with over 50% of the items being changed or amended in some way (Conn & Rieke, 1994), as some of the scales were found to have poor internal consistency. This makes comparisons of findings between research using the original version and the revised version difficult. However, the original version of the questionnaire did have evidential support. For example, the 16PF was found to predict success in different school subjects (Barton, Dielman & Cattell, 1971).

Cattell's work on personality was prolific and he suggested a number of other classifications of traits (Cattell, 1950), including traits relating to the 'nature–nurture' debate (Chapter 3).

Points to consider

- Cattell's 16 PF system has a strong empirical basis, with clearly documented methodology. This means that his methodology for identifying traits and their structure is replicable.

- Although the model appears to have evidential support, failure by Cattell and other researchers to replicate the primary factors and second-order factors suggests that the traits may be less reliable and stable than desired.

- Cattell emphasised the empirical and objective nature of his method of identifying traits. However, the subjectivity of certain aspects of this method is overlooked. These include: the selection of descriptors included in the analysis from Allport's lexical list; the choice of traits identified as belonging to the factors; and the choice of names for the factors.

- Cattell's taxonomy allows for a detailed assessment of personality. However, the sheer size of the taxonomy means it is difficult to manage. In fact, a smaller number of traits would probably satisfactorily capture the differences between individuals (consider Eysenck's PEN model, discussed next).

- Cattell's approach in general has been criticised for not simplifying the issue – other researchers have found it difficult to follow his work. This has meant that his work has not had as great an impact as you might expect.

• It has also been criticised for using obscure trait labels, making his classifications less intuitive.

Hans Eysenck's PEN model

Eysenck also used a combination of the three methods to identify traits. He was interested in the biological underpinnings of personality (see Chapter 3 for further details) and was influenced by behaviourist principles (see Chapter 4). Eysenck's theory suggests that people react to incidents in specific ways (specific behavioural responses), and when these reactions become typical, a habitual response is formed. Eysenck's theory directed him to identify the behavioural and habitual responses which were of importance, and then, like Cattell, he used factor analysis as a data reduction method and to identify the structure of his trait taxonomy.

Unlike Cattell, Eysenck developed one of the smallest taxonomies available; it contains only three core dimensions: Psychoticism, Extraversion and Neuroticism. The model derives its name PEN from these three dimensions and is also known as the **Gigantic Three model** and **tripartite trait model**. Eysenck's model was constructed in the form of a hierarchy, with a large number of these specific behavioural responses being grouped into a smaller number of **habitual responses**, which in turn produced a number of traits. These traits are used to infer personality types, or supertraits (Eysenck & Eysenck, 1985a). Figure 2.1 shows how this processes works.

Eysenck used the term 'types' in this theory, since there were just the three dimensions of Psychoticism, Extraversion and Neuroticism. The fewer labels allowed the grouping of individuals into classes.

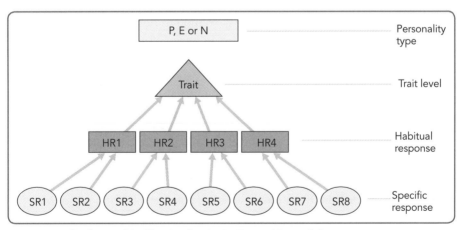

Figure 2.1 The hierarchical basis of traits in Eysenck's model
Source: Adapted from H. Eysenck, *The Biological Basis of Personality*, 1967. Courtesy of Charles C. Thomas Publishers, Ltd., Springfield, Illinois.

The traits associated with the three types or supertraits (Psychoticism, Extraversion and Neuroticism) are outlined in Table 2.5.

Table 2.5 **Traits comprising Eysenck's types/supertraits**

Psychoticism	Extraversion	Neuroticism
Aggressive	Sociable	Lack of autonomy
Cold	Lively	Unhappiness
Egocentric	Active	Pessimistic
Impersonal	Assertive	Anxious
Impulsive	Sensation-seeking	Health concerned
Unempathic	Carefree	Obsessive
Creative	Dominant	Low self-esteem
Tough-minded	Outgoing	Moody
Antisocial	Venturesome	Guilt prone

Source: Adapted from Eysenck & Wilson (1976) and *Personality, Individual Differences and Intelligence*, 2e, Maltby et al., Pearson Education Limited, © Pearson Education Limited 2010.

Eysenck's PEN model forms the basis of a number of questionnaires, including the Eysenck Personality Questionnaire (EPQ; Eysenck & Eysenck, 1975), which has been used extensively in research. However, owing to problems with the reliability of the Psychoticism scale (see Chapter 10 for a discussion of reliability), a revised version of the questionnaire was published in 1985 (EPQ-R; Eysenck, Eysenck & Barrett, 1985).

Points to consider

- The model provides a manageable number of traits in comparison to other taxonomies. However, the comprehensiveness of the model has been questioned; are three dimensions really enough to describe personality?

- There is evidence to support the cross-cultural universality of Eysenck's PEN model. Eysenck and Eysenck (1982) translated their questionnaire into African-, Asian-, Northern American- and European-based languages and found the same underlying PEN structure in 24 of the cases. The same structure was also obtained for both male and female participants (Eysenck & Eysenck, 1982).

- The PEN traits have been found to show moderate heritability (Reevy, Ozer & Ito, 2010), supporting the rationale for the model. However, other traits have also been found to show moderate heritability (Matthews, Deary & Whiteman, 2003) but are not included in the PEN model.

- In the PEN model, the three dimensions are conceptualised as orthogonal (unrelated), but other research has found a potential overlap between Psychoticism and Extraversion in the form of *impulsivity* (Wiggins, 1979).

Wiggins' Circumplex

Jerry Wiggins believed that people differ in *different ways* and he conceptualised a number of traits to describe this, as shown in Table 2.6.

Table 2.6 Jerry Wiggins' trait classifications

Trait name	Refers to ...
Interpersonal traits	The characteristic ways in which people interact with each other
Temperament traits	The 'nature' of a person, e.g. 'optimistic', 'excitable', 'nervous'
Character traits	The 'moral' character of an individual, e.g. 'honest' or 'dishonest'
Material traits	An individual's characteristics with material goods, such as 'generous' or 'miserly'
Mental traits	Perception of an individual's cognitive abilities, such as 'clever'
Physical traits	An individual's physical characteristics, such as 'healthy' or 'unhealthy'

Wiggins was primarily interested in *interpersonal traits*, which he felt were based upon social exchanges. Wiggins (1979) used the lexical and statistical approaches to produce a taxonomy based upon these traits, which he conceptualised as a **circumplex** (circular) theory.

The Circumplex taxonomy is based on the two dimensions which Wiggins believed defined social exchange: *love* and *status*. Using these dimensions, Wiggins created an 'interpersonal map' on which different behaviours, and therefore traits, could be located. This allowed him to identify:

- traits that were *adjacent* (related) to one another – the closer traits are to each other, the more highly correlated they are;
- traits that were *bipolar* (opposite) – traits which are bipolar are negatively correlated;
- traits that were *orthogonal* – traits which are completely unrelated or independent of one another.

Points to consider

- The model explicitly defines interpersonal behaviour; many taxonomies do not attempt this.
- Wiggins' 'interpersonal map' is limited to two dimensions, excluding some important traits (e.g. conscientiousness).
- The model makes explicit the relationship (e.g. adjacent, bipolar or orthogonal) between each and every other trait in the model; again, many taxonomies do not attempt this.
- Wiggins' Circumplex has evidential support: for example, it has been used successfully to identify maladaptive personal functioning strategies (Hennig & Walker, 2008).
- The Circumplex provides a framework for identifying under-researched topics in personality.

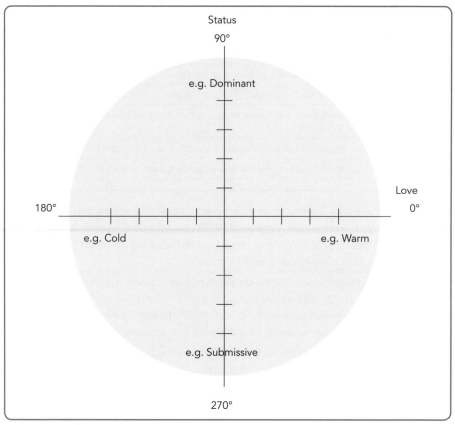

Figure 2.2 **Wiggins' Circumplex**

The Five Factor Model (FFM)

The FFM (also known as the 'Big Five') emerged as a 'consensus' from amongst competing models that seemed to measure very similar constructs (Funder, 2001). Like Cattell's 16 PF and Wiggins' Circumplex, the FFM also has its basis in the lexical and statistical approaches, which lead to *Openness to Experience, Conscientiousness, Extraversion, Agreeableness* and *Neuroticism* being identified and adopted as the named traits for the model (acronym OCEAN). These factors are best characterised as broad dimensions that incorporate more specific facets (see Table 2.7).

The FFM has formed the basis of a number of measures, including the Big Five Mini Marker (Saucier, 1994) and the NEO-PI-R and the NEO-FFM (Costa & McCrae, 1992).

Using the NEO-FFM, growing evidential support for the model has been revealed and many theorists feel that it offers the strongest predictive capacity for behaviour. For example, research has identified an association of low Conscientiousness and low Neuroticism with anti-social behaviour (Ge & Conger,

Table 2.7 The trait and facet structure of the FFM of personality

Openness (O)	Conscientiousness (C)	Extraversion (E)	Agreeableness (A)	Neuroticism (N)
Fantasy (O_f)	Competence (C_c)	Warmth (E_w)	Trust (A_t)	Anxiety (N_a)
Aesthetics (O_{aes})	Order (C_o)	Gregariousness (E_g)	Straightforwardness (A_s)	Depression (E_d)
Feelings (O_f)	Dutifulness (C_{dut})	Assertiveness (E_{ass})	Altruism (A_a)	Impulsiveness (N_i)
Actions (O_{act})	Deliberation (C_{del})	Activity (E_{act})	Compliance (A_c)	Vulnerability (N_v)
Ideas (O_i)	Self-discipline (C_{s-d})	Excitement seeking (E_{e-s})	Modesty (M_m)	Angry hostility (N_{a-h})
Values (O_v)	Achievement-striving (C_{a-s})	Positive emotions (E_{p-e})	Tender-mindedness (A_{t-m})	Self-consciousness (N_{s-c})

Practical application of theory **Applying the five factor model**

The FFM profile of an individual is presented in Figure 2.3. Using the information provided in this profile, explain why you would consider such a person to be well or poorly suited to the role of pub quiz host and that of a nursing care assistant. What further information would you like to have about the individual?

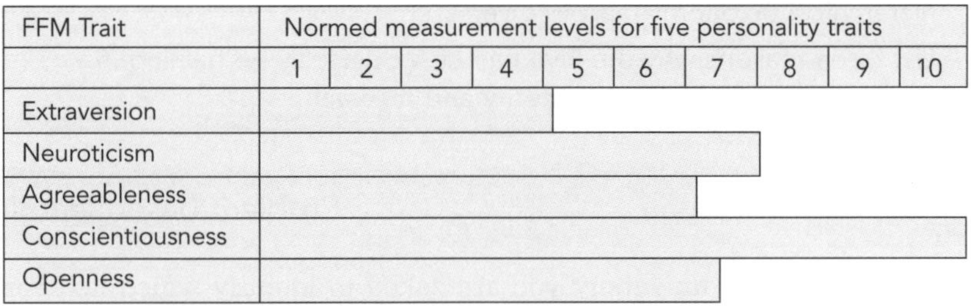

FFM Trait	Normed measurement levels for five personality traits									
	1	2	3	4	5	6	7	8	9	10
Extraversion										
Neuroticism										
Agreeableness										
Conscientiousness										
Openness										

Figure 2.3 **Illustrative profile employing the Five Factor structure**

1999; Walton & Roberts, 2004; Wiebe, 2004; Verona, Patrick & Joiner, 2001), whereas Extraversion and Agreeableness have been associated with pro-social behavior (Carlo et al., 2005). Low Openness to experience has been associated with both conservatism and authoritarianism (Riemann et al., 1993; Van Hiel & Mervielde, 1996; McCrae, 1996; Trapnell, 1996).

There is also evidence for the FFM's cultural universality; the NEO-PI-R has been translated into numerous languages and has found the same underlying factor structure (McCrae & Costa, 1997; McCrae et al., 1998, McCrae et al., 2000).

Points to consider

- There is a growing and substantial body of evidence for the FFM's predictive capacity.
- The basis of the Five Factor Model within the lexical and statistical approach has a number of implications:
  - Other important factors have been identified, such as positive and negative evaluation (Almagor, Tellegen & Waller, 1995) and spirituality/religiosity (Goldberg & Saucier, 1995), but these are not included in the model.
  - It does not examine the causal properties of personality.
  - Are five factors sufficient comprehensively to describe and explain individual differences in personality?

 Sample question   ***Essay***

Critically compare Cattell's 16PF and Eysenck's PEN personality taxonomies. Providing relevant examples from theory and research, discuss which taxonomy you feel provides the most comprehensive account of personality.

Test your knowledge

1. In what ways are Cattell's 16 PF, Eysenck's PEN and the Five Factor Model similar and in what ways do they differ?
2. What might be the advantages of a circumplex taxonomy over a hierarchical taxonomy (and vice versa)?
3. List three reasons why the Five Factor Model may be gaining in popularity in contemporary theory and research.

 Sample question   ***Problem-based learning***

In an assignment at university, you are asked to identify which taxonomy would be most useful for helping a counsellor who wishes to explore a patient's risk-taking behaviour, and an HR manager who wishes to include a personality questionnaire in selection and recruitment days, to help identify which candidate will be the best for the job they are applying for. You are asked to choose from the following list: Allport's approach to personality, Cattell's 16 Personality Factor system and the Five Factor Model. Which taxonomy do you think would be best for each situation? What information would you need to consider (or find out) before you could make your decision?

Further reading

Topic	Key reading
Review of Cattell's 16 Personality Factors	Cattell, R. & Krug, S. (1986). The number of factors in the 16PF: a review of the evidence with special emphasis on methodological problems, *Educational and Psychological Measurement, 46(3)*, 509–22.
Discussion of the core personality dimensions	Eysenck, H. (1991). Dimensions of personality: 16, 5 or 3? – Criteria for a taxonomic paradigm, *Personality and Individual Differences, 12(8)*, 773–90.
Comparison of personality scales based on Wiggins' Circumplex and the Five Factor Model.	Eysenck, H. (1991). Dimensions of personality: 16, 5 or 3? – Criteria for a taxonomic paradigm, *Personality and Individual Differences, 12(8)*, 773–90.
Overview of the Five Factor Model	McCrae, R. & Costa, P. (2008). Empirical and theoretical status of the Five-Factor Model of personality traits. In G. Boyle, G. Matthews & D. Saklofske (eds), *The SAGE handbook of personality theory and assessment: (volume 1): Personality theories and models*. London: Sage.
Critique of the Five Factor Model.	Norem, J. (2010). Resisting the hegemony of the Five-Factor Model: There is plenty of personality outside the FFA, *Psychological Inquiry, 21(1)*, 65–8.

Measuring traits

Measuring traits and types has become a major focus of theorists working within the dispositional approach and typically involves the construction of self-reported measures of behaviour, attitudes and cognitions. Some of the key personality measures have already been mentioned, including Cattell's 16PF questionnaire, Eysenck and Eysenck's EPQ-R, and Costa and McCrae's NEO-PI-R. The methods used to develop these questionnaires (and other questionnaires examining intelligence, motivation, etc.) form the basis of the field of psychometrics. As this is a topic in its own right and of great importance to Individual Differences psychology, a separate chapter is devoted to evaluating it (Chapter 10). Importantly, our understanding of personality is reliant on the effectiveness of the tools we use to measure it.

Critique of the dispositional approach and trait theories

Mischel (1968) questioned whether the dominant dispositional trait theories were adequate to describe and capture personality. He questioned whether:

- traits actually exist;
- traits are culturally universal;
- traits actually explain or predict behaviour.

Mischel (1968) reviewed a large number of studies exploring the correlation between personality traits and behaviour and found that the majority of studies reported only low correlations (typically r = 0.3). He argued that traits were therefore only able to predict *negligible* amounts of variance in personality. Haslam (2007) argues there is growing evidence to suggest that personality is consistent across situations and stable across time, strengthening the claim that traits are 'influential and predictively valuable sources of behaviour' (p. 49).

However, Mischel's argument has been challenged on the following points. Rosenthal (1990) argued that correlation of r = 0.3 can have important implications and is therefore far from negligible. Also, Mischel only looked at the correlation between traits and specific instances of behaviour, when most personality theorists and theories are more interested in *patterns* in behaviour, emotion and cognitions. Fleeson (2001) argues that greater consistency in behaviour will be observed when traits and situational factors are considered in combination (i.e. interactionism).

Cultural universality?

The **relativist critique** (or cultural-relativist critique) questions whether some theories, or even the concept of traits in general, are applicable outside specific western cultures (Haslam, 2007). For example, cultures differ in terms of their emphasis on individualism or collectivism (Miller & Schaberg, 2003), the extent to which people use internal or external factors to explain behaviour and the size of 'trait vocabularies' (Lillard, 1998; Fiske et al., 1998). This is evidenced by the findings from some translation studies of personality questionnaires that similar results and structures are identified for European countries, but not for non-European cultures (Haslam, 2007). This has led some theorists to argue that to develop an effective personality test you should adopt an ethnographic methodology and study personality indigenously (Haslam, 2007).

Alternatives to traits

A number of alternatives to traits have been proposed by dispositional theorists, including the following:

Traits versus types

Types represent an alternative way of describing personality to traits. Although many of the debates considered above regarding traits are also applicable to types (e.g. conceptualisation as internal causal properties versus descriptive summaries), the two concepts differ in a number of key ways (see Table 2.8).

Table 2.8 **Differences between traits and types**

Traits	Types
• Dimensions	• Categories
• Degree (how)	• Discrete (what)
• Quantitative	• Qualitative
• Apply to everyone to some extent	• Apply only to people exhibiting specific characteristics
• E.g. score on 'Extraversion–introversion' scale	• E.g. classifying an individual as an extravert or not.

An example of personality 'types' is Friedman and Rosenman's (1974) Type A and Type B personalities. People with Type A personality are said to be driven and competitive individuals, whereas people with Type B personality are said to be relaxed and laid-back. In this case you are classified either as having a Type A or Type B personality.

Types are derived using the same methods as traits (lexically, statistically and theoretically) and type classification systems are usually referred to as **typologies**. One of the most famous typologies is the Myers-Briggs Type Inventory (Myers et al., 1998) which is based on the typological theories of Carl Jung and is also discussed in Chapter 6. According to Funder (2001), types have enjoyed a growth in popularity over recent years.

The difference between trait and type theories is not always clear-cut. For example, Eysenck's PEN model refers to both traits and types. Some argue that whether a theory specifies traits or types may merely be an artefact of the statistical method adopted by a theorist (Chamorro-Premuzic, 2007). There is a tendency in personality theory and research to assume that personality characteristics are best understood in terms of continua (i.e. traits). However, research suggests that categorical distinctions are valuable and have evidential support (Haslam & Kim, 2002).

Values

Values reflect abstract goals that apply across different situations and motivate people to behave in ways that pursue them (Schwartz, 1992, 1994). They differ from traits in a number of ways:

- They are conceptualised as more changeable than traits.
- They describe *cognitions* rather than behavioural tendencies.
- They can only be described as 'desirable' for that person, whereas traits can be negative or undesirable.

- They are easier to put into words than traits, as they are likely to be embedded within an individual's belief system.

Character strengths

Character strengths can be thought of as 'Values in Action' (Peterson & Seligman, 2002). They differ from traits in terms of being more evaluative in nature. This could address the issue outlined previously regarding the lexical approach to identifying traits and could lead to a fuller 'personality vocabulary' (Benet-Martínez & Waller, 2002). For example, Benet-Martínez and Waller (2002) administered a list containing evaluative personality descriptors to large samples of people and found five dimensions (four negative and one positive), which were different from those identified using non-evaluative descriptors.

States

Theorists such as Raymond Cattell (1957) suggest examining **states**, as this could prove to be the key to understanding why people behave differently in different situations. Cattell argued that there are two types of 'states': moods (transient feelings) and motivational states (forces that direct our behaviour). A criticism of the trait approach is that *behavioural consistencies* are used to infer dispositions; they therefore offer insights into *how* people behave rather than *why*. Cattell believed that examining motivation in relation to personality could resolve this issue.

Two distinct fields of research have grown in this area:

1 research exploring motivational drives which people are unaware of (e.g. instincts or needs); and

2 those motivational drives which people are aware of (e.g. goals).

Instincts and needs

Instincts and needs represent another way of conceptualising the forces *driving* behaviour (Murray, 1938; Markus and Nurius, 1986). Examples include Murray's (1938) 20 basic needs and McClelland's three fundamental needs (achievement, affiliation and power) models. Another branch of the field includes 'goals and strivings' models, such as Markus and Nurius' (1986) 'possible selves' model. These models suggest that people are motivated to act in ways that move them closer to their goals and this is why patterns in behaviour, thoughts and feelings evolve.

> ### Test your knowledge
>
> 1 List three strengths and three weaknesses of the 'trait' concept.
> 2 What might the impact be of excluding 'evaluative' descriptors from personality research?
> 3 Why might it be beneficial to conduct research that looks at traits or types, as well as character strengths, values and instincts?

Further reading

Topic	Key reading
Overview of different approaches to describing dispositions	Meehl, P. (1992). Factors and taxa, traits and types, difference of degree and differences in kind, *Journal of Personality, 60(1)*, 117–74.
Example of a taxonomy based on an alternative to traits (values)	Schwartz, S. (1992). Universals in the content and structure of values: Theoretical advances and empirical tests in 20 countries. In M. Zanna (ed.), *Advances in experimental social psychology* (pp. 1–65). New York: Academic Press.
Example of a model of personality based on vocational interests	Holland, J. (1997). *Making vocational choices: A theory of vocational personalities and work environments* (3rd edn). Odessa, FL: Psychological Assessment Resources.

Conclusion

Trait theories represent the dominant approach to exploring and assessing personality in psychology. However, dispositional theorists approach trait theory in different ways: some theorists use theory to direct them to explore certain traits, whereas other theorists use the traits they identify to develop theory.

Theorists tend to use a range of methods to identify traits and trait taxonomies, which impact on the way in which we understand personality. Currently the most popular model of personality appears to be the Five Factor Model. However, this is not without criticism. There is a growing recognition of the importance of understanding the impact of interactions between dispositional and situational factors.

Traits may also represent only one *level* of personality description (McAdams, 1995). Incorporating other dispositional attributes, such as motivation, into trait theories may shed further light on the patterns in the way people think, feel and behave.

An important issue is that the methods used to identify traits and how traits are ultimately measured will provide the boundaries for how effective a model of personality is.

Chapter summary: putting it all together

→ Can you tick all the points from the revision checklist at the beginning of this chapter?

→ Attempt the sample question from the beginning of this chapter using the answer guidelines below.

→ Go to the companion website at www. pearsoned.co.uk/psychologyexpress to access more revision support online, including interactive quizzes, sample questions with answer guidelines, 'you be the marker' exercises, flashcards and podcasts you can download.

Answer guidelines

Guidelines on answering the sample questions presented at the start of the chapter are given below.

 Sample question   **Essay**

Critically discuss the extent to which the method(s) theorists use to identify traits impacts upon our understanding of personality.

Approaching the question

Firstly, you need to describe what traits are and how they are conceptualised (e.g. internal causal properties versus descriptive summaries of characteristics). You also need to discuss the issues that arise from these different conceptualisations. You could also refer to the 'accessibility' debate mentioned in the previous chapter.

Next, you need to outline the three key methods of identifying traits which you will need to evaluate in the essay: the lexical approach, the statistical approach and the theoretical approach. You will then need to evaluate each of these approaches systematically; examine their strengths and limitations; and provide well-chosen examples from theory and research to evidence the points you make.

Important points to include

- Explore the lexical hypothesis as it underpins the lexical approach to identifying traits. For example, discuss the assumption that all *meaningful* ways of describing Individual Differences can be discovered from examining language.
- Refer to the contribution of Gordon Allport to the lexical approach:
  - You could highlight the impact of the lists he developed on future researchers (e.g. Cattell), discuss the potential impact of excluding evaluative personality descriptors and nouns on how we understand personality, and examine the fact that there is a question about the degree of cultural universality of personality descriptor words.
- Refer to the contribution of Raymond Cattell to the statistical approach to identifying traits.
  - You could discuss the strengths and limitations of factor analysis. For example, you could explore the impact of the objective and subjective

elements of the technique on our understanding of personality. This includes aspects such as deciding which items to include in the analysis and the criteria used to determine how many factors to extract, the names given to each factor and the criteria upon which this is based.

- You could also discuss the implications of the reliance of this approach on self-report measures and the debate concerning whether data reduction methods such as factor analysis lead to a loss of individual 'uniqueness'.

- Explore the theoretical approach to identifying traits, such as the way Eysenck's theory directed him to study situational and habitual responses, which he then used to develop his personality taxonomy.

  - Highlight the fact that taxonomies developed using the theoretical approach 'pick up' the strengths and limitations of the theory upon which they are based.

- You could discuss the ways in which theorists have used combinations of the three approaches to identify traits, and how this has affected subsequent theory: for example, compounding or ameliorating limitations.

- You could discuss the differences in the conceptualisation and application of traits identified through a nomothetic approach versus an idiographic approach and how this impacts on the way in which we view personality.

- Make the implications of the concept of traits clear – highlight the potential applications of the trait taxonomies developed: for example, psychometric tests used in clinical, health, educational, counselling, occupational and forensic contexts. Therefore, any strengths and limitations which accrue as a result of the method of identifying traits will have significant consequences for the people in these situations.

- Use trait taxonomies developed using the different approaches to highlight the approaches' strengths and weaknesses: for example, the size of trait taxonomies, their comprehensiveness and completeness.

Make your answer stand out

For a strong answer you should evaluate the trait theory approach in general. This could include: examining the impact of the situationist and interactionist debates on how 'dispositions' are understood (see Chapter 7 for further information on this); the discussion concerning whether types provide a better description of individual differences than traits; and the debate over whether different 'units' of personality (such as values, character strengths, motives, goals or instincts and needs) would provide a better account of personality.

You could end your essay with a brief discussion of where you feel future research in trait theory should be directed and why.

Notes

3

Biological theories of personality

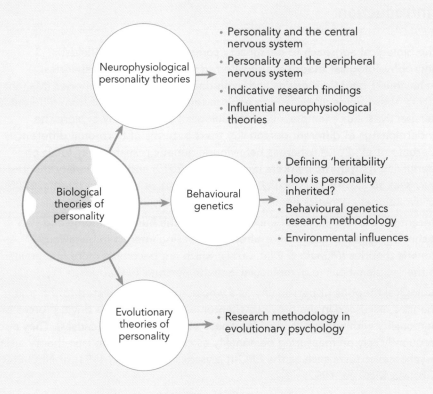

Neurophysiological personality theories
- Personality and the central nervous system
- Personality and the peripheral nervous system
- Indicative research findings
- Influential neurophysiological theories

Biological theories of personality

Behavioural genetics
- Defining 'heritability'
- How is personality inherited?
- Behavioural genetics research methodology
- Environmental influences

Evolutionary theories of personality
- Research methodology in evolutionary psychology

A printable version of this topic map is available from:
www.pearsoned.co.uk/psychologyexpress

Revision checklist

Essential points you should know:

☐ The key features of the neurophysiological, behavioural genetic and evolutionary approaches to personality

☐ Evidence for the biological basis of personality traits

☐ Methodology associated with biological approaches to personality and their strengths and limitations

☐ What heritability estimates are and what they suggest about the contribution of genetic and environmental factors to personality

☐ Current developments in evolutionary theory

Introduction

The biological approach to personality comprises three main fields: **neurophysiological theories** (also referred to as physiological theories), **behavioural genetic theories** and **evolutionary personality theories** (Mahoney, 2011). These fields often seek to explore the same issues, but from different perspectives. For example, neurophysiological theories may explore the underpinnings of different personality traits in terms of **hormonal differences** (Barbato et al., 2012), whereas behavioural genetic research may focus on identifying its **genetic markers** (Smillie et al., 2010) and evolutionary theories may seek to explain personality in terms of adaptive behaviour (Nettle, 2005) or evolutionary genetics (Penke, Denissen & Miller, 2007).

Recent breakthroughs in our understanding of the **human genome** and technological advances have resulted in increasing interest in behavioural genetic theories (Munafò & Flint, 2011), which are becoming more fine-grained in their explanations (e.g. **molecular-genetic** personality theories).

Biological theories of personality as a whole are strongly related to the trait theories discussed in the previous chapter, as they locate the driving forces of personality within the individual (as innate *abilities*, *drives* or *causes*). They also frequently rely on measuring personality as conceptualised in trait theory, using psychometric tests such as the EPQ-R (Eysenck & Eysenck, 1991) or NEO-PI-R (Costa & McCrae, 1992).

Increasingly, attempts are being made to interlink and unify the three approaches (Mahoney, 2011). As you read through this chapter, think about how theories could link together and whether an 'ultimate' theory is possible. Also think back to what you read in Chapter 2 about the strengths and weaknesses of trait theories and the dispositional approach. This will help to add another 'layer' to your understanding of the debates concerning the contribution of biology and environment to personality.

Assessment advice

This topic has a rich research and empirical foundation; there is probably more research material from which to select in this topic than any other within individual differences, so the danger is that you will be overwhelmed by it. It is likely that a question in this field will ask you to address, at least in part, the contribution of biological and **environmental factors** to personality. To stand out, your assessment needs to cover the classical theories (e g. Eysenck's PEN model) and debates (the adequacy of heritability estimates) and also current developments, such as sociogenomic personality research (Roberts & Jackson, 2008).

Questions will therefore generally seek demonstration of your understanding of conceptual matters relating to the methods of enquiry used and your awareness of their strengths and limitations. So, make sure you have a good grasp of popular methodology such as twin/adoption/family studies and that you can describe and evaluate them succinctly. Your capacity to present well-ordered and integrated evidence is a necessity for assessment in this topic to be effective, so be selective in your choices of examples.

Sample question

Could you answer the question below? It is a typical essay question that could arise on this topic. Guidelines on answering the question are included at the end of this chapter, whilst a sample problem question and guidance on tackling it can be found on the companion website at www.pearsoned.co.uk/psychologyexpress.

 Sample question   *Essay*

Do you consider personality to have a stronger genetic or environmental basis? Provide evidence for this view and critically consider the arguments for the interaction of genetics and environment.

Neurophysiological personality theories

Neurophysiological/physiological theories of personality have a long history in Individual Differences psychology: Hippocrates' and Galen's 'four temperaments' theories were based on different biological types.

- A revolution in biopsychological theories came in the form of the **structuralism** versus **functionalism** debate. Early biopsychological theories tended to seek to identify the organisation and structure of the mind, and how these influenced behaviour and experiences, whereas functionalism attempts to understand the functions which behaviour and experiences serve.

- Neurophysiological theories root their explanations of personality in physiological systems, such as the **central nervous system** (CNS; the brain and spinal cord) and the **peripheral nervous system** (PNS; all the sensory and motor neurons and receptors, muscle and glands which connect the surface of the body with the nervous system). The PNS contains further subsystems, such as the cardiac system and musculoskeletal system.

- Most modern physiological theories attempt to identify which personality traits are associated with specific physiological systems, and under what conditions or stimuli this occurs (Larsen & Buss, 2010). For this reason, and owing to advances in technology, a plethora of research methods, measures and theories have developed.

We will now look briefly at the main areas of contemporary neurophysiological research and the key methodologies they employ.

Personality and the central nervous system

Research and theory in this area has tended to focus on whether specific anatomical structures within the brain are associated with different personality traits or types. More recently, research has explored issues such as **brain asymmetry**.

Research measures

Measures tend to focus on exploring the structure of the brain (**structural neuroimaging techniques**) or measuring some metric of brain activity (**functional neuroimaging techniques**).

Structural neuroimaging

- *Computed Tomography* (CT): a non-invasive technique which measures tissue density and is used to detect areas of brain damage.
- *Structural Magnetic Resonance Imaging* (MRI): a non-invasive technique which also measures brain density but can provide better tissue delineation and allows you to determine the volume of different brain regions or regions of brain damage.

Functional neuroimaging

- *Electroencephalogram (EEG)*: measures 'spontaneous' electrical activity (e.g. when no, or limited, stimuli are presented to an individual) in the brain.
- *Evoked EEG*: measures electrical activity in the brain which results from directed, pre-determined tasks, such as looking at emotion-provoking stimuli.
- *Functional Magnetic Resonance Imaging (fMRI)*: measures activity-related blood-flow changes in the brain.

Personality and the peripheral nervous system

The PNS refers to the 'rest' of the nervous system – including the immune, cardiac and musculoskeletal systems. The PNS can be subdivided into the **somatic nervous system** and the **autonomic nervous system**. In turn, the autonomic nervous system can be further subdivided into the **sympathetic nervous system** and the **parasympathetic nervous system** (Andreassi, 2006).

Research measures

PNS research tends to focus on physiological measures of responses that are controlled by the autonomic nervous system (Andreassi, 2006), including:

- *Electrodermal activity (skin conductance/response)*: measures sweat gland activity (controlled by the sympathetic division of the nervous system). Typically, 'painful' stimuli or stimuli requiring mental effort (e.g. puzzle solving) are used.

- *Cardiovascular activity*: measures blood pressure and heart rate (controlled by the autonomic division of the nervous system). Typically, stress-inducing stimuli are employed in this research.

- *Antibodies*: measures immune system responses. Research typically involves complex sets of stimuli including, for example, the introduction of a virus (or naturally occurring virus), measuring stress levels and exploring the impact on immune effectiveness.

- *Hormones and neurotransmitters (e.g. testosterone and cortisol)*: measures hormone system activity (e.g. adrenal) and communication between neurons. Typical stimuli include inducing (or observing naturally occurring) stressful life events, or tasks which induce emotions, anxiety, attraction, competition or aggression.

Indicative research findings

CRITICAL FOCUS

Temperament versus personality

A fundamental aspect of human nature, which is taken as evidence for the biological basis of personality, is the concept of **temperament**. Temperament refers to Individual Differences in emotional and behavioural styles which are evident very early in life (Buss & Plomin, 1975, 1984), and are therefore believed to be innate. As such, temperament is viewed as the factors which influence the development of personality. For example, Kagan (1999) found that approximately 20% of infants under the age of 4 months demonstrated inhibited behaviour (shy, react to unfamiliar people or situations with distress and avoidance) whereas 40% of infants did not. He also observed that, for many of these infants, these patterns of behaviour persisted into later childhood. Of these children, those who showed greater levels of shyness were found to exhibit higher levels of physiological arousal in unfamiliar environments or situations.

- Different regions of the brain may be involved in different aspects of personality and emotionality. For example, the frontal lobes have been implicated in forward planning and anticipation (Damasio, 1994), the amygdala has been associated with aggression and inhibition (Buck, 1999; Schwartz et al., 2003); the hypothalamus has been associated with aggression, sexual behaviour, fear, panic and 'calming' mechanisms (Hart, 2008).

- A substantial portion of research aims to understand the relationship between brain asymmetry, personality and emotion regulation, owing to the different psychological functions controlled by the left and right brain hemispheres. In particular, many researchers are interested in frontal lobe activity asymmetry (measured by EEG and evoked EEG).

  - Research suggests that when an individual is experiencing pleasant emotions there will be greater activity in the left frontal lobe, but when an individual is experiencing negative emotions there will be greater activity in the right frontal lobe (Davidson et al., 1990; Fox & Davidson, 1987). These findings have demonstrated good test/re-test correlations (Davidson, 1993, 2003), suggesting that frontal lobe asymmetry may be relatively stable and reflect the biological mechanisms underpinning some aspects of personality.

- Hormones and neurotransmitters appear to play a key role in personality. For example, testosterone has been linked to aggressiveness, sexuality and sociability (Dabbs, Strong & Milun, 1997; Dabbs, Alford & Fielden, 1998), and serotonin has been found to relate to emotion regulation (Knutson et al., 1998).

KEY STUDY

The case of Phineas Gage

A substantial body of research in this area explores the impact of brain damage on psychological functioning. Studies like this seek to ascertain whether some regions of the brain may be more or less involved in different aspects of psychological functioning. A classic example of this is the case of Phineas Gage.

Phineas Gage was a railway foreman in the nineteenth century. In 1848 he was severely injured in an accident which resulted in a large metal bar (1.25 inches in diameter, over 3 feet long and weighing around 14 pounds) being propelled through his skull (below the left cheek, behind his left eye and through the top of his skull). He survived the accident, but the frontal lobes in his brain were severely damaged. When he had recovered from his initial injuries, many of his cognitive capacities appeared intact; however, his personality was reportedly unrecognisable. He went from being a hard-working, agreeable and conscientious individual to being highly aggressive, impulsive and unable to plan ahead and achieve goals (Macmillan, 2000).

1   What do you think are the implications of the story of Phineas Gage?
2   What do you think are the strengths and limitations of using research from 'damaged brains' to infer normal functioning?
3   What other explanations could there be for Phineas Gage's behaviour?

Influential neurophysiological theories

The work of two theorists has been particularly influential in the neurophysiological approach to personality: Hans Eysenck (1916–1997) and Jeffrey Gray (1934–2004). These theorists examined how different aspects of both the CNS and PNS may interact in relation to personality.

Eysenck's PEN model/Gigantic Three

We looked at Eysenck's personality taxonomy briefly in Chapter 2 because it is one of the popular trait personality theories. Eysenck's theory originally focused on the Extraversion/Introversion dimension of personality and suggested that:

- Extraverts are characterised by lower levels of activity in the ascending reticular activating system (ARAS – located in the brain stem), when compared to introverts (Eysenck, 1967).
- The ARAS controls cortisol arousal levels and acts as a gateway to the cortex.
- Extraverts require greater levels of stimulation to increase the activity in the ARAS (and therefore the cortex), which is why their behaviour is characterised by 'sensation seeking'.

However, it was later observed that extraverts' and introverts' arousal levels were not different at resting levels (Stelmack, 1990), but did differ when varying levels of stressful situations were experienced. To incorporate this finding Eysenck utilised Hebb's (1955) theory of 'optimal arousal level', which suggests that to perform any given task effectively you need to be alert enough, but not so physiologically aroused as to become overloaded by sensation.

Eysenck's revised theory suggested that:

- Difference between extraverts and introverts lay in their *arousability* (Eysenck & Eysenck, 1985a). This was supported by the fact that under moderate stressful situations introverts tend to show greater levels of physiological reactivity than do extraverts (Gale, 1987).
- The revised theory provides a potential explanation for the behavioural differences observed between extraverts and introverts.
- The predictions made by Eysenck regarding how extraverts and introverts will react to situations of different levels of stressful situation have received evidential support (Geen, 1984).

Gray's reinforcement sensitivity theory – or Behavioural Activation System (BAS)/Behavioural Inhibition System (BIS) theory

Gray developed his personality theory initially as an extension of Eysenck's PEN model (but it is now seen as an alternative) which borrows from the behaviourist concept of 'conditioning' (discussed in Chapter 4).

Gray developed his theory from the findings of his research with animals, which investigated the impact of reward and punishment on the brain and developmental effects of conditioning on (mainly) anxiety. He believed that Eysenck's dimensions of extraversion and neuroticism were useful to describe personality but did not provide a useful means of *explaining* personality. Gray argued that these two dimensions were actually based on overlapping neurophysiological systems which could better be understood in terms of *impulsivity* and *anxiety* (Haslam, 2007).

Gray (1991) observed different patterns of neural activity when organisms learned under punishment versus reward and suggested this was evidence that different brain mechanisms underpinned the two forms of learning.

- The Behavioural Activation System (BAS) biologically compels people to desire objects/events and seek to act in a way that brings about achieving them; people are biologically compelled to increase activity in the BAS.
- The Behavioural Inhibition System (BIS) biologically compels people to act in ways that will avoid punishment (or cease activity which is unlikely to result in reward); people are biologically compelled to decrease activity in the BIS.
  - The mechanism linking the BAS and BIS is *arousal,* which Gray proposed was carried out by the reticular formation (the dorsal noradrenergic bundle) in the brain (Gray, 1987a).
  - This model suggests a possible overlap between extraversion and psychoticism in terms of impulsivity, presenting a problem for Eysenck's model which suggests that extraversion and psychoticism are orthogonal.

CRITICAL FOCUS

Gray's reinforcement sensitivity theory and alcohol and illicit drug use

Franken and Muris (2005) explored the relationship between the BAS and students' alcohol and illicit drug use. They administered three questionnaires (the BAS/BIS scale, a questionnaire about drinking over the past six months and a forced choice questionnaire (yes/no) about illicit drug-taking behaviour across the lifespan). The BAS/BIS questionnaire was split into three sections: BAS drive, BAS fun-seeking and BAS reward.

- The authors identified a positive correlation between BAS fun-seeking and number of illegal substances taken, quantity of alcohol consumed per occasion and frequency of binge-drinking episodes.
- BAS drive was found to correlate positively with illegal substance use, but was not as strong a predictor as BAS fun-seeking.
- The BIS scale was weakly negatively correlated with alcohol quantity consumed per occasion and frequency of binge-drinking episodes, but not drinking frequency.

Test your knowledge

1   What do you think are the implications of Franken and Muris' study?

    Sample question   *Problem-based learning*

Based on neurophysiological theory and research, develop an intervention which aims to help people overcome gambling addictions. What information would you need in order to develop a well-evidenced programme and where could you find it? What sorts of things would you need to consider that could help avoid relapse?

Further reading

Topic	Key reading
Example of recent neurophysiological approach to researching personality	Wright, C.I., Williams, D., Feczko, E., Barrett, L.F., Dickerson, B.C., Schwartz, C.E. & Wedig, M.M. (2006). Neuroanatomical correlates of extraversion and neuroticism, *Cerebral Cortex 18*, 1809–19.
Research exploring the relationship between a hormone (dopamine) and personality.	Barbato, G., Monica, C., Costanzo, A. & Padova, V. (2012). Dopamine activation in neuroticism as measured by spontaneous eye blink rate. *Physiology & Behavior, 105 (2)*, 332–36.
Research examining the relationship between extraversion, cortical arousal and situational factors	Hagemann, D. & Naumann, E. (2009). States vs traits: An integrated model for the test of Eysenck's arousal/arousability hypothesis. *Journal of Individual Differences, 30(2)*, 87–99.
Study examining the neurophysiological underpinnings of introversion and extraversion	Gray, J. (1970). The psychophysiological basis of introversion–extraversion, *Behaviour Research and Therapy, 8(3)*, 249–66.

Points to consider

- Many neurophysiological studies are carried out in laboratory settings, owing to the requirements of the equipment used to measure responses; such research may lack ecological validity.

- Tasks that people are asked to complete may seem arbitrary (e.g. solving puzzles), which may limit the applicability of research findings to 'real life' situations.

- Many studies only focus on a limited selection of neurophysiological measures, making it difficult to synthesise research findings.

- Many neurophysiological theorists infer 'normal functioning' from damaged brains – the implications of this for our understanding of personality are unclear.

- A substantial number of neurophysiological theories have been developed from research with animals, which has a number of implications (see the 'Critical focus' box on p. 71).

- Matthews and Gilliland (1999) highlight three issues with both Eysenck's and Gray's theories:
  - Measuring the exact neurophysiological systems underpinning personality is extremely difficult and research has revealed contradictory findings.
  - Predictions from these models are often ambiguous.
  - Robust research has often failed to identify the physiological differences between people with different personalities which the two theories suggest should exist.

Behavioural genetics

Behavioural genetics is the study of the degree to which your observable characteristics (your **phenotype**) can be attributed to your inherited, genetic makeup (your **genotype**) and your environment (Plomin & Caspi, 1999). Phenotypic variance is usually assessed using self-report personality questionnaires, which is why some theorists argue that behavioural genetics should be renamed *trait genetics* (Funder, 2001).

Before we continue, we need to explore a concept upon which behavioural genetics and evolutionary theory are based: **heritability**.

Defining 'heritability'

- 'Heritability' refers to the estimate of the average variance in a specific behaviour (phenotypic variance) across a population, which is accounted for by genetic factors (Maltby, Day & Macaskill, 2010).
- The heritability estimate is denoted by h^2.
- '**Environmentality**' refers to the estimate of the average variance in a specific behaviour across a population, which is accounted for by environmental factors (Larsen & Buss, 2010).

Bouchard & McGue (1981) suggest that heritability comprises three aspects:

1 Additive genetic variance

2 Dominant genetic variance

3 Epistatic genetic variance

Additive genetic variance is underpinned by the **additive assumption**. This assumption suggests that heritability is determined by the relative strength of genetic and environmental factors, and that these factors will always account for 100% of the variance in behaviour. Although potentially a useful starting point for calculating heritability, the additive assumption is now believed to be too simplistic and obsolete (Plomin, 2004).

Research now seeks to understand dominant and epistatic variance, which are both forms of *non-additive* variance.

- **Dominant genetic variance** refers to the fact that some genes will be expressed (dominant genes), but others will not (recessive genes).
- **Epistatic genetic variance** refers to the fact that some genes act in combination and interact to effect the expression of other genes.

Bouchard & McGue (1981) argue that only by understanding all three types of genetic variance will we achieve a comprehensive picture of heritability (i.e. *total genetic variance*).

Research and literature often make a distinction between:

- **Narrow heritability**: refers to research which explores additive genetic variance only.
- **Broad heritability**: refers to research which explores all three forms of genetic variance.

How is personality inherited?

It is believed that personality is inherited through genetic material coded in DNA (deoxyribonucleic acid). DNA is located within the nuclei of the 23 chromosomes (46 chromosome cells) which you inherit from your parents and is the chemical 'basis' for heredity.

The process through which genetic information contributes to phenotypic variance between people is referred to as **phylogenic inheritance**. The important point here is that phylogenic inheritance is influenced by environmental as well as genetic factors (Plomin & Caspi, 1999).

Bouchard & Loehlin (2001) suggest six sources of population variance in behaviour: genetic, environmental, gene–environment interactions, developmental, **assortive mating** and evolution. Each of these factors may have an effect on phenotypic variance and makes the job of establishing heritability a difficult.

Behavioural genetics research methodology

Measuring variation in observable characteristics usually involves collecting data using self-report measures and identifying variation using statistical techniques. The self-report measures used are typically based upon the trait taxonomies outlined in the previous chapter (Loehlin, Horn & Willerman, 1990; Loehlin et al., 1998; 1990; Plomin & Caspi, 1999).

Behavioural genetic theorists seek to develop methods of separating out the contribution of **genetic** factors from **non-genetic factors**. The main method of investigating this is the 'twin study', the foundations of which were originally proposed by Francis Galton (Galton, 1876).

The logic of twin, sibling and family studies is that genetic heritability (the extent to which any phenotype is passed on to you by your parents as a result of the genes you inherit) can be established by looking at the extent to which parents and their child (or siblings) differ, as this will allow you to see the **proportion of shared variance**.

The proportion of shared variance is usually expressed as a percentage and represents the degree of similarity of a particular characteristic between individuals: the greater the similarity, the less variability there is and the higher the proportion of shared variance.

Sibling and family studies use the naturally occurring experiments that arise when measurements of personality are taken and comparisons made between individuals with whom there is genetic and environmental similarity. Further sophistication is introduced with studies of monozygotic (MZ; identical) and dizygotic (DZ; non-identical) twins when living in the same and differing environments.

CRITICAL FOCUS

The principles of twin, sibling, family and adoption studies

You can't establish the contribution of genetic factors from looking only at biological parents and their child (Figure 3.1), because they share the same environment and therefore the two things are confounded. You need to be able to find a way of separating out genetic and environmental variables.

In an adoptive family study (Figure 3.2), you can compare the phenotype of the child with their biological and adoptive parents. The logic of these studies is that if the child shares similar phenotype with their adoptive parent then environmental factors may have a greater impact on phenotypic variance than genetic factors. However, if the child's phenotype is similar to their biological parent, despite the lack of shared environment, it suggests that genetic factors may play a greater role in phenotypic variance than environmental factors.

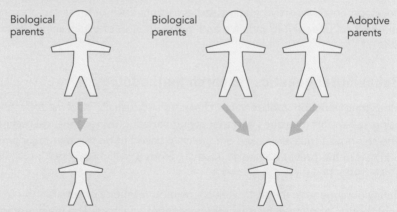

Figure 3.1 **Family studies**   Figure 3.2 **Adoption studies**

Non-identical twins share 50% of their genes, whereas identical twins share 100% genes. Comparing the phenotypic variance between these two types of twins (Figure 3.3) will provide an indication of the contribution of genetic factors.

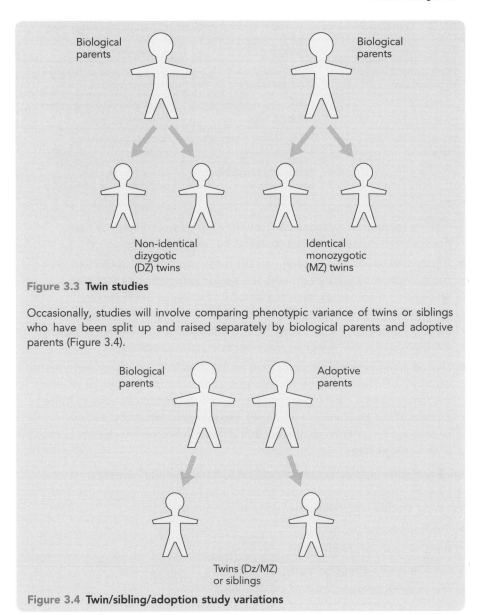

Figure 3.3 **Twin studies**

Occasionally, studies will involve comparing phenotypic variance of twins or siblings who have been split up and raised separately by biological parents and adoptive parents (Figure 3.4).

Figure 3.4 **Twin/sibling/adoption study variations**

The argument adopted is that if the proportion of genes held in common between two individuals is high, then we would anticipate that there would be a high similarity in personality. Table 3.1 presents a decision table of possible judgements based on findings and hypotheses.

- A key feature of the twin study method is the **equal environments assumption** (Larsen & Buss, 2010). This assumption asserts that the environments experienced by twins are *no more similar* than the environments experienced by siblings. If this assumption is violated and twins experience environments

Table 3.1 Genetic/environmental additive combinations with outcome judgements

Hypothesis	Findings	Judgement
Strong genetic 'explanation' for personality	Personality similarity is high amongst twins	Strong genetic explanation for personality
	Personality similarity is low amongst twins	Weak genetic explanation for personality
Strong environmental 'explanation' for personality	Personality similarity is high amongst siblings	Strong environmental explanation for personality
	Personality similarity is low amongst siblings	Low environmental explanation for personality

that are more alike (perhaps because they are treated differently from siblings), this makes it difficult to assess heritability.

- A potential issue with adoption studies is the possibility that children are placed with adoptive parents who are similar (referred to as **selective placement**). This could inflate the amount of variance attributed to environmentality. However, Plomin, Chipuer & Loehlin (1990) suggest that there is no evidence that more similar environments cause twins to be any more similar, or that selective placement occurs in practice.
- **Shared environmental influences** are all those aspects which are experienced equally by twins or siblings: for example, where the family lives, or whether the family owns a car. **Non-shared environmental influences** refer to those aspects of the environment which are experienced differently, such as favouritism by parents, or the fact that different children may be encouraged in different abilities.

Since adoption studies require considerable database administration, several large-scale studies have been designed to enable continuing research. The following studies are widely referred to in the literature:

- the Texas adoption study;
- the Colorado adoption study;
- the Minnesota adoption study;
- the Swedish adoption/twin study of ageing

KEY STUDY

Genetic, environmental and person-by-situation interaction patterns

Borkenau et al. (2006) conducted groundbreaking research exploring the relationship between genes, environment and interactionism. They observed the behaviour of 168 monozygotic and 132 dizygotic twins in reaction to 15 different situations. They then compared the degree of similarity between the two types of twins in their reactions to the different situations and suggested that approximately 25% of the variation in behavioural reactions could be attributed to genetic factors.

Further reading

Topic	Key reading
Update on contemporary research methods; the case of parenting	Collins, W., Maccoby, E., Steinberg, L., Hetherington, E. & Bornstein, M. (2000). Contemporary research on parenting: The case for nature and nurture, *American Psychologist, 55(2)*, 218–32.
Adoption study showing associations between parents' divorce and children's adjustment	Connor, T., DeFries, J, Caspi, A., & Plomin, R. (2000). Are associations between parental divorce and children's adjustment genetically mediated? An adoption study. *Developmental Psychology, 36(4)*, 429–37.

Test your knowledge

1 Specify the advantage that twin and adoption studies have over family studies.
2 Explain why the figure given for heritability is only given as an estimate.
3 Why is the heritability derived for a population not applicable to any one individual?

Environmental influences

In addition to considerations of gene–gene combinations, there are also environmental–gene variants to consider. There are multiple forms of environmental contributions to Individual Differences, depending upon what aspects of the environment are included (see Table 3.2 for a classification of potential combinations).

Environment may have positive/nurturing or negative/destructive effects on the various genetic contributions to personality. Additionally, environmental effects may not have an equal effect on all individuals.

Reiss (1997) identified three ways in which the family environment influences how genotypes form phenotypes:

1 **Passive model**: Personality is explained by the 50% overlap in genes between child and parents. This overlap is sufficient to explain any similarities in behaviour.
2 **Child-effects model**: The parent and child share genes, which brings about similar behaviour. However, in this model the child's behaviour is seen as having an impact on the parent's behaviour, but this change does not impact on the child's behaviour.
3 **Parent-effects model**: The parent and child share genes, which brings about similar behaviour. However, in this model the child's behaviour impacts on the adults' behaviour and this change in the adults' behaviour *does* have an impact on the child's behaviour. In this model, the parent's response to the child's behaviour will have an effect on how that behaviour develops.

Table 3.2 **Example combinations of types of environment**

Environmental type		Duration of environmental engagement		Intensity of engagement
Biological aspects of the environment		Instantaneous but repeated		Low emotional or intensity of impact
Family-influenced environmental factors		Short term and frequent		High emotional impact
Those involving school/education	X	Medium term and occasional	X	Neutral impact
		Long term		Reinforcing positively
Friends, acquaintances and others with varying degrees of engagement		Frequent		Reinforcing negatively
Impact of culture, arising from interests and activities		Repeated		
		Occasional		
Occupation and career influences		Continuous		

Child effects and parent effects can lead to over- and under-estimations of heritability and therefore pose a problem for researchers.

Scarr (1992) argued that generalisations of environmental influence hold for the average and typical conditions, but that dysfunctional environments can have a detrimental effect. For example, abusive families do not promote normal development.

Further reading

Topic	Key reading
Overview of the nature–nurture debate and behavioural genetics	Plomin, R. (2004). *Nature and nurture: An introduction to human behavioural genetics*. London: Wadsworth.
The impact of non-shared environmental influences on personality	Baker, L. & Daniels, D. (1990). Nonshared environmental influences and personality differences in adult twins, *Journal of Personality and Social Psychology*, 58(1), 103–10.
The effects of twins reared apart on measures of difference.	Bouchard, T., Lykken, D., McGue, M., Segal, N. & Tellegen, A. (1990). Sources of human psychological differences: The Minnesota study of twins reared apart, *Science*, 250, 223–8.

Test your knowledge

1   Explain the 'additive assumption' in behavioural genetics.
2   Specify two alternative forms of genetic interactions.
3   Specify examples of common and unique environmental experiences that act on siblings.

Points to consider: issues with estimating heritability

- Heritability is an *estimate*; it is not a perfectly accurate statistic.
- Statements of the 'heritability' of Individual Differences should only be made in reference to a population, or group of people. It is not meaningful to make statements about the characteristics specific to an individual. For example, although it is possible to say that 60% of personality across a population is heritable, it is not possible to say that 60% of an individual's personality is inherited.
- Calculating heritability is a complex process and there is no consensus on exactly how this should be done.
- Heritability estimates are applicable only to the particular groups they have been calculated for, at that particular point in time and under the specific circumstances under which the characteristic of interest was examined.
- Heritability is not static or fixed.
- Heritability is affected by the *range* of genetic and environmental differences in the population.
- The amount of genetic variance found in a population is likely to be affected by assortive mating, which poses a problem for research which tends to treat genetic variance as 'random'. Assortive mating refers to the fact that people do not 'mate' randomly. They tend to choose people with whom they either share characteristics (**positive assortive mating**) or with whom they contrast (**negative assortive mating**). These means that assortive mating has an impact on the *range* of genetic variance in any given population.

Evidence for the heritability of personality

Whilst the genetic and environmental contributions to *intelligence* have generally been determined using intelligence quotient (IQ) as measurement (see Chapters 8, 9 and 10), personality lacks this single index. However, the Five Factor Model (FFM) has typically been employed in recent studies. Studies in the heritability of personality traits have produced varying results:

- Twin studies have consistently shown individual differences in personality, but little evidence has been found for genetic influence in parent/offspring and sibling adoption studies (Plomin et al., 1998).
- Research suggests that *non-shared* environmental influences may play a greater role in Individual Differences in personality (Plomin, Chipuer &

Neiderhiser, 1994). However, shared environmental influences have still been associated with smoking and drinking behaviour (Willerman, 1979) and adjustment (Loehlin, Neiderhiser, & Reiss, 2003).

● The number of studies conducted with MZ or DZ twins or with shared and specific environments is considerable. Turkheimer & Waldron (2000), for example, list 39 studies with varied characteristics during the period from 1985 to 1997 within their own area of research interest only. Overall shared environmental influences were low, whereas non-shared environmental contributions were substantial.

Table 3.3 summarises findings on heritability on a number of studies for each of the five factors in the FFM.

Table 3.3 **Summary of personality heritability findings across five studies**

	Jang, Livesley & Vernon (1996)	Waller (1999)	Loehlin et al. (1998)	Rieman, Angleitner & Strelau (1997)	Review by Loehlin (1992) of earlier studies
	{rank}	{rank}	{rank}	{rank}	{rank}
Extraversion	0. 53{2}	0. 49 {2}	0. 57 {2}	0. 56{1}	0. 49 {1}
Neuroticism	0. 41{4}	0. 42 {4}	0. 58 {1}	0. 52{4}	0. 41 {3}
Agreeableness	0. 41(4)	0. 33 {5}	0. 51 {5}	0. 42{5}	0. 35 {5}
Conscientiousness	0. 44{3}	0. 48 {3}	0. 52 {4}	0. 53{2}	0. 38 {4}
Openness	0. 61{1}	0. 58 {1}	0. 56 {3}	0. 53{2}	0. 45 {2}
Number of MZ	123	313	490	660	–
Number of DZ	127	91	317	304	–

Source: Adapted from Bouchard & Loehlin (2001). Republished with permission of Taylor & Francis Group LLC – Books, from *Development, Genetics and Psychology*, T. Bouchard and J. Loehlin, 2001; permission conveyed through Copyright Clearance Center, Inc.

The researchers specified in Table 3.3 used the NEO five factor questionnaire to test personality for differing national groups. The table shows a convergence of findings in that personality traits are significantly influenced by genetics, but the rank order for the most significant traits differs.

CRITICAL FOCUS

Future developments

Molecular genetics is one of the newest directions in behavioural genetics, and aims to identify the specific genes associated with personality traits.

DRD4 is one of the most commonly researched genes, which codes for the dopamine receptor. Dopamine is a neurotransmitter and has been associated with novel stimuli- and sensation-seeking behaviour (Zuckerman, 2006) and individuals with the long repeat version of the DRD4 gene have been found to show greater sensation-seeking behaviour (Benjamin et al., 1996) than individuals with the short repeat version. It has been suggested that the mechanism underpinning these relationships is that individuals with the long repeat version of the DRD4 are less responsive to dopamine and require more stimulation to achieve the same level of activation as those with the short repeat version of DRD4.

Further reading

Topic	Key reading
Example of behavioural genetic personality research	Campbell, J., Schermer, J., Villani, V., Nguyen, B., Vickers, L. & Vernon, P. (2009). A behavioral genetic study of the dark triad of personality and moral development, *Twin Research and Human Genetics, 12(2)*, 132–6.
Genetic contributions in personality traits along with the evolutionary explanation	Bouchard, T. & Loehlin, J. (2001). Genes, evolution and personality, *Behavior Genetics, 31(3)*, 243–73.
Overview of the heritability of personality	Zuckerman, M. (1991), *Psychobiology of personality.* Cambridge: Cambridge University Press.

Is there a theoretical explanation for the high genetic influence in personality traits? The findings in Table 3. 3 support the view that traits are an important 'causal agency' for personality (Bouchard & Loehlin, 2001). The authors elaborate upon an evolutionary perspective to account for the formation of traits. Central to this is the view that traits serve an evolutionary purpose and in this respect they are a product of adaptations; since human adaptation involves a social dimension then responding to differences in a social context is a feature of necessary adaptation.

Evolutionary theories of personality

Evolutionary theory as a 'grand theory' adopts an explanation applicable for a whole population. However, it is a perspective that recognises the importance of Individual Differences explanations in the process of natural selection.

In comparison with other theories, the evolutionary approach is a relatively recent model and further empirical research is required into its central ideas.

The origin of the evolutionary approach is based upon the notion that since the major goal of the species is reproductive success, psychological mechanisms emerge to facilitate this (Buss & Hawley, 2011).

Evolutionary theory rests on a number of key premises: **functionality** (adaptations serve a practical function), **domain specificity** (adaptations evolve to be specific, to 'solve' specific issues) and **numerousness** (organisms develop many adaptive mechanisms to solve the variety of issues faced).

Evolutionary personality theories are based upon two key theoretical mechanisms (based on the work of Charles Darwin): **natural selection** and **sexual selection**.

- Broadly speaking, the theory of natural selection suggests that over time mutations arise which may better enable an organism to survive. In turn, this makes it more likely that the organism will survive to reproductive maturity and therefore ensure its genes enter the next generation. These *adaptations* may then be inherited by the organism's offspring, which increases the likelihood of their survival and reproduction, and eventually the beneficial mutations may spread throughout a population. Organisms which inherit deleterious (harmful) mutations will be less likely to survive and reproduce and over time these organisms will disappear from the population. The process of reproductive success relative to others is referred to as **differential gene reproduction**.

- Sexual selection refers to the process by which some organisms appear to develop characteristics which are viewed as advantageous when competing for mates. Although these characteristics may provide benefits in terms of mating success, they may not provide *survival* advantages (e.g. the peacock's tail is highly important in the peahen's choice of mates but presents a survival hazard for the peacock).

Darwin's theories have been adapted and the current evolutionary theory is referred to as *inclusive fitness theory* (Hamilton, 1964). It is through mechanisms such as this that personality and individual differences evolve and manifest themselves, and upon which evolutionary theories of personality are founded.

Processes such as these are used by theorists to explain the types and diversity of personality, and Buss and Hawley (2011) refer to several areas of support for this contention:

- the stability of personality;
- the predictive success in measured behaviour (Fleeson & Gallagher, 2009);
- evidence from multiple genetic studies showing important genetic contributions (Plomin et al., 2008);
- cross-situational species comparisons which have demonstrated similarities (Gosling, 2001).

Table 3.4 identifies several features which have commonality between human and non-human animals (Buss, 1988), presented side-by side with indicative personality trait-labels.

Buss (1991) argued that evolutionary theory provides a clear framework for understanding personality because it allows us to explore humans' major goals and obstacles, and the mechanisms which humans have evolved to meet these demands. For example, Buss argued that characteristics such as being active, sociable and co-operative have evolved because they allowed people to work together in groups to achieve goals (Buss, 1991).

Table 3.4 **Indicative links of Buss' animal features with personality labels**

Activity	Extraversion (Cattell factor A)
Dominance	Assertiveness (Cattell factor E)
Sociability	Extraversion (all trait models)
Aggressiveness	Assertiveness(Cattell factor E)
Nurturance	Agreeableness (FFM factor A)
Impulsivity	Enthusiasm (Cattell factor F)
Fearfulnes	Suspiciousness (Cattell factor L)

For the comparisons to truly be valid, though, we need to be able fully to explain human/non-human *dissimilarities* too. A large amount of theory and research focuses on identifying and explaining sex differences in relation to such things as displays of aggression (Buss & Duntley, 2006), jealousy (Schutzwohl & Koch, 2004; Miller & Maner, 2009) and sexual partner preferences (Regan & Atkins, 2006; Buss & Barnes, 1986).

Examining Individual Differences and personality within an evolutionary theory framework is a relatively new approach, which comprises four main strands:

1 Viewing Individual Differences as arising from environmental factors impacting on psychological mechanisms.

2 Viewing Individual Differences as arising from contingencies among traits (Bouchard & Loehlin, 2001). This refers to the fact that the expression of any particular trait may be contingent on the presence/absence of other traits.

3 Viewing Individual Differences as arising from frequency-dependent selection of traits: that is, some traits may be 'rare' and give a person 'the edge' over competitors.

4 Viewing Individual Differences as arising from traits which have been inherited and maintained within a population because they were optimal at different times and situations during evolution.

Research methodology in evolutionary psychology

Two research methodologies are particularly characteristic of evolutionary psychology personality theories: **life history** and **selective breeding** studies.

Life history

The life history method is a key feature of evolutionary theories. It was developed by theorists such as Wilson (1975) to provide a means of documenting the schedule of growth, survival and reproduction throughout an individual's life. It has been adapted to research personality and individual differences, such as MacDonald's (1997) and Rushton's (1985) approaches to understanding different parenting strategies.

Animal personality research

- *Within-species comparisons*: Making comparisons between animals of the same species (e.g. comparing a dog with another dog) on their typical responses/behaviour to situations.

- *Cross-species comparisons*: Making comparisons between animals of different species (e.g. comparing a dog with a wolf) on their typical responses/behaviour to situations.

  - Comparing within and across species is useful because it allows evolutionary personality psychologists to explore how personality has developed to enable an organism to survive and thrive (e.g. differences in aggressiveness between a pet dog and guard dog, or a pet dog and a wild wolf, may indicate what is required to survive in the different environments). Exploring these two forms of variation can allow a psychologist to examine the possible origins of personality traits and how traits evolve (Gosling, 2001).

- Assessing personality in animals is usually achieved either by coding (recording) how animals respond to different situations (e.g. Mather and Anderson, 1993) or by asking animal observers to identify traits which are relevant to a particular species and then asking them to rate specific animals on these traits (Gosling, 1998).

  - Assessing personality in animals is open to the same issues as all observational research (e.g. validity and reliability). These issues can be mitigated (or at least measured) through assessing such things as **inter-rater reliability** and **intra-rater reliability**.

- A key concern in animal personality research relates to **anthropomorphism**, which is the process of projecting/attributing human characteristics on to animals. This raises the question of whether animals really do have personalities, or whether it is an artefact of the researcher/observer merely imposing personalities on them through their own beliefs and expectancies.

Selective breeding studies

Some evolutionary personality research involves selective animal breeding (also known as artificial selection). This involves breeding animals for desired qualities (such as temperament or physical characteristics). If such characteristics were not heritable, this would not be possible. Selective breeding has therefore been used to provide evidence for evolution on a quicker timescale.

Points to consider

- Evolutionary processes take shape over enormous periods of time which makes it difficult to understand them fully and means that psychologists must make inferences about historical environments and how they may have affected selection processes.

- It is not clear whether the differences between contemporary environments and those experienced by our ancestors will have any impact on the way in which psychological mechanisms evolve.

- As the application of evolutionary theory is still in its infancy, there are many competing theories for the same phenomena. Further research is required to shed light on this situation.

- Greater emphasis is now being placed on developing empirically testable hypotheses, to move away from the image of evolutionary personality theories as vague and under-defined.

- Research is particularly needed to understand better the mechanism by which genetic material translates to person characteristics.

CRITICAL FOCUS

The use of animals in research

Many fields within the biological approach conduct research with animals (e.g. selective breeding studies), which raises a number of issues:

- For ethical reasons it is not possible to do some kinds of research with human participants, and therefore some psychologists feel that there is no viable alternative but to use animals in research (Gallup & Suarez, 1985).

- There are ethical and moral concerns over the welfare of animals used in research. For example, some experimental research with animals (such as some of the experiments conducted by Watson, which involved taking away animals' senses one-by-one to examine the effect of this on learning) have been found to inflict untenable cruelty on animals. There are now ethical guidelines published by the American Psychological Association (2003) and British Psychological Society (2007) which psychologists are expected to adhere to.

- A further issue concerns the value of animal research. Questions are asked concerning the generalisability of animal research findings to humans. A common argument for the acceptability of animals in research is that they are less complex organisms than humans (Goodwin, 2009). For example, the ability to develop language and culture appears unique to humans. However, these very differences may mean that findings regarding 'personality' from rats, cats and dogs (for example) may not be applicable to humans.

Further reading

Topic	Key reading
Overview of evolutionary personality psychology	Buss, D. (1991). Evolutionary personality psychology, *Annual Review of Psychology, 42*, 459–91.
Evolutionary account of sex differences	Buss, D., Larsen, R., Westen, D. & Semmelroth, J. (1992). Sex differences in jealousy: Evolution, physiology, and psychology, *Psychological Science, 3(4)*, 251–5.
Life history methodology	Wilson, E. (1975). *Sociobiology: The new synthesis.* Cambridge, MA: Harvard University Press.
The role of animal research	Gosling, S. (2001). From mice to men: What can we learn about personality from animal research? *Psychological Bulletin, 127(1)*, 45–86.

Test your knowledge

1   What are the arguments of evolutionary personality theories?
2   Why might evolutionary theories of personality be controversial?
3   Why do evolutionary personality psychologists use animals in their research?
4   What are the key issues encountered in animal personality research?

Chapter summary: putting it all together

→ Can you tick all the points from the revision checklist at the beginning of this chapter?

→ Attempt the sample question from the beginning of this chapter using the answer guidelines below.

→ Go to the companion website at www.pearsoned.co.uk/psychologyexpress to access more revision support online, including interactive quizzes, sample questions with answer guidelines, 'you be the marker' exercises, flashcards and podcasts you can download.

Answer guidelines

Guidelines on answering the sample questions presented at the start of the chapter are given below.

 Sample question   *Essay*

Do you consider personality to have a stronger genetic or environmental basis? Provide evidence for this view and critically consider the arguments for the interaction of genetics and environment.

Approaching the question

The key requirement for this assessment is to be able to provide a comprehensive discussion of the 'nature–nurture' debate, including: why it is important, what the methodology employed to assess genetic and environmental contributions to personality is, what the strengths and limitations of this methodology are, and what the evidence derived from such research suggests about personality.

The debate concerning the impact of genetic and environmental factors on personality is vast, so you need to be selective in the approaches and evidence you choose to evaluate. You need to avoid spreading your focus too thinly;

a strong essay will move beyond merely describing the field to critically appraising it. To ensure your assessment has a strong and coherent structure, you could examine evidence from the three different strands of the biological approach in turn. However, it would be a good idea to start with behavioural genetic theory and research, as this strand contains a lot of information which is particularly relevant and important to this topic. Including information from neurophysiological personality theories and evolutionary personality theories will strengthen your answer by providing evidence and critiques from slightly different perspectives on the same topic.

Important points to include

- To describe and evaluate behavioural genetic theory and research you should define what the aims and scope of this approach is and discuss the impact of developments in technology (e.g. sociogenomic personality approaches). You should define the key terms of genotypic and phenotypic variance and why they are crucial concepts to this field.

- Describe and evaluate the proposed mechanisms underpinning the inheritance of personality (i.e. through DNA).

- Describe heritability estimates, how they are calculated and their strengths and limitations.

- Describe and evaluate (with examples of research) the methodology of twin, sibling, family and adoption studies, and the results generated from this research. This is the key approach within behavioural genetics, so it is important to emphasise this issue.

- Describe how genes can interact (e.g. additive, epistatic and dominant genetic variance) and evaluate how this is measured in research. Also explain the consequences of the different types of genetic variance for calculating heritability.

- Describe how environmental factors can influence genetic factors and phenotypic variance: shared and non-shared environments, parent effects, equivalent environments and selective placement (in adoption). Explore how they can make estimating heritability difficult.

- Describe and evaluate personality research findings, referring to key issues already highlighted in the assignment as appropriate. Explicitly state what they suggest about the relative contributions of environmental and genetic factors to individual differences in personality.

Make your answer stand out

To really stand out you should include information from neurophysiological approaches (e.g. Gray's reinforcement sensitivity theory and findings from brain asymmetry research) and evolutionary approaches (e.g. animal personality research, evolutionary perspectives on genetics, and natural and sexual selection) and make links to behavioural genetic theory and research. Also,

73

remember that a strong essay will impartially provide the evidence for the two sides of the debate (nature versus nurture) and will then conclude with a statement regarding which side of the debate is believed to be the best and why the interaction effect is so important.

Notes

4

Learning theory models of personality

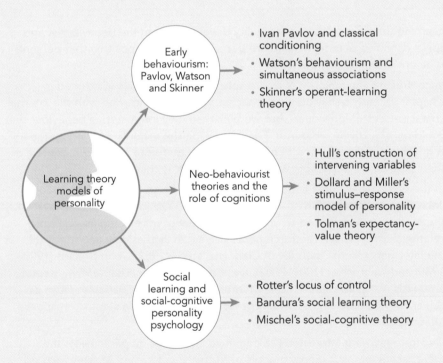

- Early behaviourism: Pavlov, Watson and Skinner
  - Ivan Pavlov and classical conditioning
  - Watson's behaviourism and simultaneous associations
  - Skinner's operant-learning theory

- Learning theory models of personality

- Neo-behaviourist theories and the role of cognitions
  - Hull's construction of intervening variables
  - Dollard and Miller's stimulus–response model of personality
  - Tolman's expectancy-value theory

- Social learning and social-cognitive personality psychology
  - Rotter's locus of control
  - Bandura's social learning theory
  - Mischel's social-cognitive theory

A printable version of this topic map is available from:
www.pearsoned.co.uk/psychologyexpress

Revision checklist

Essential points you should know:

❑ Key features of the behaviourist, social learning and social cognitive approaches to personality

❑ How the concepts of *behavioural potential*, *expectancy* and *locus of control* contribute to our understanding of personality

❑ How the concepts of *observational learning*, *reciprocal causation* and *self-efficacy* contribute to our understanding of personality

❑ Key features of the Cognitive-Affective-Personality System (CAPS) model

Introduction

Learning theory models of personality developed from the behaviourist and social-cognitive paradigms, and are based upon the proposition that personality is 'learnt' from life experiences.

In contrast to the majority of trait-dispositional approaches (discussed in Chapter 2), early behavioural approaches were not concerned with the internal characteristics of individuals, but were instead only interested in behaviour that could be *objectively measured*. For this reason the majority of learning theory is not directly concerned with personality, and therefore only those aspects of theory which are applicable will be explored in this chapter.

In the early behaviourist **conditioning** theories of Ivan Pavlov (1849–1936), John Broadus Watson (1878–1958) and Burrhus Frederic Skinner (1904–1990), the mechanisms proposed to underpin personality were **stimulus–response relationships**, in which **reinforcements** played an increasingly important role. In the later behaviourist theories of Clark Hull (1884–1952), John Dollard (1900–1980) and Neal Miller (1909–2002), and Edward Tolman (1886–1959), greater emphasis was placed on the role of intervening cognitive variables (such as **drives, motivations** and **mental representations**), in these stimulus–response relationships.

Owing to growing interest in the cognitive influences on personality, the more recent learning theory models of Rotter, Bandura and Mischel focused on *interactions* with *personal goals*, **expectancies** and **beliefs**, rather than on reinforcements.

The learning theory approach has had considerable influence in clinical contexts, owing to the fact that it provides a useful framework for exploring and facilitating behavioural change (Haselgrove & Hogarth, 2011).

Assessment advice

An understanding of the developments in the behaviourist and social-cognitive traditions is often assumed for assessments addressing learning theory personality models, and personality in general. For example, a key feature of this field is the debate concerning the role ascribed to behaviour in personality theory. In early behaviourist theory, behaviour formed the focus of research as it provided a variable capable of measurement and therefore was seen as satisfying the emphasis on scientific inquiry. However, owing to the growing dissatisfaction with the lack of these theories' interest in internal mental processes, later behaviourist and social cognitive models placed greater emphasis on intervening cognitive variables. A strong essay will reflect these issues where appropriate.

When discussing the early behaviourist approaches, the danger is that you become bogged down with describing the stimulus–response relationships and reinforcements, and lose sight of the fact that the question is about *personality*. Similarly, when discussing the social cognitive models you need to avoid an undue emphasis on describing cognitive processes at the expense of their implications for our understanding of personality. So, make sure that when you are constructing your essay or answer each of the points you make links back explicitly to personality.

Sample question

Could you answer the question below? It is a typical essay question that could arise on this topic. Guidelines on answering the question are included at the end of this chapter, whilst a sample problem question and guidance on tackling it can be found on the companion website at www.pearsoned.co.uk/psychologyexpress.

 Sample question   *Essay*

Identify and evaluate the additional contributions provided by the social-cognitive learning theories of personality to those of behaviourism.

Early behaviourism: Pavlov, Watson and Skinner

An understanding of the early behaviourist theories of Pavlov, Watson and Skinner is required to fully appreciate learning theory models of personality, as many of the concepts proposed heavily influenced later developments in the field.

A key feature of early behaviourist approaches was the emphasis placed upon *objective behaviour*; theorists such as Watson and Skinner chose to focus exclusively on objective behaviour because they felt it was unnecessary and unscientific to try to study the hypothetical, latent constructs (such as 'consciousness') which interested other psychologists. Although this allowed researchers to ground their theories in variables which could be empirically identified and measured, it led to the criticism that behaviourism was too *reductionist* (Richards, 2009) and therefore missed the complexity and totality of human experience.

The exclusion of internal mental processes from these early theories means that many theorists had little to say directly about personality. For example, Skinner (1948) simply did not accept the concept of personality. Learning theories therefore provide a useful counterpart to many of the dispositional theories outlined previously, but to fully appreciate the following debates you need to understand how the mechanisms they proposed underpin learning.

Ivan Pavlov and classical conditioning

Pavlov used the experimental method to assess the way dogs learnt to respond to objects and people (Pavlov, 1906, 1927, 1928). Pavlov's research involved presenting meat-paste (the stimulus) to dogs and noting the extent to which they salivated (the response).

Pavlov observed that:

- The dogs' salivation response was natural and automatic, representing the relationship between an **unconditioned stimulus** (the food) and an **unconditioned response** (salivation).
- If you repeatedly presented another unconditioned (neutral) stimulus before presenting the food, such as a light or a bell, the dog would begin to salivate when this new stimulus was presented: *before* the food was seen (Pavlov, 1906, 1927, 1928). This represented a **conditioned response**, developed through reinforcement, which Pavlov termed *classical conditioning*.

Pavlov explained the occurrence of this process as the combination of two actions in the brain's cerebral cortex:

- excitation – a process leading to arousal in the nervous system;
- inhibition – a process of suppression.

Pavlov related the principles he observed in dogs to personality in humans and concluded that personality was the manifestation of the excitation/inhibition balance.

- The excitation/inhibition dimension corresponds to the person characteristic of 'responsiveness'.
- It is this 'inner person' explanation that represents the link between experience, learning and personality.

Pavlov also demonstrated that conditioned responses could be:

- generalised (within limits) to similar stimuli (potentially accounting for why people enjoy similar events);
- reversed, which he termed **extinction**. Extinction occurs when the conditioned stimulus is repeatedly presented without the food reward and the conditioned response becomes weaker and weaker until it eventually dies out.

Generalisability and extinction are concepts which many clinical interventions draw upon to encourage behavioural change.

Ultimately, Pavlov used these principles to explain how human beings' emotional responses and patterns of emotional responses arise. Therefore, in Pavlov's theory a person who exhibits demanding behaviour does so not because they have a *demanding personality*, but because they have *learnt* this type of behaviour.

- Importantly, whereas personality is viewed by many other approaches as relatively unchanging, Pavlov's view suggests that patterns of behaviour can be *unlearnt*.

Watson's behaviourism and simultaneous associations

Watson felt that for psychology to be a true science the emphasis on introspection and 'interpretation' should be avoided. For Watson, it was *inappropriate* to make hypotheses about internal mental processes because there was no objective way of measuring them (Watson, 1913).

Watson (1913) believed that:

- Humans are born without any innate tendencies and therefore develop patterns of behaviour, called **habits**, through well-learned associations of responses with external stimuli (Watson, 1927).
- The main influential force in learning processes is your childhood environment and how the significant people in your life treated you.
- Personality should be viewed as 'the sum of activities that can be discovered by actual observation of behaviour over a long enough time to give reliable information. In other words, personality is but the end product of our habit systems. Our procedure in studying personality is the making and plotting of a cross section of the activity stream' (Watson, 1927, p. 220).

The essence of Watson's approach was that habits occur because of simultaneous occurrences of responses and stimuli.

- Unlike other behaviourist theories, this approach has no need for the concept of reinforcement; the correspondence of stimuli and response is sufficient.
- What determines the priorities in what we learn is how recent and how frequent responses have been to a particular stimulus. Therefore, even emotional responses such as anxiety and fear do not necessitate conscious feelings, but represent several pairings of a new stimulus to an original stimulus that have joined a *repertoire* of habits.

KEY STUDY

Little Albert

To demonstrate that anxiety and fear are learnt, Watson and Raynor (1920) conducted an experiment which has come to be known as the Little Albert study. This study involved banging a hammer on a metal plate behind the head of an 11-month-old boy (Albert) every time he reached for a white laboratory rat. Initially Albert did not show any fear of the rat, but produced a startle response each time the banging noise was made. However, after repeated pairings of reaching for the rat and the loud noise, Albert showed a fear response of the rat, even without the noise.

Points to consider

There are many ethical issues with this study, including that no 'debriefing' was given to Albert and his fear of white rats (which actually transferred to other white objects) persisted after the study (Maltby, Day & Macaskill, 2010). However, this study provided the foundations for research exploring how negative emotional reactions develop and how they can be overcome in clinical interventions (e.g. systematic desensitisation).

Skinner's operant-learning theory

Skinner felt that classical conditioning could not explain all types of learning and that it was more meaningful to consider how the *consequences* of a response affect learning (Skinner, 1971, 1972, 1976).

- Skinner proposed a new concept called **operant conditioning**, which involves two forms of reinforcement.
  - **Positive reinforcement**: when a response is rewarded and its repetition encouraged.
  - **Negative reinforcement**: when a response results in punishment and you are discouraged from repeating it.

In this respect, **operant behaviour** is not a passive-responsive behaviour like **respondent behaviour** (behaviour arising from classical conditioning).

Much of Skinner's research was conducted with animals, as he believed that the principles of animal learning could be applied to human learning. Experiments tended to involve different versions of the **Skinner box** (Skinner, 1938), which was a box in which an animal (usually a rat or pigeon) was placed and which contained a lever. If the animal pressed this lever, they would be rewarded with food. Skinner noted that the more the animal's behaviour was reinforced with food, the rate of 'lever-pressing' would increase.

Skinner was particularly interested in the impact that different *schedules of reinforcement* (i.e. the rate/frequency of reinforcement) had on learning. He found that:

- **Random** or **partial reinforcement schedules** produced behaviour very resistant to change (Maltby, Day & Macaskill, 2010). These are schedules whereby rewards are not given every time the behaviour of interest is performed. An example would be when a child learns that having a tantrum sometimes results in their parent giving in to their wishes, and it is therefore worth performing this behaviour in case it is rewarded.

- **Shaping** also occurs, which refers to situations when a response that approximates a desired response is rewarded, until the behaviour becomes closer and closer to the desired response (at which point only the desired response is rewarded).

Skinner believed that ultimately a behaviour could become **self-reinforcing**, i.e. producing the desired response becomes a reward in itself.

Skinner's work is perhaps most useful for understanding the motivational aspect of personality, i.e. why people perform certain behaviours consistently. Skinner believed that people behave in ways designed to increase positive events and avoid negative events. Therefore, patterns of behaviour from which personality is usually inferred can be better understood by examining the circumstances in which the behaviour of interest occurred.

Points to consider

Early behaviourist theories suggest:

- The impact of early childhood experiences is profound.
- Traits are useful as descriptions (Skinner, 1953) but do not *explain* behaviour.
- 'Intentions' would be better thought of as responses to *internal stimuli*, therefore making the concept of personality redundant.
- 'Personality' can be unlearnt.
- People are passive recipients of learning.
- Animal 'personality' and learning is comparable with that of humans: but whether or not this is actually the case is highly debatable.

Early behaviourist theories do not provide a coherent and complete explanation of why people approach the same situation in different ways. Also, why do some people from similar situations develop maladaptive behaviour and others do not?

Test your knowledge

1. What role do early behaviourist theorists view behaviour as playing in understanding personality?
2. Why did behaviourist theorists such as Watson and Skinner disagree with the concept of personality?
3. What mechanisms did Pavlov, Watson and Skinner propose as underpinning the development of patterns of behaviour which are usually used to infer personality?

Neo-behaviourist theories and the role of cognitions

Hull's construction of intervening variables

Hull presented a theory which included *intervening variables* (latent constructs including 'drives', 'incentive motivation' and 'habit strengths') to help explain behaviour more effectively. He believed that:

- All behaviour can be reduced to stimulus–response connections, which he termed 'habits'. Therefore behaviour requires stimulus variables, response variables and intervening variables (which were tied to the stimulus variables).
- A set of stimulus–response relationships constitutes a *hierarchy* of habits, and chains of stimuli and responses equate to 'feedback' loops (Powell, Symbaluk & Honey, 2008).
- The likelihood of a behaviour being performed rests on a number of criteria, including how *habitual* a stimulus–response relationship has become.

Hull's ultimate aim was to develop a general theory of learning which could be applied across situations. He attempted to develop algebraic equations which could be used to express the relationship between stimulus variables, intervening variables and response variables. For example:

behaviour = drive × habit

where drive is a motivational and incentivising force and habit is the result of learning from stimulus–response pairings (Fiske, 2007).

However, owing to criticisms from contemporary researchers (such as Tolman), he was forced to modify and expand his equations until they became too complex and unwieldy (Powell, Symbaluk & Honey, 2008).

In Hull's terms, personality represents habits (the more permanent associations of stimulus–response relationships) which have been bonded by rewards (operant conditioning). The extent to which these patterns in behaviour are consistent depends on the *habit strength* (the extent to which the stimulus–response associations have been reinforced).

Despite the criticisms, Hull's approach represented a marked a departure from earlier research, which had excluded variables that were not directly observable, and paved the way for other neo-behaviourist theories.

Dollard and Miller's stimulus–response model of personality

Dollard and Miller both trained as Freudian analysts and worked collaboratively to explore psychoanalytic concepts within a learning theory framework. Like Hull, they envisioned learning in the form of stimulus–response links, and they borrowed Hull's concept of *habit*: they viewed personality as mainly comprising learned habits.

According to Dollard and Miller (1950), habits are influenced by drives, which are *unconscious processes*. They agreed with Freudian theory which suggested that unconscious processes helped to shape people's behaviour, but conceptualised them differently. They argued that drives are located within the unconscious for a number of reasons, including the following:

- They develop before we can talk and we are therefore unable to *label* them or the cues which stimulate them.
- The drives we acquire and their cues are not given a label in the society to which we belong.
- The drives or their cues are repressed, to make it difficult to recall to conscious thought.

Dollard and Miller's theory also suggests:

- We inherit drives (called **primary drives**), which are physiological and help to ensure our survival.
  - Satisfying these drives (such as hunger or thirst) is a powerful reinforcement and helps to develop patterns of behaviour. The reinforcements to these drives are referred to as **primary reinforcers**, and typically take the form of food, water, rest, etc.
- **Secondary drives** develop to help us cope with our primary drives (which are largely unobservable) and are satisfied by **secondary reinforcers**, which take the form of events that were originally neutral but have come to hold a specific value to the individual.
  - Secondary reinforcers can come in many forms, including money, hugging, specific smells which remind an individual of a positive event, and so on.

Dollard and Miller (1950) suggested that there are four parts to learning habits:

- the *drive*, which initiates the whole process;
- *cues* to act;
- the individual's *response* to the cue; and
- the *reinforcement* of the response.

Cues were treated as both innate and capable of being learnt; any stimulus could serve as a cue and determine the responses that emerged. Dollard and Miller believed that responses and reinforcements form a hierarchy and vary according to the probability of occurrence. Learning has the effect of adjusting this hierarchy; an initially strong probability of occurrence can become weak as a result of learning.

It is important to note that drives were not viewed as directional – they merely alert an individual that action is required, but do not direct *what* that action should be.

Dollard and Miller (1941) were also interested in what happened if we were frustrated in our attempts to satisfy our drives. They proposed four conflicts which an individual might face:

1 **Approach–approach conflict** – having to choose between two equally desirable, yet incompatible goals.
2 **Avoidance–avoidance conflict** – having to choose between two equally undesirable goals.
3 **Approach–avoidance conflict** – having one goal which is partly desirable and partly undesirable.
4 **Double approach–avoidance conflict** – having to choose between many goals which are both desirable and undesirable.

The essential concern of Dollard and Miller was with the learning process rather than with personality, and so the authors did not attempt to characterise it overtly. The authors' attention was to those conditions that *facilitated* personality development.

Tolman's expectancy-value theory

Tolman's work gave considerably greater emphasis to cognitive *processes* over stimulus–response connections. He introduced the notion of **cognitive maps** as mental representations acquired from experience (Tolman, 1948). There was also an emphasis on motivation in the achievement of goals. From this perspective, insufficient attention had been given to beliefs, the striving towards goals and the expression of attitudes. Tolman considered that these factors played a part in 'purposeful behaviour'. Whilst the author was still concerned with objective behaviour as opposed to conscious experience, this approach recognises the relationship of behaviour to goals. Tolman believed that:

- 'Striving' to achieve a goal acts as a stimulus; an impetus for action.
- Behaviour is organised around the purposes we establish for it.

In order to explain the complexity of behaviour associated with broader rather than narrower and specific behaviours:

- Tolman introduced 'associated perception', suggesting that cognitions from different learning environments may be combined to create more generalised beliefs.
- He suggested that generalised beliefs influence behaviour over a wider field.
- He suggested that personality and social maladjustments could be thought of in terms of cognitive maps which had become 'narrowed' owing to motivations which exerted too much strain on an individual or the experience of extreme frustrations in attempting to achieve goals (Tolman, 1948).

Lewin advanced Tolman's thinking further by reference to goals. In the publication on level of aspiration, Lewin et al. (1944) used the term 'valence' to reflect emphasis given to expectancies and values. The concept introduced positive (direct towards) and negative (retreat from) behaviour. Lewin et al.'s (1944) study addressed individuals' compulsions to goals and also allowed for assessment of task difficulty.

Points to consider

- Some theorists, such as Dollard and Miller (1941, 1950), focused first on psychopathological behaviour and used insights from this to hypothesise about 'normal' behaviour and development. The implications of this should be considered.
- A number of neo-behaviourist theories (e.g. Hull) were still based on research findings from animal studies. It is not clear whether the learning mechanisms demonstrated by animals are applicable to human learning (e.g. in complex social situations).
- Many early learning theorists sought to identify universal and general laws underpinning learning (and, by default, personality), which conflicts with the aims of the main Individual Differences theories of personality.
- Ultimately, the inclusion of drives, inner thoughts, anxiety and reinforcements encouraged a growth in the consideration of cognitive aspects and led to the development of **social learning theories** of personality.

Social learning and social-cognitive personality psychology

Rotter, Bandura and Mischel are the three theorists most strongly associated with the social-cognitive learning approach to personality. Their theories placed greater emphasis on both cognitive processes and situational context.

Rotter's locus of control

Rotter attempted a synthesis of behaviourism and personality theory by replacing the notion of the drive as motivator, with the notion of *goal seeking*. Rotter's approach differs from that of dispositional trait theories because it does not treat personality as an internal phenomenon *independent* of the environment.

There are four main components to Rotter's theory:

1 *Expectancy*: the subjective assessment that a particular behaviour leads to a favourable outcome or reinforcement (based on past experience).

2 *Reinforcement value*: the subjective value we attach to the outcomes of our behaviour. If we desire them highly then they are said to have high reinforcement value.

3 *Behavioural potential*: the possibility that a particular behaviour will occur in a situation. The actual behaviour chosen in any one situation is that which has the highest potential to be exhibited. *Behavioural potential* increases with *expectancy* and also increases with *reinforcement value*. This is expressed as:

$$BP = f\,(E\ \&\ RV)$$

4 *Psychological situation*: the concepts of expectancy, reinforcement value and behavioural potential rely on the situational influence on personality. However, Rotter's notion of *situation* constituted a subjective interpretation of environment, as opposed to an objective formulation independent of person perspective.

Specific expectancy, generalised expectancy and locus of control

Rotter presented two forms of expectancies: broad and abstract; and narrow and concrete. The narrower the expectancy, the more precise the behavioural prediction possible. However, Rotter suggested that broad classifications are easier to use in terms of generally *explaining* the behaviour.

Rotter identified a particular form of **generalised expectancy** for the control of favourable outcomes which he called **locus of control**. Locus of control is formed on a scale reaching from an internal to an external pole:

● High **internal locus of control** arises when individuals see that the outcomes of a behaviour/event are the result of their own actions. An example would be where the explanation for an employee achieving a promotion is seen as the consequence of their hard work.

● An **external locus of control** arises in those situations where individuals believe the explanations arise from the actions of others or events that are not of their own making, e.g. where a promoted employee has achieved her situation through 'luck'.

Rotter believed that individuals would demonstrate stable individual differences when faced with the same situation, and a test was produced which reliably measured the extent to which an individual possessed an internal or an external locus of control (Rotter, 1966). The test consisted of 23 pairs of contrasting general statements, and seeking selection of one from the pair. An example is given below:

A Getting a good job depends upon being in the right place at the right time.

B The candidates most successful in job applications are those who have good qualifications and experience and prepare themselves well for the interview.

Test your knowledge

1   With what concept did Rotter replace the notion of drive in the early behavioural theories?

2   Specify the relationships between behavioural potential and (a) expectancy and (b) reinforcement value.

3   From examining Rotter's theory, what do you think is the theoretical justification for cognitive behavioural therapy?

KEY STUDY

Psychological aspects to situation

Phares and Rotter (1956) devised a study demonstrating that students' perceptions of subject interests changed depending upon the class groups to which they were attached. Three lists each of six reinforcements were presented to groups of students, who were asked to rank them in order of their preferences. Six were related to a manual skill, i.e. woodwork; six were related to academic skills, i.e. Maths test results; and six were concerned with a sport performance result, i.e. physical competition. Students were asked to rank them in each of three conditions: a carpentry workshop; a classroom; and a gym. It was shown that the ranks (reinforcement value to the students) varied according to the situation in which they found themselves.

Further reading

Topic	Key reading
Underlying theory and limitations of the construct of 'locus of control'.	Rotter, J. (1975). Some problems and misconceptions related to the construct of internal versus external control of reinforcement, *Journal of Consulting and Clinical Psychology* *43(1)*, 56–67.
Contributions of Rotter's 'locus of control' variable to psychological theory.	Rotter, J. (1990). Internal versus external locus of control, *American Psychologist, 45(4)*, 489–93.
Application of the 'locus of control' concept.	Crothers, L., Kanyongo, G., Kolbert, J., Lipinski, J., Kachmar, S. & Koch, G. (2010). Job stress and locus of control in teachers: Comparisons between samples from the United States and Zimbabwe, *International Review of Education, 56(5–6)*, 651–69.

Sample question **Problem-based learning**

Individuals who are considerably overweight are often advised by doctors to begin diets and yet many of those who start give up. If we were to use questionnaires to measure Rotter's expectancy and reinforcement value for a group of individuals, what would you expect to find concerning correspondence of the findings with successful and less successful dieters?

Bandura's social learning theory

Bandura's social learning theory can be understood through the concepts of **observational learning, vicarious reinforcement, reciprocal determinism** and **self-efficacy**. These concepts constituted what Bandura considered to be a unified theoretical framework for the analysis of thought and behavioural change (Bandura, 1977). Bandura's social learning theory was different from many of the theories which preceded it because it viewed the forces controlling behaviour as more equally distributed between internal and external stimuli.

Observational learning and vicarious reinforcement

Bandura believed that the simple notion of reinforcement could not account for more complex behaviours and that people are capable of learning the benefits of reinforcements without needing personal and direct experience of them. In Bandura's theory, merely observing the effects of other people's experiences (i.e. vicariously) would be sufficient to serve as reinforcement: a process he termed **observational learning**.

Bandura called the overall process of social learning **modelling**.

KEY STUDY

The 'Bobo' study

Bandura conducted a study (1965) to show that reinforcements administered to a participant-model influenced the performance of groups of observing children. A film was shown to children, in which a plastic 'Bobo' doll was subjected to four different verbal and physically aggressive behaviours. Bandura predicted that the presence or absence of rewards would influence imitation by the groups of observing children. One group saw the participant-model rewarded for aggression. A second group saw the participant experience reprimanded for the behaviour. A third group was a control with no consequences. The findings demonstrated that the children's observation of punishment for the aggressive acts performed resulted in fewer aggressive acts when they were given later opportunities to carry them out.

Observational learning as a four-stage process

Bandura considered observational learning as a four-stage process, in which each stage was treated as a necessary condition for modelling (Bandura, 1971, 1977):

1 *Attention processes*: refers to the capacity to recognise, differentiate and attend to different models – to be able to imitate a model, you must first be able to see it!

2 *Retention processes*: refers to the capacity to recall the modelled behaviour. Mental images are retained only if we have the capacity to store them and have cues to retrieve them.

3 *Reproduction processes*: refers to the capacity to translate mental images and act on cues to actions. This therefore requires that we have the motor skills to be able to carry the actions out.

4 *Motivational processes*: the observer must be motivated to carry out the action they have observed and recalled from memory, and they must also have the opportunity to do so. Past reinforcement of the action, expected positive outcomes, and vicarious reinforcement may all act as motivations to modelling.

Bandura (1977) identified three factors important to modelling:

1 *Characteristics of the model*: simpler models and models which exhibit aggressive or hostile behaviour are more likely to be imitated. Also, the more similar the model is to you, the more likely you are to imitate them.

2 *Attributes of the observer*: if you are low in self-esteem, low in self-confidence, highly conformist or dependent, you will be more likely to imitate a model.

3 *Consequences of imitating the behaviour*: if you believe imitating the model will be likely to result in a positive outcome, you will be more likely to imitate it. This is the most influential factor.

Reciprocal determinism

Bandura believed that characteristics of the person (*personal factors*) and their environment (*environmental factors*) interact to motivate behaviour (*behavioural factors*), a process which he called **reciprocal determinism** (Bandura, 1989).

He extended the concept of the characteristics of the person to include psychological processes and suggested that individuals be viewed as creators of their environment and seekers of preferential environments (Bandura, 1995, 1998). This represented a fundamental break from behaviourism, which had tended to view people as passive recipients of environmental influences.

Bandura (1999) referred to the mutual influence of person, environment and behaviour as **triadic reciprocal causation**. Exhibited behaviour will, for instance, affect the environment and cognitions of the person. For example, an aggressive person may behave aggressively (behavioural factor), which will invoke a response from others (environmental factor) and these responsive consequences contribute towards the reinforcement of the trait of aggression, as well as to expectations of reactions from others (personal factor). The model of reciprocal determinism is represented in Figure 4.1.

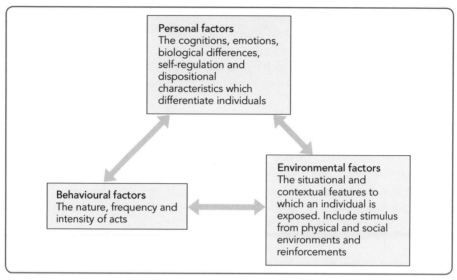

Figure 4.1. **The mutually interactive factors in Bandura's reciprocal determinism**

Self-efficacy, goals and motivation

Enhanced levels of motivation can be achieved with the setting of goals. Successful individuals in physical performance, dance and sport, for instance, have developed the skill of setting appropriate, realistic goals – sufficient that they can be steadily improved through training regularly.

Bandura believed that the level of achievement was strongly affected by internal self-regulation. Achievement also promotes an individual's sense of internal confidence or, more specifically, self-efficacy (Bandura, 1982). This concept refers to the expectation that an individual will conduct a given behaviour and that it will result in the preferred outcome. Achievement has made important contributions to the field of health and occupational psychology. In occupational psychology, performance training programmes have used and adapted goal-setting objectives to improve performance (Locke & Latham, 1990).

Several criteria were added as necessary elements for achievement:

● Goals should be specific to behavioural performance rather than an outcome.

● They need to be realistic and positive, and to be staged as short-term steps to a longer-term goal with time spans for delivery.

● They need to be observable and measurable.

Bandura (1989, 1994) described self-efficacy as the beliefs that we hold about the extent to which performing a specific action will result in the positive outcome we desire. It relates to your belief in your ability to perform. Beliefs affect our emotions and motivations and so also affect our behaviours.

Bandura suggested that four sources inform self-efficacy beliefs, as shown in Figure 4.2.

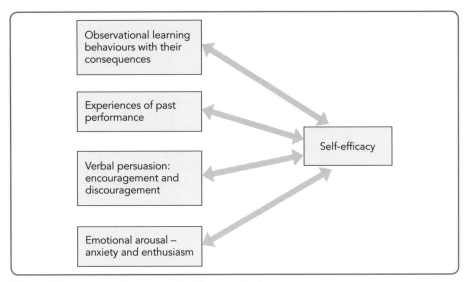

Figure 4.2 **Sources informing self-efficacy beliefs**
Source: Bandura (1989 and 1994).

The concept of self-efficacy is important to the social learning theory's model of personality because it sheds light on how people self-regulate and maintain their motivation. For example, self-efficacy has been found to predict success in smoking cessation (Schnoll et al., 2011) and educational performance (Caprara et al., 2011).

Test your knowledge

1   What were the four necessary cognitive stages considered by Bandura to be necessary for effective observational learning?

2   What are the key features of reciprocal determinism and how does this concept impact on our understanding of personality?

3   What sources of information did Bandura believe inform beliefs about the successful performance of goals?

KEY STUDY

Effects of goals and feedback on improvements in physical performance

The hypothesis in a study by Bandura and Cervone (1983) was that self-evaluative and self-efficacy mechanisms mediate the effects of goal systems and performance motivation. Personal standards and cognitive comparisons were said to be involved. Participants were required to perform strenuous physical activities (exercise bike tasks). The different conditions were: the setting of goals and performance feedback; goals alone; feedback alone; and the absence of both factors. It was found that performance information and a standard had strong motivational effects. There was no significant motivational effect with either goals alone or feedback alone. It was also found that perceived self-efficacy for goal achievement was greater and produced greater exertion of effort when there were higher levels of personal dissatisfaction. The findings of the study have made important contributions to sports psychology, but comparative findings have also found relevance in occupational psychology, where a number of analogous studies have been conducted.

 Sample question   *Problem-based learning*

The most successful call centre bonus schemes have operated on the basis that rewards for increased job performance are provided soon after the production has been earned. The setting of goals and the close accompaniment of the payments have been found to produce the best incentives. In what way would goal-setting theory be able to explain how performance is maintained by sporting champions at the Olympic Games?

Further reading

Topic	Key reading
Expectations of personal efficacy on behavioural change	Bandura, A. (1977). Self-efficacy: Towards a unifying theory of behavioural change, *Psychological Review, 84(2)*, 191–215.
Self-evaluative and self-efficacy mechanisms governing the motivational effects of goal systems	Bandura, A. & Cervone, D. (1983). Self-evaluative and self-efficacy mechanisms governing the motivational effects of goal systems, *Journal of Personality and Social Psychology, 45*, 1017–28.
Human agency and triadic reciprocal causation	Bandura, A. (1989). Human agency in social cognitive theory, *American Psychologist, 44*, 1175–84.
Application of the social efficacy concept	Schnoll, R., Martinez, E., Tatum, K., Glass, M., Bernath, A., Ferris, D. & Reynolds, P. (2011). Increased self-efficacy to quit and perceived control over withdrawal symptoms predict smoking cessation following nicotine dependence treatment, *Addictive Behaviours, 36(1–2)*, 144–7.

Mischel's social-cognitive theory

Mischel's theory integrates several aspects of cognitive and social psychology and as such could have been discussed under cognitive models (Chapter 5). He was heavily influenced by Rotter and Bandura's work (Maltby, Day & Macaskill, 2010), and his theories and challenges to trait personality theories have had lasting impact on Individual Differences psychology (see Chapter 7 for a further discussion).

Mischel had traditionally held the view that situational variables were the dominant factors in the determination of behaviour, but increasingly recognised the importance of individual cognitive style. As a result he adopted an interactionist perspective and incorporated cognitive psychological concepts into his theory to explain how individuals differ.

Instead of using traits to describe individual differences, he suggested using social-cognitive person variables (Mischel, 1973), which he described as: *constructs and encoding strategies*; *expectancies and beliefs*; *emotions*, *goals and values*; *competencies* and *self-regulatory systems*. Behaviour was seen as the outcome of how the mind works in particular social contexts.

To explain how and why people's behaviour appears consistent across situations, Mischel (Shoda, Mischel & Wright, 1993, 1994) proposed the following concepts:

- *Functionally equivalent class of situations*: refers to the fact that some situations are perceived as similar, suggesting that people may behave similarly in them. This will also influence how people choose to describe themselves, as they will use functionally equivalent situations to identify how they behave in specific situations and whether they are, for example, a 'sociable' or 'shy' person.

- *Behavioural signature of personality*: refers to our characteristic reactions to situations – that is, stable situation–behaviour relationships.

Mischel believed that to capture personality required the development of a dynamic model that could evolve, and incorporated emotions and the notion of personality function as a whole system. As a result, Mischel and Shoda (1995) proposed the Cognitive-Affective Personality System (CAPS) which:

- aims to go beyond merely describing personality and provide greater predictive power of behaviour;

- comprises Cognitive-Affective Units (CAUs), which are mental representations of self, other people, situations, goals, expectations, values, memories, abilities and self-regulatory systems.

CAPS has the following features:

- CAPS variables account for how individuals respond to the situation in which they find themselves (Mischel & Shoda, 1995).

- Encoding strategies assist with categorisation and understanding of events, helping to explain why individual differences exist in how people interpret, represent and construe situations.

- The behavioural choices people make are strongly influenced by expectations and beliefs. So, the likelihood that certain occurrences take place arises because of our beliefs and expectancies.

- The motivation to engage in or avoid experiences arises from our goals and values.

- The behavioural capacity to address experiences encountered is met by our competencies and with our self-regulatory processes.

- The self-regulatory process involves the capacity to make the necessary adaptations and adjustments in order to cope.

- The selection of goals is a feature of self-regulation; individuals differ in the balance between short- and long-term regulation, capacities and levels of cognitive competence.

It is the dynamic interaction between Mischel's factors and the situational characteristics which explains individual differences in behaviour. Distinctive behavioural signatures result from the interactions between situations and the individual's characteristic way of responding.

Sample question   **Essay**

Critically evaluate the extent to which learning theory models sufficiently describe and explain personality.

Further reading

Topic	Key reading
CAPS theory	Mischel, W. & Shoda, Y. (1995). A cognitive-affective system of theory of personality: reconceptualizing situations, dispositions, dynamics and invariance in personality structure, *Psychological Review, 107(2)*, 246–68.
Behavioural signature	Shoda, Y. (1999) Behavioural expressions of a personality system: generation and perception of behavioural signature. In D. Cervone & Y. Shoda (eds), *The coherence of personality: social-cognitive bases of consistency, variability and organization.* New York: Guilford Press.
Application of CAPS theory	Eaton, N., South, S. & Krueger, R. (2009). The Cognitive-Affective Processing System (CAPS) approach to personality and the concept of personality disorder: Integrating clinical and social-cognitive research, *Journal of Research in Personality, 43(2)*, 208–17.

We have seen how behaviourist, social learning and social-cognitive theories have each conceptualised personality and why. To help with your revision about the rough progression of theories (from behaviourist to social-cognitive theories), see Figure 4.3.

Chapter summary: putting it all together

→ Can you tick all the points from the revision checklist at the beginning of this chapter?

→ Attempt the sample question from the beginning of this chapter using the answer guidelines below.

→ Go to the companion website at www. pearsoned. co. uk/ psychologyexpress to access more revision support online, including interactive quizzes, sample questions with answer guidelines, 'you be the marker' exercises, flashcards and podcasts you can download.

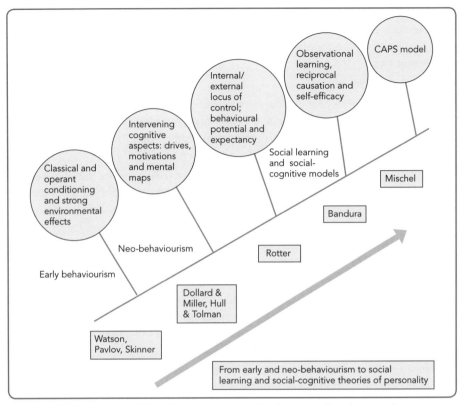

Figure 4.3 **Progression of learning theory models of personality: from early behaviourist to social-cognitive theories**

Answer guidelines

Guidelines on answering the sample questions presented at the start of the chapter are given below.

> ✳ *Sample question*   *Essay*
>
> Identify and evaluate the additional contributions provided by the social-cognitive learning theories of personality to those of behaviourism.

Approaching the question

In essence, this question is asking you to demonstrate your understanding of all aspects of social-cognitive learning theories of personality. Notice that the means by which you are asked to do this is by demonstrating the extent of the growth of thinking that social-cognitive learning theories of personality represent over the foundations of behaviourism. This allows you to use the comparator as a platform against which to evaluate social-cognitive learning. Notice that the wording of the question asks you both to identify and to evaluate, so you need to make sure you do both. In order to demonstrate the advancement of social-cognitive learning theory over behaviourism, you need to provide an outline of its key features.

Make sure that you briefly:

- Provide recognition of the stimulus and response relationships, both unconditioned and conditioned, and the role of reinforcements. This would include reference to the Watson's conceptualisation of habit formation and the reinforcement connectionism of Skinner.

- Discuss your appreciation of intervening variables. This can be demonstrated initially by reference to the drive and incentive motivation of Hull, but most importantly the strength with which habits are formed. In this latter idea, a clearer link with the structure of personality emerges.

- Highlight the leap in the extent of contribution from cognitive aspects to personality theory introduced by Tolman's mental representation, in the form of cognitive maps and the achievement of goals.

The heart of the response to the question comes with the contributions of Rotter, Bandura and Mischel, who present a full coverage of personality as seen through the person, the environment and the determination of behaviour.

- Rotter introduced the concepts of expectancy, reinforcement value, behavioural potential and psychological situation. With the concept of locus of control, the discussion moved most clearly from learning to characteristics of personality (expectancies become generalised).

- Bandura introduced observational learning with the implication of representation in the absence of direct experience, through the stages of: attention, retention, reproduction and motivation. Bandura formed the relationship between behaviour, person and environment. Bandura also introduced self-efficacy and goals as motivators.

- Mischel's CAPS model was the most rounded theoretical framework, offering an integration of the five components of: emotions, encoding strategies, expectancies and beliefs, goals and values, and self-regulatory processes and competencies.

> Make your answer stand out

Your answer will stand out if you are able to progress beyond description of the contributors: that is, if you are able to show concisely the progression in thinking to an increasing level of personality formation that even extends to emotions. As such, personality fully emerges into an entity distinct from that which can be observed directly from behaviour.

Notes

Notes

5

Cognitive and humanistic (phenomenological) models of personality

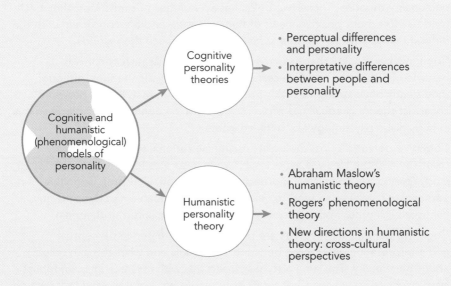

Cognitive and humanistic (phenomenological) models of personality

- Cognitive personality theories
  - Perceptual differences and personality
  - Interpretative differences between people and personality

- Humanistic personality theory
  - Abraham Maslow's humanistic theory
  - Rogers' phenomenological theory
  - New directions in humanistic theory: cross-cultural perspectives

A printable version of this topic map is available from:
www.pearsoned.co.uk/psychologyexpress

> **→ Revision checklist**
>
> *Essential points you should know:*
> ❏ How cognitive psychology models of personality are linked with humanistic models of personality and social learning theory
> ❏ Key cognitive models of personality
> ❏ Key humanistic models of personality
> ❏ The clinical applications of cognitive and humanistic personality models
> ❏ The strengths and limitations of cognitive and humanistic approaches to personality

Introduction

In this chapter we will explore cognitive and humanistic (phenomenological) personality theories. These two fields have a number of similarities: they both tend to offer more positive views of human nature and are concerned with the different ways in which people *subjectively* experience their worlds.

Cognitive personality theories arose as a result of dissatisfaction with behaviourist theories and to a certain extent humanistic theories, although they clearly have strong ties with both paradigms. In fact, Kelly's personal construct theory is equally as often located within cognitive psychology as it is in humanistic psychology textbook chapters.

Cognitive personality psychologists recognise rationality, consciousness, creativity and the free-will aspects of human nature as legitimate topics for study (previously denied by approaches such as behaviourism). Cognitive personality models also tend to view people as malleable and dynamic, in contrast with other approaches (e.g. psychodynamic and trait theories).

Cognitive personality theorists are particularly interested in perceptual and interpretative differences between individuals and what this can reveal about personality. This area also has strong ties with research into emotional intelligence (discussed in Chapter 8), so it would be useful to read that section after this chapter.

You should consider the social-cognitive and social learning theories discussed in the previous chapter, as these are inherently linked to the theories here. They are particularly useful for understanding another area of interest to cognitive psychologists: goals and motivations.

Humanistic theories are based upon **existential philosophy**, which is concerned with how we find meaning for our existence and what motivates us. For this reason, humanistic theories are particularly interested in what constitutes 'uniqueness', 'free will' and responsibility. The two psychologists who have had the greatest impact on humanistic psychology are Abraham Maslow and Carl Rogers, so their theories will be explored here.

Some argue that the humanist approach has made a rod for its own back with its censure and dismissal of mainstream psychology's 'narrow-minded, scientific values' (Funder, 2001, p. 202). Shunning the scientific method has raised questions about the validity, reliability and evidence supporting humanistic theories, which may explain its dip in popularity. However, since the 1980s efforts have been made to develop a 'scientific' branch of humanistic psychology (Rychlak, 1988).

Assessment advice

Assessments in this area require you to demonstrate an understanding of what makes the cognitive and humanistic approaches similar, whilst being aware of how they differ from each other, and how they compare with other approaches. They are likely to focus on the role that these theories give to internal mental processes (such as perceptions, cognitions and needs) in the development and expression of personality. Assessments may also ask you to consider how these approaches have contributed to our understanding of personality change, in which case it is important to be aware of the clinical applications associated with them (such as Albert Ellis' Rational-Emotive Behaviour Therapy and Carl Rogers' person-centred therapy).

An understanding of these approaches is also extremely important for those assessment questions which ask you to identify approaches of your choice to evaluate a specific topic. This is because they offer a strong contrast to the behaviourist, psychodynamic and biological approaches (amongst others), owing to their focus on positive growth, and do not tend to view people as passive recipients of their biology or their environment. A strong essay or answer to a problem-based learning question will cover these issues.

Sample question

Could you answer the question below? It is a typical essay question that could arise on this topic. Guidelines on answering the question are included at the end of this chapter, whilst a sample problem question and guidance on tackling it can be found on the companion website at www.pearsoned.co.uk/psychologyexpress.

 Sample question   *Essay*

Critically evaluate the contribution of the idiographic and phenomenological theories of Kelly, Ellis and Rogers to our understanding of personality. Discuss the implication of these theories by comparison with other approaches where appropriate.

Cognitive personality theories

Perceptual differences and personality

There are differences between people in the way they see things, even when looking at the same object, event or scene. These represent individual differences in perception which have been found to have meaningful, consistent and stable associations with other areas in life (Larsen & Buss, 2010). Two key theories which shed light on this topic are the field dependence/independence theory (Witkin et al., 1954) and the sensory reducer/augmenter theory (Petrie, 1967).

Field dependence versus independence

Herman Witkin (Witkin et al., 1954) believed that personality is revealed through the different ways in which people perceive their environment, particularly how people use different *cues* (i.e. internal versus external) to judge orientation in space. To help him explore this further he developed the Rod and Frame Test (RFT).

CRITICAL FOCUS

Witkin's RFT

The RFT involved seating a participant in a darkened room and asking them to watch a glowing rod which was surrounded by a glowing square frame. The researcher would then manipulate the angle of the rod, the frame and the chair the participant was sitting on. The participant would then be asked to adjust the angle of the rod (using a dial) until it was perfectly vertical. If the participant ignored the external cues (cues in their visual field, such as the angle of the square frame) and used their internal cues (e.g. the angle of their body in the chair) to align the rod, they were said to be field independent. If, however, they ignored their internal cues and used the external cues, so adjusting the rod to align with its square frame, they were said to be field dependent.

Points to consider

- The RFT method was cumbersome and ultimately replaced by the Embedded Figures Test (EFT), which involved asking people to identify as many smaller pictures hidden within a large picture as possible: the greater the number of pictures identified, the more field independent you are said to be. Substantial correlations have been identified between the RFT and EFT (Cronbach, 1970), suggesting that the two are comparable. A further test was developed to increase the efficiency of the EFT, which was called the Group Embedded Figures Test (GEFT; Witkin et al., 1971).

- The EFT and GEFT have been criticised for potentially measuring cognitive *ability*, rather than just cognitive *style*.

- Field dependence/independence has been found to relate to educational performance (Witkin, 1977; Witkin et al., 1977; Weller et al., 1995) in part because this relates to how people 'pick out' relevant information from 'background noise'. Also, cognitive style has been found to predict educational subject preferences: people tend to choose courses which are congruent with their cognitive style (Witkin et al., 1977).

- Cognitive style has been shown to relate to interpersonal relationships (Witkin & Goodenough, 1977; Bastone & Wood, 1997). For example, field independent people have been found to be more likely to display autonomy and ignore social cues in socially ambiguous situations, and field dependent people have been found to be more likely to make greater use of external social referents.

Sensory reducers versus sensory augmenters

Further differences in perception were identified in tolerance of pain, leading Petrie (1967) to develop her sensory reducer/augmenter theory.

Petrie attributed differences in pain thresholds to differences in people's nervous systems:

- People with high pain thresholds were thought to have nervous systems which reduced (dampened) sensory stimulation.

- People with low pain thresholds were thought to have nervous systems which augmented (amplified) sensory stimulation.

This theory suggests that sensory reducers would be likely to try to find ways of enhancing their sensory reactivity, and this idea has gained some support. For example, in numerous research studies sensory 'reducers' have been found to be more likely to use substances (i.e. alcohol and drugs) to 'compensate' artificially for their reduced sensory experiences (Haslam, 2007).

Points to consider: individual differences in perception

- Taken together, cognitive style and tolerance to pain suggest that there are individual differences in the way that people perceive and experience their world, which in turn affect how they react to it. This may explain, in part, why there are individual differences in personality and patterns of behaviour.

- It is not clear whether personality affects the way that people perceive their world, or whether the way in which people perceive their world affects the 'expression' of personality.

Interpretative differences between people and personality

A further interest of cognitive personality psychologists lies in how people differ in terms of their *interpretation* of perceptual information and events. A pioneer in this field was George Kelly, whose work also straddles the humanistic (or experiential/phenomenological) domain.

Further reading

Topic	Key reading
Personality differences and field dependence/ independence.	Lipperman-Kreda, S. & Glicksohn, J. (2010). Personality and cognitive-style profile of antisocial and prosocial adolescents: A brief report, *International Journal of Offender Therapy and Comparable Criminology*, 54(5), 850–6.
Personality differences and cognitive style	Konrath, S., Bushman, B. & Grove, T. (2009). Seeing my world in a million little pieces: Narcissism, self-construal, and cognitive-perceptual style, *Journal of Personality*, 77(4), 1197–228.
Example of reducer/ augmenter theory	Schwerdtfeger, H. (2007). Individual differences in auditory, pain, and motor stimulation: The case of augmenting/reducing, *Journal of Individual Differences*, 28(3), 165–77.

Test your knowledge

1   In what ways might cognitive style affect the way in which an individual approaches academic achievement?

2   Why do you think substance misuse has been linked to individual differences in pain thresholds?

3   What do you think are the strengths and limitations of using cognitive style and pain thresholds to explain individual differences in personality?

 Sample question   Essay

Critically discuss the extent to which cognitive personality theories are able to account for personality development and change.

George Kelly's personal construct psychology

Kelly's (1955) theory is based on the view that people actively seek to understand the world around them. To do this we generate and test hypotheses gained through observation. However, because we do not have an *objective* interpretation of the world to work with, we must use our *personal experiences*. Therefore, our understanding of the world is gained through *subjective cognitive* interpretations.

Kelly believed that we keep our observations, hypotheses and perceptions (called **personal constructs**) private, and it is often only when we do choose to share our views that we realise that they are not held universally.

● Personal constructs represent the criteria we use to interpret events and direct our behaviour: adjustments are made according to confirming or conflicting information.

● They are considered to be bipolar in that they are characterised at one of two opposing positions, e.g. good/bad or enjoyable/boring.

- They are hierarchical in nature, with constructs at a higher level described as **superordinate**, and those at a lower level described as **subordinate**.
  - For example, a personal construct relating to an evaluation of a lecturer might be described in terms of engagement or disengagement relating to the subject matter of his/her lectures. This superordinate construct is accompanied by subordinate constructs, such as different lecture topics. Superordinate constructs also represent our long-term goals, which have the greatest impact on our subsequent choices and behaviour.
- Personal constructs are permeable: our interpretations are capable of adaptation and change with new experiences or observations. As a result, all constructs are open to new situations, people and events, and are capable of adaptation to experience (called **constructive alternativism**).

Kelly believed that we adopt a futuristic orientation – the effects of our personal constructs influence the future behaviours we adopt. This approach is very different from many others we have looked at (e.g. early learning theories), as it suggests that we are motivated to act in certain ways because of the ways in which we *anticipate* future events. So, we behave in ways to achieve our long- and short-term goals, rather than because of early learning experiences or innate drives. Kelly referred to this concept as the **fundamental postulate**.

Kelly suggested that when we use personal constructs, we organise our experiences in terms of similarities and differences, of which Kelly argued there must be three elements: two which are similar and one with which they contrast. To understand how people go about identifying similarities and differences, and ultimately how constructs are formed, Kelly (1955) specified 11 interpretative processes called **corollaries** (Table 5.1).

The way in which we see the world is therefore a unique product of the operation of the interpretative processes, which form the constructs that we uniquely acquire.

According to Kelly, your *personal construct system* is your personality (1963); this system governs the way in which you view the world around you and how you behave. Personality can change; this occurs when the construct system fails in some way, such as when there is a discrepancy between what the construct system suggests you should be feeling and experiencing in a particular situation or event, and what you actually experience. To amend this situation, you can re-evaluate the situation, elements or characteristics in question, to bring your personal construct system in line with your experiences. In this respect, Kelly's conceptualisation of personality is a dynamic one.

Assessing personal construct systems: repertory grids

One key measure which emerged from Kelly's personal construct theory was the **repertory grid**, which was originally used solely for the determination of personal constructs. The repertory grid allows you to address four key questions:

Table 5.1 **Kelly's 11 corollaries**

Corollary name	Description
Dichotomy	We state a phenomenon simultaneously with a notion of its contrast.
Range of convenience	Constructs exist within a range or limited number of contexts.
Organisation	Constructs are hierarchical for any one person.
Personalised	Constructs exist in relation to our individualised experiences.
Sociality	Where a construction is mutually held then each person plays a role in that interpretative process.
Choice	Meaning is acquired by selecting which of the bipolar alternatives suits the situation.
Clustering	Attribution of information arises as we cluster information.
Fragmentation	Inconsistencies exist within our constructs and may result in what appear to others as logical inconsistencies.
Experience	New experiences allow for changes.
Permeability	Openness to change.
Construction	Constructs may not always be readily understandable or adequately verbalised.

1 What constructs do people use and what aspects of other people are most important to an individual?

2 How does an individual understand key *elements* (e.g. themselves, friends, family) in their life?

3 How do constructs relate to one another?

4 How do elements relate to one another?

The repertory grid involves asking a participant to take on a title role, such as themselves, or a family member, and can represent people whom they like or dislike. The participant must usually select three roles at a time (e.g. 'myself', 'my mother', 'my father'), and take on each role in turn. In clinical applications a therapist may also ask an individual to take on title roles such as 'myself now', 'myself in the future' and 'myself in the past'. The participant is then asked to think of one important psychological way in which two of the individuals are similar (e.g. my mother and I are trusting of people), but differ from the third (e.g. my father is suspicious of everyone). This process is used to develop the bipolar terms (e.g. Trusting versus Suspicious) which constitute the grid, and is repeated until a sufficient number of constructs are developed, or the participant is unable to think of any more.

It is the multiple production of such constructions as ambitious/laid-back, friendly/unfriendly and shy/outgoing that enables the formation of a general interpretation of how people characterise their world (Fransella, Bell & Bannister, 2004). Figure 5.1 illustrates such a grid. For researchers, it is the sufficiency of the combinations of constructs that helps inform individual perceptions and overall views.

An alternative (more refined) use of grids involves the ranking of all the elements (people or events) rather than just assessing similarity/dissimilarity with triads (Fransella, Bell & Bannister, 2004). This technique allows for analysis of relationships between elements through correlation.

Practical application of theory Repertory grids

In practical application, the REP test is a tool employed to explore the constructs individuals use to understand their world. Respondents are asked to identify a number of people (elements) with whom they have a relationship, which are then presented as the headings for the columns in the grid (Figure 5.1). The bipolar constructs presented in the final columns of the grid are generated by asking the respondent, 'in what way are the people (elements) in groups of three (triads) alike (similarity = X) and differ from the third (contrast = 0)?' The responses become the similarity/contrast pole and can be used to understand an individual's personality.

The first six rows in Figure 5.1 demonstrate this approach to constructing and using repertory grids; the final three rows demonstrate an alternative version which allows for ranking of elements, and therefore correlation analysis.

self	mother	sister	boyfriend	former school friend	a disliked teacher	boss	work colleague	partner	cousin	Similarity	Contrast
X		X					O			conscientious	lapse
	X			O				X		active	responsive
			O	X		X	X			cooperative	competitive
		O	X					X		impulsive	guarded
	O				X				X	sensitive	distant
		X				O	X			warm	threatening
8	2	7	9	1	4	10	3	5	6	optimistic	discouraging
2	3	1	5	4	10	8	6	9	7	ambitious	relaxed
6	1	7	9	2	3	9	4	5	6	conforming	argumentative

Figure 5.1 Illustration of REP grid construction

The earlier part of the grid shows that the major concerns of the respondent are conscientiousness, activity, co-operation, impulsiveness, sensitivity and warmth (rows 1–6). It is also interesting to note that the last dimension, warmth, is contrasted with threat rather than with distance. This demonstrates how the respondent perceives it and reveals something of that individual's perception of their surroundings. It can be seen from the ranking of elements in rows 7–9 that there is some correlation between rows 7–9, but not with row 8. This suggests that the respondent associates optimism/discouragement with conformity/argumentativeness, but not with ambition/being relaxed.

<table>
<tr><td colspan="2">Further reading</td></tr>
</table>

Topic	Key reading
Uses and technique of the repertory grid	Fransella, F., Bell, D. & Bannister, D. (2004). *A manual for repertory grid techniques* (2nd edn). Chichester: Wiley.
Background information to personal construct theory	Butler, R. (2009). Chapter 1: Coming to terms with personal construct theory. In *Reflections in personal construct theory*. Chichester: Wiley-Blackwell.
Example of the use of Kelly's personal construct theory in sport	Gucciardi, F., Gordon, S. & Dimmock, J. (2009). Advancing mental toughness research and theory using personal construct psychology, *International Review of Sport and Exercise Psychology*, 2(1), 54–72.
Example of the use of repertory grids in identifying personality characteristics of effective information services professionals.	Siau, K., Tan, X. & Sheng, H. (2010). Important characteristics of software development team members: An empirical investigation using repertory grid, *Information Systems Journals*, 20(6), 563–80.

Test your knowledge

1   How did Kelly believe that we construct hypotheses of the world around us?
2   According to Kelly, how are adjustments made to our interpretations?
3   What is the general purpose of the REP grid and what do you think its strengths and limitations are?

Albert Ellis' rational-emotive behaviour therapy

Ellis' theory of personality (1958a, 1958b) evolved from his clinical practice and the development of his therapeutic approach, which is known as **rational-emotive behaviour therapy (REBT)**. The REBT approach came about from Ellis' interest in learning theorists' approaches to behavioural change, and his own experience of practising psychoanalysis. However, Ellis felt that learning theories at the time were too simplistic and could not account for the entirety of people's behaviour.

Ellis was interested in helping people overcome their fears, anxiety and other disturbances, and believed the following:

- Helping people merely identify the cause of their anxiety will not be enough to overcome it.
- Most people reinforce their anxiety by telling themselves how frightened or upset they are.
- Our cognitions reinforce our disturbances and are therefore the key to understanding our emotions and behaviour.
  - Specifically, disturbances arise from *irrational* cognitions: by thinking and acting more rationally, we can alleviate distress (Ellis, 1958a, 1958b).

● Irrational behaviour is that which prevents us from achieving our goals, and causes distress through its demanding nature. An example would be demanding that another person changes their behaviour, because we have no control over this.

Like Kelly, Ellis believed that we create our own *subjective* view of the world, which guides how we think, feel and behave in different situations.

He believed that empowering people to see that they had free will, and to take responsibility for their own actions, would encourage them to think and behave more rationally (Ellis, 1978).

Ellis also believed that we are oriented to **hedonism**, as everyone's main goals in life are to survive and be happy. He suggested two forms of hedonism that motivate us, short term and long term, and argued that we often sacrifice our long-term goals for short-term hedonism. This may cause distress in the long term.

Ellis' ABC model

To understand human behaviour in more detail, Ellis (1979) proposed the ABC model of emotional and behavioural responses:

A = the Activating event

B = the person's Belief system

C = the emotional and behavioural Consequences that arise

According to Ellis, C does not actually occur directly from A, but is influenced by B. So, it is the way that people believe about an event or situation that affects emotional and behavioural responses and consequences.

In line with this model of behaviour (and personality), Ellis' REBT therapy adopted a logico-empirical approach that stressed the importance of having evidence to support our beliefs. This therefore requires the individual to be aware of their thoughts, feelings and behaviour, and may help to avoid 'faulty thinking'. It also demonstrates the link between cognitive and humanistic personality theories.

So, REBT involves two further stages:

D = helping the person think differently about an event which causes them distress (referred to as Disputation)

E = helping the person to understand new and alternative beliefs through Educational homework

Points to consider: Ellis' approach

● Ellis' REBT is one of the most researched therapies in this field and has a strong evidence base supporting its effectiveness (e.g. Macaskill & Macaskill, 1996).

● Ellis' theory and approach have been criticised for putting too much emphasis on an individual's thought processes, without considering other aspects of personality.

109

Think back to Chapter 4 when we discussed social learning and social-cognitive theories, such as Rotter's locus of control and Bandura's self-efficacy. How do you think they fit with what we have discussed here?

 Sample question   *Problem-based learning*

You are assisting a counselling psychologist who is exploring the effectiveness of different methods of counselling to support 'dysfunctional' families. The counselling psychologist asks you to write a brief report on whether using the repertory grid or Ellis' REBT approach would be most beneficial for helping a stepmother, father and adolescent son who are experiencing difficulties in the home to resolve their issues. Provide evidence to support your claims from relevant theory and research.

Points to consider: strengths and limitations of the cognitive approach

- Kelly's repertory grid and Ellis' ABC model provide valuable insights into the way we see our world, how we organise our attitudes and beliefs, how we generate emotional responses and how these influence our behaviour.
- These theories conceptualise everyone as operating within the same framework, yet allow for an understanding of the *uniqueness* of individuals.
- There is a fair amount of research evidence supporting the value of Kelly's repertory grid for exploring people's thoughts, feelings and behaviours. However, the repertory grid test is complex and requires the expertise of a therapist to be used effectively.
- Both theories offered a challenge to the dominance of the learning theory paradigm and have clear applied value.
- Kelly's 11 corollaries are described using complex language and are not always easy to follow.
- These models tend to focus too greatly on the individual at the expense of other aspects of their personality.
- Much of the research examining the effectiveness of Kelly's repertory grid is correlational, rather than experimental, and it has been criticised for this.
- Kelly's theory focuses almost exclusively on the internal factors affecting an individual and therefore is not comprehensive.
- Both theories may be too simplistic.

Further reading

Topic	Key reading
Application of REBT	Brown, G., Have, T., Henriques, G., Xie, S., Hollander, J. & Beck, A. (2005) Cognitive therapy for the prevention of suicide attempts: A randomized controlled trial, *Journal of the American Medical Association, 294(5)*, 563–70.
Examination of the relationship between personality and cognitive behavioural therapy (CBT)	Sava, F. (2009) Maladaptive schemas, irrational beliefs and their relationship with the Five-Factor Personality Model, *Journal of Cognitive and Behavioral Psychotherapies, 9(2)*, 135–47.
Critique of two different approaches to REBT	Dryden, W. (2010) Elegance in REBT: Reflections on the Ellis and Dryden sessions with Jane, *Journal of Rational-Emotive and Cognitive-Behavior Therapy, 28(3)*, 157–63.

Test your knowledge

1   In what ways are Kelly's personal construct theory and Ellis' REBT similar and in what ways are they different?
2   Why do you think people may interpret the same situation in different ways?
3   Write a paragraph stating what personality is in terms of Kelly's and Ellis' theories.

Humanistic personality theory

Humanistic personality theories arose from dissatisfaction with both the Freudian psychodynamic and the learning theory approaches to personality. The humanistic approach holds a 'future positive' view of human nature and acknowledges the capacity for positive growth. Humanistic theories are described as phenomenological given their concern with people's awareness of their own perception of their thoughts and feelings and the recognition of people's unique experiences.

Abraham Maslow's humanistic theory

Maslow was dissatisfied with the Freudian view of personality and proposed that people are essentially driven to further positive growth, i.e. the full realisation of individual potential. Whilst he recognised that psychoanalysis could make important contributions for disturbed clinical patients, Maslow was concerned with the positive features of human nature and motivation for all. To explain these phenomena, Maslow proposed a hierarchy of six needs: meeting a need provides satisfaction, but opens up a need at a higher level, until the highest need is met (self-actualisation).

Maslow's hierarchy of needs

Maslow's hierarchy of needs is divided into:

● needs arising from deficiencies (e.g. safety, nutrition); and
● needs that advance human fulfilment (e.g. belongingness, esteem).

These needs form a pyramid, with the two lower tiers representing deficiency needs and the higher tiers representing the 'promotion' needs (see Figure 5.2).

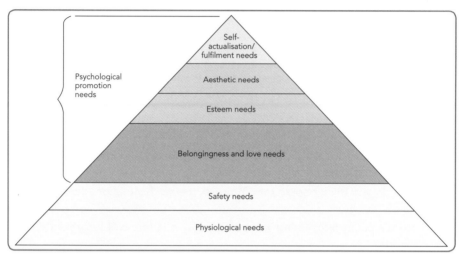

Figure 5.2 Representation of Maslow's hierarchy of needs

● Physiological needs refer to the basic needs that we share with the animal kingdom. These include needs to satisfy thirst, hunger, sleep, elimination of waste and sex. Although it may be possible to have a concern with a higher-level need before basic needs are met, it will only be a *temporary* concern.

● Safety needs involve the need for ordered surroundings and security; and the avoidance of pain. Concern with safety and security in a disruptive environment will be greater in a well-organised community and this will be especially observed in children and the elderly.

● Once deficiency needs have been generally satisfied, the concern for 'psychological promotion' needs becomes greater. These needs involve firstly the need to belong, i.e. have relationships and friends; secondly, the need to gain esteem and respect from others; and further, the need for self-fulfilment. These latter needs differ between individuals, but include aesthetic and cognitive needs and may involve appreciation of beauty and justice, for example.

Maslow's needs classification is not treated as a static model, since it is accepted that our needs change: the needs of an individual living a very fulfilled life can suddenly change if they become ill. As a dynamic model then, the theory allows for complexity of behaviour, which may fulfil a range of needs. There is often no one-to-one relationship between behaviours and needs.

Constituents of self-fulfilment

Maslow identified characteristics of self-actualisation by interviewing those who were considered to have attained high levels of self-fulfilment. Key figures in history were also subjected to analysis to add to this understanding. No one combination of factors that constituted self-fulfilment was found, but an indication of a number of such features was presented. Table 5.2 presents a selection of those characteristics.

Table 5.2 **Selected characteristics of fully fulfilled persons**

• Ease of acceptance of self and others
• Self offers little distraction to dealing with day-to-day issues
• Accurate perceptions of reality with a meaningfulness gained from everyday experiences
• Are ethical, are creative in their approach to life, experience peak experiences, and enjoy a sense of harmony with others

Points to consider: Maslow's theory of self-actualisation

There are a number of challenges to Maslow's model:

- Maslow's theory was essentially based on a concept of his own derivation: independent verification of the concept would add to its validity.

- The theory as a whole has additionally lacked empirical support, in part due to some concepts being difficult to define (e.g. peak experiences). There are few recent works that use the theory of Maslow, but other concepts such as 'subjective wellbeing' and associations with positive psychology have parallels with Maslow's work.

- It is not clear why Maslow included the needs he did in his theory, but excluded others.

- Maslow focused almost exclusively on positive growth, and therefore little is known about how psychopathology (e.g. personality disorders) 'fits' into this theory.

Further reading

Topic	Key reading
Hierarchy of needs theory and parallels with drug use	Best, D., Day, E., McCarthy, T., Darlington, I. & Pinchbeck, K. (2008). The hierarchy of needs and care planning in addiction services: What Maslow can tell us about addressing competing priorities, *Addiction Research and Theory, 16(4)*, 305–7.
Update and revision of interpretation of Maslow's theory	Koltko-Rivera, M. (2006). Rediscovering the later version of Maslow's hierarchy of needs: Self-transcendence and opportunities for theory, research, and unification, *Review of General Psychology, 10(4)*, 302–17.
Beyond the thinking of Maslow – subjective wellbeing	Diener, E., Oishi, S. & Lucas, R. (2003). Personality, culture and subjective wellbeing: Emotion and cognitive evaluations of life, *Annual Review of Psychology, 54*, 403–25.

Test your knowledge

1 How did Maslow see deficiency needs distinguished from 'promotional' needs?
2 Provide an example of a way in which the model allowed for change to reflect the complexity of behaviour.

Rogers' phenomenological theory

Whilst Maslow's concern was with 'typical' populations, Carl Rogers' contributions were developed from his work with disturbed children. Both the tendency and the capacity of individuals for self-fulfilment were accepted by Rogers (1961). From his experiences Rogers formed the view that we all had a natural tendency for achieving our potential, unless there were external constraints to this achievement. The model of motivations adopted reflected the structure provided by Maslow together with the inclusion of 'satisfiers' (essentially physiological) and 'motivation promoters' (psychological).

● Motivation promoters are the product of individual unique interpretations, i.e. the product of individual differences.
● The perceptions we hold of situations are products of our beliefs and experiences and will differ from one individual to another. With respect to troubled children, their perceptions will not only reflect their experiences but result in destructive and aggressive behaviour as a consequence of the effects of negative environmental factors.
    ● Such environments act as a constraint or block on development.

Rogers' basic theory and concepts

The person-centred (phenomenological) approach was formed from Rogers' explanations for the interactions he experienced in client psychotherapy. Rogers believed:

● The most valid statements about personality are those which come from the individuals themselves.
● An individual's view of their surroundings cannot be distinguished from any other notion of reality.

In breaking from the roots of psychoanalysis, Roger argued that all that was important were the current and subjectively perceived experiences, and not those derived from the past.

Rogers introduced a distinction between the concepts of the 'self' and of the 'ideal' self: the correspondence of self with ideal self is called *congruence*. The only way of uncovering another person's notion of self was through empathy, promoted in non-directive counselling. In counselling Rogers sought to free individuals from the restraints imposed by others and their surroundings.

He believed that the development of self depends upon acquiring *regard* from others. In adolescence, in particular, pressures to conform may act in tension with the development of independent self-worth. At home a child learns about the conditions for self-worth, i.e. those activities which gain approval, attention and reward. In the counselling process, the counsellor will need to promote the atmosphere as one of 'unconditional positive regard'.

Practical application of theory Q-sort (Block, 1961)

The Q-sort technique can be employed to determine the self-concept of a client in therapy. A series of statements with key adjective descriptors of personality are presented separately on each of a large number of cards. Individuals are required to organise each of the cards along a scale from 1 to 9 according to the extent to which the statements are a reflection of their own personality or have no relationship to their personality.

Most like me   Least like me

$$\longleftarrow \hspace{8cm} \longrightarrow$$

9   8   7   6   5   4   3   2   1

After some opportunity to organise their cards, the respondent is required to distribute them along a normal curve distribution, i.e. the central position occupying a large number of statements and the extremes containing a small number. The forced distribution ensures an idiographic classification and that each statement is not considered in isolation. The way this is achieved is that the extreme positions are allocated five statements each; positions 2 and 8 have eights statements each; 4 and 6 have 16 statements each; and the central position is allocated 18. The clustering of the descriptive statements enables the counsellor to organise the responses to elicit the characteristics of an individual's personality.

Rogers used pre- and post-therapy classifications to identify change in the client as a result of these sessions.

KEY STUDY

Person-centred personality theory, positive psychology and self-determination theory

Patterson and Joseph (2007) conducted a review of person-centred personality theory and explored how recent developments in the new paradigm of positive psychology have impacted on our understanding of Carl Rogers' conceptualisation of personality. In particular, the authors focused on self-determination theory (SDT), which 'is a more contemporary organismic theory of human motivation and personality functioning that emphasizes the central role of the individual's inner resources for personality development and behavioral self-regulation' (Patterson & Joseph, 2007, p. 119). They conclude that SDT and person-centred approaches provide similar theoretical frameworks for investigating personality and therefore that SDT research findings provide further insight into personality as conceptualised by Carl Rogers. Their paper suggests that findings from SDT research provide a strong empirical evidence base for person-centred therapy – particularly regarding the impact of positive regard. However, the authors argue that person-centred theory does not adequately account for some aspects of personality development or vulnerability to psychopathology. In particular, it does not adequately explain why not all individuals who are exposed to negative social environments develop psychopathology.

Points to consider: Rogers' person-centred approach

- There is an essential difficulty with the evaluation of any therapeutic process in that it requires revealing client information from recorded interviews. Phenomenological approaches are concerned with conscious processes and the clients' participation in those processes, but there is no explanation of how interviewer preconceptions are eliminated or limited in the process.
- Support for Rogers' non-directive therapy has been weakened by arguments that achievement is only rarely demonstrated satisfactorily.
- Rogers has also been criticised for replacing objective evaluation with optimism.
- Recent commentary on Rogers' work has generally been confined to practical applications of his theory (e.g. DeRoberts, 2006), rather than wider discursive themes.
- Similarities can be noted with concepts in Maslow's theory, despite their quite separate and distinct origins.

Further reading

Topic	Key reading
An application of the theory of Carl Rogers	DeRoberts, E. (2006). Deriving a humanistic theory of child development from the works of Carl Rogers and Karen Horney, *The Humanistic Psychologist, 34(2)*, 172–99.
Beyond the thinking of Maslow – subjective wellbeing	Diener, E., Oishi, S. & Lucas, R. (2003). Personality, culture and subjective well-being: Emotion and cognitive evaluations of life, *Annual Review of Psychology, 54*, 403–25.

Test your knowledge

1 For Rogers what is the meaning of the concept of congruence?
2 How did Rogers attempt to minimise the destructive effects of negative environmental influences in his therapy?

New directions in humanistic theory: cross-cultural perspectives

According to Funder (2001), humanistic personality theories have influenced the growing interest in cross-cultural issues, due to their emphasis on phenomenology. This has resulted in the development of two new cross-cultural approaches:

- The first approach argues that we will never be able to obtain a 'true' picture of other cultures because it is impossible to untangle our own world view from our interpretation. Also, just as Allport (1961) argued that one set of personality traits is unique to one individual and should not be applied to others, this viewpoint suggests that we cannot make comparisons between cultures because there are no descriptors which are common to all (Shweder & Sullivan, 1993).

- The second approach suggests that we should be aiming to identify **etics** and **emics** (Triandis, 1997).
  - Etics are those psychological characteristics which are common to all cultures.
  - Emics are the psychological characteristics that are unique to a particular culture.

This new direction of the humanistic approach is linked to the cultural universality of traits debate, which was discussed in Chapter 2. In contemporary research these efforts have centred on exploring the cultural universality of the Five Factor Model of personality (Funder, 2001).

Chapter summary: putting it all together

→ Can you tick all the points from the revision checklist at the beginning of this chapter?

→ Attempt the sample question from the beginning of this chapter using the answer guidelines below.

→ **Go to the companion website at** www.pearsoned.co.uk/psychologyexpress to access more revision support online, including interactive quizzes, sample questions with answer guidelines, 'you be the marker' exercises, flashcards and podcasts you can download.

Answer guidelines

Guidelines on answering the sample questions presented at the start of the chapter are given below.

 Sample question   *Essay*

Critically evaluate the contribution of the idiographic and phenomenological theories of Kelly, Ellis and Rogers to our understanding of personality. Discuss the implication of these theories by comparison with other approaches where appropriate.

Approaching the question

The first part of the question is inviting you to elaborate on the contributions to personality offered by the idiographic and phenomenological approaches to personality. In particular, you should examine the premise of the humanistic and cognitive traditions that personality, behaviour and emotion can be understood only through exploring an individual's subjective experience of their world. You should then examine each of the theorists' conceptualisations of personality in turn – what are their key themes? What are their theories' strengths and limitations? How are their theories applied in practice?

The second part of the question allows you to explore these theories (and the overall idiographic/phenomenological approach) in relation to other key approaches within Individual Differences.

As this assignment asks you to consider other approaches, it would be easy to lose sight of the fact that you are primarily evaluating the theories of Kelly, Ellis and Rogers; remember that including theories from other approaches should be a means of providing context for the discussion and of highlighting the important issues, so don't wander off topic!

Important points to include

- An outline of the distinctive approach of George Kelly and the role of constructs in personal construct psychology:
  - A summary of the propositions associated with the constructs and how their multiplication makes up an individual's unique interpretation of the world.
  - How and why Kelly believed personality change occurs.
  - The therapeutic approach developed by Kelly based upon his theory (e.g. the repertory grid test).
- Ellis' ABC (and DE) model of behavioural and emotional responses, and his rational-emotive behaviour therapy:
  - Implications for how and why personality change occurs.
- Rogers' congruence theory and the motivating effect of overcoming incongruence:
  - Rogers' contributions to counselling and to perceived weaknesses in the psychodynamic approach to counselling.
  - The central role of individual experience in the determination of future behaviour and the potential for self-fulfillment.
- What do these approaches have in common?
  - They have a future positive orientation (e.g. we are motivated to act in ways that fulfil our potential or help us better understand the world around us). This views human personality more positively than approaches such as Freud's psychoanalytic theory.
  - These theories suggest that people are not just passive recipients of their environment (e.g. early behaviourist theories) or biology (e.g. Freud's psychoanalytic theory).
  - Taken together, these propositions support the suggestion that it is only through exploring the experiences of an individual *holistically* that you can understand personality. However, this has serious implications for how personality should be measured and researched, and for how the effectiveness of therapeutic interventions should be assessed.
  - These approaches suggest that what describes personality for one person cannot be used to describe personality for another. However, each of the

approaches works within the same framework, which can be applied to understanding personality.

- There are a considerable number of criticisms of idiographic theories. You should use the opportunity to contrast these phenomenological theories with one or possibly two 'grand' theories. This is both to extract their strengths and to tease out their weaknesses.
- Examples of alternative theories that could be used as comparisons:
  - Psychoanalysis – to highlight differences in the perception of human nature, the sequential nature of human development (which everyone goes through in the same order), the role of therapist and patient in counselling, and the view of the potential for personality change.
  - Learning theories – to highlight differences in the focus on past versus present and future behaviour, the appearance of behavioural and emotional consistencies in responses, the impact of childhood experiences on adult personality, internal mental processes, individuals as passive recipients or active participants of their environment, and the stimulus or individuals' beliefs about the stimulus as the cause of behavioural and emotional responses.

Make your answer stand out

Capturing the additional contributions of idiographic and phenomenological theories of personality to the nomothetic theories is a centrally important aspect of your answer. This represents a very different approach from many of the typical approaches within Individual Differences psychology: for example, a key part of your answer should be the implication this has for the use of the scientific method in personality assessment and also for how personality can be compared across individuals (if this is even possible). The key issue with these theories is their shortfall in both empirical support and validity, which you should examine (e.g. the implications of methodology used in research). A well-constructed essay will identify theories developed through alternative approaches to use as comparators that highlight the key assumptions underlying the humanistic and cognitive traditions (and hence why they are so different). This will also help to underscore why the cognitive and humanistic approaches mainly developed from frustration with the theories which were dominant at the time. A strong essay will also identify the significance of each contribution to the field of personality, such that they stand out despite their inadequacy as complete personality theories.

Notes

6

Psychodynamic personality theories

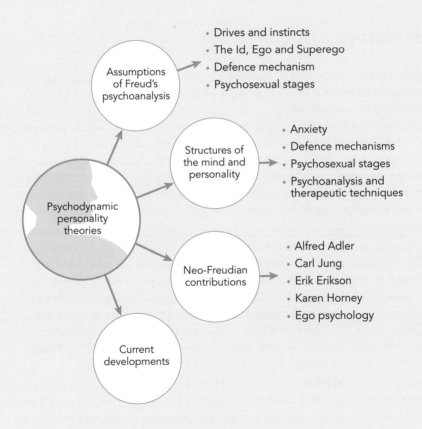

- Drives and instincts
- The Id, Ego and Superego
- Defence mechanism
- Psychosexual stages

Assumptions of Freud's psychoanalysis

- Anxiety
- Defence mechanisms
- Psychosexual stages
- Psychoanalysis and therapeutic techniques

Structures of the mind and personality

Psychodynamic personality theories

- Alfred Adler
- Carl Jung
- Erik Erikson
- Karen Horney
- Ego psychology

Neo-Freudian contributions

Current developments

A printable version of this topic map is available from:
www.pearsoned.co.uk/psychologyexpress

Revision checklist

Essential points you should know:

- ❑ Fundamental assumptions of psychoanalytic theory
- ❑ Freud's structure of personality
- ❑ The role of psychosexual stages·and defence mechanisms in personality development
- ❑ The neo-Freudian contributions of Adler, Erikson, Jung and Horney
- ❑ Psychodynamic approaches to abnormal personality treatment
- ❑ The strengths and limitations of psychodynamic personality theories

Introduction

Sigmund Freud attempted to develop a theory which provided a comprehensive explanation for the functioning of the human mind and behaviour. He was additionally concerned with the correction of people's inner disorders and the resolution of inner conflicts which caused them. Central to Freud's explanations was the role of unconscious drives – particularly the libido. The libido is present at birth and is the source of sexual energy, the will to live and aggression. This drive has the potential to cause conflicts when energy is misdirected. Conflicts arise between the structures within the mind, and formation of the person is the result of development of psychosexual stages through which we progress into healthy individuals.

Freud's are some of the most heavily criticised theories of personality (Haslam, 2007), in part owing to the fact that for many years his was the dominant approach to understanding personality. Freud also proposed a number of controversial concepts, such as **penis envy**, which led later proponents of psychoanalysis (**neo-Freudians** such as Adler and Horney) to develop his theories in new directions. Another fundamental criticism of psychoanalysis is its reliance on 'untestable' and vague concepts (Haslam, 2007), although researchers such as Westen (1998) now seek to address this issue.

In recent years there has been a revival of the psychodynamic approach to personality (Funder, 2001), with some arguing for recognition of Freud's theories which predicted parallel-processing models of consciousness and that many mental processes are unconscious (Westen, 1998).

Assessment advice

Assessments on the topic of psychodynamic personality theory are likely to be framed in one of the following ways: evaluate Freud's psychoanalytic theory of personality (or personality development), evaluate the impact of the psychoanalytic approach on personality psychology as a whole, critically discuss the contributions of the neo-Freudian theorists to psychodynamic personality theories, or compare the psychodynamic approach to personality with one or more other approaches (e.g. trait, biological, cognitive or learning theory approaches).

In each case it is important that you have a strong understanding of Freud's theory of personality development (including the concepts of defence mechanisms and psychosexual stages), and the core criticisms (and strengths) of Freud's psychoanalytic theories. A strong assignment will also be able to demonstrate an awareness of current developments in the field (such as the growing body of empirical research examining Freud's concepts).

Sample question

Could you answer the question below? It is a typical essay question that could arise on this topic. Guidelines on answering the question are included at the end of this chapter, whilst a sample problem question and guidance on tackling it can be found on the companion website at www.pearsoned.co.uk/psychologyexpress.

 Sample question   *Essay*

Critically discuss the contribution made by Freud, and two other psychodynamic theorists of your choice, to our understanding of personality.

Assumptions of Freud's psychoanalysis

Freud's psychoanalytic theory rests on a number of fundamental assumptions:

- People possess 'psychic energy', which remains constant across the lifespan and motivates people to act, and act in certain ways.
- Psychic energy is produced and maintained by innate forces, referred to as *instincts*.
- Instincts can be broadly categorised as the **life instinct** (libido) and the **death instinct** (thanatos).
- The life instinct is associated with urges to satisfy needs, sustain life and seek pleasure; however, the death instinct is associated with urges to harm or destroy oneself or others.
- Freud initially believed that the life and death instincts acted against each other, but later suggested that they could work in combination.

- The amount of psychic energy spent on directing behaviour (in relation to an instinct) cannot be used to direct other behaviour – in this sense, psychic energy is finite. However, changes in personality represent a rechannelling of psychic energy.

- Freud believed that the mind consists of three parts: the **pre-conscious**, the **conscious** and the **unconscious**. This model is referred to as the **topographic model** of the mind (Haslam, 2007).

- The pre-conscious mind is where information that we can access 'on demand' but are not currently using is stored.

- The conscious mind contains all of the thoughts and feelings that we are currently aware of; the unconscious mind is where our 'hidden' thoughts, feelings, base urges and instincts reside. It was this aspect of the mind that Freud was particularly interested in.

- Freud believed in **psychic determinism**, the supposition that everything happens for a reason. Therefore, everything we think, feel and do is the result of activity in our pre-conscious, conscious or unconscious mind (even if we are unaware of it).

Structures of the mind and personality

Freud believed that our urges and drives are primitive and in their natural form are socially unacceptable. For this reason, our mind finds ways to modify them and make their expression more acceptable.

Freud conceptualised the mind as comprising three systems that work together to achieve this: the **id, ego** and **superego** (Figure 6.1). This model is referred to as the **structural model** of the mind (Haslam, 2007). The three components were not considered physical entities but biological metaphors for activities.

The id
The id is innate and unconscious; it is the source of our psychic energy and contains our drives and urges. It directs us to avoid pain and seek pleasure and is the component through which **primary process thinking** (thinking without basis in reality or logical rules) operates.

If an object of desire identified by the id cannot be obtained in reality, the id may produce mental representations or fantasies of the object to satisfy needs temporarily (called **wish fulfilment**).

The ego
The ego develops as an infant, interacts with reality and is the source of rational decision-making. It operates with the **reality principle** and aims to resolve the conflict between the urges of the id and what is deemed socially and morally acceptable. It ensures that the id is constrained to reality and the individual is

safely able to go about their daily lives. It is the ego which engages in **secondary process thinking** (strategy and problem-solving).

The superego

The superego represents a person's 'conscience'. It is the source of morality, contains the values and morals of society and is associated with an individual's internalisation of what is 'right' and 'wrong'.

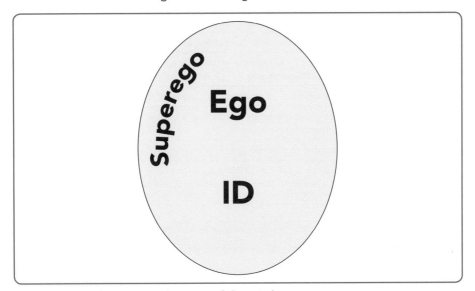

Figure 6.1 **Freud's structures/systems of the mind**

A healthy psychological state exists when the component forces are in equilibrium. Freud believed that neuroticism emerges where the superego becomes dominant and psychosis emerges when the id dominates (Baran & Davis, 2008).

Anxiety

Freud believed that three types of anxiety exist and arise because of imbalances in the three systems:

1 **Objective anxiety**: the fear experienced when there is a real threat to the person, such as when confronted by physical danger.
2 **Neurotic anxiety**: the unpleasant state experienced when there is a conflict between the id and ego, such as worrying excessively about saying or doing the wrong thing in public.
3 **Moral anxiety**: the unpleasant state experienced when there is a conflict between the ego and the superego, such as experiencing chronic feelings of worthlessness for not meeting the standards set by the superego.

Conflicts between the id, ego and superego often occur outside our consciousness and are manifested through mechanisms such as dreams.

Defence mechanisms

Defence mechanisms are the means by which conflicts are resolved or managed. These unconscious methods are adopted to protect the individual from anxiety by distorting reality in some way (see the examples in Table 6.1).

Table 6.1 **Types of defence mechanism**

Defence mechanism	Description
Repression	Removes inappropriate id instincts from consciousness
Projection	Changes attribution of faults from oneself to others
Rationalisation	Generation of acceptable reasons for allowing a socially unacceptable outcome
Sublimation	Replacement of an unattractive course by a valued one
Denial	Insisting that things are not as they seem, in response to a severe anxiety-producing situation
Displacement	Movement of unacceptable feelings to another object
Reaction formation	Displaying a number of behaviours opposite to that which is desired, in an attempt to suppress an unacceptable urge

 Sample question   *Problem-based learning*

You aim to investigate how defence mechanisms are expressed in childhood compared to adulthood. How would you go about designing a research study to do this? Whom would you recruit as participants and how? How will you 'measure' defence mechanisms? What methodological issues might you encounter and how you could overcome them?

Psychosexual stages

Personality is formed by a series of psychosexual stages (see Table 6.2). This model of personality tends to be called the **genetic model** (Haslam, 2007), which rather confusingly refers to developmental, rather than genetic, factors. The experience of the individual at each of these stages influences the type of mature personality formed; the failure to resolve conflicts at any particular stage of development results in *fixation* – a further defence mechanism.

Psychoanalysis and therapeutic techniques

Psychoanalysis is both a theory and a therapeutic approach which can be used to help people who are experiencing psychological distress. Larsen & Buss (2010) argue that psychoanalysis as a therapy can be viewed as the deliberate attempt to *restructure* personality. The key goal of psychoanalysis is to make conscious those conflicts and processes which are unconscious and a number of techniques have developed to help therapists achieve this, including:

Table 6.2 **Freud's psychosexual stages**

Psychosexual stage	Age	Description	Evidence of fixations
Oral	Birth – 18 months	The mouth, lips and tongue are the main sources of pleasure and means to reduce tension. Unresolved conflicts (e.g. in weaning) result in oral fixations that are concerned with 'taking in' and dependency.	Dependent personality; over-eating; drug/alcohol addictions
Anal	18 months – 3 years	The anal sphincter becomes the source of pleasure and is the focus during toilet training (the main source of conflict). Unresolved conflicts may result in anal fixations that are concerned with self-control.	Compulsive or obsessive disorders
Phallic	3–5 years	The genitals become the main source of pleasure and sexual desire is first manifested (and directed toward the parent of the opposite sex). For male children the main conflict at this stage is the *Oedipal conflict* (the desire of the boy to possess his mother and view his father as a competitor for her affections), which is based upon *castration anxiety* (the fear of losing the penis) and resolved through *identification* with the father. The main conflict in this stage for female children is *penis envy*, which occurs when the girl realises that she does not have a penis and blames the mother for this. The girl also wishes to possess her father, but is also jealous because he has a penis but she does not. Freud believed that women never resolve this conflict, which prevents their superego from fully developing. Freud ultimately believed this meant women were morally inferior to men (Kofman, 1985). This assumption has been heavily criticised and most contemporary psychodynamic theorists reject it.	Continuation of the Oedipal complex, Electra complex, or Castration complex
Latent	6 years old – puberty	A period of psychological rest in which children learn the skills needed to become an adult, but do not encounter specific sexual conflicts.	No specific fixations
Genital	Puberty onwards	There are no specific conflicts during this stage. The life instinct focuses on the genitals once again, but the earlier conflicts have been resolved.	No specific fixations

- **Free association**: this involves a psychoanalytic patient relaxing, allowing their mind to drift in whatever direction it chooses and then relaying their thoughts to the therapist, without censoring them. In Freudian free association the analyst's job is to help the patient recognise when something important has been revealed and help the patient focus on this.

- **Dream analysis**: this is concerned with interpreting the content of dreams (manifest content), with the aim of uncovering their underlying meanings (latent content). The psychoanalyst must identify *symbols* which signify the socially unacceptable urges being experienced by the patient and can shed light on the unresolved conflicts which may be causing psychological distress.

● **Projective techniques** (see below).

Practical application of theory TAT projective technique

The assessment of the psychodynamic method has often employed projective techniques. Two such techniques are the Thematic Apperception Test (TAT) and the Rorschach inkblots. In the TAT, clients are asked to devise stories about or explanations of pictures/images presented. The analyst has the task of interpreting the respondent's information, ensuring that intuitive or subjective influences are minimised. The TAT pictures are quite ambiguously constructed so as to encourage the respondent's own perceptions into the situation. The technique is used to explore clients' unconscious defence mechanisms. The idea is that repetition of themes across a large number of images demonstrates areas for exploration. Defence scales have been adopted including the Minnesota Multiphasic Personality Inventory (MMPI) and the California Psychological Inventory. Figure 6.2 is an example of a card offered to clients, who are then asked to explain the circumstances which led up to the picture presented. It is analysed by means of recurrent themes and images and produces working hypotheses for which corroborating evidence is sought.

Figure 6.2 An example of one Thematic Apperception Image

Projective techniques have been subjected to considerable criticism in relation to their scientific validity. However, some arguments in their defence have been presented: for example, in instances where numerous scorers produce the same consistent findings, then at least some of the requirements for validity can be demonstrated. Inter-judge agreements have been the basis for scoring systems offered by Exner (1974) and Cramer (1991).

Further reading

Topic	Key reading
Contribution of Freud's psychodynamic approach	Westen, D. (1998). The scientific legacy of Sigmund Freud: Towards a psychodynamically informed psychological science, *Psychological Bulletin, 124(3)*, 333–71.
Examination of the latency period and the impact of child sexual abuse	Hunt, S. & Kraus, S. (2009). Exploring the relationship between erotic disruption during the latency period and the use of sexually explicit material, online sexual behaviors, and sexual dysfunctions in young adulthood, *Sexual Addiction and Compulsivity, 16(1)*, 79–100.
Paper calling for the re-evaluation of Freud's concept of infantile sexuality	Zamanian, K. (2011). Attachment theory as defense: What happened to infantile sexuality? *Psychoanalytic Psychology, 28(1)*, 33–47.
Defence mechanisms	Sandstrom, M. & Cramer, P. (2003). Defense mechanisms and psychological adjustment in childhood, *Journal of Nervous and Mental Disease, 191(8)*, 487–95.

1   List the key processes through which Freud proposed that personality was formed.

2   What are defence mechanisms and how did Freud propose that they operate?

3   Why might it be difficult to test Freud's theories?

Points to consider

- Historically, Freud's theories have had an enormous impact on how we perceive the mind to operate. For example, psychoanalysis and psychotherapy are still popular in contemporary society.

- A number of Freud's concepts are still relevant in contemporary theory and research, such as the 'unconscious' (Bargh, 2005).

- Freud's view of human nature is inherently negative, which contrasts with humanist representations of human nature.

- Freud's theories tend to ignore the impact of relationships on personality development.

- Freud suggests that personality has developed by the age of around 6 years and remains relatively fixed from this point onwards

- He provides a framework for understanding how both normal and abnormal personalities develop and can be 'treated'.

- His theory has been heavily criticised for its implications for understanding sex differences (see Horney's critique below), which has resulted in neo-Freudian theorists moving away from using psychosexual stages to understand personality development.

- It has also been heavily criticised for being 'untestable'. Eysenck (2004) was a particularly notable critic. A key theme includes the criticism that the formulation of concepts does not permit measurement. Nor does the theory have the capability to predict how someone will behave in the future.

- However, some clinicians do offer more generous judgements of these contributions; Westen (1998) argued that clinical work has demonstrated a series of propositions that are empirically verifiable and that inform experimental enquiry.

Neo-Freudian contributions

A number of theorists have adopted Freud's work and, based on their conceptualisations of its strengths and limitations, have developed the theory in different directions. Key neo-Freudian theorists include Adler (individual psychology), Jung (analytic psychology), Erikson (ego psychology) and Horney (feminist critique).

Alfred Adler

Adler's primary disagreement with Freud concerned Freud's negative conceptualisation of human nature and the conflict between systems. He believed that the structures of the mind (and personality) act in unity: we strive to be the people we *know* ourselves to be.

Adler termed his approach 'individual psychology' because it viewed people as discrete whole entities and observed that:

- *Social context* is important in personality development, particularly in relation to *community*.
- People tend to recognise their weaknesses and attempt to compensate for them.
- Our concerns about weakness are derived from feelings of *inferiority* that develop in childhood, due initially to being 'helpless' as an infant (Adler, 1979).
- We seek to address our inferiorities because we are motivated to fulfil our potential and achieve *superiority*. However, because we all experience feelings of inferiority it helps us to empathise with other people who need help.
- Individuals may seek to overcome their inferiorities in a number of ways, such as through **masculine protest** (exaggerating your sense of superiority in front of others).
- The way in which we seek to commute our inferiorities demonstrates our **style of life** (attitude towards life), which is established between the ages of 3–5 years.
- If an individual (male or female) becomes fixated on their inferiorities, they are said to develop an **inferiority complex**.

Adler believed that personality develops through how we learn about work, friendship and love. This in turn is influenced by how our parents introduced us to *social life* (Adler, 1964) and how 'good' as role models our parents have been.

Adler believed that birth order of siblings was also key to understanding personality development (1927):

- The eldest child may experience being 'dethroned' as the centre of attention on the birth of siblings, but this could have a positive effect on later development as they would have a good understanding of power and authority.
- Eldest children could impact on the personality development of second children; having more supportive elder siblings will encourage healthy personality development for the second child.

- Youngest children and only children are more likely to be pampered and have a high need for approval and achievement.

Adler's personality types

Adler (1973) identified several personality types, based on tendencies to act:

- **Ruling type**: these are characterised by an intense desire for superiority and exploit others to achieve this, as they do not have the necessary social interest or courage to achieve it legitimately.
- **Avoiding type**: when faced with a problem, they deny it exists or pretend that the problem is someone else's.
- **Getting type**: they use other people to achieve their goals and put as little effort into achieving goals as possible.
- **Socially useful type**: these approach life proactively and co-operate with others in order to achieve goals.

The first three types are forms of neurotic personality, which arise when a child is unable to compensate for perceived inferiorities and instead uses them as excuses not to achieve goals, when they suffer neglect or rejection, or when they are pampered by their parents.

Points to consider: Adler's approach to personality

- Adler disagreed with Freud's deterministic view of personality and behaviour and promoted the view that *we are free to achieve our potential*.
- Adler's approach shares many characteristics with humanistic approaches because it emphasises a positive view of human nature and people's worth.
- Many of Adler's theories are underspecified and difficult to test. For example, he did not specify what a 'good' parental role model is.
- Adler's theories provide a framework for understanding personality development, motivation and change. However, the emphasis on one aspect of motivation (to achieve superiority) appears too simplistic.
- Adler provided a much more balanced view of sex differences than Freud and allocated equal worth to both males and females in the parenting role.
- Although, like Freud, Adler believed that understanding patients' past experiences was important, he recognised that the current environment and situations experienced by the individual would also contribute to psychological distress.

Carl Jung

Carl Jung adopted Freudian principles, but viewed psychic energy as comprising more than just sex and aggression instincts. He referred to this broader energy as **life-process energy** and suggested that it arose from conflicts between opposing forces in the **psyche** (personality as a whole), a process which he called the **principle of opposites**. According to Jung:

- Personality development occurs across the lifespan and only ends when we reach a stage where we have accepted ourselves and have accepted that we have reached our potential, through self-realisation (Jung, 1954).
- Life-process energy is infinite and can manifest in numerous ways, including moods and delusions.
- For each activity in one area of the psyche, there will be a corresponding decrease in other areas (the **principle of equivalence**).
- Human nature is motivated to pursue harmony between the opposing forces and achieve a state of balance (the **principle of entropy**).

Brief outline of Jung's structures of the mind

Jung adapted Freud's structure of the mind to account for his observations of similarities in people's delusions. Jung suggested:

- We inherit instincts from our ancestors (e.g. concepts of good versus evil) that are often projected on to fantasies and delusions.
- These instincts, fears and images are stored beneath consciousness in the **collective unconscious** (Jung, 1965).
- The collective unconscious also contains **archetypes** (Jung, 1954, 1964), which are universal symbols that exert influence on our dreams, fantasies, relationships and behaviour, etc.
- Examples of archetypes include:
  - The **god archetype** (Jung, 1964): an all-powerful being that humans turn to in times of distress. This is not related to whether God exists or not, but is a concept present in our collective unconscious.
  - The **persona archetype** (1964): the masks that we wear when adopting different roles (e.g. mother, friend, pupil) that help us to ensure our actions, thoughts and feelings are socially acceptable.
  - The **self archetype** (1959): the potential to achieve balance within our psyche, to accept ourselves and our own identity.
- We have a **personal unconscious** (very similar to Freud's unconscious) which contains all our 'socially unacceptable' thoughts and feelings and files them away from our awareness.
- The personal unconscious differs from the collective unconscious because it contains thoughts and feelings that have arisen from our *own* experiences, whereas the material in the collective unconscious is *innate*.
- The *ego* is what makes us *us*. It represents our consciousness: the thoughts, feelings and memories we are aware of and that shape our identity (Jung, 1965).

Jung's personality types

Jung identified a number of core personality types based on two concepts: whether people were outwardly or inwardly focused and how people relate to the world. The latter concept could be broken down into four approaches:

sensing (registering that we are experiencing something, without evaluating it), **thinking** (interpreting an experience using reason and logic), **feeling** (evaluating the desirability of what we are presented with) and **intuitive** (interpreting the world around us using premonitions or gut-instincts).

When explored, these two broad concepts resulted in the personality types listed in Table 6.3.

Table 6.3 **Description of Jung's personality types**

	Extraverted	Introverted
Sensing	Sociable; shuns introspection, prefers action and pleasure seeking.	Hyper-sensitive to stimuli and the views of other people. Can be passive and calm.
Thinking	Guided by facts and rules, tries to be objective and logical rather than emotional.	Prefers privacy and their own inner world, and finds it difficult to express themselves.
Feeling	Sociable; respects convention, authority and the views of other people.	Quiet, introspective, may experience feelings intensely. May be difficult to form relationships with.
Intuitive	Guided by gut-instinct rather than facts, keen to try new things, creative.	Withdrawn and introspective and experiences difficulty expressing themselves.

Therapy

Jung (1968) suggested that there were four stages in the treatment of psychological distress:

1 **Confession**: recognises there is an issue and seeks the help of a therapist.

2 **Elucidation**: comes to understand what the issues are.

3 **Education**: identifies ways of managing and dealing with the issues and developing their personality.

4 **Transformation**: equilibrium of the psyche's opposing forces is achieved.

Like Freud, Jung was interested in dream analysis. However, Jung believed that dreams revealed repressed material from both the personal unconscious and collective unconscious (Jung, 1965) and the individual's unconscious attempts to find healthy solutions to the problems causing the dreams. According to Jung:

● Dreams could be classed as either 'everyday' or 'archetypal'.

● Archetypal dreams and the symbols they contained were particularly important, as they could be analysed to help reveal and respond to a patient's fears.

● Dream analysis was performed through the **method of amplification**, which requires an analyst and patient to identify symbols in the patient's dream and explore these in great detail to reveal their meaning.

Jung (1964) was also one of the first therapists to employ art therapy in his treatment. This involved patients creating paintings which they and their analyst would then study, in order to help identify symbols and explore the emotions evoked.

Points to consider: Jung's individual psychology

- Jung does not specify in detail the processes or mechanism through which personality develops and focuses more on how individuals can reach the final stages of development (self-realisation) in adulthood.

- Jung's theory is very complex and his original writings are difficult to follow owing to obscure references and style.

- Although aspects of Jung's work, such as archetypes (Jung, 1959), have been found to be difficult to test, work has been undertaken to empirically examine his personality typology. For example, the Myers-Briggs Type Indicator (Myers et al., 1998) is a personality inventory based on Jung's theories and is still widely used in research and occupational selection and recruitment.

 Sample question   **Essay**

Critically discuss the impact of Freud's and Jung's conceptualisations of the unconscious mind on our understanding of personality development.

Erik Erikson

Erikson disagreed with Freud that the personality had fully developed by the age of 5–6 years and argued that personality actually developed across the lifespan (Erikson, 1975). Erikson believed that:

- Freud's 'latent' period was actually a period of great development (Erikson, 1963, 1968) because this is the period in which we go to school, learn how to achieve academically and co-operate with others.

- Rather than placing focus on the sexual aspects of the conflicts experienced by an individual at each stage of personality development, **psychosocial conflicts** are the key.
  - Psychosocial conflicts are those which are socially directed, such as learning how to interact with others and become autonomous.
  - These crises/conflicts are *developmental* because they occur across the eight stages of personality development and must be resolved before progress can continue.

Erikson's eight stages of development

Erikson described eight stages of personality development (Table 6.4).

Table 6.4 Description of Erikson's stages of psychosocial development

Stage	Crisis/ conflict	Description
Infancy (0–2 years)	Mistrust versus trust	People are born and are totally helpless and dependent on others. The extent to which they develop trust that those around them will care for them affects their ability to form trust in future relationships. Infants who have loving and caring parents are more likely to develop trust than those who have parents with poor parenting skills.
Toddlerhood (2–3 years)	Shame and doubt versus autonomy	The child develops greater motor skills and experiments with the world around them to see how much of it they can control. This will affect the extent to which they develop feelings of autonomy in adulthood. Children who have parents who support their developing mastery will be more likely to develop autonomy as they grow older than those whose parents attempt to control or limit the amount of mastery they are allowed to demonstrate.
Young childhood (3–5 years)	Guilt versus initiative	Children begin to imitate the tasks that adults perform in play. This imitation can lead to the development of co-operative skills and achieve goals. If successful, the child will grow in confidence and will start to develop initiative and ambition. If unsuccessful, the child may develop a sense of learned helplessness and expect failure in their ventures.
Elementary school (5–11 years)	Inferiority versus industry	The child develops a sense of comparison with others. If the child has experience of success, they will begin to believe that through hard work they can achieve their goals and this will translate into adulthood. However, if they have mostly negative experiences (failure), they will believe that they are not able to achieve their goals.
Adolescence (11–18 years)	Role confusion versus identity	A difficult period of time in which a child starts to become an adult. A central issue concerns developing a sense of self. If successful, an individual identifies their own values and goals. If not, an individual will experience confusion in adulthood concerning who they are, and may find relationships and identifying meaning in life difficult.
Young adult (18–40 years)	Isolation versus intimacy	The need to develop mutually caring and satisfying relationships with others is a key aspect of this stage. If successful, we are able to grow emotionally. If not, we will feel isolated and may feel less satisfied with life.
Middle adulthood (40–65 years)	Stagnation versus generativity	The search for something meaningful to care about, such as family, a career or hobby, is the main focus of this stage. Conflict arises when an individual steps back and looks at their life and either believes they have found something they care for, or are merely going through the motions.
Old age (65 years–death)	Despair versus integrity	This stage involves coming to terms with having to give up some of the roles we care about (e.g. retiring from our career) and preparing for death. We examine our past to see if we have achieved what we had hoped. This will either result in success (feeling satisfied and content) or failure (feeling despair and regret).

Sample question   *Problem-based learning*

You aim to investigate whether Freud's psychosexual stages or Erikson's psychosocial stages represent a more accurate account of personality development. What type of research design (e.g. longitudinal, retrospective, cross-sectional) would you use and why? How would you operationalise the different stages of the two studies? What other methodological and ethical issues would you need to consider?

Points to consider: Erikson's approach

- Like Freud, Erikson believed that personality development should be viewed as a sequential process.
- He labelled his stages after *life* crises, rather than parts of the body.
- He took a more positive view of human development than Freud, as he believed the 'end point' of personality development was a well-adjusted and pro-social adult.

Karen Horney

Horney was born and lived in a period of history in which it was less usual for women to pursue higher education or careers. Owing to her own experiences of psychological distress and dissatisfaction with psychoanalysis she had received (Horney, 1950), Horney trained as a psychoanalyst and examined Freud's theories in detail. She was particularly interested in how Freud had conceptualised women and their personality development.

- Freud believed women could never fully come to terms with penis envy because it was biologically *impossible* for them to do so.
- As a result, the progression of personality development would be limited and women could never have fully developed superegos.
- As the superego is the 'moral centre' of the mind, Freud argued this meant that women must be morally inferior to men.

Freud (1950) believed that penis envy affected every aspect of women's personality and life:

- The desire to have children was a woman's flawed desire to possess a penis which was symbolised by the child (Abrahams, 1927).
- Women's desires to pursue distinction in education or an occupation arose from their envy of men and demonstrated a need to compete with them.
- Female displays of modesty were expressions of shame and disgust at their own sex for not possessing a penis.

In sum, all of women's motivations, neuroses and expressions were due to penis envy.

Horney proposed that this view of women was inaccurate and unhelpful. She argued that Freud's conceptualisation of personality development was a product of his *own* views about women and the cultural beliefs of the time period that he inhabited.

Horney believed that much of psychoanalysis was based upon the work of men (Horney, 1993), which had led to women's views being underrepresented. She also argued that many of Freud's theories of women's personality development were based on work with 'neurotic' women and therefore not representative of all women. For these reason's Horney re-examined many of Freud's concepts and adapted them. She argued that:

- 'Penis envy' is better understood in terms of envy of the *privilege*, *power* and *status* that men enjoyed, rather than envy of their biology (Horney, 1993).

- Women's desire to possess masculine traits could best be understood in terms of culture and social forces; culture and society suggested that these attributes were worthy and highly valued (and feminine traits were less so), which could explain why women desired them.

- Healthy personality was when we were able to achieve our 'real self' (full potential) and were able to communicate and interact comfortably with the world around us (Horney, 1950).

- Developing a healthy personality was more likely if we had had positive childhood experiences, in particular if our parents were supportive, loving and respectful of each of their children (Horney, 1977).

- Children who have a difficult childhood and unstable or problematic relationships with their parents are at greater risk of developing neurotic personality (Horney, 1945).

- Neurotic personality develops from **basic anxiety**, which arises from negative experiences in childhood that leave the child feeling helpless and alone. As these feelings grow, the child feels more and more distrustful of the world around them and develops **defensive attitudes** (expressed as **neurotic needs** – see Table 6.5) to help them cope (Horney, 1945). Although these defensive attitudes are designed to help the child feel safer in their environment, they are *maladaptive*.

In adulthood, people with neurotic personalities can develop further defence mechanisms to reduce anxiety and help deal with internal conflicts (Horney, 1977). Horney called this process **externalisation** because it involves the person projecting their own thoughts and feelings on to others.

Horney's personality types

Horney suggested there were four main personality types, which were based on the way in which they behaved with other people: *moving towards others*, *moving against others*, *moving away from others* and *healthy*. A healthy personality was a personality which was capable of using all three behaviours appropriately to deal with the situation encountered.

Table 6.5 Description of Horney's ten neurotic needs

Neurotic need for ...	Description
Affection and approval	• Obsessive desire for affection (whether genuine or not) • Hypersensitive to criticism • Unassertive and frightened of 'making' people not like/love them
Dependency	• Need to be looked after • Not 'complete' without a partner • Incapable of a balanced, healthy and caring relationship
Narrow life boundaries	• Risk averse • Prefer routine and order
Power	• Fear of asking for help from others • Misguided belief that they can be master of any situation they encounter • Require power to mask their feelings of helplessness
Exploiting others	• Blame other people if things do not work out for them • Suspicious of other people and their motives • Expect others to help and do things for them, but will not help them in return
Prestige	• Obsessive need for status and fear of losing it
Admiration	• Experience strong levels of self-loathing and self-contempt • Feel they need to project a perfect image of themselves to others
Achievement	• Deny their own faults and wish to be perfect • Need to be the best at everything they do
Independence	• Desire not to need anyone • Estranged from everyone around them
Perfection	• Aware of high moral standards of behaviour (because parents applied excessive demands on them in childhood) but this does not necessarily relate to their actual behaviour

Table 6.6 Horney's personality types

Personality type	Description
Compliant type (moving towards others)	• Desperate need for others • Submissive, avoid criticism and confrontation, devalue themselves
Aggressive type (moving against others)	• Desperate need for power, prestige and admiration • Tough, distrustful of everyone around them and poor at relationships
Detached type (moving away from others)	• Desperate need to be independent and self-sufficient • Distance themselves from others
Healthy type (healthy use of behaviours towards others)	• Flexible approach to others • Trusting, and confident in themselves and others

Points to consider: Horney's approach

- Horney placed greater emphasis than Freud on interpersonal, social and cultural factors in personality development (Horney, 1945, 1977).
- Horney's theories have strong links to the humanistic approach, owing to their positive conceptualisation of people and their development.
- Like Freud, Horney believed that anxiety is produced by conflicts within the person and that childhood experiences are particularly important for personality development. Horney believed that *parenting style* was especially important in this respect (Horney, 1945, 1977).
- Little research has been conducted to test many of Horney's theories (Maltby, Day & Macaskill, 2010).

Ego psychology

Both Erikson and Horney can be described as *ego psychologists* because they attributed a greater role to the ego than Freud (who focused on the id). Erikson, for example, believed that the ego was the powerful part of the personality which helped to established *identity* and helps an individual to achieve their goals. When the ego fails to achieve this, an individual experiences confusion and distress, which is referred to as **identity crisis.**

Further reading

Topic	Key reading
Overview of Adler's approach to personality	Ewen, R. (2003). Chapter 4: Alfred Adler – individual psychology (pp. 89–112). In R. Ewen, *An introduction to theories of personality* (6th edn). Mahwah, NJ: Erlbaum.
Overview of Erik Erikson's theory of psychosocial development	Berzoff, J. (2011). Chapter 5: Psychosocial ego development: The theory of Erik Erikson. In J. Berzoff, L. Melano Flanagan & P. Hertz, *Inside out and outside in* (3rd edn). Plymouth: Rowman and Littlefield.
Overview of Jung's work	Bennett, E. (1983). *What Jung really said*. New York: Schocken Books.
Overview of Horney's feminist critique of Freud's work	Horney, K. (1993). *Feminine Psychology*. London: Norton.

Test your knowledge

1 What are the key differences between Freud and Jung's approaches to therapy?

2 In what ways do Freud and Jung view dream analysis differently?

3 What were the key issues that Adler, Erikson, Jung and Horney raised concerning Freud's personality theories?

▶

> **4** List one key strength and one key weakness of each of the neo-Freudian approaches to personality.
>
> **5** In what ways might a theory that focuses on the ego as the driving force of personality differ from a theory that focuses on the id?

Current developments

Funder (2001) argues that psychodynamic theory has regained popularity in recent years as some of Freud's theories gain belated recognition (e.g. Freud's conceptualisation of parallel processing of the systems of the mind). An individual who has featured strongly in the resurge in interest in psychoanalysis is Drew Westen. Westen has focused on exploring the evidence base for psychoanalysis and psychotherapy (Westen, 1998; Westen, Novotny & Thompson-Brenner, 2004), and has postulated five tenets which apply to all psychodynamic theories in general:

1 As a great deal of mental life is unconscious, people develop behaviour or symptoms which they are unable to explain consciously.
2 Mental processes act in parallel, meaning that people's thoughts, feelings or behaviours can seem contradictory or confusing.
3 Childhood experiences play an important role in personality development, as personality patterns begin to form during this period.
4 Mental representations of the self, other people and relationships guide our behaviour and interactions.
5 Personality development involves being able to regulate one's sexual and aggressive feelings and move towards maturity healthily.

It seems likely that a key focus of future effort will be the empirical investigation of the mechanisms underpinning psychodynamic theory and the effectiveness of psychotherapies.

KEY STUDY

Using psychoanalysis in personality assessment

Bornstein (2010) conducted a review of approaches to psychological testing and examined how psychoanalytic principles could be used to enhance personality assessment. He suggested that psychoanalysis could provide a framework that could be useful in three specific domains of personality assessment:

1 The role of projection in shaping Rorschach responses (projection techniques).
2 Exploring gender differences.
3 Using process dissociation procedures to help understand personality test score convergences and divergences.

Bornstein (2010) therefore suggests that psychoanalysis can be used to help explain the findings of personality assessment from other branches of Individual Differences psychology.

Points to consider: psychodynamic theories

- Many theories of 'healthy' personality are derived from theories developed from observations of 'unhealthy' or 'abnormal' personality.

- Many of the psychoanalytic theorists discussed in this chapter used their own experiences to direct their theory and conceptualisation of human nature (Maltby, Day & Macaskill, 2010). The impact of this is unclear and often appears unacknowledged.

- Many psychoanalytic theories (such as those proposed by Jung) are extremely complex and difficult to follow.

- A number of criticisms of psychoanalysis have been aimed at Freud's personal life and how he treated his patients (Haslam, 2007), which are not particularly relevant to his theories.

- Approaches within psychoanalysis can be distinguished by their conceptualisation of human nature as negative (e.g. Freud's approach) or positive (e.g. Horney's approach).

- Many neo-Freudian theorists felt that Freud's focus on sexual conflicts and instincts was unnecessary.

Chapter summary: putting it all together

→ Can you tick all the points from the revision checklist at the beginning of this chapter?

→ Attempt the sample question from the beginning of this chapter using the answer guidelines below.

→ Go to the companion website at www.pearsoned.co.uk/psychologyexpress to access more revision support online, including interactive quizzes, sample questions with answer guidelines, 'you be the marker' exercises, flashcards and podcasts you can download.

Answer guidelines

Guidelines on answering the sample question presented at the start of the chapter are given below.

Sample question   **Essay**

Critically discuss the contribution made by Freud, and two other psychodynamic theorists of your choice, to our understanding of personality.

Approaching the question

The first thing you will need to do is to outline Freud's theory of psychoanalysis. You will need to explore each of the key concepts proposed by Freud (such as defence mechanisms and psychosexual stages) and evaluate them (e.g. is there evidence for or against them, or other possible explanations for observations?). You will then need to carefully select two further psychoanalysts to explore further. You can demonstrate a strong understanding of the subject by critically discussing the ways in which these theorists' views were similar/dissimilar to Freud's and why, and ultimately the extent to which these 'neo' approaches provide a comprehensive and complete account of personality. To finish you should provide a succinct conclusion on where you feel the impacts of the psychoanalytic approach are felt in personality psychology and how they suggest personality should be viewed.

Psychoanalysis is a relatively old approach and as such has generated a number of criticisms. Notably, a large number of criticisms centre on Freud himself – so you need to try to avoid 'hearsay'. Only include criticisms of Freud if they are relevant and wherever possible support your critique with evidence from theory and research. Make sure you consider the strengths and limitations in a balanced way.

Although this question focuses on psychodynamic theories, there is potential to include issues and theories from other approaches in individual psychology, where appropriate.

Important points to include

- Describe and evaluate Freud's topographical and structural models of the mind and discuss their implications. For example, Freud was one of the first theorists to postulate that a substantial number of mental processes are *unconscious*.
  - Psychoanalysis is based on the premise that some mental processes are unconscious. This recognises (and provides a possible explanation for) the fact that sometimes people are unaware of what is causing them distress, or are unaware that they have behavioural/emotional issues.
- Describe and evaluate Freud's concept of defence mechanisms and their implications for personality.
- Describe and evaluate Freud's concept of psychosexual stages and their implications for personality.
- Highlight the fact that Freud was one of the first theorists to recognise that mental processes *operate in parallel*. This allows psychoanalytic theories to

provide an explanation of why there are inconsistencies or discrepancies in behaviour. Also, there is now a greater recognition and evidence for parallel distributing processing in neuroscience and neuropsychology.

- Identify the key criticisms of Freud's theories (and where these criticisms originated), such as the emphasis he placed on sexual issues (Erikson) above all others and the explanation of sex differences (Horney) he provided.

- Pick two neo-Freudians to evaluate with Freud (e.g. Adler, Erikson, Jung or Horney) and critically evaluate their contributions in the same way.

- Examine the impact of psychodynamic personality theories on other areas/branches of Individual Differences psychology: for example, the impact on personality assessment, on 'popular culture' perceptions of personality and on the treatment of psychopathology (e.g. **personality disorder**).

- Explicitly state what psychoanalytic theories suggest about personality, for example:

  - Freud's conceptualisation of human nature was quite negative: we are driven by our id (which contains destructive drives such as sexual and aggressive urges), which causes conflicts that we must resolve in order to develop our personality fully. Other theorists (such as Adler and Horney) suggested more positive representations of human personality and others argued that the ego (e.g. Erikson) should be viewed as the driving force behind personality (e.g. ego psychology).

  - Freud's (and Erikson's, for example) theories suggest that personality development is sequential: moving from one stage to another in order. Freud's theories also suggest that these stages are biologically based (oriented around the fixation on different parts of our body), but other theorists (such as Erikson) disagree.

  - This also suggests that personality is affected almost exclusively by internal processes, whereas other theorists (such as Adler and Horney) suggested that parenting style plays a key role in personality development.

  - Freud's theories were deterministic – for example, suggesting that women's personalities could never develop as fully owing to their biology, which is highly contentious (e.g. Horney's critique).

  - Freud's theories suggest that psychoanalysis is the process through which the unconscious processes of the mind which are causing distress (e.g. unresolved conflicts) can be discovered and treated. Conflicts are also symbolised in dreams, which can be analysed by a therapist. Importantly, in Freud's conceptualisation of therapy, the therapist was seen as the expert who could interpret the 'patient's' dreams and unravel the unconscious conflicts for them. Different therapists have had different approaches, and you could also highlight the differences with other approaches in Individual Differences psychology (e.g. person-centred counselling, where the 'patient' is seen as the expert concerning their own experiences).

Make your answer stand out

Make sure your assignment has a strong structure – the critiques of Freud's and the neo-Freudians' psychoanalysis are extensive and it would be too easy to end up with an essay that reads like a list of what 'he or she said'. Also, make sure you choose wisely which two neo-Freudian theorists to evaluate. For example, if there are key criticisms you are highlighting of Freud's work, pick two theorists who have attempted to address these issues and evaluate how effectively they do this. For example, two key criticisms of Freud are his focus on sexual issues and sex differences, so you could pick Erik Erikson and Karen Horney to explore how these issues have been dealt with by other psychoanalysts. You then need to critique these approaches effectively too.

To demonstrate a strong assessment, the implications of the fact that a large number of theories in psychoanalysis were developed from clinical practice with psychopathological symptoms, or from the therapists' own experiences, should also be considered. You could also examine the suggestion that historical and cultural factors affect theory generation (e.g. Horney's critique of Freud's views on women examined this).

Notes

Stability, consistency and change in personality traits

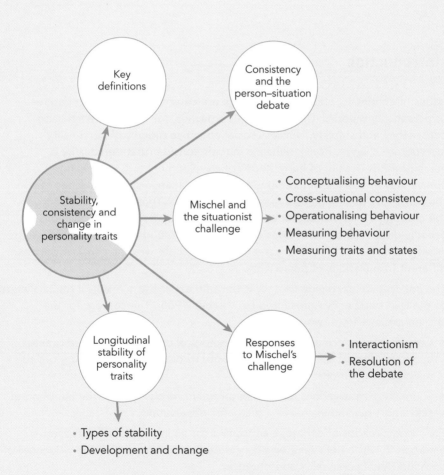

- Conceptualising behaviour
- Cross-situational consistency
- Operationalising behaviour
- Measuring behaviour
- Measuring traits and states

- Interactionism
- Resolution of the debate

- Types of stability
- Development and change

A printable version of this topic map is available from:
www.pearsoned.co.uk/psychologyexpress

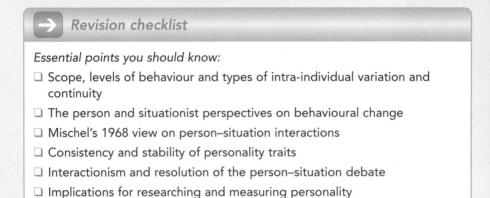

Revision checklist

Essential points you should know:
- ❑ Scope, levels of behaviour and types of intra-individual variation and continuity
- ❑ The person and situationist perspectives on behavioural change
- ❑ Mischel's 1968 view on person–situation interactions
- ❑ Consistency and stability of personality traits
- ❑ Interactionism and resolution of the person–situation debate
- ❑ Implications for researching and measuring personality

Introduction

Issues of continuity, stability and change are central distinguishing features of personality theories. Dispositional approaches, for example, emphasise consistency and stability, whereas social-cognitive models of personality incorporate change. Psychodynamic models consider that personality is established as a result of early stages of development and that change comes only as a result of intervention, whereas humanistic approaches see the possibility of change as a reason for optimism. These perspectives cover the differing views of whether personality was seen as stable dispositions, as broadly distinct of context, or as an amalgam of thoughts, actions and feelings arising from the context. The essence of the debate was the contrast between different formulations of personality.

The importance of change as a topic became explicit as a result of the challenge to the trait perspective presented by Mischel (1968). The content for the challenge came from two sources:

- Growth in influence of cognitive psychological principles provided greater understanding of the individual's capacity to discriminate and therefore to distinguish situations.
- There were reservations about measurement reliability, with the adoption of self-report questionnaires as a proxy for observation.

Following decades of debate, a consensus for an interactionist perspective emerged in which behaviour was considered a consequence of the influences of both individual personality and situation.

Issues of intra-individual variation in personality go wider than that of cross-situational consistency: longitudinal consistency in personality (for both children and adults) over time is an additional area for debate and research.

Assessment advice

Assessments in this topic area explore your understanding of the issues associated with each side of this debate as well as arguments for the interactionist resolution of the issues of continuity of personality for a fully developed adult. The debate has continued over a number of years and has been revived on several occasions. A convenient mechanism to ensure that you cover all the material is to present the discussion in historical terms as it progressed.

Sample question

Could you answer the question below? It is a typical essay question that could arise on this topic. Guidelines on answering the question are included at the end of this chapter, whilst a sample problem question and guidance on tackling it can be found on the companion website at www.pearsoned.co.uk/psychologyexpress.

✳ Sample question   *Essay*

Critically consider whether the interactionist perspective on personality has satisfactorily resolved the debate as to whether personality or situation is the primary determinant of behaviour.

Key definitions

A distinction can be drawn between the usage of the terms *consistency* and *stability*. Consistency refers to the way in which people tend to behave in similar (or dissimilar) ways *across situations* (see Figure 7.1).

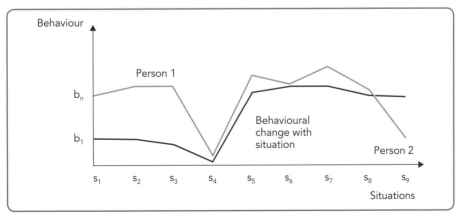

Figure 7.1 **Diagrammatical representation of personality consistency across situations**

Stability (see Figure 7.2) tends to refer to the way in which an individual's own behaviour may differ or appear constant across the lifespan (or a set period of time).

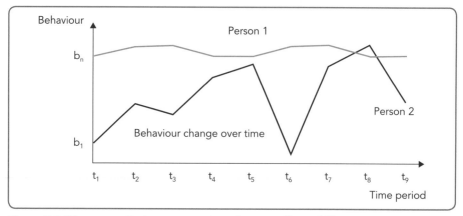

Figure 7.2 Diagrammatical representation of personality stability over time

These represent two key ways of exploring continuity or change in personality. Both formulations presented a challenge to the trait perspective on personality, which characterises personality as an enduring dispositional part of the person.

In our everyday lives we rely upon being able to predict satisfactorily the behaviours of others; when selecting groups with whom we wish to work or associate, we make decisions based upon a judgement of how they have behaved in the past and how we anticipate they will behave in the future.

Consistency and the person–situation debate

The person–situation debate centres on whether person variables (e.g. shyness or stubbornness) have a greater influence in the determination a person's behaviour than does the situation in which they find themselves. If person variables were the most dominant, then the trait perspective would anticipate an individual's behaviour to be consistent across varying situations and time periods (see Figure 7.3).

It can be seen from Figure 7.4 that behaviour act B_1 is consistent across situations a, b, and c (although not d). There is said to be cross-situational consistency. This cross-situational consistency is not repeated for any other behaviours, i.e. B_3, B_4, B_2. It will also be noted that there is temporal consistency over times t_1, t_2, and t_3 for behavioural act B_4. Behavioural act B_5 occurs in no other situation and at no other time than t_2.

Much of the debate about consistency turns on what is the term 'consistency' is actually understood to mean. In practice, the question is determined by judgements about what is required to be sufficient for there to be a consensus for consistency.

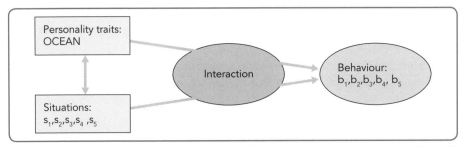

Figure 7.3 Diagrammatical representation of the interaction between personality and situational factors and the impact on behaviour

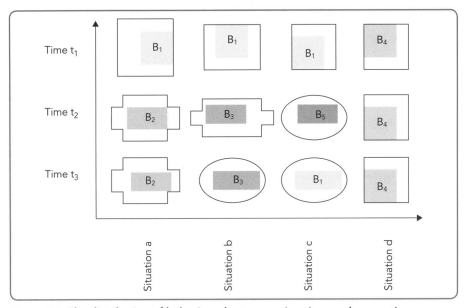

Figure 7.4 The distribution of behavioural acts over situations and across time

Mischel and the situationist challenge

Mischel's (1968) **situationist challenge** to the dispositional approach centred on a number of key issues:

- The ability of the trait concept to capture personality accurately: Mischel believed that the notion of traits did not effectively discriminate situations and did not recognise the importance of cognitive psychology.

- The view that there was evidence for consistency of behaviour sufficient to suggest the predominant influence of broad traits: Evidence from the classic Hartshorne and May (1928) study, and the Newcombe (1929) residential summer camp study gave support to Mischel's challenge on this front.

- The predictive capacity of self-report questionnaires: Questionnaires are typically the means for measurement and so are dependent upon the way we use language and the structure of that language.
  - Questionnaires reflect 'pre-existing categories' and 'organisation of language'. Mischel believed that the language we use is constructed in trait-like forms, so it was not surprising that trait-like descriptors emerged from factor analytic study.
  - The representations of behaviour in language are not empirically accurate but produce a **tautological** response. This view contains an implicit criticism of the lexical hypothesis of Galton, Allport and Cattell (discussed in Chapter 2); the forms of language in which we provide descriptions structure our representations. These representations limit our capacity to report situation-specific identifiers.
- Traits ought to be able to predict specific behaviour associated with specific situations, rather than suggesting they are essentially consistent over a broad span of situations. To illustrate, for trait theorists individuals with the high trait level of introversion would be expected to express that behaviour over a span of situations even when the behaviour may not be evidenced in a single instance.

Conceptualising behaviour

Mischel believed that behaviour is shaped by three factors:

1 the individual 'person factor';
2 the stimuli and boundaries of situations;
3 the interaction of situations with **person factors**.

According to Mischel:

- Situations elicit cues for appropriate behaviours, which are then mediated by person-factors.
- The view you take of a situation influences the actions you take and the explicit behaviour exhibited. Therefore, although person-factors mediate behaviour, it is the social context which is most important.
  - This is evidenced by the frequently low correlations identified ($r = 0.2$–0.3 correlation, later increased to 0.4) between a trait and specific behaviour.
  - The low-magnitude correlations between trait measurements and specific behavioural measurements should be called the 'personality coefficient'.
- It is the psychologically *meaningful* aspects of situations that constitute the important cues, rather than their objective measurement, and these should therefore be the focus of study.

KEY STUDY

Behavioural signatures

In a study of children over time and different settings, Shoda, Mischel and Wright (1994) found that the most salient psychological characteristics of the situation are the behaviour of the individual with whom the child was interacting; and the positive and negative experiences of these interactions. Therefore, it was *behavioural signatures* as stable patterns of responses to meaningful situations, rather than traits, which were considered to distinguish people.

Mischel believed that people show stability over time but do not show cross-situational consistency. However, he did accept that we do not approach every situation as if it were completely new: expectancies and memories are active components of our functioning.

CRITICAL FOCUS

Situational consistency of behaviour

Hartshorne and May's classic 1928 study is presented as evidence for inconsistent behaviour. The researchers studied school children's trait of honesty at a summer camp both in leisure activities and in written exams. Occurrences of dishonesty amongst the children were noted in the different situations and over time. Low correlations were reported, suggesting that behaviour could not be interpreted as consistent or stable. The researchers later extended the trait study to 'self-control' and 'preparedness to help'. The same findings were recorded.

Test your knowledge

1 What correlation finding did Mischel consider was the maximum likely to be found?
2 Why did Mischel consider that trait conceptions were not an accurate way to capture personality?
3 What aspect of situation measures did Mischel believe we should employ to capture what was most relevant?

Cross-situational consistency

A number of themes emerge from the Hartshorne and May study which later became the source of discussion. These were the breadth/specificity of behaviours appropriate to adopt for measurement. In particular, Epstein (1983) explored how broad or narrow a span of behaviour should be for it to be defined as an appropriate measure for testing correspondence with traits. Epstein's study introduced the notion of aggregation as the means by which consistency is demonstrated over a wider span of behaviour rather than specific behavioural instances.

KEY STUDY

Span of situational influence on behaviour

Epstein (1983) conducted an examination of the breadth of situational influences on behaviour, asking respondents to record their behavioural tendencies and actual behaviours daily over a period of 28 days. The question posed was how much of the behaviour was consistent on consecutive occasions. The author also asked whether behaviour varied with time. The study produced two contrasting sets of findings.

Behaviour occurring on one day was not able to predict the behaviour on a subsequent day, suggesting that there was a lack of consistency. However, when the period of behaviour was extended over a one-, two- or three-week period there was consistency with the one-, two- or three-week periods. Epstein concluded that over a broad range of behaviour there was cross-situational consistency.

Whilst broad traits did correspond with a broader range of behaviour, they did not correspond to specific situations. Transient states have a better correspondence to specific behaviours (Matthews, Deary & Whiteman, 2009).

Further reading

Topic	Key reading
Situation specificity and reliable means of measurement	Epstein, S. (1983). Aggregation and beyond: Some basic issues on the prediction of behaviour, *Journal of Personality*, 51, 360–92.
Clarifications of aggregation finding and the person–situation debate	Epstein, S. (1983). The stability of confusion: A reply to Mischel & Peake (1982), *Psychological Review*, 90(2), 171–84.

Test your knowledge

1 Explain why Epstein's investigation and arguments were able to undermine confidence in Mischel's low correlation figure for personality behaviour correspondence.

Since it is the immediate situation which is a primary behavioural determinant, changed primary circumstances will result in different behaviour on different occasions. The continuing support for the situationist perspective can be found amongst researchers many years after the debate was initiated. One reason for this persistence of view was that important situational effects regularly exceeded the personality influence (Funder & Ozer, 1983).

KEY STUDY

Situational influences on behaviour

Funder and Ozer (1983) conducted three reanalyses of the data from experiments of classic investigations to elaborate upon the significance of the situational influence upon behaviour. The cases chosen explored central themes of social psychology and used classic social psychology study designs. Case 1 involved attitude change under a forced compliance situation; case 2 involved bystander intervention in situations of crises; case 3 involved the effect of obedience on behaviour.

Case 1 involved respondents gaining different levels of reward for portraying a purposefully dull task as one of great interest to subsequent participants. Different levels of reward were offered (situations). Case 2 involved respondents being asked to provide assistance to a distressed confederate. Two conditions (situations) were established: first, the extent to which the 'helper' (respondent) was in a hurry and, secondly, the extent to which other bystanders were available. Case 3 on obedience involved the two conditions (situations): extent of isolation of the respondent to the victim; and the closeness of the instructor to the respondent. The situations employed in the Funder and Ozer study were different in nature and yet their findings were not able to show the high importance of situations to behaviour. They concluded that the size of the effects is insufficient alone to confirm their value. It was considered, therefore, that it was the practical and theoretical relevance of their effects which required attention.

Further reading

Topic	Key reading
The effect and nature of situational influences	Funder, D. & Ozer, D. (1983). Behaviour as a function of situation, *Journal of Personality and Social Psychology, 44(1)*, 107–12.

Operationalising behaviour

The term 'behaviour' spans a wide range of levels and activities, since it can be described simply as 'a response' to some event (Ajzen, 2005). Even within a narrower conception of behaviour, it has a wide range of applicability:

- It can consist of short bursts of fairly spontaneous acts with little meaning, or very purposeful, driven activity with considerable implications.
- It can be a single event or repetitive.
- It can vary in duration from long-standing actions over weeks or months, to instantaneous acts.
- The terms 'molecular' (smaller) and 'molar' (larger) are used to discriminate between the size of the units of measurement (Rosenthal & Rosnow, 1991).

Mischel has been criticised for treating all behaviour as an undivided spectrum of activity.

Measuring behaviour

The different formulations of behaviour, and the extent to which any behaviour can be effectively observed, presents different issues for measurement:

- Measurement and the accuracy of classification and frequency counts can be subject to both random and systematic error.

- Standardised methodology, trained observers and assessment of inter- and intra-rater reliability are required to help mitigate these issues.

Figure 7.5 is a representation of a typical coding sheet used for behavioural measurement. It shows the behaviour coding employed, for example, by Patterson (1977) in a naturalist observation of aggressiveness and non-co-operation.

Coding Sheet for Behavioural Observation

Participant Code no. ....

Code............   Observer...............   Date...............

Approval (AP); Attention (AT); Negative Command (CN); Compliance; presence of Crying (CR); Disapproval (DI); Dependency (DP); Destructiveness (DS); Ignore (IG); Laugh (LA); Non-Compliance (NC); No Response (NR); Play (PL); Negative physical contact (NP); Positive physical contact (PP); Shout (SH); Talk (TK); Tease (TE); Whine (WH).

Incident	Occurrences	Duration secs (1)	Duration secs (2)	Duration secs (3)	Duration secs (4)	Duration secs (5)
CN	///	5	8	10	4	
IG	//	12	15			
PL	///// //	20	22	25	30	6
TE	////	5	5	8	10	

Figure 7.5 **Representative behavioural scoring sheet**

Individual behaviour is highly variable but this does not detract from individuals acquiring typical patterns of behaviour (Fleeson, 2004). These reflect the stability that is characteristic of the person, and is used as an explanation for a distinction between traits and states.

Measuring traits and states

We briefly discussed states in Chapter 2 and it is important to understand how they differ from traits:

- Traits are relatively stable, whereas states are considered to be a transient phenomenon and are also often referred to as 'moods'.
- Traits are usually associated with broader and longer-duration occurrences.
- States are portrayed as more limited, reflect behaviour at that moment, and are measured as such.
- Traits are inferred from a series of behaviours.

The directness of measurement suggests that states can be more easily interpreted as immediate responses to external stimuli.

✳ Sample question   *Essay*

Critically evaluate the usefulness of states compared to traits in understanding Individual Differences in behaviour.

Responses to Mischel's challenge

Responses to Mischel have focused on his proposition of low correlations between personality traits and behaviour for a number of reasons, such as:

- It depends upon the bandwidth of the traits and the span of behaviour adopted for measurement.

- In respect of the small 'effect size', it was not considered reasonable to expect a single measure to predict a single behavioural outcome.

- There were issues concerning the measurement of situation; there is lack of consensus as to what constitutes situation and also no agreement on how situation should be measured.

- Whilst Mischel's characterisation assumed absolute consistency across situations, there are other formulations for consistency that are meaningful, such as individual-rank position (Caspi and Roberts, 2001).

Criticisms have been levelled at Mischel for not accurately representing the subtleties of the trait–behaviour relationship. Trait psychologists Allport, Cattell and Eysenck did not, for example, argue that personality generated rigid behaviour devoid of the environment, only that there was broad consistency in the resulting behaviour. Early personality definitions were treated as 'relatively enduring', but not absolutely rigid, which would be more reflective of a psychopathological state.

Mischel (1968) had also challenged the use of questionnaires and the reliability that can be obtained from the behaviour raters' inter-observer reliability. This criticism continues as a continuous source of concern for investigators who need to constantly demonstrate validity with each enquiry undertaken. This reliability can be increased with improved measures, well-trained judges and sufficient corroboration of findings. Kenrick and Funder (1988) attempted to bring the debate to a conclusion by presenting evidence in response to a series of arguments introduced by Mischel. These are presented in Table 7.1 which summarised those findings and rejected a number of the challenges. The authors did, however, reject the view that the debate served only to topple a 'straw man'; the authors claimed that our understanding of personality had been considerably advanced as a consequence of the debate.

Interactionism

There are a number of forms of interactions between person and situations. These include situation selection and situation adjustment. We all have the capacity to select from a number of environments according to what suits us at a particular time. Our personalities will play a part in that selection. Choosing to go fishing on an early damp morning is an environmental choice selected by many, but generally may not appeal to the same person choosing the bright lights and warm environment associated with Christmas shoppers. Even where we have selected similar environments, we may attempt to influence and change them. This is achieved by the behaviours we adopt to adapt those environments. Responses by others to our behaviour can alter the climate and effectively change all that is characteristic of the situation.

Table 7.1 **Summary of areas of hypotheses lacking evidential support**

a	Personality traits are not just in the eye of the beholder
b	Are not a product of semantic illusions
c	Are not a product of accuracy in base-line measures
d	Are not a product of shared stereotypes
e	Are not due to discussion or collaboration of observers
f	Purely products of situational consistencies
g	The small relation of traits to behaviour is still important

Source: D. Kenrick & D. Funder, Profiting from controversy: Lessons from the person – situation debate, *American Psychologist*, 43, pp. 23–24, 1988, APA, adapted with permission.

Further reading

Topic	Key reading
Evidence on findings concluding the person–situation debate	Kenrick, D. & Funder, D. (1988). Profiting from controversy: Lessons from the person–situation debate, *American Psychologist*, 43(1), 23–34.
Evidence for behavioural consistency	Funder, D. & Colvin, D. (1991). Explorations in behavioural consistency: Properties of persons, situations and behaviours, *Journal of Personality and Social Psychology*, 54, 528–50.

Test your knowledge

1 Identify three areas of Mischel's challenge for which no supporting evidence has been presented.

2 Explain why a small effect size of 0.3 to 0.4 cannot be dismissed as of no value.

3 What techniques can be adopted to increase inter-observer reliability?

Resolution of the debate

Fleeson (2004), as with Kenrick and Funder's (1988) article two decades earlier, argued that the debate is resolved. Fleeson's (2004) resolution was that both sides turn out to be correct if we take account of the importance of the situation. Fleeson (2004) gives emphasis to the need for traits to explain that a typical person acts in a similar way most of the time and on different occasions (except adaptations to momentary events). Consistent with Epstein's (1983) findings, Fleeson (2004) argued that an individual's behaviour will be similar when measured over greater periods of time such as weeks. Everyone has a distribution of behaviours rather than a single level and people differ in their 'within-person' profiles of those behaviours, i.e. portions have different central positions. These central portions are said by Fleeson (2004) to be stable over large timespans. People can be ranked consistently with respect to each other.

Further reading	
Topic	*Key reading*
Considerations of within-person variability and personality processes	Fleeson, W. (2004). Moving personality beyond the person–situation debate: the challenge and the opportunity of within-person variability, *Current Directions in Psychological Science*, *13(2)*, 83–7.
Personality dispositions and personality processes	Mischel, W. & Shoda, Y. (1998). Reconciling processing dynamics and personality dispositions, *Annual Review of Psychology*, *49*, 229–58.

Longitudinal stability of personality traits

Longitudinal stability is the alternative form of consistency to that of cross-situational consistency. Durations can vary considerably but consistency is typically considered over months or years. Stability needs to be distinguished from reliability, which is the *internal consistency* of the trait over a short time period.

Types of stability

Caspi and Roberts (2001) initiated a discussion concerning longitudinal stability and change, presenting a number of themes to which other researchers have responded. The authors alerted us to the ambiguities in findings that arise when we fail to distinguish types of continuity across the lifespan. Three of several different types of continuity are represented graphically in Figures 7.6, 7.7 and 7.8. The first is absolute continuity of traits. There has been contrasting evidence from researchers in respect of absolute continuity of individual characteristics. The second type is the individual's rank-order of traits amongst a group of individuals over time. Structural continuity refers to the continuation of the correlational relationships within the trait-profile for an individual over time.

Development and change

Consistency of traits, as opposed to stability over time, has attracted the greatest attention from researchers. However, different stability types are important:

- One form of change that occurs is a within-person comparison of a personality attribute over time (Figure 7.6). This type of stability/change presents a measure of how each individual may vary.

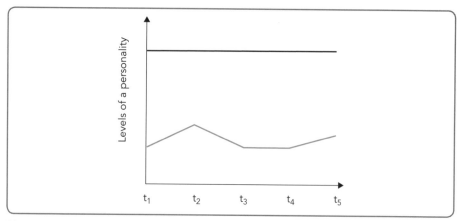

Figure 7.6 Within-person's relative constant/variable personality attribute over time

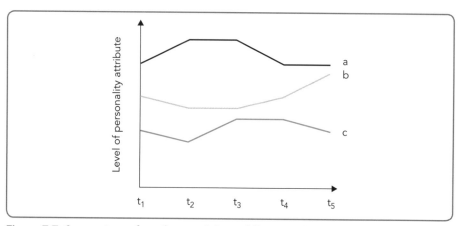

Figure 7.7 Comparison of attributes of three different individuals over time

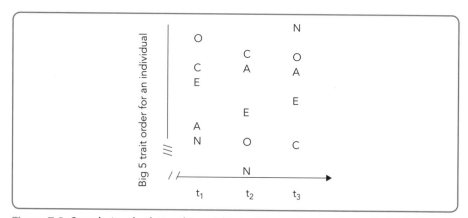

Figure 7.8 Correlational relationship: within-trait inconsistency for an individual

- A second of these can be considered as the stability relative to others with whom you could be compared (Figure 7.7). Change in this respect allows comparisons between individuals over time.
- A further type of stability is the changes in the relative levels of a number of traits for an individual (Figure 7.8). This represents coherence of personality, such that earlier behaviours are found to be consistent/inconsistent with later behaviours.

Since stability studies have taken place over long periods of time, some of the data preceded the consensus on the Big Five as an appropriate model, so different instruments have been used. Costa, McCrae and Arenberg (1980) showed six-year stability of between 0.71 and 0.83 using scales in the ten-scale Guildford and Zimmerman temperament survey. The same article showed 12-year stability that varied between 0.68 and 0.83.

Of course, results can vary depending upon the age group that is employed for surveys. An important question raised is the age at which personality is treated as fully developed such that change could be considered legitimate, i.e. contrasted with maturity. There were some differences between researchers, with McCrae and Costa (1994) claiming that personality is fixed by the age of 30. Several other theorists have challenged this with regard to specific traits, e.g. Roberts (1997) in relation to extraversion.

Caspi and Roberts (2001) raised several key issues of importance in relation to stability. At what age can we identify the characteristics about which to examine change? When is personality sufficiently developed to consider change? And what mechanisms promote continuity or change? The conclusions reached were that there is continuity from childhood to adulthood but it is small. They argued that personality does not become set at a certain age but retains the potential for change. In support of this potential, the authors say that we become more capable of interacting with our environment such that consistency increases with age.

Further reading	
Topic	*Key reading*
Stability and change	Caspi, A. & Roberts, B. (2001). Personality development across the life course: The argument for change and continuity, *Psychological Inquiry, 12(2)*, 49–66.
Debating issues in stability and change.	Paunonen, S. (2001). Inconsistencies in the personality consistency debate, *Psychological Inquiry, 12(2)*, 91–3.
Summarising debated issues in personality stability and change	Roberts, B. & Caspi, A. (2001). Personality and the personality-situation debate: It's déjà vu all over again, *Psychological Inquiry, 12(2)*, 104–9.

1   Distinguish three main types of stability.
2   Has personality been found to be stable from childhood to adulthood?
3   Is personality set at a determinable age?

Chapter summary: putting it all together

→ Can you tick all the points from the revision checklist at the beginning of this chapter?

→ Attempt the sample question from the beginning of this chapter using the answer guidelines below.

→ Go to the companion website at www.pearsoned.co.uk/psychologyexpress to access more revision support online, including interactive quizzes, sample questions with answer guidelines, 'you be the marker' exercises, flashcards and podcasts you can download.

Answer guidelines

Guidelines on answering the sample question presented at the start of the chapter are given below.

 Sample question Essay

Critically consider whether the interactionist perspective of personality has satisfactorily resolved the debate as to whether personality or situation is the primary determinant of behaviour.

Approaching the question

In approaching the question, clarity in the debate could be achieved if it is approached as a historical development of the arguments, i.e. arguments supporting the consistency of traits and the arguments supporting the influence of situations. It is necessary to provide adequate coverage of both 'person' and 'situation' sides of the argument as well as available evidence to support the points you make.

Different formulations of continuity need to be distinguished if you are to be able to tease out all the crucial aspects of the debate. However, the essay's central theme is concerned with the discussion of the forms of interactionism together with an assessment of the extent to which the debate has been resolved.

Important points to include

- In relation to the 'person' side of the argument it is important to consider a number of personality and trait models, as there is variation in the extent to which they emphasise consistency (see Chapters 1 and 2 for further ideas).

- Different trait models of personality have different numbers of traits and therefore the breadth/narrowness (bandwidth) of behaviours that they claim to represent varies. The implications of this need to be made clear in your answer.

- The distinction between states and traits and the capacity of traits as broad measurements needs to be discussed.

- Mischel's three main areas of challenge to consistency of trait formulation need to be examined.

- The impact of the scope, types and levels of behaviours and meaning attached to situations on this debate need to be considered.

- The distinctions between consistency across situations and stability over time must be made clear.

- Explore variations in the findings of research exploring different traits.

- Responses to Mischel's challenge both in the evidence for consistency and arguments for types of consistency, types of situation and range of behaviours, need to be outlined and evaluated.

- The forms of interactionism and contributors' explanations of the means by which the debate is resolved should be discussed.

Make your answer stand out

There is a temptation in this debate to give great attention to the evidence, measurements and conceptual discussions and to lose sight of real people, situations and behaviours. You need to show your understanding of the conceptual issues and evidence and the historical flow to the discussion, but your essay will stand out if you are able to show the implications of this debate across the field of Individual Differences (and applied situations). Providing concrete references to specific and general behaviours, to a range of situations and to actual people and their personalities will help to demonstrate a deeper understanding of the issues.

Some of the arguments in this essay polarise the discussion and emphasise the confrontation between the points of view. However, proponents of both sides of the debate have made valid points; it is our formulations of behaviours; characterisation of our situations; and types of personality model that form the barriers. Your capacity to demonstrate your understanding of this will help your essay to really stand out.

Notes

8

Describing intelligence: structure and composition

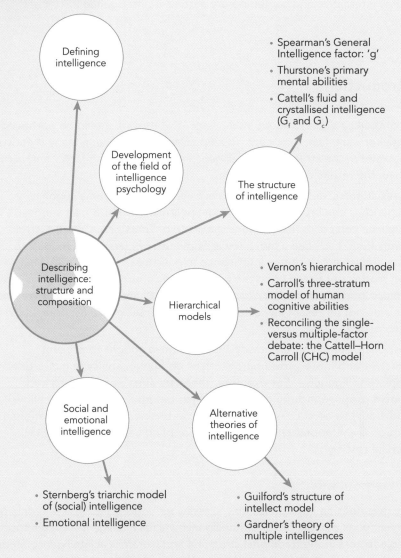

- Spearman's General Intelligence factor: 'g'
- Thurstone's primary mental abilities
- Cattell's fluid and crystallised intelligence (G_f and G_c)

Defining intelligence

Development of the field of intelligence psychology

The structure of intelligence

Describing intelligence: structure and composition

Hierarchical models

- Vernon's hierarchical model
- Carroll's three-stratum model of human cognitive abilities
- Reconciling the single-versus multiple-factor debate: the Cattell–Horn Carroll (CHC) model

Social and emotional intelligence

Alternative theories of intelligence

- Sternberg's triarchic model of (social) intelligence
- Emotional intelligence

- Guilford's structure of intellect model
- Gardner's theory of multiple intelligences

A printable version of this topic map is available from:
www.pearsoned.co.uk/psychologyexpress

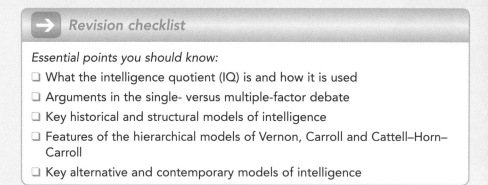

Introduction

One of the key debates about intelligence is whether it should be portrayed as a single- or multi-factor concept. To help answer this question many theorists have explored the structure of intelligence empirically, using factor analysis to examine the results of **aptitude tests**.

As a result, many different models have been proposed; some suggest intelligence is one broad construct (e.g. Spearman), whilst others suggest intelligence comprises many distinct facets (e.g. Thurstone, Cattell, Carroll). Recently there has been a move towards the use of hierarchical models to understand what constitutes intelligence (e.g. Cattell–Horn–Carroll). Many of the above models are based upon the psychometric approach to conceptualisation and measurement, which has proved controversial; some argue these traditional models do not represent laypersons' theories of intelligence (Cooper, 2002) and are too narrow.

In response, some contemporary theorists have sought to present alternative and more varied perspectives on human ability (e.g. Gardner's multiple intelligences). For example, theorists such as Sternberg and Goleman propose including abilities which tap into creativity and allow an individual to be *successful* in life (e.g. in business or social situations). Although these approaches have strong *applied* value, they often lack *empirical* testing.

Assessment advice

Essay questions on intelligence may assess your understanding of the debate between 'g' as a single factor of intelligence versus intelligence as comprising multiple factors in the traditional structural and hierarchical intelligence models. This requires an historical perspective on the two early theorists of Spearman and Thurstone and their relation to modern psychometric formulations of Carroll

(1993) and Cattell–Horn–Carroll. Underlying all the models is the argument as to whether intelligence can be presented as a single underlying phenomenon or a multi-factor phenomenon.

Assessments may also ask you to compare classic models of intelligence with more contemporary or alternative models, such as Gardner's multiple intelligences or Goleman's emotional intelligence theory (see Chapter 9 for a discussion). This is essentially tapping into the debate about what types of ability constitute intelligence (e.g. numerical and verbal comprehension versus social competence and self-regulation), and how they should be measured.

Problem-based learning questions may also be set on this topic, because it naturally lends itself to assignments that require demonstrating an understanding of the stages of test construction or how factor analytic studies of intelligence abilities are conducted.

Sample question

Could you answer the question below? It is a typical essay question that could arise on this topic. Guidelines on answering the question are included at the end of this chapter, whilst a sample problem question and guidance on tackling it can be found on the companion website at www.pearsoned.co.uk/psychologyexpress.

 Sample question   *Essay*

Critically discuss the extent to which the CHC model of cognitive abilities resolves the debate about whether intelligence comprises a single factor or multiple abilities. Present appropriate evidence to support your position.

Defining intelligence

Intelligence is the second substantive topic of interest in Individual Differences psychology. This is due to its long history, the importance placed upon it in popular culture and the impact it has on people's lives. For example, intelligence has implications for people's educational and occupational spheres (Haslam, 2007), as well as having links to health and wellbeing (Gottfredson & Deary, 2004).

A key issue in the definition of intelligence is first deciding which abilities should be included in intelligence theory and research, and which should not. This debate typically centres on identifying abilities that are deemed to require *substantial mental effort*. For example, being able to complete a crossword puzzle, structure and write an essay, or complete a maths problem is deemed to require greater mental effort than being able to clean a room or cycle in a race.

Indeed, Cooper (2002) defines the mental abilities which are usually the focus of theory and research in this area as those 'traits that reflect how well individuals can process various types of information' (p. 172).

There is also a difference between the ability to process and react to novel problems/stimuli (**aptitude**) and the ability to recall/remember information that has been learnt, such as at the end of a course (**attainment**). Many intelligence tests seek to assess aptitude, because attainment may more accurately reflect the educational resources (or quality of these resources) available to an individual, rather than the inherent qualities (or traits) they possess.

Intelligence is also likely to be defined differently in an academic context, compared with everyday 'layperson' theories (called **implicit theories of intelligence**). For example, most people have an intuitive understanding of the term 'street smart', but few intelligence models aim to explain this.

Development of the field of intelligence psychology

Intelligence theory developed originally from the work of Francis Galton and Alfred Binet, and their thinking still underpins the field today. These individuals believed that:

● people differ on their intelligence;

● intelligence could be measured directly.

Binet was interested in finding ways to identify children who would need special education at school and, together with Theodore Simon (Binet & Simon, 1905), created the first intelligence test (the Binet–Simon scale). Although a number of issues have been identified with these tests, such as cultural bias and the confounding effects of perceptual and language ability, they have shaped the field of intelligence theory and research.

From Binet's initial work, William Stern (1912) developed a standardised unit of intelligence measurement called the intelligence quotient (IQ). IQ represented the ratio of mental age to chronological age and was calculated like this:

$$IQ = \frac{\text{mental age}}{\text{chronological age}} \times 100$$

However, a crucial flaw was identified with this conceptualisation of IQ:

● Increases in performance on tests cease after the late teens, preventing individuals' mental age or IQ being scored after this point.

To circumvent this issue a new measure was developed called the **deviation IQ** (Cooper, 2002).

● This is based upon the predication that scores on ability tests follow a normal distribution (a bell-shaped curve on a graph)

- When scores are *standardised*, it is possible to calculate where an individual's score falls in relation to everyone else's (or the average).
- It can be used to see how performance on different test types falls in relation to each other.

Although deviation IQ is an extremely useful concept (and a marked improvement on the old conceptualisation of IQ), it is controversial for a number of reasons:

- Differences between different groups of people in society (e.g. based on ethnicity and gender) have been identified (discussed in more detail in Chapter 9).
- Can ability-centric test scores, and therefore IQ, ever fully explain an individual's intelligence comprehensively and completely (Ritchhart, 2001)?
- Ethical concerns have been raised over the stigma attached (in particular) to low scores, whereby an individual may be negatively 'labelled' (Vig, 2009).
- The impact of IQ (and the results of ability tests in general) can be seen in educational and occupational environments. It is therefore crucial that this concept is both reliable and valid.

The structure of intelligence

Theorists have developed numerous models of intelligence, owing mainly to the different types of ability they have chosen to include and the different research methodologies they have adopted. It is helpful to think of these different approaches in terms of the classification proposed by Mayr (1982):

- **Lumpers**: models which propose a unitary 'lump' of intelligence.
- **Splitters**: models which propose that intelligence comprises a series of *distinct* abilities.
- Hierarchical/intermediary: models which propose that intelligence comprises a number of abilities conceptualised at different *levels*.

As you read through the next section, ask yourself which of the following models would be classed as 'lumpers' and which would be classed as 'splitters' (a section on hierarchical models is provided later).

Spearman's General Intelligence factor: 'g'

Spearman investigated the nature of intelligence through exploring the relationships which underlay a number of quite distinct ability tests.

- Spearman developed a number of statistical techniques, two of which (correlation and factor analysis) continue to play a major role in empirical intelligence research today.

- He constructed tests to assess a range of abilities in school-aged children, such as mathematical ability, vocabulary and visualisation (Spearman, 1904, 1927), and analysed them using factor analysis.
- He found that results across the different types of test corresponded for each child; an average-scoring individual tended to score at that level across a number of tests, whereas a high-scoring individual tended to score highly across the batch (Figure 8.1).

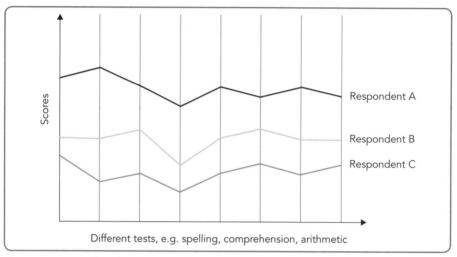

Figure 8.1 Example of scores on different tests for three respondents

- He concluded that a *single* underlying factor was influencing the school children's performance across *all* the test areas, which he called the **General Intelligence factor**, or **'g'** (Spearman, 1904, 1927).
- He suggested that the specific intelligence variations identified between different tests were due to **specific abilities**, or **'s'** (Figure 8.2).
- He believed that the positive correlations identified between specific abilities were further evidence for the underlying influence of 'g'.
- 'g' could be thought of in terms of a form of *mental energy* (1904, 1927).

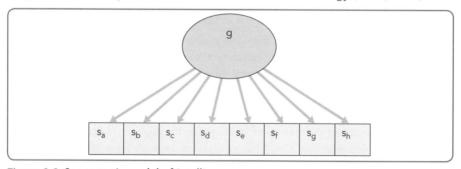

Figure 8.2 Spearman's model of intelligence

Source: Adapted with permission of Guilford Press, from The Cattell–Horn–Carroll theory of cognitive abilities, K. McGrew, 2nd ed., 2005, In D. Flanagan & P. Harrison (eds.), *Contemporary Intellectual Assessment: Theories, Tests and Issues.*

Points to consider

- The samples Spearman used in his research were limited:
  - His first research study consisted of 24 children from a village school (Spearman, 1904), chosen primarily because it was convenient for Spearman to access.
  - All the children shared the same educational experience.
- The finding for 'g' had important theoretical implications as to whether it is possible to account for intelligence by means of one broad measurement. However, it seems unlikely that a single, broad concept of intelligence can account sufficiently for all the variation observed between individuals.
- Spearman's approach was one of the first to attempt to examine intelligence *empirically*.
- The statistical methods Spearman used may have arbitrarily resulted in a single underlying factor, and later theorists, who have adopted different techniques, have identified greater numbers of distinct intelligence abilities.

Further reading

Topic	Key reading
Practical value of 'g'	Gottfredson, L. (2002). Where and why g matters: Not a mystery, *Human Performance*, 15(1/2), 35–46.
Spearman's and Thurstone's approaches to intelligence	Deary, I. (2001). *Intelligence: A very short introduction.* Oxford: Oxford University Press.

Test your knowledge

1 What techniques did Spearman use to show the associations between test results and to demonstrate the underlying intelligence 'g'?
2 What factor in addition to 'g' did Spearman introduce to account for specialised variations?

Thurstone's primary mental abilities

Thurstone used a different method of factor analysis to explore the structure of intelligence: he used a substantially larger number of discrete and separate tests, which were administered to a larger sample consisting of university students. He was unable to replicate the finding of a single, general underlying intelligence factor. Instead, he identified multiple factors which he called **primary mental abilities** (PMAs; see Figure 8.3; Thurstone, 1934, 1935, 1938). PMAs were conceived of as:

- distinct, independent, broad-group factors;
- much more general than Spearman's specific abilities, but not as broad as Spearman's 'g' factor;
- representing seven core abilities (Thurstone,1938): word fluency; verbal meaning; number; perceptual speed; spatial assessment; reasoning; and memory.

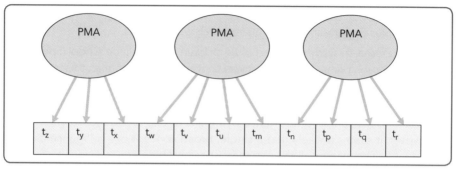

Figure 8.3 **Example of a selection of Thurstone's primary mental abilities**

Source: Adapted with permission of Guilford Press, from The Cattell–Horn–Carroll theory of cognitive abilities, K. McGrew, 2nd ed. 2005, In D. Flanagan & P. Harrison (eds.), *Contemporary Intellectual Assessment: Theories, Tests and Issues.*

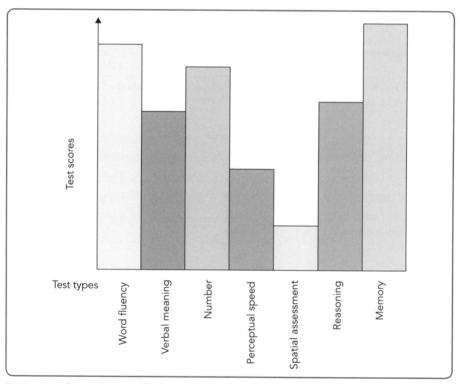

Figure 8.4 **Illustrative profile for an individual using Thurstone's PMAs**

Figure 8.4 provides an indication of how an individual's profile of performance on each of the PMAs could look.

Thurstone identified other primary abilities (Mahoney, 2011; Cooper, 2002) but they were conceptually difficult to interpret and are frequently overlooked.

Points to consider

- Thurstone's theory suggests that Spearman's 'g' is an artefact of the statistical procedures he had used.
- The statistical procedure that Thurstone used forced the PMAs to be orthogonal (independent) of each other. However, other theorists have found that if other methods are used the PMAs are correlated (Mahoney, 2011).
- Other theorists have used different methodologies and have identified different numbers of PMAs as a result (Cattell, 1971; Hakstian & Cattell, 1978), raising the question of how valid or reliable Thurstone's conceptualisation of the number of abilities underpinning intelligence is.

 Sample question   **Essay**

Critically consider Spearman's 'g' and 's' model of intelligence and the PMA structure of Thurstone. Which of the approaches do you consider to be the stronger representation of intelligence? Provide evidence to support your argument.

Test your knowledge

1   Why might it be difficult to establish whether or not PMAs are independent of each other?
2   According to Thurstone's theory, why does 'g' *appear* to exist?
3   What might the strengths and limitations of Thurstone's methodology be?

Cattell's fluid and crystallised intelligence (G_f and G_c)

Cattell (1963, 1971), and Horn and Cattell (1966), suggested that 'g' is actually composed of two types of ability: **fluid intelligence** (G_f) and **crystallised intelligence** (G_c). These different abilities allow people to perform different types of task.

- Fluid intelligence underpins the capacity for abstract reasoning, free of cultural influences. It is evidenced by people's ability to *acquire* new information and makes inferences about new patterns or relationships in stimuli. Variation between individuals is evidenced by both the speed and accuracy with which they are able to perform these tasks.
- Crystallised intelligence refers to all the knowledge and skills an individual has acquired and is evidenced by such things as knowledge of vocabulary and general knowledge. This means that crystallised intelligence is influenced by cultural factors.

G_f and G_c interact dynamically with each other, but develop differently across the lifespan: G_f is fairly innate (i.e. we are born with it) and stabilises in adulthood, whereas crystallised intelligence develops across the lifespan, as a result of learning and educational experiences (Cattell,1963, 1971; Horn & Cattell, 1966).

Many tests now aim to measure G_c as this may more accurately reflect an individual's intellectual capacity, rather than the learning experiences they have been able to access, or the cultural factors they have been exposed to. However, some theorists argue that assessing both abilities is beneficial for estimating both learning *potential* and *acquired* knowledge (Stankov, Boyle & Cattell, 1995).

Points to consider

- Cattell (1987) later believed that his model was incomplete and added a third ability labelled G_{sar}. This ability comprises short-term memory abilities, and is evidenced by people's ability to retrieve information and manipulate it.
- There is great debate about whether or not Cattell and Horn's model is hierarchical in nature.
- Cattell's (1943, 1963, 1971) conceptualisation of G_f is said to be 'culture-fair' because it is context-independent and based on abstract reasoning.

Test your knowledge

1 Briefly describe the difference between crystallised and fluid intelligence.
2 Why might the concepts of crystallised and fluid intelligence be useful for the sphere of education?
3 Classify Thurstone's PMAs according to whether you consider they are more appropriately grouped into fluid or crystallised intelligence.

 Sample question   **Problem-based learning**

You are asked to develop a measure of culture-free (fluid) intelligence. How might you go about creating such a measure and ensuring it is reliable and valid? What issues would you need to consider when developing the items (and response types) to include?

Hierarchical models

Many theorists have attempted to resolve the contradictions that single and multiple factor models of intelligence pose, by examining whether a *hierarchy* of cognitive abilities exists.

The variations in hierarchical models that have emerged arise from disagreement concerning the number of factors considered sufficient to describe intelligence, how these factors relate to each other and how they should be measured.

Vernon's hierarchical model

Vernon (1950) attempted to make the links between Spearman's 'g' and 's' abilities more explicit. As a result he proposed a four-tiered model with a general factor ('g') at the pinnacle, leading down to *major-group factors, minor-group factors* and specific factors ('s') at the base.

Vernon believed there were two major-group factors: verbal/educational (v:ed) and spatial/mechanical (k:m). The minor-group factors leading from v:ed were 'verbal', 'numerical' and 'educational' abilities, whereas the minor group factors leading from k:m were 'practical', 'mechanical', 'spatial' and 'physical' abilities (see Figure 8.5). Examples of specific factors include: spelling, mental object rotation, object recognition, and the ability to use punctuation and grammar.

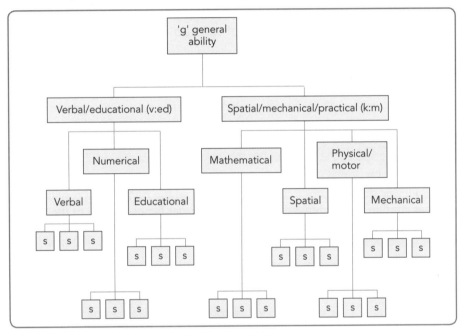

Figure 8.5 Outline of Vernon's hierarchical model
Source: Vernon, 1950.

Points to consider

● The increasing number of components on Vernon's model ensured that it was more capable of accounting for the variation between individuals. This arose because it noted a wide number of factors upon which individuals differ.

● There is evidence to suggest that Vernon's v:ed (Vernon, 1961) reflects crystallised intelligence as evidenced by academic attainment (Kline, 1996).

● Vernon's hierarchical model of intelligence provides greater flexibility to explain people's strengths and weaknesses: for example, it can account for the fact that someone may have superior spatial abilities, but is unable to read.

173

- Vernon's model provides an explicit link between Spearman's and Thurstone's models of intelligence.

- Vernon's model contains a general factor ('g') which Vernon believed was the greatest variation in intelligence – the concept of 'g' is still controversial.

 Sample question   *Essay*

Compare Vernon's hierarchical model with the formulations of Spearman and Thurstone. Do you consider that Vernon's model is capable of accounting for the findings provided by the earlier theories?

Carroll's three-stratum model of human cognitive abilities

Carroll (1993) proposed a hierarchical model of intelligence comprising three tiers (see Figure 8.6 for a horizontal representation), which he called *strata*. 'Strata' refers to the breadth, or bandwidth, of the abilities at each level.

In this model, stratum III lies at the pinnacle and refers to a single, general ability (analogous to 'g') which, according to Carroll, accounts for 50% of ability. Stratum II represents eight broad abilities which arise from a number of specific abilities; these specific abilities (of which Carroll identified around 70) represent stratum I: the narrowest ability level.

Stratum II was derived from a factor analysis run on the original test results, whereas stratum III was derived from a second-order factor analysis of the grouped data (i.e. stratum II). Carroll's work confirmed the three second-order factors identified by another researcher (Gustafsson, 1984), lending further credibility to the model.

Points to consider

- The validation of the model lies in the confirmation of factor analytic procedures of data derived for the analysis.

- One weakness of the model was that the three-stratum theory has not been translated into specifically designed tests and remains primarily used for research on cognitive abilities.

- Carroll systematically brings together Spearman's, Cattell's and Thurstone's models, within Vernon's hierarchical framework.

Reconciling the single- versus multiple-factor debate: the Cattell–Horn–Carroll (CHC) model

Cattell, Horn and Richard Woodcock developed a model that integrated Cattell and Horn, and Carroll's theories (Flanagan, McGrew & Ortiz, 2000; Lohman, 2001). This new model, called the Cattell–Horn–Carroll (CHC) theory of cognitive abilities, abandoned the concept of 'g' and instead proposed a hierarchy of

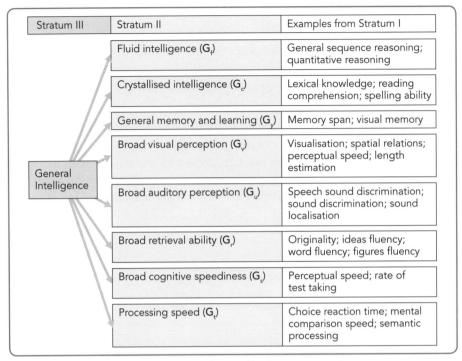

Stratum III	Stratum II	Examples from Stratum I
General Intelligence	Fluid intelligence (G$_f$)	General sequence reasoning; quantitative reasoning
	Crystallised intelligence (G$_c$)	Lexical knowledge; reading comprehension; spelling ability
	General memory and learning (G$_y$)	Memory span; visual memory
	Broad visual perception (G$_v$)	Visualisation; spatial relations; perceptual speed; length estimation
	Broad auditory perception (G$_u$)	Speech sound discrimination; sound discrimination; sound localisation
	Broad retrieval ability (G$_r$)	Originality; ideas fluency; word fluency; figures fluency
	Broad cognitive speediness (G$_s$)	Perceptual speed; rate of test taking
	Processing speed (G$_t$)	Choice reaction time; mental comparison speed; semantic processing

Figure 8.6 Horizontal representation of Carroll's three stratum factors

Source: Adapted from J. Carroll, *Human Cognitive Abilities*, 1993. Courtesy of Cambridge University Press, USA.

abilities (see Table 8.1), with two levels: stratum II (broad stratum) and stratum I (narrow stratum).

Stratum II contained 16 intelligences which were each composed of a number of abilities (see Table 8.1 for examples).

Table 8.1 The CHC model of cognitive abilities

Broad stratum (stratum II)	Narrow stratum (stratum I)
Fluid intelligence/reasoning (Gf) – the use of mental operations to solve novel and abstract problems	e.g. general sequential (deductive) reasoning, logical thinking and speed of reasoning
Crystallised intelligence/knowledge (Gc) – intelligence that is incorporated by individuals through a process of culture	e.g. language development, listening ability, information about culture
General (domain-specific) knowledge (Gkn) – breadth and depth of acquired knowledge in specialised (not general) domains	e.g. knowledge of English as a second language, knowledge of singing, general science information
Visual-spatial abilities (Gv) – the ability to invent, remember, retrieve and transform visual images	e.g. spatial relations, closure speed, length estimation

Points to consider

- Some of the abilities in the model are more abstract and are less easily understood (e.g. tactile abilities). For this reason it is more difficult to see how they can be applied.

- The model resolves a number of issues with previous models (e.g. the issue concerning the 'realness' of 'g').

- The model makes explicit the similarities between Cattell and Horn's and Carroll's models.

- The introduction of hierarchical models allowed for the possibility of a single, general, factor and multiple factors to exist simultaneously, through asserting that intelligence abilities fall at different levels and bandwidths.

Further reading

Topic	Key reading
Nature of abilities and cognitive diversity	Horn, J. (1989). Cognitive diversity: A framework for learning. In P. Ackerman, R. Sternberg & R. Glaser (eds), *Learning and individual differences: Advances in theory and research* (pp. 61–116). New York: Freeman.
Three-stratum theory	Carroll, J. (2005). The three stratum theory of cognitive abilities. In D. Flanagan & P. Harrison (eds), *Contemporary intellectual assessment: Theories, tests and issues* (pp. 69–76). New York: Guilford.
Cattell–Horn–Carroll theory	McGrew, K. (2005). The Cattell–Horn–Carroll theory of cognitive abilities. In D. Flanagan & P. Harrison (eds), *Contemporary intelligence assessment: Theories, tests and issues*, 2nd edn (pp. 136–81). New York: Guilford.
Single-factor/multiple-factor debate	Ch. 2 of Cooper, C. (1999). *Intelligence and abilities*. London: Routledge.

Test your knowledge

1 In what ways is the CHC model an improvement on Cattell and Horn's (1966) model, Carroll's (1993) model and Vernon's (1950) model?

2 In what way do items in stratum I differ from those in stratum II of Carroll's (1993) model and the CHC model?

3 Do you consider that Carroll's hierarchical model reflects more of the multiple-factor or single-factor model of intelligence?

4 What accounts for the limitation of the applications of Carroll's model to the workplace?

5 What was the number of factors identified as broad groupings in the CHC model?

6 Why might it be difficult to develop a psychometric test that comprehensively measures all aspects of the CHC model of intelligence?

Sample question   *Problem-based learning*

Explain, stage by stage, the steps you would go through in order to replicate findings of the early intelligence researchers to determine the structure of aptitudes that constitute intelligence. How would you ensure that this specifies the number of ability factors you have found?

Alternative theories of intelligence

We will now look at a number of other theories of intelligence which are considered 'alternative' for various reasons.

Guilford's structure of intellect model

The structure of intellect model subscribed to the notion of multiple abilities. However, abilities were portrayed as acting in *parallel* rather than in the form of a hierarchy. Guilford conceived of intelligence as a number of subcomponents, which were grouped into one of *three* categories of abilities or *facets*. The three facets were identified as: *operations* (of which there are 5), *contents* (of which there are 6) and *products* (of which there are also 6).

- Each intellectual activity performed was said to be composed of one ability from each of the three facets. Figure 8.7 presents the three facets along with their components and an illustration of a specific combination that would constitute a complete mental activity.

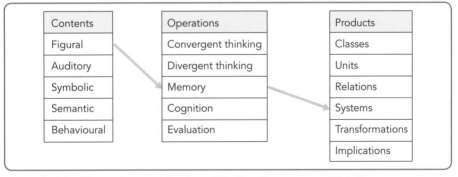

Figure 8.7 An illustrative combination of Guilford's structure of intellect

'Contents' are what we think about the source material we use, in which various mental processes (operations) are conducted. 'Products' are the form in which information is held in cognition, or results from the action of mental ability.

Points to consider

● An important strength of Guilford's model was its capacity to link combinations of abilities to that of intelligence in the absence of a hierarchy.

● The model recognises the growing emphasis being placed on parallel distributed processing in models of cognition.

● It also provides a basis for developing an understanding of the different forms in which intelligence may express itself. However, it is a demanding feat of analysis to securely provide evidential support for such a sophisticated model. The complexity of the model may potentially make the facets feel disjointed (i.e. appear as separate faculties) and may make the concept of the model as an integrated whole appear redundant.

Further reading

Topic	Key reading
The three facets of intelligence	Guilford, J. (1968). Intelligence has three facets, *Science, 160,* 615–20.

Test your knowledge

1 Distinguish Guilford's 'contents' from 'operation' and 'products' and use the facets to explain the conduct of intelligent thinking.

2 Identify a strength and a weakness of the structure of intellect model.

 Sample question **Essay**

Critically evaluate what Guilford's structure of intellect model adds to our understanding of the nature of intelligent thinking.

Gardner's theory of multiple intelligences

Whilst previous discussion of the psychometric theories of intelligence accepted the possibility of multiple abilities, Gardner went further by proposing a model of *multiple intelligences*. He considered the human mind to be a loosely related collection of distinct components. These components represented eight distinct and separate intelligences (see Table 8.2) which were:

● rooted in distinct areas of the brain (Gardner, 1983);

● outside the control of each other but could interact with each other if needed.

Gardner did not believe that psychometric intelligence was capable of adequately representing abilities found in different cultures. As a result he:

● believed we should model intelligence by behaviour but did not believe it should be benchmarked against the cultural priorities of a particular community;

- based his model on observations of brain-trauma patients and individuals from different cultural groups;
- argued that his model was universal and lacked bias to western ethnic groups; and
- rejected the proposition that pencil and paper psychometric tests could capture the many different ways people go about solving problems.

This approach therefore led to the rejection of the possibility of uncovering a single underlying general intelligence (i.e. 'g').

Table 8.2 **Gardner's eight types of intelligence**

Type of intelligence	Example behaviour
Linguistic	Capacity to learn language
Logic–mathematical	Ability to work with numbers, both concretely and abstractly
Spatial	Ability to visualise and work with spatial information
Musical	Ability to absorb and transmit rhythm and pitch
Kinaesthetic	Capacity for bodily coordination
Interpersonal	Strength in recognising and perceiving emotions and intention
Intrapersonal	Ability to distinguish and appreciate our own emotions

One of Gardner's most significant contributions was the method used to identify intelligence. Multiple sources for data collection were employed. The approach determined criteria (see Table 8.3) for concluding that a phenomenon constituted an intelligence. These criteria were then matched to 'intelligences' that were identified by rigorous empirical review of that which was considered in the literature.

Table 8.3 **Gardner's criteria for determination of an intelligence**

- Isolated avoidance of brain damage
- Evidence of extraordinary talent (e.g. musical)
- Identifiable core human operation (identification of musical tone)
- Distinctive developmental activity (expert)
- Distinctive evolutionary theme with likely associations
- Supportive experimental cognitive evidence
- Psychometric evidence
- Susceptibility to encoding with symbols for culturally expressed forum (e.g. dance)

Points to consider

- Gardner (1999, 2004) later extended the range of intelligences to include:
  - 'natural intelligence' (the capacity to interact well with natural phenomena);

- 'existentialist capacity' (a cognisance of our place in the context of a grand scheme);
- 'mental searchlight' (an ability to scan wide spaces efficiently and ensure society runs smoothly), and;
- 'laser intelligence' (an ability that allows individuals to generate the advances and disasters in society).
- Gardner's theory of multiple intelligences has been heavily criticised for the lack of empirical evidence to support it (Sternberg, 1994; Allix, 2000). In the absence of a test or measurement tool based on the model, evidence is unlikely to be forthcoming.
- Gardner has not postulated a link between the old intelligences and the new intelligences, making it difficult to see how they all relate and operate together.

Practical application of theory Optimising learning in the classroom

Despite some criticism of Gardner's theory, it has on occasions been adopted by educationalists as providing practical ways of adjusting classroom teaching to optimise learning. Using Gardner's framework of eight types of intelligence, design a scheme of coaching for a group of psychology students wishing learn about Gardner's theory. Would some items of the framework be more successful than others and would some not apply at all?

Further reading

Topic	Key reading
Multiple intelligences	Gardner, H. (1983). *Frames of mind: The theory of multiple intelligences.* New York: Basic Books.
The theory of multiple intelligences	Gardner, H. (1993). *Frames of mind* (2nd edn). London: HarperCollins.

Test your knowledge

1. Present three sources you would employ to demonstrate validating evidence for a number of Gardner's distinct aspects of intelligence.
2. What are the features that distinguish Gardner's theory from that of hierarchical multiple-factor theorists?

 ### Sample question   *Essay*

Critically consider Gardner's theory of multiple intelligences. Do you consider that the approach has more to offer to trainer-practitioners than to psychologists?

Social and emotional intelligence

Sternberg's triarchic model of (social) intelligence

Sternberg's interest in intelligence was grounded in the different aspects of our everyday functioning, and what he termed 'Social Intelligence' (Sternberg, 1985). In particular, he was interested in three mental activities: information processing, experience, and interaction with the external world. Together, these processes represented Sternberg's triarchic theory of intelligence (Sternberg, 1985).

Sternberg named the three processing functions within the model the **componential subtheory** (analytic intelligence), **contextual subtheory** (practical intelligence) and **experiential subtheory** (creative intelligence) (See Figure 8.8).

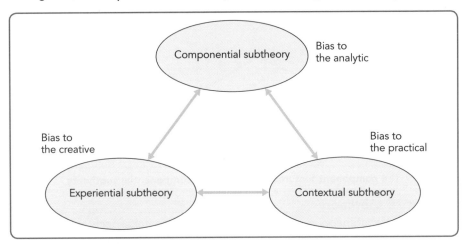

Figure 8.8 Sternberg's triarchic theory of intelligence

Componential subtheory

The term 'component' was used by Sternberg to indicate a process rather than an actual entity. The componential subtheory refers to the mental mechanisms that underlie intelligence and is composed of three further subcomponents (see Figure 8.9):

- **Knowledge acquisition components** – represent how we learn from experience. They are involved in:
  - **selective encoding** (sifting out relevant from irrelevant information);
  - **selective combination** (synthesis of information); and
  - **selective comparison** (comparison of old and new information).
- **Performance components** – specific processes involved in problem solving. They are directed by the metacomponents and come in three forms depending upon the type of task being executed:
  - **encoding components** (recognition);
  - **comparison components** (identification of similarities); and
  - **response components** (determination of action).

181

● **Metacomponents** – operate at a higher level than both knowledge acquisition and performance subcomponents, and allow an individual to identify a problem and act to resolve it. This involves time and resources planning and evaluation of the success of strategies. Sternberg used these components as an explanation for the distinction between experts and novices.

The componential subtheory utilises these three subservient processes to form what may be characterised as *analytic intelligence*.

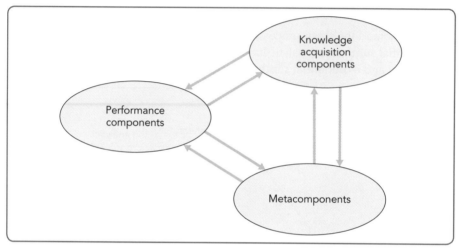

Figure 8.9 **The component features of Sternberg's componential subtheory**

Contextual subtheory

The contextual subtheory is concerned with environmental aspects and the performance of intelligent behaviour. Sternberg identified three ways in which we interact with our external environment:

1 *shaping* (modifying our environment);

2 *adaptation* (adapting to our environment);

3 *selection* (choosing a new environment).

The linking of the contextual subtheory with information-processing components arises because adaptation, shaping and selection occur in a *context*, i.e. in the 'real world'. This explains why Sternberg associated this subtheory with *practical intelligence*.

KEY STUDY

Mathematical capacity amongst street children

Carragher, Carragher & Schliemann (1985) conducted a study assessing the importance of context in learning and performance amongst a group of Brazilian 'street children'. The study was able to demonstrate that children who were not able to work abstractly with mathematics in a school context had been able to show high levels of mathematical capacity when they were engaged in international currency transfers as street vendors.

Experiential subtheory

Sternberg believed that the subtheories interact and that internal functioning is tied to experience. Therefore, to explain intelligent behaviour the level of experience, internal processing and external context need to be considered simultaneously (Sternberg et al., 2000). An individual's experience is important because:

- It promotes **automation**; when tasks become familiar they acquire an automatic capacity. We develop the capability to conduct them in the absence of significant internal allocation of time and effort; this is the basis of expertise. Novel challenges, on the other hand, demand significant attention for completion.

- The distinction between the two types of intellectual demand has been aligned to the distinction in 'g' between fluid intelligence (novel challenges) and crystallised intelligence (automated challenges).

Points to consider

- The triarchic theory of intelligence incorporates existing analytic intelligence within a framework that allows for the inclusion of a wider range of intelligence types (e.g. social/practical and creative).

- The complexity of combinations of serial and parallel processing means the model is difficult to test empirically and therefore lacks evidential support.

- The evidence for the experiential and contextual subtheories is not equal to the evidence for the componential subtheory (i.e. analytic intelligence).

- The model has practical and applied value as it recognises the importance of context in intelligence and therefore enables us to consider intellectual engagement beyond the laboratory. However, by opening up the discussion of contextual factors, the number of potential variables that need to be considered complicates the task of designing research and tools to investigate their role in intelligence.

- An important factor in the pursuit of gaining evidence for a theory is the capacity to offer a means of measurement based upon it. Sternberg developed a test called the Sternberg Triarchic Abilities Test (STAT) to measure those wider aspects of intelligence (Brody, 2006). Whilst the test has been trialled in a variety of different educational environments, it has not been in mainstream use and few research studies using it have been published (Brody, 2006).

Practical application of theory Tacit knowledge

Sternberg has operationalised the practical aspect of his model in the form of tacit knowledge. Tacit knowledge was considered to be a necessary ability to adapt to, select or shape the environment. Whilst the concept was introduced and developed by Polanyi (1966, 1976), Sternberg and colleagues developed inventories for the measurement of tacit knowledge amongst a number of distinct occupational groups. Two of these were the Tacit

▶

Knowledge Inventory for Managers (TKIM) and the Tacit Knowledge Inventory for Sales (Wagner & Sternberg, 1989). The inventories were constructed such that it was possible to measure expertise amongst these three professional groups. Tacit knowledge was employed in these situations as a proxy for the wider notion of intelligence inherent in the triarchic model.

Test your knowledge

1 Present the rationale for the contextual subtheory being aligned with 'practical' intelligence and the experiential subtheory being aligned with 'creative' intelligence.

2 From your understanding of the triarchic theory of intelligence, would you anticipate that its test measurements would be able to generate a measure like the IQ scale? In what way might it differ?

3 In gaining ready acceptance as a measure of intelligence, what advantage would you see for a profile score for intelligence? Why would the profile scores limit its value for research?

Further reading

Topic	Key reading
Triarchic theory of intelligence	Sternberg, R. (2005). The triarchic theory of successful intelligence. In D. Flanagan and P. Harrison (eds), *Contemporary intellectual assessment: Theories, tests and issues.* New York: Guilford.

 Sample question   *Problem-based learning*

You have been asked to counsel a student on those areas about which she seems to have acquired strength through preparation and those areas for which she seems to have a natural talent. Using your knowledge of theories in this and in other chapters, what advice could you give her to improve her performance in her studies?

Emotional intelligence

Emotional intelligence typically refers to an individual's ability to understand and manage their emotions, and those of the people around them (Maltby, Day & Macaskill, 2010). For example, Salovey and Mayer (1990) suggest that emotional intelligence comprises four key abilities:

1 accurately perceiving emotions;

2 using emotions to facilitate thinking;

3 understanding emotional 'meanings';

4 effectively managing emotions.

A number of theories have evolved relatively recently in this area, one of the most influential of which was developed by Goleman in 1995.

Goleman's emotional intelligence (EI/EQ)

Goleman linked emotional intelligence to the amygdala in the brain (part of the limbic system), which has been linked to *emotional responses*. Goleman believed that the extent to which we are able to develop, control and employ these emotional responses effectively determines how 'successful' people are in life (Goleman, 1995, 2001; Goleman, Boyatzis & McKee, 2002).

Goleman's current model of emotional intelligence is hierarchical (see Figure 8.10) and comprises four key domains, which are sequential. That is, it is not possible to sustain good interpersonal relationships if you are not able to identify your own emotional states first (Goleman, 2001; Goleman, Boyatzis & McKee, 2002).

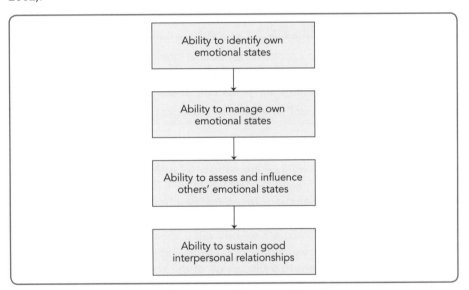

Figure 8.10 **Goleman's hierarchical model of emotional intelligence**

Goleman suggested that these abilities reflected personal, social, recognition and regulation competencies.

Points to consider

- Goleman's theory has been particularly influential within the sphere of business, and two widely used questionnaires have been developed: the Emotional and Social Competencey Inventory (ESCI; Goleman & Boyatzis, 2005) and the Emotional and Social Competence Inventory – University Edition (ESCI-U; Boyatzis & Goleman, 2001).
- The model has been criticised for attempting to combine intelligence and personality factors (a so-called 'mixed' model).

185

- Eysenck (2000) argues that if such a model is found to predict a certain behaviour, it will not be possible to tell whether this is owing to the ability or personality factors it encapsulates.

- Although Goleman suggests that emotional intelligence has biological underpinnings, he does not attempt to test this empirically (Matthews, Zeidner & Roberts, 2004). Therefore, further research is required in this area to be able to tell whether this is actually the case.

Further reading	
Topic	*Key reading*
Triarchic theory of intelligence	Sternberg, R. (2005). The triarchic theory of successful intelligence. In D. Flanagan and P. Harrison (eds), *Contemporary intellectual assessment: Theories, tests and issues.* New York: Guilford.

Test your knowledge

1 Why might Goleman's model of emotional intelligence have become popular within a business/occupational context?
2 What might the strengths and limitations of this theory be?
3 What is a 'mixed model' of emotional intelligence?

Points to consider: Howe's critique of intelligence theories

Alternative models of intelligence are criticised for their lack of empirical support. The validation of these models lies largely in the adequacy of the observations and explanations for everyday intelligent behaviour and performance. A debate on the nature of the scientific enquiry into intelligence took place between two dominant theorists in a special issue of the *British Journal of Psychology* (Howe, 1988a; Sternberg, 1988; Howe, 1988b). The issues remain important to a discussion of the scientific enquiry into the nature of intelligence. They remain especially important in respect of the alternative models of intelligence because for those models they are especially poignant.

Howe's (1988a) contention was that whilst intelligence as a concept serves well as a description, the concept does not meet the requirements for an explanatory concept in human affairs. Howe (1988a) identified ten states of affairs that had to be met if the concept was to serve as an adequate explanation (see Table 8.4).

Sternberg's response was to present indicative evidence for all ten criteria to show that evidence was available and substantial. However, this evidence did not suffice for Howe (1988b) since each illustration was methodologically a correlational investigation. Whilst correlational evidence was considered satisfactory for decriptive purposes, it was not sufficient to serve as an explanation. Howe asserted that the concept remained tautological (circular) until explanatory evidence was provided, i.e. any of the above criteria were met.

Table 8.4 **Ten criteria for an explanatory concept**

1	Observable physiological variable
2	Variability in basic mental-processing mechanisms
3	Capacity to learn or remember
4	Fundamental thinking skills
5	Ability to reason abstractly
6	Complexity of a person's cognitive functions
7	Adaptability or neural flexibility
8	Executive controlling functions
9	Unspecified biological mechanism
10	Indications of measured intelligence levels which precisely identify intellectual qualities of individuals

Alternative models of intelligence have attempted to correspond more with everyday observations. They have done this by introducing a more complex variable structure. The challenge for alternative models of intelligence then becomes secure with evidential support which meets scientific criteria.

Further reading

Topic	Key reading
Criteria for intelligence to serve as an explanatory concept	Howe, M. (1988a). Intelligence as an explanation, *British Journal of Psychology, 79*, 349–60.
Evidence demonstrating the value of intelligence	Sternberg, R. (1988). Explaining away intelligence: A reply to Howe, *British Journal of Psychology, 79*, 527–33.
Weaknesses of correlational evidence and the danger of intelligence as a tautological construct	Howe, M. (1988b). The hazards of using correlational evidence as a means of identifying the causes of individual differences: A rejoinder to Sternberg and a reply to Miles, *British Journal of Psychology, 79*, 539–45.
Discussion of the strengths, limitations and future direction of emotional intelligence theories	Murphy, K. (2006). *A critique of emotional intelligence: What are the problems and how can they be fixed?* Mahwah, NJ: Erlbaum.

Chapter summary: putting it all together

→ Can you tick all the points from the revision checklist at the beginning of this chapter?

→ Attempt the sample question from the beginning of this chapter using the answer guidelines below.

→ Go to the companion website at www.pearsoned.co.uk/psychologyexpress
to access more revision support online, including interactive quizzes,
sample questions with answer guidelines, 'you be the marker' exercises,
flashcards and podcasts you can download.

Answer guidelines

Guidelines on answering the sample question presented at the start of the
chapter are given below.

 Sample question   **Essay**

Critically discuss the extent to which the CHC model of cognitive abilities
resolves the debate about whether intelligence comprises a single factor or
multiple abilities. Present appropriate evidence to support your position.

Approaching the question

In order to answer this question you need to provide the context of the debate.
This will involve briefly exploring the issues involved in defining intelligence and
identifying what constitutes an intelligent ability. The next step will be to outline
the development of traditional models of intelligence, from single-factor theories
to multi-factor theories, and providing their strengths and limitations.

You need to state explicitly that to answer the question fully, you need to
examine the development of intelligence theories, from single, to multi-factor, to
hierarchical models (with the CHC model representing the pinnacle of these).

The potential danger of this assignment is that you will lose track of the central
question and will become bogged down with providing a list of models and
their descriptions. To avoid this you need explicitly to link each point you make
back to the question and how it sheds light on the empirical and practical value
of the CHC model.

Important points to include

- Firstly you need to provide an explanation of the fact that traditional
  models of intelligence focus on abilities involved in processing information,
  particularly those which can be said to be analytic or academic (referred to
  as ability-centric). This point will form part of the critique of the traditional
  models of intelligence that will be presented later in the discussion.

- You need to briefly explain the origins of intelligence testing (i.e. Binet and
  IQ) and highlight that this has shaped the pursuit of decades of theory and
  research seeking to identify the structure of intelligence.

- Examine Spearman's theory of the General Intelligence factor ('g'): explore
  how he researched the concept, and what methodologies (e.g. factor analysis)
  he employed. Explore the concept of the specific 's' abilities. Provide an

evaluation of the strengths and limitations of Spearman's approach, for example:

- Highlight the issues with the samples and tests he used to gather data.
- Examine the suggestion that a broad measure of intelligence is insufficient to explain all variation between individuals.
- Discuss the lasting impact of the concept of 'g' (e.g. in research and applied settings).

- Examine the development of multi-factor theories, including:
  - Thurstone's primary mental abilities, which were discovered following the failure to replicate Spearman's finding of a single factor of intelligence. Highlight that Thurstone believed that each of the PMAs was independent of the others, but that later research casts doubt on this.
  - Cattell's theory of 'g' as actually comprising two abilities: fluid and crystallised intelligence. Examine the impact on psychometric tests of intelligence and what research findings suggest (i.e. later inclusion of further intelligence abilities, which highlights the impact of the methodology adopted on the number of abilities identified).
  - Discuss the importance of the evolution of hierarchical models and the role they have played overall in resolving the debate. Primarily, this is to illustrate that hierarchical models allowed theorists to explain why a general factor has been observed by some theorists, whilst other identify separate abilities. To achieve this, you need to examine the following models.
  - Vernon's hierarchical model identified the link between specific abilities, major- and minor-group factors and a general factor.
  - Carroll's three-stratum model of cognitive abilities represented a major step towards resolving the debate concerning single versus multiple factors because it combined elements of Spearman's, Thurstone's, Vernon's and Cattell and Horn's models. Examine the strengths and limitations of this model and explain why the further development of the CHC model arose.

- Examine the structure of the CHC model of cognitive abilities: what does it suggest about intelligence and how it should be measured? What are the model's strengths and limitations – are there any issues raised by earlier models which it has not resolved satisfactorily? Remember, the discussion of this model needs to provide the focus of the essay, so be explicit about why the context to the argument needed to be discussed in order to answer the assignment question fully.

Make your answer stand out

To provide a really strong answer you need to examine the impact of other 'alternative' models on our understanding of intelligence, and what this means for the CHC model. This may involve examining the idea of abilities operating in parallel (proposed by Guilford's structure of intellect model), the concepts of practical/social intelligence (e.g. Sternberg's triarchic theory of intelligence) and emotional intelligence (e.g. Goleman's model), and the theory of the existence of distinct multiple intelligences (e.g. Gardner's theory), and identifying the implications of these models for how we currently understand intelligence.

To finish, you should consider where future efforts should be directed. This will demonstrate the ability to recognise where the gaps in our understanding of intelligence are and how they can be addressed.

Notes

9

Explaining intelligence: development, determinants and controversies

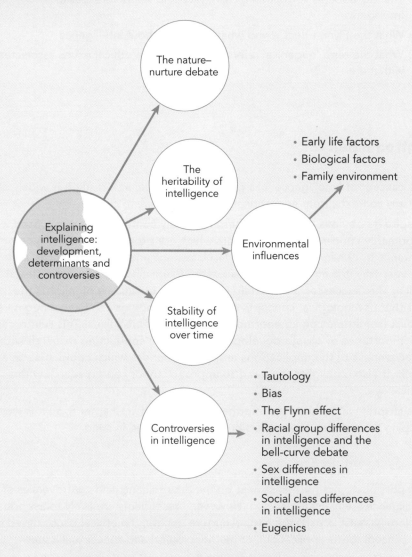

- The nature–nurture debate

- The heritability of intelligence

- Environmental influences
  - Early life factors
  - Biological factors
  - Family environment

- Explaining intelligence: development, determinants and controversies

- Stability of intelligence over time

- Controversies in intelligence
  - Tautology
  - Bias
  - The Flynn effect
  - Racial group differences in intelligence and the bell-curve debate
  - Sex differences in intelligence
  - Social class differences in intelligence
  - Eugenics

A printable version of this topic map is available from:
www.pearsoned.co.uk/psychologyexpress

> **→ Revision checklist**
>
> *Essential points you should know:*
> - ❑ How twin, family and adoption study methodologies are used in intelligence research
> - ❑ What research findings suggest about the relative contributions of genetic and environment factors to intelligence
> - ❑ How intelligence develops across the lifespan
> - ❑ The key debates surrounding class, race and sex differences in intelligence
> - ❑ What the Flynn effect is and what it implies about intelligence
> - ❑ What the term 'eugenics' refers to and what the ethical issues associated with it are.

Introduction

The concept of 'intelligence' has great applied value; as a result it is widely used in many contexts, from educational, to occupational, to clinical.

Despite its obvious usefulness, there are many controversies associated with it; primarily concerning those factors which are proposed to determine or influence it, observed group (such as class, race and sex) differences and the very way it is measured and assessed. Examining the controversies as well as the 'successes' in this field is important because it highlights the fact that psychological concepts and research findings can have a negative impact (sometimes on an enormous scale) on people's lives. This reinforces the importance of always developing theory and conducting research with an awareness of the implications and consequences which could arise as a result. It also highlights the need to approach theory and research with a critical eye.

This chapter will build on the information presented in Chapter 8, so it is worth keeping the debates and models previously discussed in mind.

Assessment advice

The possible topics for assessment on the determinants and controversies of intelligence are many and varied. However, assessments are likely to ask you to explore (at least in part) the nature–nurture debate, the ethical issues raised by the concept (or its application), or methodological and conceptual issues.

The debates concerning intelligence as a construct and the ethics of how it is applied in practice are complex and intricate, and have sparked heated exchanges between theorists in the past. To be a strong answer your assessment needs to have a clear structure, should impartially explore the different perspectives in each argument and should provide relevant (and current) research to evidence the key points made.

Sample question

Could you answer the question below? It is a typical essay question that could arise on this topic. Guidelines on answering the question are included at the end of this chapter, whilst a sample problem question and guidance on tackling it can be found on the companion website at www.pearsoned.co.uk/psychologyexpress.

 Sample question   *Essay*

Critically evaluate the extent to which the concept of intelligence constitutes a reliable, valid and 'real' construct. Provide evidence from theory and research to support your argument.

The nature–nurture debate

One of the key pursuits in the field of intelligence is to identify the factors that influence its development and expression, which often involves the *nature–nurture* debate. Many of the issues that are explored in relation to intelligence are the same as those encountered in Chapter 3 in relation to personality, so make sure you are familiar with that chapter when reading through the information presented here (particularly the sections on research methodology).

The majority of information in the 'nature' argument focuses on the principles and findings from behavioural genetics research. As with personality, the heritability of intelligence is assessed according to the proportion of shared variance between a child and their parents (or other family member), which represents the degree of variance between their genotype and phenotype.

The heritability of intelligence

There is reasonable agreement amongst independent researchers concerning the genetic–environmental distribution of influence upon intelligence. Table 9.1 provides a consensus view presented by two such researchers acting independently.

Evidence for high genetic influence on intelligence is given by twin studies, adoption studies and familial studies. The table shows a higher heritability of

IQ between identical twins than fraternal twins, both reared together and apart. Indeed, identical twins reared apart show a higher heritability than fraternal twins reared together.

Table 9.1 Concordance rates of intelligence scores between relatives living together and apart

Relationship	Environment	Intelligence correlation (Devlin et al., 1997)	Intelligence correlation (Ridley, 1999)
Same person (twice)		–	0.87
Identical twins (mz)	Reared together	0.85	0.86
Identical twins (mz)	Reared apart	0.74	0.76
Fraternal twins (dz)	Together	0.59	0.55
Biological siblings	Together	0.46	0.47
Biological siblings	Apart	0.24	–
Parents/child	Together	0.50	0.40
Parents/child	Apart	-	0.31
Single parent/child	Together	0.41	–
Single parent/child	Apart	0.24	–
Adoptive parent/child	Together	0.20	–
Adoptive children	Together	–	0
Cousins	–	–	0.15
Unrelated individuals	Apart	–	0

Results such as this are persuasive, but should be interpreted with caution because they may (at least in part) be an artefact of the research methodology used. For example, samples may be subject to bias by the ease with which they can be accessed and may be not be representative.

From the findings of the reviews above, it would appear that there is strong evidence for the heritability of intelligence and many early heritability estimates were high. For example, Eysenck proposed the estimate of 69% (1971, 1991). However, early estimates were calculated based on the additive assumption (see Chapter 3 for a discussion) which has since been dismissed as too simplistic (Plomin, 2004). Contemporary estimates now typically 'cover' both additive and non-additive genetic variance and report estimates of intelligence in the form of a *range* of values. Modern estimates of the heritability of intelligence have been produced in the region 40–50% (Neisser et al., 1996) or 30–75% (Mackintosh, 1998).

Environmental influences

Evidence for the environmental contributions to intelligence comes from several sources. The American Psychological Association task force suggested four critical areas of environmental effects on intelligence (Neisser et al., 1996): biological variables, family environment, school/education and culture.

Early life factors

Early life factors, such as family environment, have an impact on a number of biological variables and so are intertwined.

Biological factors

Important biological variables include prenatal factors and nutrition:

- Lifestyle factors of pregnant women can impact on the development of intelligence in their children. For example, continuing to smoke and consume alcohol through a pregnancy has been associated with *Foetal Alcohol Syndrome (FAS)*, growth reduction, facial abnormalities, and brain damage and reduced intelligence in the child (Neisser et al., 1996). This result persists even after parental socioeconomic status and educational factors are controlled for (Mortensen et al., 2005).
- Duration of breastfeeding period has been related to intelligence in children, with those children who were breastfed fully for over 6 months being more likely to have higher IQ scores than those children who were breastfed for shorter periods of time (Smith et al., 2003).
- Improvements in nutrition and healthcare (Lynn, 1990) may be associated with the general increase in intelligence observed over time, a phenomenon referred to as the **Flynn effect** (discussed later in this chapter).
- Taking vitamins and minerals has been associated with increases in children's intelligence (Benton & Roberts, 1988).
  - Research into differences in intelligence associated with nutrition has been criticised for not taking into account the host of other variables (such as socioeconomic status, educational opportunities and parenting styles) which may also be associated with good versus poor nutrition (Lynn, 1990).

Family environment

Research into the impact of family environment on intelligence has typically focused on: shared versus non-shared environments (see Chapter 3 for a discussion), family socioeconomic status, birth order and family size.

The adoption studies cited by Devlin, Daniels & Roeder (1997) and Ridley (1999) have been used to show that siblings or twins who share the same home

195

environments have a greater correlation than those siblings or twins reared separately.

In addition to the twin and adoption studies, evidence can be found from comparisons on the effects of different environments (e.g. enriched versus deprived) and changes in environment over time (e.g. the Flynn effect).

- It has been suggested that the shared environments of twins and siblings who are raised together play only a minor role in phenotypic similarity between individuals (Bouchard, 1994). Instead *non-shared environments* (those environments which are different for individuals, even if they live together, such as different friendship groups) are now believed to affect individual differences in intelligence to a greater extent (Braungart et al., 1992). This finding may provide a possible explanation for why members of the same family, living together, differ.

- In Chapter 3 we encountered the child–parent-effects models devised by Reiss (1997); they also offer a means of explaining individual differences in intelligence. For example, the child-effects model has been expanded by Harris (1995) to examine *child-driven* effects:

  - These occur when a parent reacts differently to children who display different natural intelligence tendencies through either a *positive* or *negative* feedback loop. A positive feedback loop occurs when a parent reacts in supportive ways to a child who demonstrates strong intelligence abilities and facilitates their development. A negative feedback loop occurs when a parent reacts by attempting to stop development of a child's natural tendencies by encouraging them to engage in alternative activities.

- There is no clear agreement on how socioeconomic status should be measured, which can make comparisons between research findings from different studies difficult. One of the most commonly used methodologies is to use parental (usually father's) occupation as an indicator.

  - Research in this area typically finds that children whose fathers have unskilled professions tend to have lower IQs than children whose fathers have professional occupations (e.g. Mackintosh, 1998).
  - Individuals from professional occupations also tend to have higher IQ levels than individuals from less skilled or unskilled occupations (e.g. Rushton & Ankney, 1996).
  - The findings above may reflect the impact of different opportunities (e.g. educational opportunities) available to people of different socioeconomic status.

Practical application of theory **The Carolina Abercedarian Project**

Following the observation that a deprived or impoverished environment may affect the educational opportunities available to children, the 'Carolina Abercedarian Project' was established. This project involved studying the impact of a 5-day-a-week 'out of home' intervention on 111 pre-school-aged children's cognitive abilities. The project was different

---

from many other interventions (such as Project Head Start; Lee et al., 1990) because it was longitudinal (a 5-year programme starting when the children were 6 months old). The study identified that the children who were part of the intervention scored higher on cognitive ability tests than a group of control infants of the same age who had not, at age 2, and that this finding was still observed when the children were 12 years old (Ramey & Ramey, 2004). This suggests that long-term, cognitive interventions may have a positive impact on raising children's cognitive abilities, and that this impact can be long-lasting.

- Some research suggests that children from larger families are more likely to have lower IQ levels (e.g. Bjerkedal et al., 2007), and that first-born children are likely to have higher IQ levels than their siblings (Zajonc, 2001; Belmont & Marolla, 1973). However, others have suggested that findings such as these are due only to the way in which the research was conducted, which may explain why other research has failed to replicate these findings (Rodgers et al., 2000).
- Three models have been proposed to account for birth-order effects:
  - The **admixture hypothesis** (Page & Grandon, 1979; Rodgers, 2001): this suggests that the apparent relationship between birth-order and intelligence is an artefact, simply produced by the fact that parents with lower IQ scores tend to have more children than parents with higher IQ scores.
  - The **confluence model** (Zajonc, 1976; Zanjonc & Markus, 1975): this suggests that a number of factors affect the relationship between birth-order and intelligence. This includes the fact that first-born children may have initially received greater attention and resources than other siblings who have had to share this. First-borns may be given greater responsibility by their parents and may need to develop skills in order to care for and help their younger siblings which may also facilitate the development of intelligence abilities.
  - The **resource dilution model** (Blake, 1981; Downey, 2001): the more children who are born, the greater the impact on parents' resources. Therefore children of high birth-order are likely to have far less parental resources available to them than first-borns or only children.

School/education

As might be expected, the relationship between educational experience and intelligence has been explored intensively. However, Neisser et al. (1996) highlight that education is not examined uniformly across all studies: sometimes education is viewed as an 'independent' variable and in other cases it is used as a 'dependent' variable. This suggests that the relationship between the two variables is somewhat circular.

- Length of educational experience has been found to predict performance on a range of ability tests, above and beyond age (Cahan & Cohen, 1989).
- Children who attend school regularly are more likely than children who do not attend regularly to score high on ability tests (Ceci, 1991).
- Intelligence test scores have been found to predict educational achievement and attainment (Kaufman & Lichtenberger, 2005).

Culture

There are three main features of culture which appear to impact on intelligence:

- **Decontextualisation**: this refers to the fact that many western cultures value abstract thinking and the removal of context from decision making, whereas other cultures place greater value on incorporating contextual information. Therefore, in western cultures decontextualised thinking is seen as an indicator of intelligence, but whether this is appropriate or not is debatable (Serpell, 2001).

- **Quantification**: this refers to the overreliance of the field of intelligence on quantifying intelligence, intelligence measurement and the process of assigning 'numbers' to people. This issue has important consequences for the way in which we view intelligence, but also for how we apply the concept in practice (e.g. recruitment and selection tests).

- **Biologisation**: this refers to the growing emphasis placed on biological and evolutionary theories of intelligence.

KEY STUDY

Piaget's developmental theory of cognitive ability

Jean Piaget (1896–1980) was dissatisfied with the psychometric approach to understanding intelligence and developed his own theory which sought to explain why children's intelligences appeared to develop in the same way. Piaget's belief that all children's intelligence developed in the same way was based on the observation that children of the same age appeared to make the same *mistakes* in their thinking. Although Piaget was interested in examining universal laws of intelligence development (which may therefore seem to conflict with Individual Differences psychology's focus on uniqueness), it is still of relevance because it may shed light on how childhood experiences can affect the development of cognitive abilities. In essence, Piaget believed that intelligence developed through the interaction of biological and environmental factors (Piaget, 1952).

From observations about the way children think, Piaget suggested that intelligence develops through four universal stages, shown in Table 9.2.

Table 9.2 **Piaget's stages of development**

Stage	Brief description
Sensorimotor (0–2 years)	Mental representations of objects/people are restricted to those in the immediate view of the child.
Preoperational (3–7 years)	Mental representations of objects/people currently outside the view of the child emerge.
Concrete operational (8–12 years)	The abilities to employ deductive reasoning and distinguish between one's own and other people's perspectives emerge.
Formal operational (13–15 years)	The ability to employ 'abstract reasoning' emerges.

This model represent a child's development from a non-verbal, pre-conceptual developmental stage, to a complex, language acquisition and conceptual reasoning (early adolescence) stage. Although the stages of development are pre-programmed in children, their environment will affect the progress from one stage to the next (Piaget, 1952).

It can be seen that evidence for the specific factors outlined above is difficult to ascertain due to the multitude of factors that could be operating (i.e. confounds), or the variable time durations of occurrence of the phenomena of interest. However, Plomin and Spinath (2004) argue that environmental factors have been said to account for a *third* of total phenotypic variance.

KEY STUDY

Effect of shared environment on intelligence

Segal (1997) conducted a study demonstrating the variants of investigation designs that emerge from the behavioural genetics principles. Entitled 'Same-age unrelated siblings: A unique test of within-family environmental influences on IQ stability' (published in the *Journal of Educational Psychology*), the study shows a new behavioural design. Pairs of unrelated siblings with matched ages were reared together from early childhood and their IQ was assessed. The findings showed low IQ similarities, $r = 0.17$, which contrasted with 0.86 for MZ twins, 0.60 for DZ twins and 0.50 for siblings. This finding was used as evidence to support the claim that shared environment has a small influence on intelligence and was used to challenge the argument that the high correlations between MZ twins' IQs is merely a product of their shared experiences.

Test your knowledge

1   What do you think the consequences of 'biologisation' may be for our understanding of intelligence?

2   Describe how child-driven effects may influence the development of intelligence in children.

3   Why is it important to examine both shared and non-shared environments when examining the effects of environmental factors on intelligence?

4   Why might Piaget have been dissatisfied with the psychometric approach to explaining the development of intelligence in children?

Further reading

Topic	Key reading
Heritability of intelligence	Bouchard, T. & McGue, M. (1981). Familial studies of intelligence: A review, *Science*, *212*, 1055–8.
Top-down and bottom-up studies of intelligence	Plomin, P. & Spinath, F. (2004). Intelligence: Genetics, genes and genomics, *Journal of Personality and Social Psychology*, *86(1)*, 112–29.
What is known and what has not been established in intelligence	Neiser, U., Boodoo, G., Bouchard, T.J., Boykin, A.W., Brody, N., Ceci, S.J., Halpern, D.F., Loehlin, J.C., Perloff, R., Sternberg, R.J. & Urbina, S. (1996). Intelligence: Knowns and unknowns, *American Psychologist, 51*, 77–101.

CRITICAL FOCUS

Twin study methodology and intelligence

Richardson's (1991) 'understanding of intelligence' challenged a number of assumptions, and was supported by Howe's 1997 statement of accuracy and inaccuracy in the study of intelligence.

In relation to twin and adoption studies, a number of challenges were identified. The selection basis of children's adoption may not, for instance, be representative; also children may be adopted into similar social situations to their 'biological' home. This continuation of environmental influence may thus challenge the statistical separation of the biological parents from those with variable environmental continuity. Not all adopted children are adopted from birth and therefore it is unreasonable for studies to ignore early and contrasting environmental experiences. In relation to separated twins, account needs to taken of actual contact that can occur between such twins.

Further methodological weaknesses in the studies need to be noted. Firstly, the model of intelligence used in studies is a model represented by measured IQ. The model presumes only an additive formulation, i.e. not dominant genes, and gene combinations (epistatic). Second, environment is often treated as within the 'normal' range of experiences, whereas seriously detrimental, or exceptionally enriching environments, may have a more dominant impact.

Stability of intelligence over time

Intuition might suggest that the ratio of genetic influence to environmental influence over time would move in favour of the environmental contribution, as life experiences increase over the life course both in breadth and in depth. Plomin (1986) has shown the reverse to be the case: heritability actually increases over the lifespan (see Table 9.3).

Plomin (1986) used the information presented in the table to argue that genes are involved in *change* as well as in continuity of development in intelligence. This may be because, as we grow older, we exercise greater control over our environments

Table 9.3 **Change in genetic influences (heritability) on intelligence over time (Plomin, 1986)**

Age in years	Heritability of intelligence
1	0.10
2	0.17
3	0.18
4	0.26
Adulthood	0.50

Source: Republished with permission of Taylor & Francis Group LLC – Books, from *Development, Genetics and Psychology*, R. Plomin, 1986; permission conveyed through Copyright Clearance Center, Inc.

and the effects of family and other environmental factors are reduced. In fact, other researchers have suggested that heritability estimates increase across the lifespan to reach a pinnacle of around 0.80 at 60 years of age (Haslam, 2007). McGue et al. (1993), who conducted longitudinal adoption studies, suggested that correlations between adopted siblings drop dramatically after childhood.

A key issue with heritability research such as this is that certain groups (such as people of the lowest socioeconomic status and individuals from minority ethnic groups) are underrepresented (Haslam, 2007). This must make us question the representativeness of heritability estimates and is an area of interest for future research.

Despite the apparent changes in the contribution of genetic and environmental influence on cognitive ability, intelligence appears to have high rank-order stability across the lifespan. This is evidenced by the fact that research has reported very strong correlations between test scores administered years apart. For example, Deary et al. (2000) identified a correlation of $r = 0.73$ between two test scores for a group of 100 individuals, who had taken the test when they were 11 years old (in 1932) and again 66 years later when they were all 77 years old.

CRITICAL FOCUS

Molecular genetics

In their article, 'Intelligence: Genetics, genes and genomics', Plomin and Spinath (2004) present new areas for study arising from the integration of findings from the Human Genome Project into the genetic study of intelligence. The authors identify the two most important genetic findings as the increase in the effect of heritability on intelligence throughout the lifespan; and the genes' effect on different cognitive aptitudes, i.e. intelligence measures are only one branch of the impact upon cognitive performance. For the authors, this promotes the next area for research as the understanding of the path between genes and intelligence. As such they promote the possibility for bottom-up molecular study to meet top-down psychological research. This may also be a means of identifying the specific genes which underpin intelligence (Deary, Spinath & Bates, 2006).

Test your knowledge

1   Provide an estimate of heritability for the intelligence of twins living together and apart.

2   Why may the results for the determination of IQ proportions amongst twins raised together and apart not necessarily be translated to the individual?

3   Why might the influence of environmental factors on intelligence decrease over the course of an individual's life?

Further reading

Topic	Key reading
Exploration of the development of intelligence	Berg, C. (2004). Chapter 6: *Intellectual development in adulthood.* In R. Sternberg (ed.), *Handbook of intelligence.* Cambridge: Cambridge University Press.
Examination of the relationship between cognitive abilities across ability level and lifespan	Tucker-Drob, E. (2009). Differentiation of cognitive abilities across the lifespan, *Developmental Psychology, 45(4)*, 1097–118.

Controversies in intelligence

There are many controversies in intelligence, some of which have been touched upon already. We will now explore some of the issues which have caused the greatest concern.

Tautology

A key debate regarding the intelligence quotient, and intelligence and ability tests in general, is whether they measure intelligence, or *define* what intelligence is. Some theorists have suggested that intelligence is merely whatever intelligence tests measure (Boring, 1923), calling into question the validity of such tests. However, it would appear that intelligence and ability tests are relevant because they are often found to correlate with 'useful real-life criteria' (Cooper, 2002, p. 188). For example, intelligence is found to correlate with performance at school (Frey & Detterman, 2004) and to predict performance at work (Ree & Earles, 1992).

Bias

Establishing the 'fairness' of psychometric tests designed to measure intelligence is extremely important (see Chapter 10 for further discussion). Tests need to be fair to ensure that they fulfil the task they are supposed to and to help ensure that people are not discriminated against. For example, if part of the selection process for a job is based on the results of an intelligence test, but this test is biased against a particular group of individuals, this would be unethical and discriminatory.

Another criticism is that intelligence tests cannot provide all the information that is required to explain an individual effectively. For example, knowing an individual's IQ may tell you in part whether they would have the capacities to complete a specific task or perform a certain job, but it would not tell you whether an individual would be *motivated* or *interested* to perform this task (or to perform it *well*). This narrow focus on 'academic' abilities was one of the impetuses for theorists to develop new 'nonacademic' or 'real-world' intelligences (Sternberg, 1997a, b, 1988).

Despite the controversies surrounding the ways in which intelligence tests have been developed, Vernon (1979) argues that they still measure a *stable* component of human functioning.

The Flynn effect

The Flynn effect (named after the political scientist James Flynn) is the year-on-year rise in measured intelligence, which was noted during an exercise to update intelligence test norms. Intelligence test scores are raw scores which need to be standardised using norm tables before they can be validly applied in comparisons between individuals and over time.

Flynn discovered that higher standards for *average* IQ scores were being set in newer IQ tests compared to previous versions. So, you would need to be more intelligent to score 100 IQ on a newer test than on a previous version of the test. Fascinated by this observation, Flynn investigated further and found the following:

- Over the course of a generation (1948–72), a representative sample of US residents' IQ scores increased by 8 IQ points (Flynn, 1984).
- Through examining the results of 73 studies conducted in the USA which had required their samples to complete two or more versions of the same IQ test, Flynn identified a 0.30 point increase per year in white American individuals' IQ scores (Flynn, 1984).
- The year-on-year rise in average IQ was not restricted to the USA, with the same phenomenon being observed across a number of other countries (Flynn, 1987, 1994).
- Greater increases were indentified in non-verbal tests of intelligence (an average of approximately 15 points per generation) compared to verbal tests (an average of approximately 9 points per generation).

Flynn did not consider the explanation that the human race was getting more intelligent as plausible. His attention turned to the intelligence tests themselves and what they measure. He suggested that the phenomenon may be a result of environmental factors, such as: the improvement in nutrition over the generations; parenting and schooling advances; adaptations over generations to the style of tests adopted in intelligence test taking; and advances in environmental factors that stimulate intellectual functioning.

Flynn believed that intelligence tests do not *measure* intelligence, but instead *correlate* with it.

Further reading

Topic	Key reading
Flynn effect	Flynn, J. (1999). Searching for justice: The discovery of IQ gains over time, *American Psychologist, 54*, 5–20.

Test your knowledge

1 Describe the Flynn effect.
2 Where did Flynn direct his attention to search for explanation?
3 Specify two explanations for the Flynn effect.

Racial group differences in intelligence and the bell-curve debate

In 1994 Herrnstein and Murray published a controversial book called *The bell curve: Intelligence and class in American life*. This book sparked a great deal of controversy and debate owing to the premises and conclusions stated. The bell curve was a reference to the shape of the standard normal statistical distribution, which applies to intelligence test scores. Figure 9.1 presents this curve.

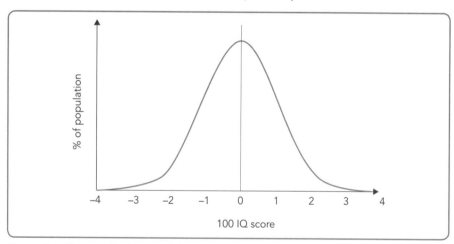

Figure 9.1 The standard normal distribution curve

Herrnstein and Murray (1994) make a number of statements in this book that, when taken together, suggest that IQ and tests that measure IQ are reliable and valid. These statements therefore imply that observed differences between groups of people (e.g. ethnic, socioeconomic) are real, rather than artefacts of measurement. On this basis they go on to explore four key ideas:

- *The cognitive elite*: From looking at those individuals who fell into the higher end of the bell curve (individuals with higher IQ scores), Herrnstein and Murray concluded that higher IQ was the overriding factor contributing to academic and career success. For this reason they believed that a new class system would evolve based on intelligence with those at the higher end of the bell curve representing the 'cognitive elite'.

- *Socioeconomic status and IQ*: Herrnstein and Murray suggest that intelligence is a more important predictor in an individual's eventual economic and social position than socioeconomic status.

- *Race and IQ*: Herrnstein and Murray identified differences between Asians and Asian Americans, and White Americans, with the former scoring approximately 5 IQ points higher on average than the latter, and found that White Americans scored an average of approximately 1 standard deviation higher than Black Americans on different intelligence tests. They also found that immigrants to the USA scored lower than US residents on IQ. They concluded that this, coupled with the observation that women with lower IQs tended to have more children, was resulting in the 'dumbing down' of America. They also suggested that many of the social problems of America (such as poverty and crime) were attributed to individuals with lower IQs. As a result these conclusions implied that individuals from certain ethnic backgrounds were therefore the cause of social problems in America.

- *Implications for social policy*: Herrnstein and Murray suggested that trying to improve IQ does not work (and cited different projects that had unsuccessfully attempted to increase access to education and educational performance for disadvantaged or minority groups). For this reason they suggested that rather than trying to address inequality, resources should be redirected to ensure that the gifted in society reach their full potential (as they felt they were hitherto being marginalised). Herrnstein and Murray believed that this would increase the intelligence of the nation overall and would ultimately lead to a reduction in social problems.

Points to consider: The bell-curve debate

- Many of the premises upon which Herrnstein and Murray base their arguments have been challenged (e.g. Gould, 1995). For example, the authors assume there is a general factor of intelligence, but from the previous chapter it should be clear that whether or not a General Intelligence actually exists is far from clear. This conceptualisation also disregards other forms of intelligence, or different forms of cognitive processes that may exist.

- The analysis of the book presented arguments for the presence of a genetically determined 'cognitive elite' in the USA. This group of highly intelligent individuals were conceptualised as society's successes, whereas individuals with lower IQ were proposed as being the cause of problems in society. This interpretation has obvious ethical implications.

- Some researchers and theorists criticised Herrnstein and Murray's book because the core arguments it contained appeared reminiscent of the arguments underpinning the concept of **eugenics** (e.g. Fraser, 1995). However, it should be noted that the authors never directly asserted this as a conclusion from their work.

- Crucially, differences in the average IQ of different groups as defined by race have been observed by a number of researchers (Mackintosh, 1998). The fact that some differences between groups are evidenced is a product of the fact that groups comprise individuals who *differ* from each other, and so some groups' averages will be higher than others (Chamorro-Premuzic, 2011).

  - The controversy and ethical quandaries that arise from this finding really centre on how these differences are *interpreted*: what factors are proposed as *causing* or reflect a *consequence* of these differences (e.g. some aspect of biology or social or economic factors), whether they are of *practical* significance, and how these findings affect social policy and practices.

  - For example, Herrnstein and Murray's conclusions appear to be that differences in IQ between racial groups are in some way biologically or genetically determined. However, another explanation might be that individuals from different ethnic backgrounds may have different educational, social and economic opportunities available to them. Also, some research suggests that an individual's perception of the negative stereotype about their racial group's expected performance on a cognitive ability test can impair that individual's performance on the test.

  - Cooper et al. (2000) argue that using the concept of race as a 'real', biological grouping variable is misleading. This is because groups defined in such a way as 'Black', 'White' and 'Asian' actually comprise individuals from large and diverse ranges of countries, each with their own language and culture. The impact of this must be considered.

Further reading

Topic	Key reading
Discussions of Herrnstein and Murray's arguments and conclusions, presented by noted authors in the field of intelligence	Fraser, S. (1995). *The bell curve wars: Race, intelligence and the future of America*. New York: Basic Books.
Themes in the bell-curve debate	Thematic papers in Devlin, B., Fienberg, S., Resnick, D. & Roeder, K. (1997). *Intelligence, genes and success: Scientists respond to the bell curve*. New York: Springer.
Response to Herrnstein and Murray's arguments	Devlin, B., Fienberg, S., Resnick, D. & Roeder, K. (1997). *Intelligence, genes and success: Scientists respond to the bell curve*. New York: Springer.

Sample question   *Essay*

Society would benefit to a greater extent if social policy and practices re-directed resources away from widening participation activities, to supporting and encourage the 'cognitive elite' in society. Critically discuss this position, providing appropriate evidence from theory and research to support your argument.

Sex differences in intelligence

Sex differences in intelligence are controversial because they have been used historically to justify discrimination and inequality in such spheres as education, politics (Haslam, 2007) and the labour market. However, there is a great deal of debate in the literature (and media) regarding whether or not sex differences in intelligence actually exist:

- Court (1983) conducted a systematic review of 120 research studies and found no clear pattern of sex differences; some studies suggested that men scored higher than women, others found the opposite pattern, but the majority of studies found no significant differences.

- Lynn and Irwing (Lynn & Irwing, 2004; Irwing & Lynn, 2005) conducted a meta-analysis of a smaller sample of studies (57) examining General Intelligence and found that men scored an average of 5 IQ points higher than women. However, the effect size for this relationship was small ($d = 0.30$).

- Other research suggests that the mean IQ score may be the same for men and women, but that men's IQ scores may show greater variability than women's (Lubinski & Humphreys, 1990).

A number of explanations have been proposed to account for sex differences, including:

- *Differences in brain size and weight*: Lynn (1994a) suggested that the fact that men on average may score higher on intelligence tests may be related to the fact that their brains are on average larger (approximately 8% bigger) than women's.

  - This argument has been criticised for being misleading and too simplistic (e.g. Jensen, 1998). For example, when controlling for the fact that men are

207

also more likely to have greater body size/mass, the same results are not found (Halpern, 2000).

● *The result of evolutionary adaptation* (e.g. Buss, 1995a): Evolutionary theories argue that sex differences have arisen as a result of different adaptive needs of men and women across history (Buss, 1994). For example, Buss suggests that differences in spatial rotation abilities (where males appear to score higher than females) are a result of the skills required to be an effective hunter in hunter-gatherer societies (Buss, 1995b). Evolutionary theories of this nature have been criticised because it has been suggested that many of the abilities that humans possess today are a result of adaptive solutions for living in a particular technologically complex cultural context, rather than a result of evolution directly (Geary, 1996, 2007)

● *Socialisation processes and role stereotyping*: The role stereotypes concerning the way in which male and female children and adults should behave that are prevalent in a culture will affect the way people treat them, and therefore the way in which they develop. It is known that boys and girls are encouraged to play with different toys and engage in different play activities. These different toys and activities may require the development of different skills (Levine et al., 2005). Socialisation processes may also affect the choice of subject selected to study in school (Halpern & LaMay, 2000) and whether people feel they will be able to excel at a subject or not, and may result in self-fulfilling prophecies (Plucker, 1996).

Test your knowledge

1 If sex differences in IQ do exist, does this mean that they are meaningful?

2 What are the ethical issues concerning the identification of sex differences in IQ?

3 Compare two key explanations of sex differences: what are their strengths and weaknesses?

Further reading

Topic	Key reading
Examination of the methodology used to identify sex differences	Molenaar, D., Dolan, C. & Wicherts, J. (2009). The power to detect sex differences in IQ test scores using multi-group covariance and means structure analyses, *Intelligence, 37(4)*, 396–404.
Examination of alternative explanations of sex differences	Dykiert, D., Gale, C. & Deary, I. (2009). Are apparent sex differences in mean IQ scores created in part by sample restriction and increased male variance? *Intelligence, 37(1)*, 42–7.
Sex differences in intelligence	Halpern, D. (2009). Chapter 3: Intelligence. In D. Halpern, *Sex differences in cognitive abilities* (3rd edn). Mahwah, NJ: Erlbaum.

Social class differences in intelligence

We have already explored some of the factors related to social class (under family and environmental effects) and its relationship with intelligence. However, there are a number of other issues which it is important to be aware of in this topic.

One of the key issues is whether intelligence is a *consequence* or *cause* of social class. Historically, research has suggested that those individuals with a low socioeconomic status are likely to have lower IQ scores than individuals with higher socioeconomic status (Scarr, 1981). However, there are so many factors which could be underpinning this pattern that interpreting the relationship between socioeconomic status and intelligence is difficult.

KEY STUDY

Socioeconomic status and children's intelligence

A seminal piece of research was conducted by Capron and Duyme (1989) to systematically investigate the relationship between socioeconomic status and children's intelligence. They assessed the intelligence of four groups of adopted children, who were identified as comprising:

1 Children born into a low social class family, adopted into a low social class family

2 Children born into a low social class family, adopted into a high social class family

3 Children born into a high social class family, adopted into a low social class family

4 Children born into a high social class family, adopted into a high social class family

The result indicated that the social class of the children's biological and adoptive family affected their IQ similarly. The children with the highest IQ were those in group 4, and the children with the lowest IQ were those found in group 1.

Test your knowledge

1 Why might it be difficult to establish whether socioeconomic/class status is a cause, or consequence, of intelligence?

2 How does the observation of class differences potentially tie into the debate about racial group differences in IQ?

Further reading

Topic	Key reading
Discussions of the relationship between social class/socioeconomic status and intelligence (as well as other key factors in the debate)	Scarr, S. (1981). *Race, social class and individual differences in IQ*. Mahwah, NJ: Erlbaum.
The relationship between IQ and social mobility	Forrest, L., Hodgson, S., Parker, L. & Pearce, M. (2011). The influence of childhood IQ and education on social mobility in the Newcastle Thousand Families birth cohort, *BMC Public Health, 11(895)*, 1–9.

Eugenics

The term 'eugenics' was coined by Sir Francis Galton (1869) from the Greek meaning 'good breeding'. Galton was interested in the theory of evolution proposed by his cousin Charles Darwin, particularly in the nature of heritability. From his own observations of the way in which intelligence appeared to pass down through generations of eminent families, Galton suggested that intelligence (amongst other qualities) was heritable. He published a book on the subject, entitled *Hereditary Genius* (1869), in which he suggested it was important to explore the ways in which the intelligence, health and moral character of the population could be improved through the use of eugenics (using social factors to steer the inheritance of traits). Galton wrote prolifically on the subject of eugenics and explored many of the consequences and issues which arise from it. He believed that the population of the time had begun to deteriorate genetically (Galton, 1865) and proposed different methods of developing selective breeding as a solution. He proposed two mechanisms through which to achieve this:

- **Positive eugenics** involved finding methods of increasing the fertility of 'desirables'. Desirables were individuals who were exceptionally intelligent or healthy or had extraordinary moral character. Galton believed that this would be the most effective strategy for increasing desirable characteristics within the population.

- **Negative eugenics** involved finding methods of decreasing the fertility of 'undesirables' (individuals who demonstrated poor qualities in relation to intelligence, health and moral character).

'Passable' (average) individuals required no action to be taken (Galton, 1908).

Galton's arguments were adopted by other notable psychologists (e.g. Lewis Terman) and have been extremely influential; the concept of eugenics has been used as the basis of extreme social policies, politics and laws. For example, it was used by Hitler and the Nazi Party as the basis of a sterilisation law which resulted in 20,000 'feeble-minded' or 'mentally unworthy' people being sterilised between 1933 and1939 (before the holocaust).

The controversial and ethical issues raised by the concept of group differences on intelligence and eugenics are clear and are likely to continue to spark debates in the future.

Test your knowledge

1 What is the core premise of the eugenics argument?
2 List three reasons why the concept of eugenics is controversial.
3 What impact might the debate about eugenics have on human genome research and technologies?

Further reading

Topic	Key reading
Overview of Richard Lynn's work concerning Individual Differences variables and work on eugenics	Thompson, J. (e-pub. ahead of print). Richard Lynn's contributions to personality and intelligence, personality and Individual Differences, available online 2 April 2011, ISSN 0191-8869, 10.1016/j.paid.2011.03.013.
Individual Differences in perceptions of genetic influence and policies	Shostak, S., Freese, J., Link, B. & Phelan, J. (2009). The politics of the gene: Social status and beliefs about genetics for individual outcomes, *Social Psychology Quarterly, 72(1)*, 77–93.
Discussion of the impact of perception of ability on educational policy	Gillborn, D. (2010). Reform, racism and the centrality of whiteness: assessment, ability and the 'new eugenics', *Irish Educational Studies, 29(3)*, 231–52.

Chapter summary: putting it all together

→ Can you tick all the points from the revision checklist at the beginning of this chapter?

→ Attempt the sample question from the beginning of this chapter using the answer guidelines below.

→ Go to the companion website at www.pearsoned.co.uk/psychologyexpress to access more revision support online, including interactive quizzes, sample questions with answer guidelines, 'you be the marker' exercises, flashcards and podcasts you can download.

Answer guidelines

Guidelines on answering the sample question presented at the start of the chapter are given below.

 Sample question   *Essay*

Critically evaluate the extent to which the concept of intelligence constitutes a reliable, valid and 'real' construct. Provide evidence from theory and research to support your argument.

Approaching the question

This assignment provides a large amount of scope for you to choose how to construct your answer: this is good because it will allow you free rein to choose

211

the debates and evidence to support your discussion, but it could result in you trying to include too much. For this reason it may be helpful to structure your question according to the key debates in the field that may either lend support to the existence of the construct, or spread doubt about whether the construct is genuine (or has been conceptualised appropriately in theory and research).

Important points to include

You need to include some background about why the reliability, validity and 'realness' of the concept of intelligence are important. To do this you could include information on:

● stigma and self-fulfilling prophecy;
● the applied value of intelligence, e.g. in educational attainment and occupational selection and recruitment;
● the 'dark side' of psychology and eugenics.

Following this you could highlight the fact that a key debate in establishing the reliability, validity and reality of intelligence concerns the lack of a single, consensus definition of intelligence. To discuss this debate you could include information from the previous chapter on:

● the single- and multi-factor debate (and evidence for and against these positions);
● whether multiple intelligences exist and the criticism of focusing only on 'analytic' intelligence in traditional theory;
● methodological issues arising from model construction (e.g. lack of instrument measuring in Guilford's structure of intellect model).

Following this you could outline the concept of the intelligence quotient (IQ) and discuss:

● how the deviation IQ concept was developed from the concept of mental age and the controversies associated;
● how IQ is the most commonly used piece of information in intelligence research and what the implications of this may be;
● Boring's criticism of the tautology of intelligence measurement and the implications of this for theory, research and social policy.

You also need to consider the wealth of research findings which provide fairly consistent support for the existence of intelligence:

● It remains fairly stable across the lifespan.
● There is evidence to support heritability and fairly consistent information on how environmental factors can affect phenotypic variance (discuss the strengths and limitations of research, where appropriate) from:
   ● twin studies and
   ● adoption studies.
● Consistent correlations exist with educational and occupational performance and socioeconomic status.

- A person tends to perform comparably across different ability tests (although variations do occur).
- Observations of differences between groups (e.g. based on race, class and sex) have been linked to other 'real life' variables (e.g. deprived versus enriched environments).

Provide the critique of the research and its findings. Consider:

- methodological issues in research (e.g. potentially biased samples in twin and adoption studies);
- confounding variables: i.e. racial differences may be confounded by socioeconomic status, access to educational opportunities and cultural factors;
- no consensus of agreement about the determinants of intelligence;
- the Flynn effect – how to explain the year-on-year rise in intelligence;
- Flynn's suggestion that intelligence tests do not *measure* intelligence, but merely *correlate* with an abstract reasoning ability;
- the controversy over using certain socially constructed variables (such as race) as grouping variables to investigate differences in intelligence;
- cross-cultural issues in intelligence theory and research.

The final stage in the answer should be to consider the implications of the intelligence construct (i.e. whether it is real or an 'artefact' of methodology). Issues include:

- the statistical versus practical significance of intelligence research findings (particularly observed group differences);
- ethical issues in the field;
- the impact of intelligence research findings on social policy, practice and psychometrics (e.g. education, selection and recruitment, welfare, eugenics).

> ### Make your answer stand out
>
> *Using the controversies highlighted in this chapter to illustrate the key issues in intelligence theory and research will provide a useful framework within which to construct your answer. However, the debates concerning the 'realness' of intelligence and the extent to which group differences in intelligence are actually observable have sparked much heated debate in the literature (and more generally in public media). Many theorists who argue that race and sex differences (for example) do actually exist have experienced an extremely negative backlash from both the public and academic communities. In some cases their theories and research findings have been dismissed by default. Therefore, to provide a strong answer that is persuasive, you need to look impartially at the evidence for both sides of the argument and provide a well-reasoned discussion if you feel the evidence for a particular topic is flawed or not persuasive. This will allow the person marking your assignment to see that you have fully considered the debate and have understood the*

complicated nature of the issues that assignments on this topic can often reveal.

Notes

Psychometrics: tests, testing and measurement

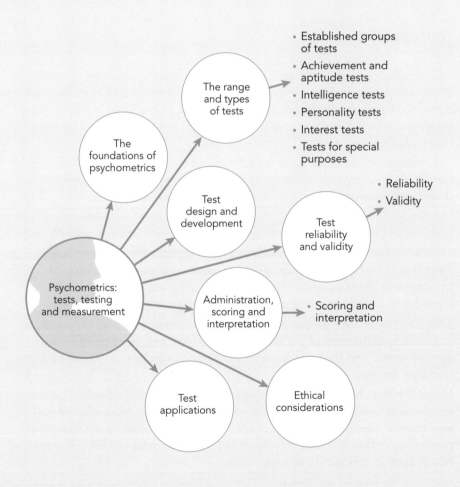

- Established groups of tests
- Achievement and aptitude tests
- Intelligence tests
- Personality tests
- Interest tests
- Tests for special purposes

The range and types of tests

The foundations of psychometrics

- Reliability
- Validity

Test design and development

Test reliability and validity

Psychometrics: tests, testing and measurement

Administration, scoring and interpretation

- Scoring and interpretation

Test applications

Ethical considerations

A printable version of this topic map is available from:
www.pearsoned.co.uk/psychologyexpress

➡️ *Revision checklist*

Essential points you should know:
- ❑ The principle of scaling
- ❑ Range and types of tests
- ❑ Stages of test design and development
- ❑ Test reliability and validation
- ❑ Administration, scoring and interpretation
- ❑ Ethical matters in test construction and the testing process

Introduction

The compilation of psychometric tests is an important area within the study of Individual Differences as they offer the potential to validate the individual difference variables employed. Most conceptions of intelligence and the trait-dispositional models of personality (for instance) are substantiated by means of rigorously designed tests.

The tests employed differ quite considerably in a number of ways. The range of test types are considered in this chapter, along with the stages involved in test design and development.

The discussion of test construction is the framework within which the concepts of reliability and validity can be examined. There are several forms of reliability and validity which will be discussed in relation to test design and the process of testing.

The conduct and administration of testing sessions presents a number of challenges to the standardisation of the test-taking environment and also therefore to the scoring, interpretation and contextualisation of findings.

Ethical concerns are especially important in relation to test use; the sensitive and confidential nature of the data collected, together with retention and storage issues, and the uses to which the findings can be put, invoke strong reactions amongst participants.

Material in this chapter is wide ranging and presents issues associated with both existing and well-established psychometric tests, and the production of new instruments. These are issues which are relevant across Individual Differences psychology and so a strong understanding of these topics will be useful to most assessments in this branch of psychology.

Assessment advice

The discussion of psychometrics (and psychological testing in general) in individual differences is most typically presented as supporting material for the subject of the main question. In some instances, therefore, it may constitute the second part of a question or serve as a supplementary theme. Measurement issues are nevertheless integral to many individual differences themes even when they are treated implicitly. More specialist courses devoted to measurement and testing will give full attention to test themes. But it is rare in a course on personality and individual differences that a full question is devoted to measurement and testing. Outside of those specialist courses, the coverage of testing topics is closely associated with the specific Individual Difference concept being explored, e.g. personality or interests.

Tests and testing will emerge in practical investigations of Individual Difference concepts; therefore, an understanding of the key debates and issues in this field is important to demonstrate a strong understanding of Individual Differences psychology as a whole.

Sample question

Could you answer the question below? It is a typical problem question that could arise on this topic. Guidelines on answering the question are included at the end of this chapter, whilst a sample essay question and guidance on tackling it can be found on the companion website at www.pearsoned.co.uk/psychology express.

 Sample question   *Problem-based learning*

You are required to design an interest inventory that is to be used to determine the career preferences of a group of undergraduate students. Identify and outline the stages you would adopt for the production of such a questionnaire.

The foundations of psychometrics

The fundamental premise of this field is that Individual Differences can be 'turned into' measurable qualities and can be assigned numbers (referred to as *scaling*). Assigning numbers to different qualities (e.g. a score on conscientiousness) allows us to produce descriptive and inferential statistics that tell us about the relationships between a person's 'score' on different Individual Differences, and between people's scores on the same Individual Differences, or across time points or situations. However, this assumption is very controversial because it is unclear whether we can measure accurately hypothetical, unobservable constructs (such as intelligence) from observable phenomena such as behaviour. This is referred to as the *accessibility debate*. There is also a great deal of debate about how the error involved in scaling (e.g. random or systematic) should be controlled for (Mahoney, 2011) – a debate which has shaped the ways in which many statistical techniques have been developed (Howell, 2006). You should keep these background debates in mind when reading the rest of this chapter, because they ultimately represent the underpinnings (and controversies) of all psychometric tests.

The range and types of tests

There are a number of different ways in which psychometric tests can be distinguished. We could, for instance, distinguish them by the person characteristics, i.e. measured aptitude, personality, behaviour, interest or attitude. We could distinguish them by the purposes to which they are to be put, i.e. counselling, business and personnel selection, or clinical purposes. We could classify tests by the way they are scored or measured, e.g. rater-observations, performance measurement or self-rating evaluations. Tests can be administered either to individuals or to groups; either with or without time constraints; some employ instruments or equipment; others are paper and pencil tests. Also, client responses may allow for open choice, or categorical or constrained answers.

Whilst some tests are open access, many tests have restrictions on *how* they can be used and *who* is allowed to administer, score and interpret them. Restrictions come in the form of certification with general or specific test training; the British Psychological Society's Psychological Testing Centre (PTC) maintains a register of qualified test users at different qualification levels (the Register of Qualifications in Test Use; RQTU). The PTC also conducts regular reviews of the major tests instruments through its Committee on Test Standards (CTS). Over 140 such tests have been reviewed, an example being the review of personality test instruments for use in occupational settings (Lindley, 2001), although online updates are now the standard for knowledge dissemination. The PTC provides information for psychologists and non-psychologists on appropriate test development procedures, and standards for the administration and use of psychological tests (including training and certification).

Established groups of tests

There are two broad categories of psychometric test: **tests of maximal performance** and **tests of typical performance**.

Tests of maximal performance are those which are designed to assess what we have learned and our capacity to learn new things, whereas tests of typical performance are those which aim to assess how we typically think, feel and behave (Bartram & Lindley, 2007).

These two broad categories of test contain further subgroups of tests:

- Examples of tests of maximal performance include: intelligence, achievement, ability and aptitude tests.

- Examples of tests of typical performance include: personality tests, and tests of interests, preferences and motivations.

The two types of test require different skills to interpret and therefore require different levels of qualification (Bartram & Lindley, 2007); to be able to administer, score and feedback tests of maximal performance you are required to achieve a Level A certificate of competence in occupational testing. To be able to administer, score and feedback tests of typical performance requires a further qualification: a Level B certificate of competence in occupational testing. You may also be required to undertake training on specific tests, to ensure you have the skills to use the tests appropriately and *ethically*.

Achievement and aptitude tests

Achievement tests measure current capability, i.e. what we are capable of at the time of the testing. These tests contrast with *aptitude tests*, which are a measure of potential, i.e. what we are potentially capable of. Clearly these can show different results distinguishing actual performance from projected possibilities. Both achievement and aptitude tests are employed in areas where maximal performance is sought. Maximum performance can be contrasted with tests which seek assessment of preference or personality, for example. Examples of achievement tests include the car driving theory test and many of the school and university-type assessments, whether coursework or examinations. Examples of aptitude tests include tests of cognitive or verbal reasoning and manual dexterity.

Intelligence tests

Intelligence tests necessarily correspond to the particular theoretical and intellectual basis for the model. Chapter 8 shows that there are quite different conceptions of what constitutes intelligence. If intelligence is treated as a single dimension 'g', then measurement will be determined by a number of items that can be shown to be measures for 'g'. Where intelligence is treated as in the three-stratum theory, G_c, G_f, G_m, then items that test crystallised intelligence, fluid intelligence and memory are generated. The most established, recent test is the Weschler Adult Intelligence test (WAIS-IV), (Weschler, 2008). The WAIS-IV contains 14 distinct scales that form Weschler's model of intelligence. Figure 10.1 illustrates the Weschler intelligence profile showing how scales are used for interpretation. In this example we are looking at the Full Scale Intelligence Quotient (FSIQ), which comprises the 10 core subsets of the Verbal Comprehension Scale (VCS), the Perceptual Reasoning Scale (PRS), the Working Memory Scale (WMS) and the Processing Speed Scale (PSS).

A completely contrasting model of the concept of intelligence and corresponding test is Sternberg's Triarchic Abilities Test (STAT) (Sternberg, 1993). This test is modelled on the three different components of intelligence which Sternberg (1993) believed existed: practical, analytical and creative (Sternberg et al., 2001), and therefore represents another way of 'grouping' intellectual abilities.

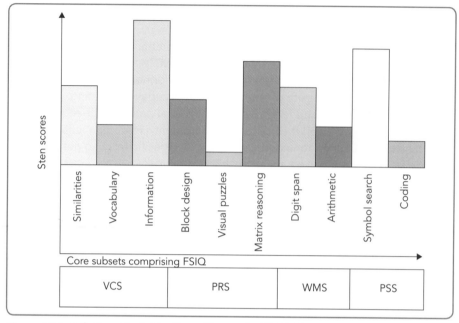

Figure 10.1 **A fictional individual's profile on the WAIS-IV**

CRITICAL FOCUS

Sten scores

Sten scores are a form of standardised test score, which are commonly used in psychometric testing. They have a range of 1–10 (with a mean of 5.5) and can be calculated from the manual of the specific test you are using (Chauhan & Ahmad, 2007).

Test your knowledge

1   What distinguishes tests of achievement from tests of aptitude?
2   For which groups of tests is maximum performance an essential requirement and for which tests is typical performance an essential requirement?

Personality tests

Preceding chapters have demonstrated the range of personality models that exist, and have shown the variations in the extent to which they are suitable to be 'turned into' psychometric measures. Phenomenological, humanistic and psychodynamic models, for example, do not easily lend themselves to 'scientific' measurement. Behaviourist models are capable of measurement with the use of behavioural observation assessment. The social-cognitive personality models present more complications for measurement than more traditional behavioural schemes of trait-dispositional models of personality, e.g. Eysenck's PEN Model and Cattell's 16PF, the Costa and McCrae Five Factor Model are the best examples of a concept formulation that allows measurement. Each of those models presents a manageable number of traits which can be measured in isolation, or in combinations, depending upon the hypotheses being tested.

Practical application of theory **Items in Cattell's 16PF Personality Questionnaire (IPAT, 1993)**

6. I tend to get embarrassed if I suddenly become the centre of attention in a social group.

11. I get into trouble because I sometimes pursue my own ideas without talking them over with the people involved.

44. It seems that more than half the people I meet can't really be trusted.

It will be noted that the forms of these questions are not transparently associated with the particular traits they measure. This feature is purposeful in acting as a disguise to avoid faking. The approach adopted by Cattell contrasts with the more transparent question formulations of the FFM.

Interest tests

An example of a preferential interest model that attempts to accommodate person characteristics with environmental characteristics for the purpose of career decision-making is Holland's (1973) RIASEC model (discussed in more detail in Chapter 11). Holland's model comprises six scales: Realistic, Investigative, Artistic, Social, Enterprising and Conventional. These scales are person characteristics and based upon the groups of interests that individuals declared in items of career interests. These scales have also been adopted by other inventories: for example, the Strong Interest Inventory (SII). The SII has progressed through many stages of development since its introduction following the First World War with a current version dating from 1927. The Strong Inventory has been used extensively for job selection purposes, although it has also been employed for career counselling.

The Kuder Occupational Interest Survey (KOIS) contrasts with the SII in that it adopted a forced choice method for determining preferences amongst paired options. The KOIS also used the principle of correspondence of interests to existing job-holders, i.e. the alignment of interests with actual jobs selected. The KOIS therefore used average interest score measures from existing and satisfied post-holders in occupational groups. These scores then allowed future respondents' interest scores to be matched and possibly correlated with suggested job titles.

Tests for special purposes

In addition to established tests designed for general ability, personality and interests, tests are also designed for measures of specific aptitudes or to assist with selection for particular purposes. Such tests will typically begin with determination of scales that correspond to the requirements of a job. A job analysis will precede the test design. It is expected that items generated will demonstrate reliability and validity, and also correspond to job performance criteria. Special purpose tests are commonly developed for use in selection of staff for training, e.g. the Clinical Aptitude Test for entry to medical training. In a volume designed to assist such applicants in their preparation for the selection tests, Green and Jethwa (2009) provided practical examples in the several fields. These are verbal and quantitative reasoning; abstract reasoning; decision analysis; and non-cognitive analysis. The categories of examples included correspond with those of the examination. In the design of such a test it was necessary for the authors to ensure validity. This was achieved by corroboration of results with actual performance of students in their degree training; and indeed in their actual clinical performance when taking up positions.

Practical application of theory Entrance test for medical school (Green & Jethwa, 2009)

The item below is taken from the practice test version of the actual UK Clinical Aptitude Test. It includes a verbal reasoning subtest; quantitative reasoning subtest; abstract reasoning subtest; and decision analysis subtest.

Verbal reasoning example question 10

'To be an effective leader, you need to have a vision to know how you are going to bring people together to understand it. Charisma plays a vital role in leadership; charismatic leaders are admired by others and are concerned with others around them. A good leader also needs to understand when and when not to take risks, and how to portray success. Good leaders will usually pass down the glory to their teams, so that the teams feel satisfied with their winnings. When unforeseen circumstances come about, good leaders will also need to have the ability to claim a level of responsibility over strategies and related items which do not flow according to plan. True leaders are eager to offer power to get things done rather than handling power.'

Are the following true, false or cannot tell?

A. Good leaders should create a collective sense of achievement.
B. Good leaders should hand over complete power.
C. Charismatic leaders make better leaders.
D. Good leaders need to claim responsibility over events that do not go according to plan.

The above verbal example of the test has demonstrated that it is a valid predictor of performance of test takers with the performance of post holders.

Test your knowledge

1 What techniques could you employ to corroborate selection test results with performance in medical training?

2 What are the strengths and limitations of having practice test versions for occupational and educational recruitment and selection purposes?

Further reading

Topic	Key information
Range of tests and validity and reliability measurements	BPS Psychological Test Centre: www.psychtesting.org.uk

Test design and development

The production of psychometrically valid and reliable tests is presented in Figure 10.2 as a series of stages, beginning with conceptualisation of the variable being measured. A number of challenges have to be addressed to progress successfully from this stage. Cohen and Swerdlik (2002) present these challenges in the form of a number of questions to be addressed at each step.

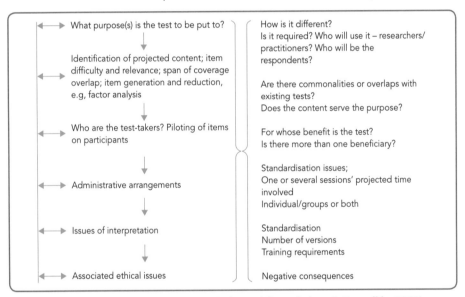

Figure 10.2 Stages in test construction (adapted from Cohen & Swerdlik, 2002)

Figure 10.2 presents the stages in the construction of a test for measuring an Individual Difference variable. Although the chart presents the thinking as linear, it will more typically be an iterative process, with the backward and forward steps being revisited for greater refinement. At each stage a number of questions emerge, the answers to which help with refinement of the test.

Further reading

Topic	Key reading
Test construction	Chapter 3 in Rust, J. & Golombul, S. (2009). *Modern psychometrics: The science of psychological assessment* (3rd edn). London: Routledge.

Test reliability and validity

Reliability

Reliability in testing is a measure that demonstrates consistency in the replicability of test results. Because exact replication in any measurement rarely occurs, there is a specified margin of acceptable variation. There are a number of forms in which reliability can be assessed in test construction. The most common are: item analysis; split-half reliability; test–retest reliability; and multiple-form comparability.

Item analysis is a procedure used to help identify items on a questionnaire which do not perform in the way the test-developer intends (Cooper, 2002). This may be because they do not differentiate between individuals (e.g. they are too easy, in which case everyone gets them right, or they are too hard, in which case everyone gets them wrong), or they do not appear to 'tap into' the construct of interest (e.g. they are measuring another construct, questions are worded ambiguously, socially desirable responding is induced).

There are four main types of item analysis:

1 *Criterion keying*: involves identifying items which predict a criterion (e.g. correlating each item with a known outcome variable which represents the characteristic of interest). Items which predict the criterion (correlate highly with it) are retained and all those items which don't are dropped.

2 *Factor analysis*: this has been discussed in Chapter 2 and refers to identifying items that have substantial **factor loadings** with factors (representing hypothetical constructs) which will be retained. All those items which have low factor loadings are dropped.

3 *Item response theory*: involves assuming that all questions aim to measure a single construct and removing all those items which do not appear to tap into it.

4 *Classic item analysis*: attempts to estimate the correlation of each item with an individual's 'true score', which is the score that would have been obtained had the individual completed every question which could ever have been written to measure the characteristic of interest. As this is not possible, an estimate of the true score is calculated from the total score of the subset of questions the individual has completed (e.g. a questionnaire total score) and correlating each item with this (which involves calculating **Cronbach's alpha**). High correlations are retained and low correlations are removed. To avoid merely correlating each item with a product of itself, we have to 'correct' the questionnaire total score and then examine removing each item individually and re-running the correlation. Luckily, statistical packages such as IBM SPSS do this for you; otherwise it is an extremely lengthy process!

Split-half reliability is another way of exploring how well items relate to each other. It involves dividing the test into two halves and comparing the results of one half with the results of the other (and is usually also assessed using Cronbach's alpha). This is treated as a reliability check on the test as a whole. The technique seeks to split the test in such a way that no systematic distortion is created by the split. In a numbered questionnaire (for example, in a personality inventory), a common mechanism is to separate odd and evenly numbered items. This division enables the scores on one-half of the test to be compared (randomly) with those of the other half, although strictly speaking this is a reliability check on just one half of the test.

An alternative form of reliability measurement, which has similarity with the split-half, is the multiple-form retesting. Multiple-form retesting is also known as parallel-form testing. The idea is that a comparison is made between two distinct versions of the same test. A Pearson correlation measure is used on the tests administered to the same respondents on different occasions (with controls for the order effect). If the tests from the two occasions correlate highly, this would suggest that the measure is reliable.

Test–retest reliability occurs when the same group of respondents takes the same test on two distinct occasions. A correlation calculation is made between the scores on those distinct occasions and this is treated as an assessment of the extent of the reliability of the test. That is, the stronger the correlation, the greater the reliability of the test.

There are other measures such as observational assessments where the only forms of reliability measurements are the *inter*-rater reliability between independent assessors and the *intra*-rater reliability within the same individual across cases/time. These are typically assessed through calculating **kappa** or **intraclass correlations**.

Validity

Validity is an assessment of the extent to which a test measures that which it claims to measure. There are a number of different forms of validity. Important forms include: face validity, content validity, predictive (criterion and concurrent) validity, convergent and divergent/discriminant validity, and construct validity.

Face validity is the most basic form of validity 'test' and refers to the everyday acceptability of items of the test. Candidates need to be convinced that tests do, at a minimum, appear to have relevance to the purpose for which they are adopted. Test designers need to be aware of the confidence that clients may or may not have in the tests being used, if they wish to encourage attention and effort in their completion.

Content validity is also one of the more basic validity tests, and refers to the extent to which a test adequately reflects the purposes for which it is employed. We would, for example, wish a careers interest test to consist of items that explore client interests which have a bearing upon potential career choice. Content validity is also sometimes referred to as criterion validity, as it uses relevant (external) criteria as its means for measurement.

Convergent validity refers to the extent to which the scores on a test correlate with scores on other variables with which theory suggests they should correlate. Divergent validity refers to the extent to which scores on a test *do not* correlate with scores on other variables, with which theory suggests they should not.

Predictive validity refers to the test's ability to predict the outcome on external criteria (e.g. a separate measure) and is also referred to as criterion validity. This may involve examining the correlation between an individual's test score on a future result or outcome (e.g. an exam result), or the correlation between an individual's test score and scores on a measure gathered at the same point in time. For example, in occupational recruitment an individual's scores may be compared to the scores of individuals who are already employed by an organisation to see how they relate to each other. This latter form of predictive validity is referred to as *concurrent* validity.

The use of the term *'construct'* in construct validity refers to a latent, hypothetical variable which cannot be directly observed. It is therefore one of the most complex forms of validity. An example of a 'construct' is intelligence because it cannot be observed separately but must be inferred from some notion of what constitutes high intelligence and low intelligence. The test designer is therefore required to specify in advance what indicator would be employed to distinguish high from low intelligence. In the case of a complex variable such as intelligence, several such indicators are more likely to be employed. The example of intelligence is a very illuminating one because there are many variations of view and controversies concerned with whether it is a single construction or a multiple formulation. The single personality trait conscientiousness is a single trait construction and also cannot be directly measured. Conscientiousness is also inferred from the formulation of high and low poles of indicators. If a mixed group of employees have been assessed on independent work-based tasks as high and low in conscientiousness and this outcome corresponds with the high and low test measures then the subsequently produced test can be considered a valid construct. Construct validity typically subsumes all the forms of validity outlined previously (Larsen & Buss, 2010).

Further reading

Topic	Key reading
Discussion of reliability and validity	Chapters 4, 12 and 17 in Cooper, C. (2002). *Individual differences* (2nd edn). London: Hodder Arnold.

Test your knowledge

1 How would you distinguish reliability from validity?
2 Distinguish content validity, construct validity and predictive validity from each other.

Administration, scoring and interpretation

Environmental conditions and administrative arrangements are a potential source of error in accurately representing a client's scores. Disturbances or discomfort in the conditions can distort performance. The absence of well-organised and smooth-running arrangements can induce tension and anxiety and thereby affect performance. Lack of seriousness by the administrator may affect motivation.

There are also a number of person factors which impinge upon the level of a client's performance. Whilst discomfort can be minimised, the person's dispositional anxiety in such surroundings is unavoidably a feature of the way they perform. An individual's current emotional preoccupations or the level of their previous night's sleep, for example, are unavoidably incorporated in the test scores. The number of 'distorting' factors that do occur during administration can, however, be reduced. Are candidates clear about what to do should they make an error in recording their response? Do they know what to do in the event of missing a question as a result of carelessness? The professionalism, projected confidence and ease of approach of the administrator help establish an appropriate environment for the best performance of candidates.

Scoring and interpretation

The type of scoring reflects the design of the type of each test. Each of the tests noted earlier in the chapter will have an accompanying form in which data should be collected. Self-report questionnaires often employ an 'agree, neutral or disagree' decision. Other rating scales may employ a Likert-type rating (e.g. 1–7, with 1 being strongly disagree and 7 being strongly agree). Both manual scores and computer administrative systems are employed in many test manuals and most tests will come with scoring templates which aim to ease the collation of data.

In the visual or pictorial comparison style of decision-making, a simple count of similarity or dissimilarity will be the method of scoring.

Behavioural measures typically have a categorical agree–disagree count. Raw scores on such tests may not be the appropriate means for comparison and norm tables are typically adopted in such situations. Norms are required when a comparison of one individual with another individual or a group is sought (see the critical focus box on p. 228). Norms are produced for a population group and are often presented in norm tables to enable the individual's score to be set against a standard or an appropriate context for evaluative purposes. A score of 40 has little interpretative meaning unless we know how this compares with a comparator group. The group from which the individual is drawn could have a mean of 50, with a maximum and minimum of 60 and 35 respectively. This would make the individual's score look quite different to the situation where the maximum and minimum was 42 and 20 respectively, with a mean of 38. The **standard deviation** of the data is an important component of the production of normative information.

CRITICAL FOCUS

The concept of standardisation

The term 'standardisation' typically refers to two concepts in psychometrics:

1 Standardising scores on a test, so that a group of scores is transformed to having a mean value of 0, allowing individual scores to be located in terms of where they lie in relation to this. This is a little like locating cities in terms of where they fall in relation to the equator on a globe (e.g. above/below and by how much). This process 'removes' the original units of measurement from the picture and makes directly comparable those variables which had previously been measured in different ways.

2 Standardising test procedures to try to ensure that all individuals have the same experience (e.g. same instructions, delivered in the same way, under the same conditions and in the same environment). If this is achieved, any variation in scores could potentially be attributed to genuine Individual Differences.

Once raw or standardised scores have been determined, it is possible to consider their interpretation. To make the appropriate interpretation, the scores obtained are referenced to that which was measured, e.g. a spatial ability test score has meaning only in reference to the visual; a career interest score can only be referenced to career preferences. More complex constructs such as intelligence and personality produce multiple scores and in such instances interpretation reports are compiled using a *profile* of results. Specific information is considered alongside other specific information, introversion being seen alongside conscientiousness and anxiety, for example. Personality trait interpretation is typically based upon a personality profile as demonstrated in Figure 10.3.

Practical application of theory **Profile used for intepreting reports**

The interpretative report will note the correspondence of extraversion (low) and conscientiousness (high) for the candidate's profile. Similarly, there may be comment on low correspondence of anxiety with high agreeableness. The contrast between high conscientiousness and low openness to experience will be noted, for example, as an interpretative feature for a narrative report.

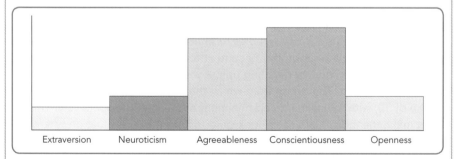

Figure 10.3 **Five factor personality profile – basis for a narrative report**

Similarly the Weschler intelligence test will be used to examine how an individual will use their abilities in perceptual organisation and verbal comprehension based on the interaction of the subtests.

Further reading

Topic	Key reading
Test design	Rust, J. & Golombok, S. (2009) *Modern psychometrics: The science of psychological assessment* (3rd edn). London: Routledge.

Test your knowledge

1   What are the implications of an absence of standardised arrangements for the organisation and administration of tests?
2   In what circumstances is it necessary to use standardised scores rather than raw scores in test results?

Ethical considerations

Ethical matters require attention at several stages of test design and use. These commence prior to test construction and continue during administration and scoring, and in interpretation and application. The issues of ethical concern and examples of good practice will be found in the test providers' guidance notes and manuals, as well as those provided by independent or professional bodies (such as the BPS). The legal system has also contributed to expectations through data protection and discriminatory legislation. Some of these concerns mirror those found in other social and medical areas of practice and some are more centred in psychometrics.

Ethical concerns encompass a wide range of issues. There are concerns that arise from the profession; those of the respondents themselves; and those of other public bodies. There are also a number of matters that can be considered ethical in that a breach devalues the application or interpretation of findings, i.e. poorly administered instructions lead to invalid application of results and breach of copyright law may mean that tests are used by unqualified people in inappropriate ways.

Prior to the beginning of the test, the administrator needs to ensure accuracy in the recording of all details for the candidate, i.e. relevant biographic information and the administrative matching of test results to candidates. This may involve anonymity.

During the testing session, assurances about the standardisation and commonality of environmental experience will be sought and distracting factors will be minimised. Respondents need to be given full information on the purpose and nature of the tests and details of the arrangements prior to attendance at the sessions. Candidates arriving with anxiety about any of these matters may have their performance affected. Candidates also need to be assured about what happens upon completion of the tests, i.e. if and how the data is to be stored; the form in which it will be stored; the duration of storage; the confidentiality of the data; the uses to which it will be put; and the form that feedback to them will take.

The testing environment should ensure consistency between candidates to ensure reliability of findings, both for single subject testing and for group tests. Efforts should be made to recreate a natural environment by avoiding contrived formality and through the creation of rapport by the test administrator. This includes assurances about the test duration and such matters as whether all questions require a response.

An important task of the test administrator is to promote the candidate's attention to the test and adherence to instructions for efficient and accurate completion. The administrator should note variations to normal standardised routines for possible allowance in any post-test analysis. A particular challenge arises where candidates ask questions, the responses to which could have implications for altering the standard conditions for other test takers on different occasions.

Table 10.1 provides a summary of a number of wide-ranging ethical matters.

Table 10.1 **Selected areas of ethical concern**

- Confidentiality, e.g. recording and storage, minimum intrusion, dissemination.
- Relationships: participation and informed consent.
- Role, function and participation in ethical committees; ethical approval; organisational arrangements; resolution of conflict.
- Organisational and administrative arrangements prior to testing.
- Design and construction of tests.
- Standards and conduct of sessions during testing.
- Scoring, interpretation and feedback.

Test your knowledge

1   Why are standardised arrangements an important feature in the conduct of tests?

2   What factors in the candidate's state of mind may affect test performance?

Further reading

Topic	Key reading
Ethical decision-making and conduct	BPS (2010). *Code of human research ethics*. Leicester: BPS

Test applications

Tests have application to a wide range of activities, not just single application of a variable to a discrete action, experience or behavioural outcome. Clearly intelligence, personality and interest tests will be employed where information about those measures of the person is required. All Individual Difference measurements can, however, be employed in multiple ways: tests can be employed in other areas of life. For example, motivation is important for sports performance – but so is personality through the manner in which athletes respond to pressure. Interest preferences are important for career decision-making, but so is the range of aptitudes that direct orientation. Personality additionally affects the confidence to pursue such options. So whilst test measures are used for single measurement of discrete activities, Individual Difference test measures have mutually interactive effects.

Points to consider: psychometric testing

- The information from psychometric tests can be associated with stigma and prejudice. For example, having a personality disorder diagnosis can result in an individual being excluded from therapeutic interventions in prison (Bell et al., 2003).

- The results of psychometric tests are used to make important decisions, such as for career, education or therapeutic purposes. They can therefore have serious implications for people's lives. If decisions are made upon the basis of tests which are flawed or inappropriately administered or interpreted, this is unethical and misleading. For example, in occupational testing this could lead to the best individuals for the job not being recruited.

- There is a concern over whether psychometric tests measure the constructs we define, or whether the constructs of interest to us are merely products of the tests we create (tautology).

- Can psychometric tests capture the totality of human experience?

- Psychometric tests do not merely assume that we can measure hypothetical constructs from behaviour (the accessibility debate); they assume that *self-report* measures can be used in place of the observation of behaviour.

Figure 10.4 is a diagram to help with your revision.

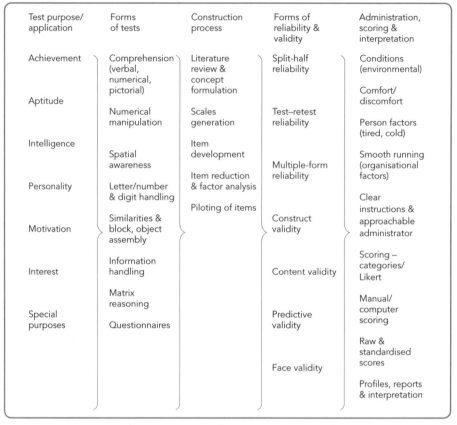

Figure 10.4 Overview of concepts in psychometrics revision aide

Chapter summary: putting it all together

→ Can you tick all the points from the revision checklist at the beginning of this chapter?

→ Attempt the sample question from the beginning of this chapter using the answer guidelines below.

→ Go to the companion website at www.pearsoned.co.uk/psychologyexpress to access more revision support online, including interactive quizzes, sample questions with answer guidelines, 'you be the marker' exercises, flashcards and podcasts you can download.

Answer guidelines

Guidelines on answering the sample question presented at the start of the chapter are given below.

Sample question   *Problem-based learning*

You are required to design an interest inventory that is to be used to determine the career preferences of a group of undergraduate students. Identify and outline the stages you would adopt for the production of such a questionnaire.

Approaching the question

The question is expecting you to show your appreciation of the stages of compilation of the inventory and your understanding of details and some of the complexities involved in the practical construction. Note that the question did not require you to present a completed questionnaire with accompanying research.

Important points to include

Figure 10.2 provided the framework for your response to this problem and also presented a number of challenging questions. The questions guide you to appropriate areas for elaboration. The task is to adapt the steps in a general framework for test construction to the specific context of a career inventory (questionnaire).

The first stage of this process is the identification of relevant content, i.e. the scales that capture career interest. You would need to determine the key dimensions of career preferences. The sources of information for this will usually involve a review of relevant literature and could be supplemented by exploratory interviews. These could include individual self-awareness; job and career opportunity information; clients' decision-making capacity; and the necessary skills to conduct that analysis.

For each of the above scales and any additional ones you have derived, it is necessarily to generate distinct items that measure those scales, both individually and collectively. Self-awareness, for example, can be made up of items reflecting general interests; awareness about your own abilities and capacity; awareness about those things which may or may not be important over a longer period of time; and what motivates you on a daily basis. Each of those items is illustrative of what can be listed and formed into questions. Figure 10.2 alerts you to the need to ensure relevance; the avoidance overlap; and provision of sufficient balance of generality and specificity. Good item and question generation is an acquired skill that comes with practice. You should not be concerned about the several drafts and redrafts you may have to make. This exercise would be repeated for each of the proposed scales of self-awareness; opportunity information; and decision-making skills and any other scales introduced. In a more sophisticated questionnaire than this trial, factor analysis on a large sample would be employed to reduce the number of items and seek out overlapping areas. For the purposes of this trial, inventory refinement through piloting is deemed appropriate. Once a manageable number of items have been developed they need to be presented in questionnaire format. Further refinement will be gained by seeking responses from those who match the test-takers. Improvements to the wording for clarity and understanding can therefore be made.

The outcome of a typical questionnaire of this sort would have four or five scales, each having four or five items. Such a design balances manageable size with adequacy in the breadth of coverage. You will need to identify what you consider to be the appropriate environment for taking the test and whether this is done individually or in groups. You need to specify how each of the questionnaire items should be scored and combined, and how this information could be interpreted. Finally, you should specify the ethical issues that you believe the administrator should take into account.

Although this particular question did not ask you to provide a guide for test administrators, in your list of steps for development this could be included along with notes on appropriate content.

Make your answer stand out

Your answer to this problem question comes in the form of a number of steps that should be taken to design a questionnaire, along with an elaboration of those associated themes. To make your answer stand out, you need to ensure that you have elaborated sufficiently on the number of themes associated with each step. This is your opportunity to show that you have a good understanding of the underlying issues and have advanced beyond just following the pure mechanics of the process. A neat and concise solution to demonstrate this would be the provision of an administrator's guide that systematically addresses the issues.

Notes

Applications of personality and individual differences

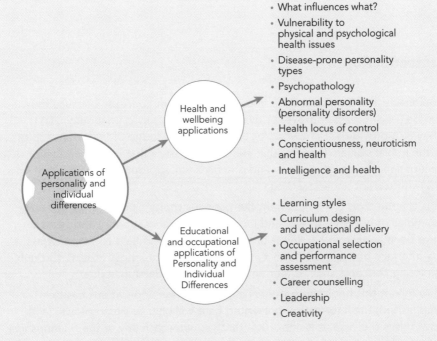

- What influences what?
- Vulnerability to physical and psychological health issues
- Disease-prone personality types
- Psychopathology
- Abnormal personality (personality disorders)
- Health locus of control
- Conscientiousness, neuroticism and health
- Intelligence and health

Health and wellbeing applications

Applications of personality and individual differences

Educational and occupational applications of Personality and Individual Differences

- Learning styles
- Curriculum design and educational delivery
- Occupational selection and performance assessment
- Career counselling
- Leadership
- Creativity

A printable version of this topic map is available from:
www.pearsoned.co.uk/psychologyexpress

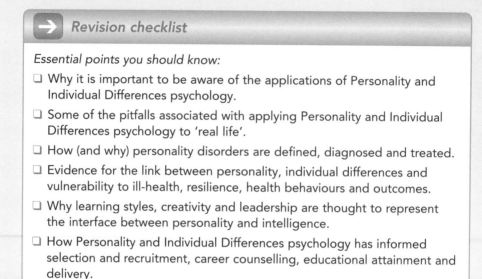

→ **Revision checklist**

Essential points you should know:

❑ Why it is important to be aware of the applications of Personality and Individual Differences psychology.

❑ Some of the pitfalls associated with applying Personality and Individual Differences psychology to 'real life'.

❑ How (and why) personality disorders are defined, diagnosed and treated.

❑ Evidence for the link between personality, individual differences and vulnerability to ill-health, resilience, health behaviours and outcomes.

❑ Why learning styles, creativity and leadership are thought to represent the interface between personality and intelligence.

❑ How Personality and Individual Differences psychology has informed selection and recruitment, career counselling, educational attainment and delivery.

Introduction

Personality and Individual Differences are important concepts because they can be used to help improve, or even save, people's lives (Mahoney, 2011). They also provide a framework for improving knowledge of important topics in the public domain (and popular culture), to ensure that health, educational, occupational and legal policies and practices are appropriate and brought into line with current understanding.

This chapter aims to complement the previous topics examined, by providing examples of how Personality and Individual Differences theory and research have been applied in a number of contexts. It will also help to demonstrate the interface between personality and intelligence (amongst others), through exploring concepts such as **learning styles** and **leadership styles**.

Throughout this book the potential impact of these applications has been emphasised; the information presented here will help to illustrate why (and how) this is the case. It is important that you approach any of the relationships identified between personality, individual differences and health, educational, occupational or forensic factors with a critical eye; you need to consider whether there are other possible explanations for the relationships and whether the theory and research upon which the application is based are reliable and valid. Also think about what the implications of suggesting these relationships are: for example, what positive and negative outcomes might there be for suggesting (and evidencing) the concept of a **disease-prone personality type** or diagnosing someone as having a **personality disorder**?

The number and type of applications are too vast to examine in their entirety, so we will focus on two overarching themes that have generated enormous amounts of interest: health and wellbeing, and educational and occupational applications. However, you should also keep in mind the applications you have encountered in previous chapters, such as the clinical and counselling approaches developed from the work of Freud, Rogers and Ellis (amongst others).

If you are interested in exploring other applied areas, personality and intelligence have been considered by Kanfer et al. (1995) in relation to industrial and organisational psychology; by Braden (1995) in educational psychology; by Balin and Hirschi (2010) in relation to career counselling; by Baxter, Motiuk and Fortin (1995) in relation to criminal behaviour; and by Tenenbaum and Bar-Eli (2007) in relations to sports psychology.

Assessment advice

Assessments in this area will typically ask you to either explore the implications of Personality and Individual Differences psychology on a particular applied area (such as health programmes) or will ask you to explore applications of theory and research as a means of highlighting important issues in the field. For this reason it is important that you demonstrate a critical appreciation of the topics discussed here. These topics also provide you with a means of identifying where future efforts in the field should be directed (i.e. under-researched areas).

Remember that a strong assignment is one that is able to integrate issues in theory, research practice and applications, so this chapter will provide you with a number of ideas about how to do this for assessments on a number of Individual Differences topics.

Psychological applications are successful only when they are able to address individual variations. General theories in cognitive, developmental, social and biological spheres frequently provide explanations of commonalities, but do not necessarily apply equally to all individuals. Wherever appropriate in your assessment, you need to highlight these issues, as this reinforces the uniqueness of the Individual Differences approach and the value it adds to psychology as a whole.

Sample question

Could you answer the question below? It is a typical essay question that could arise on this topic. Guidelines on answering the question are included at the end of this chapter, whilst a sample problem question and guidance on tackling it can be found on the companion website at www.pearsoned.co.uk/psychologyexpress.

Sample question — *Essay*

Critically examine how Personality and Individual Differences psychology can be applied to help understand career choice and success. Provide examples from relevant theories and research to support your discussion.

Health and wellbeing applications

The domain of health clearly demonstrates the impact of Personality and Individual Differences psychology. For example, many psychologists have sought to identify relationships between individual differences and health because they provide a potential explanation for differences in:

- vulnerability to illness;
- risky behaviour/health protective behaviours;
- health outcomes and
- experience of illness.

Findings from research into these issues can be used to inform interventions to improve:

- longevity;
- survival and
- quality of life.

What influences what?

In response to this question a number of models have been proposed to understand the relationships between individual differences and health, including:

- **Somatogenic models**: these suggest that physical factors cause (or influence) psychological differences (Shontz, 1975).
- **Psychogenic models**: these suggest that individual differences cause (or influence) physical factors (Alexander, 1939).
- **Biopsychosocial models** (Engel, 1977): these suggest that *biological*, *psychological* and *social factors* interact to influence health.

CRITICAL FOCUS

Causality

In contemporary research the premise of the **circular causality** of individual differences and health is increasingly accepted.

Circular causality suggests that individual differences can influence the way in which physical factors are expressed, and physical factors can also influence the ways in which individual differences are expressed. For example, the experience of ill health (e.g. hypertension) may change people's typical patterns of thoughts, feelings and behaviour (e.g. the reaction to conflicts and frustration), but people's typical thoughts, feelings and behaviour (e.g. typically suppressing anger and hostility) may influence the risk of experiencing ill health (e.g. hypertension) in the first place (Shontz, 1975; Jorgensen et al., 1996).

Vulnerability to physical and psychological health issues

To further explain why some people appear to be *more likely* to experience ill health than others, theorists have proposed **diathesis-stress** or **vulnerability-stress** models (Monroe & Simons, 1991; Ingram & Loxton, 2005). These models propose that **pre-morbid characteristics** influence how a person will react to stressful stimuli, which in turn influences whether an individual will develop a health issue or not. This may explain why not all individuals develop health issues following exposure to **stress**: some people are simply *predisposed* to physical ill health or **psychopathology**.

Pre-morbid characteristics come in many forms, including personality. Three key mechanisms by which *personality* may influence health outcomes (Caspi, Roberts & Shiner, 2005; Contrada, Cather & O'Leary, 1999) are as follows:

1 Certain traits are intrinsically associated with psychological processes that put an individual at greater or lesser risk of developing negative health outcomes.

2 Certain traits may be more associated with the adoption of risky behaviours, which in turn may put individuals at greater risk of negative health outcomes.

3 Certain traits may be associated with adaptive or maladaptive reactions to health problems, which in turn may put an individual at greater or lesser risk of developing negative health outcomes.

Some researchers have extended this thinking to see if specific *types* of personality exist that make people more vulnerable to physical (and psychological) health problems.

Disease-prone personality types

Theory and research in this area has tended to view personality as a *causal* factor in the development of illness, although more recently correlational links and interactions with other variables have been explored. Individuals who are identified as being at greater risk of developing illness have been said to have 'disease-prone personalities' (Alexander, 1950).

Type A personality (Friedman & Rosenman, 1957, 1959)

- This characterises people who are extremely competitive, strive excessively for achievement or recognition, repress aggression and frequently experience feelings of frustration and restlessness (Jenkins, Rosenham & Friedman, 1968).

- It is proposed as an explanation for why there were increases in cases of cardiovascular disease, which could not be explained in terms of other known risk factors.

Type B personality (Friedman & Rosenman, 1957, 1959)

- This characterises people who exhibit the 'opposite' features of Type A (e.g. being relaxed and laid-back) and who are less likely to develop cardiovascular disease.

Type C personality

- This personality type is believed to put people at risk of developing cancer.
- Research initially focused on individuals high on extraversion and low on neuroticism (Amelang, 1997), but research now indicates that the relationship is more complex (e.g. Hansen et al., 2005).

Type D (Distressed) personality (Denollet, 2005)

- This characterises people who exhibit high levels of negative affect and social inhibition.
- It has been found to relate to poor disease progress, poor quality of life and poor health outcomes (i.e. **clinical outcomes** and **patient-centred outcomes**).

KEY STUDY

Review of Type A personality evidence

Lachar (1993) published a seminal review examining the evidence for and against Type A personality and its relationship to elevated risk of developing cardiovascular disease (CVD). His paper suggested that:

- Five main research methodologies are adopted to explore this issue, providing varying degrees of evidential support:
  - epidemiological and longitudinal population studies of healthy people;
  - studies which seek to explore specific characteristics of the Type A personality and health outcomes;
  - studies which examine individuals at high risk of developing CVD;
  - research looking at the similar health issue referred to as 'coronary artery disease'.
- Research produced conflicting findings, with epidemiological and longitudinal population studies providing evidential support for the power of Type A personality to predict the onset of CVD (e.g. Rosenman et al., 1975), but research examining high-risk CVD individuals often finding no relationship with Type A personality (e.g. Shekelle et al., 1985).
- The different methodological strategies adopted by researchers may therefore in part influence whether the relationship Type A personality and CVD is identified.

Points to consider

- Identifying disease-prone personalities could help pinpoint individuals who are at risk of developing particular diseases.

- It could be used to develop interventions to improve survival, longevity and quality of life for individuals who develop diseases and to design interventions to reduce vulnerability to ill-health. However, exactly *how* it could be used to improve health outcomes is less clear.
- There has been a great deal of controversy over these personality types, for example:
  - What might the impact of being labelled with a disease-prone personality be on people (e.g. stigma, perceptions of risk and feelings of helplessness/hopelessness)?
  - What might the impact of knowing whether an individual is diagnosed with a disease in the first place (e.g. cancer) be on whether the characteristics of a disease-prone personality (e.g. Type C personality) are identified as being present or not (Amelang, 1997)?

CRITICAL FOCUS

The 'hardy' personality

In recent years greater emphasis has been placed on identifying protective factors (characteristics which mitigate or reduce risk) against developing illness.

One suggestion is that certain personality factors may protect against the development or progression of disease. Based on this premise, Kobasa (1979) proposed the positive psychological concept of the 'hardy personality' to describe a person's relationship with other people, their own goals and the challenges they face (Kobasa-Ouellette & Di Placido, 2001).

A hardy personality is defined by three variables:

1 engagement with life (commitment);

2 perceptions of your own influence over the events in your life (control); and

3 the way you approach change (challenge).

Individuals with a hardy personality are more resilient to stressful events (Kobasa-Ouellette & Di Placido, 2001) owing to a more optimistic perception of events (Allred & Smith, 1989) and the types of coping mechanism adopted (Westman, 1990).

Coping styles, which are suggested to be particularly protective against the effects of stress (and consequently the development of physical illness or mental health issues such as **burnout**) involve either changing the stressful event (e.g. to reduce or remove its impact) or changing the way you think and feel about the event (e.g. introducing more positive attributions).

Hardiness in relation to physical illness could involve either taking steps to improve the likelihood of a positive health outcome (e.g. increasing healthy lifestyle habits or adhering to medical advice) or changing the way you feel about an illness you are suffering from (e.g. finding a way to make sense of an illness in a way which improves your quality of life).

The shift in focus from exploring disease-prone personalities to resilient personalities reflects a general shift in definitions of 'health' (i.e. health as 'wellbeing' rather than the absence of disease).

Further reading

Topic	Key reading
Links between Type D personality, depression and heart failure	Schiffera, A., Pedersen, S., Widdershoven, J., Hendriks, E., Winter, J. & Denollet, J. (2005). The distressed (Type D) personality is independently associated with impaired health status and increased depressive symptoms in chronic heart failure, *European Journal of Preventative Cardiology,12(4)*, 341–6.

Test your knowledge

1 In what ways might individual differences be related to health?

2 What is the premise of a diathesis-stress model?

3 Why might researching disease-prone personalities be difficult?

 Sample question   **Essay**

Critically compare and evaluate the notions of disease-prone and resilient personality types: which do you feel has more applied value and why?

Psychopathology

The term 'psychopathology' is usually taken to refer to disturbances of emotion, mood, thinking and behaviour which can cause great distress. For example, **depression, schizophrenia** and abnormal personality (i.e. **personality disorders**) are considered to be forms of psychopathology.

Examining the entire range of research into the relationship between personality, individual differences and psychopathology is beyond the scope of this revision guide. We will instead examine abnormal personality in some detail because it provides a useful illustration of many of the key issues on this topic. For information on other forms of psychopathology see the further reading box.

Further reading

Topic	Key reading
An approach to investigating individual differences in psychopathology	Bijttebier, P., Beck, I., Claes, L. & Vandereycken, W. (2009). Gray's reinforcement sensitivity theory as a framework for research on personality–psychopathology associations, *Clinical Psychology Review, 29(5)*, 421–30.
The formation of individual differences in stress responsiveness (linked to psychopathology)	Claessens, S., Daskalakis, N., van der Veen, R., Oitzl, M., de Kloet, E. & Champagne, D. (2011). Development of individual differences in stress responsiveness: an overview of factors mediating the outcome of early life experiences, *Psychopharmacology, 214(1)*, 141–54.

Abnormal personality (personality disorders)

Personality disorders represent severe disturbances across the life-course in an individual's patterns of cognition, affect and behaviour (Paris, 2003), and are often viewed as extreme expressions of 'normal' personality dispositions which are maladaptive. These disturbances can cause great distress for the individual and the people with whom they interact.

According to Zimmerman and Coryell (1989), between 10 and 15% of the population have personality disorders.

Diagnosing personality disorders

Diagnosis of a personality disorder is usually based on the classification system outlined in the *Diagnostic and statistical manual of mental disorders* (DSM-IV-R, American Psychiatric Association, 2000), under the Axis II category. However, the International Classification of Diseases (ICD-10; World Health Organisation, 2011) is also used.

Points to consider: diagnosing personality disorders

- Some individuals exhibit severe personality problems, but do not meet the criteria proposed in the DSM-IV-R: this phenomenon is referred to as 'Personality Disorder Not Otherwise Specified' (PDNOS).

- Many individuals receive more than one personality disorder diagnosis (co-morbidity). For example, antisocial, narcissistic and paranoid personality disorders frequently co-occur (Haslam, 2007).

The determinants of personality disorder

In recent years, research efforts have tended to focus on whether the Five Factor Model of personality is able to describe and explain personality disorders.

Research suggests that personality disorders have a sizeable genetic basis: Torgersen et al. (2000) estimated the heritability of different personality disorders by comparing 92 pairs of monozygotic and 129 pairs of dizygotic twins to a baseline sample of 2000 individuals.

Early life experiences may be important in the development of personality disorders: parental neglect and abuse have been linked to antisocial, avoidant, borderline and schizotypal personality disorders (Cohen et al., 2006; Rettew et al., 2003; Zanarini & Frankenberg, 1997; Anglina, Cohenab & Chena, 2008).

Several biological and neurophysiological factors have been proposed to explain personality disorders. For example, Siever and Davis (1991) suggest that *neurotransmitters* may be involved.

Sex differences in the prevalence of personality disorders have been identified; Morey, Alexander & Boggs (2005) found higher prevalence rates for men in six of the ten DSM personality disorders compared to women. However, prevalence rates for borderline personality disorder were found to be higher for women.

There is a great debate about whether these sex differences represent real or arbitrary differences arising from research bias, or **criterion bias** in diagnostic tools (Morey, Alexander & Boggs, 2005).

Points to consider: personality disorder

- Personality disorders (and other mental, development and learning disorders) are ever-changing concepts, as evidenced by the number of editions of the DSM and ICD (the DSM-V is due to be published in 2012).
- Do personality disorders really exist, or are they arbitrary labels?
- The **continuity hypothesis**: Many theorists conceptualise personality disorder in terms of extremes on a dimension of characteristics (i.e. running from normal to abnormal), yet the current tools used to diagnose them provide *categorical* classifications.
- Personality disorder classification systems rely on unstructured interviews (Westen, 1997), leading many to call for the development of *psychometric inventories*, for parity with the way other forms of mental, developmental and learning disorder are diagnosed (Widiger & Samuel, 2005).
- Garb (1997) found that clinicians were more likely to diagnose antisocial personality disorder in men than women, and were more likely to diagnose histrionic personality disorder in women than men, even when the symptoms were identical. What does this suggest about sex differences in personality disorder?

Further reading

Topic	Key reading
Correlates of the Five Factor Model of personality and personality disorders	Saulsman, L. & Page, A. (2004). The five-factor model and personality disorder empirical literature: A meta-analytic review, *Clinical Psychology Review, 23(8)*, 1055–85.

Test your knowledge

1 What does the 'continuity hypothesis' suggest about the currently most commonly used methods of personality diagnosis?

2 How could the stigma associated with a diagnosis of personality disorder be mitigated?

3 Some researchers have identified links between personality disorders and criminal behaviour (e.g. Perkins & Bishopp, 2003) – why do you think this might be?

Health locus of control

Rotter's (1966, 1982) concept of *locus of control* has been tailored to the field of health (health locus of control; Wallston & Wallston, 1982) and has been used to explore differences in vulnerability to ill-health, disease progression, health behaviours and outcomes.

Studies typically focus on differences between individuals with 'internal' (where an individual feels they have control over their health and health outcomes) versus 'external' health locus of control (where an individual feels they have no control over their health or health outcomes). The suggestion is that if one type of locus of control appears more beneficial to the quality of life and health outcomes of people who are ill, then interventions can be developed to help promote this type of locus of control. However, the results of research have been mixed. To explain this, theorists have suggested that an internal locus of control is only adaptive when individuals can *actually* exert control over their situation. If this is not the case, an internal locus of control may actually have a detrimental impact on quality of life and wellbeing (Christensen et al., 1991).

People with an internal health locus of control have been associated with exercising more (Norman et al., 1997) and better diet (Steptoe & Wardle, 2001). External locus of control has been associated with delayed help-seeking behaviours (O'Carroll et al., 2001). However, external locus of control has also been associated with greater adherence to medication routines (Evans et al., 2000) and compliance to dietary regimes for terminally ill individuals with renal disease (Schneider, 1992). These contradictions may reflect the debate highlighted above regarding degree of control over health outcomes.

Practical application of theory **Locus of control, self-efficacy and smoking cessation**

Stuart, Borland & McMurray (1994) explored whether the success of a group-facilitated smoking cessation programme could be predicted by people's health locus of control and level of self-efficacy. The results indicated that both variables predicted whether an individual would attempt to quit smoking, and whether they had been able to remain abstinent for at least one day at the end of the treatment. However, only self-efficacy predicts whether an individual would still be abstinent six months after they finished the cessation programme. Interestingly the authors found that 'high self-efficacy is inversely related to making attempts to quit, but positively related to the success of attempts' (Stuart, Borland & McMurray, 1994, p. 1).

The relationship between health locus of control and 'success' was more difficult to conceptualise. However, it would seem reasonable to suggest that an individual with an internal locus of control would be more likely to view themselves as having control over quitting and may therefore be more likely to attempt to quit smoking in the first place.

The results of this research suggest that improving an individual's self-efficacy could provide a means of increasing the effectiveness of smoking cessation behaviours and is therefore of important applied value.

Conscientiousness, neuroticism and health

Research suggests that personality variables, particularly conscientiousness and neuroticism, correlate with longevity and survival; typically, higher scores on conscientiousness are positively associated with longevity (Kern & Friedman,

2008), whereas higher scores on neuroticism are associated with greater risk of worse physical health and poorer wellbeing for both men and women, and increased mortality risk for women (Friedman, Kern & Reynolds, 2010).

Intelligence and health

In relation to intelligence, Gottfredson (2004) found that 'g' was positively correlated with longevity and negatively correlated with infant mortality. In addition, Gottfredson (2004) found that 'g' was positively correlated with a number of health protective behaviours, including:

- physical fitness (e.g. exercise);
- low-sugar diet and
- low-fat diet

and negatively correlated with:

- smoking and
- obesity.

Other researchers have suggested that intelligence is able to predict health outcomes above and beyond other variables, such as socioeconomic status (Hart et al., 2003). For example, higher IQ has been associated with increased likelihood of survival (Deary, Whalley & Star, 2003), whereas lower IQ has been associated with:

- increased risk of cancer (Deary, Whalley, & Starr, 2003);
- increased risk of lung cancer-related death (Hart et al., 2003);
- increased risk of cardiovascular and coronary heart disease (Hart et al., 2003) and
- increased risk of heart-disease related death (Hart et al., 2003).

Further reading

Topic	Key reading
Review of the links between personality and longevity	Chapman, B., Roberts, B. & Duberstein, P. (2011). Personality and longevity: Knowns, unknowns, and implications for public health and personalized medicine, *Journal of Aging Research*, 1–24.
Personality, intelligence, illness and mortality	Deary, I., Weiss, A. & Batt, D. (2010). Intelligence and personality as predictors of illness and death: How researchers in differential psychology and chronic disease epidemiology are collaborating to understand and address health inequalities, *Psychological Science in the Public Interest, 11(2)*, 53–79.
Exploration of individual characteristics and quality of life within a positive psychology framework	Keyes, C., Fredrickson, B. & Park, N. (2012). Positive psychology and the quality of life. In K. Land, A. Michalos & M. Sirgy (eds), *Handbook of social indicators and quality of life research* (pp. 99–112). London: Springer.
Investigation of personality, coping, health locus of control and emotional intelligence (EI) links with health behaviours	Saklofske, D., Austin, E., Galloway, J. & Davidson, K. (2007). Individual difference correlates of health-related behaviours: Preliminary evidence for links between emotional intelligence and coping, *Personality and Individual Differences, 42(3)*, 491–502.

Educational and occupational applications of Personality and Individual Differences

A number of topics under the headings of educational and occupational applications represent an interface between personality and intelligence theory and research.

Intelligence (as measured by 'g') is the most robust and consistent predictor of academic performance. Although this might seem obvious, a number of issues have been raised in relation to the links between IQ and academic performance:

- A tautology debate (see Chapter 9 for further details) arises between the concept and assessment tools.
- It is not clear whether intelligence predicts all forms of assessment (e.g. exams versus coursework) equally. Chamorro-Premuzic and Furnham (2005, 2006) argue that performance on coursework-based assessments may be influenced more by personality characteristics than intelligence (e.g. motivation).
- Jensen (1980) argued that although IQ is a good predictor of academic performance at lower academic levels, it is less effective at predicting success at higher educational levels (e.g. degree level).

To address some of these issues, psychologists have sought to identify the relationship between educational performance and personality, using the Five Factor Model.

Two personality traits appear to play a key role in academic performance:

1   *Conscientiousness*: less conscientious individuals are less likely to perform well (Chamorro-Premuzic & Furnham, 2003a, 2003b, 2005).
2   *Neuroticism*: more neurotic individuals may experience greater amounts of subjective stress evoked by assessment procedures. This may have a detrimental effect on how an individual perceives a stressful situation (i.e. an assessment) and reacts to it (Lazarus & Folkman, 1984; Matthews, Derryberry & Siegle, 2000).

Learning styles

Interest in the study of individual differences in learning (the acquisition of knowledge and expertise) has been growing since the 1970s. It is an important area because if people learn in different ways, an educational curriculum (and its delivery) must be flexible enough to ensure all children (and adults) have equal opportunity to learn.

Kolb (1981) proposed the experiential learning theory (ELT), which suggests there are two key factors contributing to individual differences in learning:

1 **Learning processes:** there are four main mechanisms underpinning learning styles:
   - concrete experience/feeling – learning through involvement in new experiences;
   - reflective observation/watching – learning through thinking about our own experiences, or the experiences of other people;
   - abstract conceptualisation/thinking – learning through the creation of theories to explain our behaviour and observations and
   - active experimentation/doing – learning through using our theories to solve problems.
2 **Learning styles:** there are four types of learning style, which are characterised by the way we learn (i.e. preferences for the learning processes outlined above). These are best understood in diagrammatic form (see Figure 11.1).

	Active experimentation	Observation and reflection
Concrete experience	Accommodating (practical, 'hands-on' approach)	Diverging (thinking from different perspectives approach)
Abstract conceptualisation	Converging (practical problem-solving approach)	Assimilation (theoretical and logical problem-solving approach)

Figure 11.1 **Kolb's (1981) four learning styles**

Points to consider: Kolb's theories

- Kolb's theories are influenced by neo-Freudian, cognitive, humanistic and intelligence theories.
- Kolb recognises the active participation of the learner in the learning process (not just as a passive recipient of educational delivery).
- He does not refer to other important Individual Differences aspects of learning, such as motivation, goals and intentions.
- He does not provide a mechanism for assessing the actual extent of learning.

Kyllonen and Shute (1989) proposed a model of learning in which four dimensions combine to produce individual differences in learning: subject matter, learning environment, desired knowledge outcome and learner attributes. Learner attributes include such things as background experience and personality traits. This model recognises that all learners have their own unique characteristics, which will be better suited to certain learning environments and will therefore affect performance (Shute & Glaser, 1990).

Researchers have formulated several classification of learning styles, with varying degrees of evidential support (Table 11.1).

Table 11.1 **Classification of notable styles**

Style/dimensions	Meaning	Originating source
Levelling/sharpening	Sensitivity to detail and sharpen small differences	Klein (1954)
Constricted/flexible control	Ability to disregard a cue when presented with conflicting information	Klein (1953)
Scanning	Attempts at judgement verification	Gardner & Moriarty (1968)
Field dependence/ independence	Capacity to integrate or separate background/contextual features	Witkin (1964)
Reflection/impulsivity	Extent of review of range alternatives	Kagan (1966)
Cognitive complexity	Degree to which cognitive complexity addressed	Gardner & Schoen (1962)
Conceptual integration	Relating parts to other parts and to the whole	Harvey, Hunt & Schroder (1961)
Splitters/lumpers	Analytical or global interpretations	Cohen (1967)
Tolerance for experiences	Readiness for perceptual variance with reality	Klein, Gardner & Schlesinger (1962)
Convergent/divergent	Orientation to deduction or open-ended thinking	Guilford (1967)
Dynamic/literal	Preference for the dynamic and emotive rather than the static and literal	Klein (1970)
Compartmentalisation	Tendency to compartmentalise	Messick & Kogan (1963)
Verbaliser/visualiser	Orientation to verbal visual processing	Paivio (1971)
Serialist/holist	Tendency for incremental or global problem solving	Pask (1976)
Abstract/concrete	Tendency for the abstract rather than the concrete	Harvey, Hunt & Schroder (1961)
Activist/reflector	Concrete-abstract perception in contrast to activist-reflector processing.	Kolb (1976)

Source: Adapted from Grigorenko & Sternberg (1995); Riding & Raynor (1998); Miller (1987); Allinson & Hayes (1996).

As you can see, these classifications are based upon different aspects of individual differences in learning.

Points to consider

- The study of individual differences alerts us to the fact that one style of learning may not be effective for all individuals and for all types of learning material. Also, it appears reasonable to believe that learning chess strategies may encourage a different learning style from learning Origami.

- The relationship between individual styles and dispositional-based traits is not well established and this is because styles incorporate personal preferences.

- There is no guarantee that our *preferences* necessarily produce the most effective performance.

Further reading

Topic	Key reading
Learning styles	Kyllonen, P. & Shute, V. (1989). A taxonomy of learning skills. In P. Ackerman, R. Sternberg & R. Glaser (eds), *Learning and individual differences: Advances in theory and research* (pp. 117–63). New York: Freeman & Co.

Test your knowledge

1   In what ways are learning styles different from intelligence and personality traits?

2   Why is it important to investigate individual differences in learning style/cognitive orientation?

Curriculum design and educational delivery

Along with other professions in education, educational psychologists contribute to curriculum design and methods of delivery as well as 'clinical' work and assessments of individuals. This can either be for special needs assessment (e.g. dyslexia and development of study skills), or for behavioural purposes (e.g. challenging behaviour). Educational psychologists are also called upon as consultants for the evaluation of educational provision, in-service training and adolescent counselling.

Intelligence tests (amongst a range of other tests) are useful for understanding performance within education; general aptitude can be matched against actual scholastic performance to assess whether a pupil is performing at, above or below the expected level of achievement, and emotional disturbance can often be revealed by mismatches in expected performance.

Occupational selection and performance assessment

Individual Differences psychology can be applied to occupational psychology to predict and understand consequential outcomes. For example, it can help to understand and improve career success.

According to Ozer and Benet-Martinez (2006), career success arises from the balance between job satisfaction (intrinsic rewards) and associated benefits, such as performance, salary and status (extrinsic rewards). This balance is referred to as 'satisfactoriness' (Dawis & Lofquist, 1984).

Personality and aptitude measures have helped with the selection of suitable employees from amongst a number of applicants. This often requires a **job analysis** and matching the tasks typical of the job in question to those characteristics which are believed to predict good performance in the role.

Psychometric test information has also informed follow-up training for those recruited and offers further assurance in the decision-making process.

The overall objectives of aptitude and personality tests have been to improve person–job fit, although they have not replaced the need for interviews and real-life 'assessment centre' tests.

Consideration of individual differences within occupational psychology has also informed performance assessment and training programmes. The interface between the concepts of intellectual competence and personality introduces 'real world' assessment of the ways in which we perform.

KEY STUDY

Relationship of personality traits to performance

Mount, Barrick and Murray (1998) investigated the relationships of the 'Big Five' personality dimensions to three performance criteria (job proficiency, training proficiency and personnel data), for each of five occupational groups (professionals, police, managers, sales and skilled/semi-skilled groups). The results showed that one personality dimension, conscientiousness, had a relationship with all five occupational groups; extraversion was a predictor for two occupations, managers and sales staff. The relationship was found across all performance criteria. Openness to experience predicted the training proficiency criterion. This was across all occupations. The level of predictions for some occupations was proven but was not large.

Further reading

Topic	Key reading
Predictions of the Big Five's relationship to performance across occupations	Mount, M., Barrick, M. & Murray, R. (1998). Five reasons why the 'Big Five' article has been frequently cited, *Personnel Psychology*, *51*, 849–57.
Example of predicting 'career success'	Musson, D., Sandal, G. & Helmreich, R. (2004). Personality characteristics and trait clusters in final stage astronaut selection, *Aviation, Space, and Environmental Medicine, 75(4)*, 342–9.

Career counselling

In relation to career counselling there are a number of areas where individual differences inform decision-making especially well. Pre-counselling information involves assessing individual differences and the requirements of specific occupations. If performed appropriately, career counselling can help to expand the range of options being considered by a client, in order to maximise career success and satisfaction (Prediger & Johnson, 1979).

The process requires an individual to understand the requirements of a job and how their own personal qualities (which can be identified by different psychometric tests) relate to this.

Practical application of theory **Holland's RIASEC model**

Holland (1973) introduced what became a widely adopted scheme that accommodated person characteristics with those of the environment for careers decision-making. The measure of the person, which also corresponds to measures of the environment, has six poles forming an hexagonal model (see Figure 11.2). Those poles are listed as realistic (R), investigative (I), artistic (A), social (S), enterprising (E) and conventional (C). The distances between the poles in the model represent the correlations between the poles.

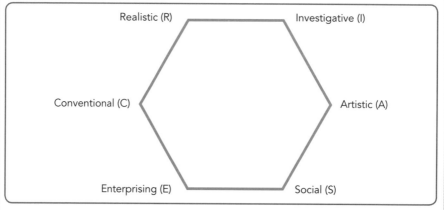

Figure 11.2 Diagrammatic representation of Holland's RIASEC model

---

KEY STUDY

Relationship of personality to Holland's types

Barrick, Mount and Gupta (2003) considered the relationship between two widely employed models for classifying individual differences – the 'Big Five' measure of personality and Holland's RIASEC model of occupational types. The researchers found meaningful relationships between some of the RIASEC types and personality traits. The strongest relationships were found between enterprising and artistic occupational types and the trait of extraversion and openness to experience. Three of the RIASEC types had correlations with at least one of the 'Big Five' traits. The findings showed that although the models were related, they were not substitutes for each other.

Points to consider

● Personality and aptitude measures in careers counselling are usually used in conjunction with Holland's (1973) model as personality measures act in addition to the preferential **interests** of Holland's model.

● Interests reflect the current levels of an individual's priority, whereas personality traits correspond to more stable and deeper levels of orientation. For example, conscientiousness may help determine the appropriateness of an individual to the sustained demands of some occupations, but an individual's interests may vary over time and exposure.

Further reading

Topic	Key reading
Holland's RIASEC model	Armstrong, P., Day, S., McVay, J. & Rounds, J. (2008) Holland's RIASEC model as an integrative framework for individual differences, *Journal of Counseling Psychology, 55(1),* 1–18.

✱ *Sample question*   *Problem-based learning*

You are presented with the task of giving an informed opinion to a student colleague on how to match her interests with those of a sales occupation for which she has received a job offer. Identify the interest types in the Holland model that could potentially help. Why do the personality traits in the 'Big Five' add to the understanding?

Leadership

The study of leadership focuses on identifying those individual differences (e.g. personality and intelligence) which are able to explain why some individuals emerge as effective leaders.

Defining leadership is not straightforward: when looking at famous historical leaders (such as John F. Kennedy, Tony Blair and Mohandas Gandhi) they all appear very different. However, leadership appears to comprise two key characteristics:

1 the ability to influence others; and

2 demonstrable excellence in a career or other related area.

Beyond these common features there are two main approaches to defining leadership:

1 *Situational approaches* (also referred to as *contingency approaches*) view leadership as a *process* which is at least in part influenced by situational factors. This approach recognises that different situations may require different types, or styles, of leadership (Fiedler, 1967). For example, some tasks may require a task-oriented leadership style, whereas other tasks may require an emotional leadership style.

2 *Trait approaches* view leadership as determined by an individual's abilities or psychological characteristics. Therefore whether someone is an effective leader or not depends on the combinations of Individual Differences traits (e.g. personality and intelligence) they exhibit. For example, Carlyle's (1907) 'Great Man/Person' theory of leadership suggests that good leaders are different from non-leaders because the former possess traits that the latter do not.

As with the debates discussed in Chapter 2, a clearer understanding of leadership is likely to be achieved through an *interactionist* perspective.

Types of leadership
Three key leadership types have been proposed:

1 **Charismatic leadership** (e.g. Bass, 1997): highly expressive individuals who are motivational and emotionally appealing. They are often able to inspire optimism in their followers, who trust them implicitly.
2 **Transformational leadership** (e.g. Burns, 2003): individuals who are able to inspire others to go beyond their own self-interests, for the good of their group or society.
3 **Transactional leadership** (Avolio, 1999): individuals who practise contingent reward systems to control their followers' behaviour and exert influence. They aim to promote the interests of their own group or constituency (rather than, for example, the greater good of society as a whole).

Points to consider
Studying leadership is important because it can help to inform selection and recruitment practices and can help to find ways of increasing productivity in work teams. It can also help to understand the style of leadership required for the effective completion of different *types* of task.

Creativity

Creativity refers to the ability to produce novel (and useful) thoughts and solutions to problems (Sternberg & O'Hara, 2000), and is associated with such things as motivation, self-belief and imagination (Runco, 2004).

Creativity has been explored in four different ways by Individual Differences psychologists (Chamorro-Premuzic, 2011):

1 *Dispositional approach*: theory and research explore the personality traits and abilities associated with 'creative people', usually irrespective of context.
2 *Cognitive/process approach*: theory and research explore the *general processes* underlying creativity.
3 *Product approach*: theory and research explore creative outcomes/products and how individuals achieve these outputs.
4 *Press approach*: theory and research aim to understand the situational factors and interactions which facilitate creativity.

Creativity has been linked to intelligence and personality and may represent a link between the two concepts (suggesting they are not independent).

Intelligence and creativity

Sternberg and O'Hara (2000) suggest five ways in which creativity and intelligence might be linked:

1 Creativity and intelligence are the same construct.
2 Creativity and intelligence are completely unrelated constructs.
3 Creativity and intelligence are related constructs.
4 Creativity may be a part of intelligence.
5 Intelligence may be a part of creativity.

Each of these propositions has evidence to support it and a number of differing theories have arisen. For example, the threshold theory of creativity and intelligence (Shouksmith, 1973; Guilford, 1967) suggests that a certain level of intelligence is required for creative thinking to be possible.

Evidence supporting this theory can be found from the observation that individuals with low IQ scores tend to score low on creativity as well, but individuals with high IQ do not tend to have significantly higher (or lower) levels of creativity. Guilford's (1967, 1975) theory of intelligence and Gardner's multiple intelligences theory (1993), on the other hand, incorporate creativity as a *form* of intelligence. This theory identifies abilities such as flexibility, fluency and originality as core components of creativity, suggesting that personality and ability factors must be examined in conjunction to understand creativity.

KEY STUDY

Creativity in artists and scientists

Feist (1998, 1999) examined whether different profiles of the Big Five personality traits could be distinguished between creative versus non-creative individuals, scientists versus non-scientists and artists versus non-artists. Feist found that creative scientists scored differently from non-creative artists and non-creative scientists on openness, extraversion and conscientiousness, whereas artists and non-artists could be distinguished by differing profiles on extraversion and openness.

What does this suggest about creativity across different subject areas?

Points to consider: creativity

- Understanding the mechanisms underpinning creativity is important because it may be possible to find ways of:
  - Encouraging creativity. Creativity has been associated with flexibility (Flach, 1990); encouraging creativity may help increase people's ability to adapt to the demands of a rapidly technologically advancing culture.
  - Identifying jobs which particularly require creativity or innovation and identifying individuals who are creative and helping to improve person–job fit.

- Measuring creativity has proven difficult, as evidenced by the dearth of tests designed for this purpose.
- The traditional intelligence level concept does not ensure you will be 'successful' in life, which is why some individuals (e.g. Sternberg and Goleman) have sought to explore 'other' intelligences.
- To have a fuller understanding of intelligence we should also explore motivational aspects which are related.

Test your knowledge

1   In what ways is creativity different from intelligence?
2   Why might different types of task require different forms of leadership in order to be performed effectively by a group?
3   Why is Holland's RIASEC model useful for career counselling purposes?

Chapter summary: putting it all together

→ Can you tick all the points from the revision checklist at the beginning of this chapter?

→ Attempt the sample question from the beginning of this chapter using the answer guidelines below.

→ Go to the companion website at www.pearsoned.co.uk/psychologyexpress to access more revision support online, including interactive quizzes, sample questions with answer guidelines, 'you be the marker' exercises, flashcards and podcasts you can download.

Answer guidelines

Guidelines on answering the sample question presented at the start of the chapter are given below.

 Sample question Essay

Critically examine how Personality and Individual Differences psychology can be applied to help understand career choice and success. Provide examples from relevant theories and research to support your discussion.

Approaching the question

In approaching this question you would be wise to indicate the areas of personality and individual differences that you intend to address in your essay: this will also provide a framework for you to return to in your conclusion.

The second step will be to provide an introduction to the topic area; demonstrate why understanding career choice and success is important and outline the unique contribution of Personality and Individual Differences psychology to this topic.

Next you need to provide the relevant theory and evidence around which you intend to construct your answer. What does it suggest about career choice and success – are the findings of research in this area conclusive or are there contradictions? Are there any gaps in knowledge that need to be addressed in the future?

Finally, you need to provide a critique of the Individual Differences approach to these phenomena: for example, are the theories, research and constructs used reliable and valid? Are the tests used to assess individual differences in personality, intelligence, interests and performance also reliable and valid?

Important points to include

- Make sure you provide the relevant definitions for important concepts as they appear in your essay. For example, what is 'career success' and how is it measured (e.g. intrinsic and extrinsic rewards, 'satisfactoriness', job-fit, performance and attainment).
- Discuss the findings of research and what they indicate about the relationship between career choice, success and:
  - Intelligence: Discuss the links between people's IQ score, their occupations and socioeconomic status (see Chapter 9).
  - Educational attainment: Explore the fact that this will influence the options available to people and how this demonstrates the indirect relationship with learning styles. Learning styles may also directly influence career choice and success, owing to preferences in the way that people process information and the types of task they feel more comfortable performing.
  - Personality: Highlight the links between the FFM, performance and the relationship to stress, as this may influence the degree of career success (and job satisfaction) an individual experiences.
  - Holland's RIASEC model: Examine how this model moves beyond intelligence and personality theories to understand career choice and success.
  - Emotional intelligence: Think back to Chapter 8 and critically examine what theories of emotional intelligence (e.g. Goleman's EI) suggest about 'success'.
  - Creativity: Consider how innovation is sought after by some professions more than others; discuss the issues involved in assessing creativity and how it is different from intelligence and personality.
  - Leadership: Discuss how Individual Differences psychology can be used to identify individuals who are more likely to be effective leaders (and therefore

more successful in the roles which require leadership). Also explore how different styles of leadership may be more desirable for certain types of task.

- Crucially, you need to explore how the above research findings have been translated into practice, for example:
  - Development of job analysis and job-fit assessments and how they are used.
  - Construction and use of tests for the purposes of: identifying factors which predict job satisfaction, performance and attainment; selection and recruitment; and career counselling.
  - Impact on training programmes to enhance employees' career success and performance

Make your answer stand out

A strong answer will discuss the issue of career choice and success from the perspective of both the individual (e.g. the employee) and the organisation. This will allow you to demonstrate an understanding of how and why psychometric tests are used in selection, recruitment and career counselling, and what the implications of 'getting it wrong' are for both parties.

You could also explore the implications of poor career choice and success: where appropriate you could briefly discuss the implications for people's health and wellbeing, such as the research exploring Type A personality and diathesis-stress models of illness. You could also highlight the impact on organisational performance and discrimination. This will help to demonstrate the importance of making effective career choices and encouraging career success.

Notes

And finally, before the exam ...

How to approach revision from here

You should now be at a reasonable stage in your revision process – you should have developed your skills and knowledge base over your course and used this text judiciously over that period. Now, however, you have used the book to reflect, remind and reinforce the material you have researched over the year/seminar. You will, of course, need to do additional reading and research to that included here (and appropriate directions are provided) but you will be well on your way with the material presented in this book.

It is important that in answering any question in psychology you take a research- and evidence-based approach to your response. For example, do not make generalised or sweeping statements that cannot be substantiated or supported by evidence from the literature. Remember as well that the evidence should not be anecdotal – it is of no use citing your mum, dad, best friend or the latest news from a celebrity website. After all, you are not writing an opinion piece – you are crafting an argument that is based on current scientific knowledge and understanding. You need to be careful about the evidence you present: do review the material and from where it was sourced.

Furthermore, whatever type of assessment you have to undertake, it is important to take an evaluative approach to the evidence. Whether you are writing an essay, sitting an exam or designing a webpage, the key advice is to avoid simply presenting a descriptive answer. Rather it is necessary to think about the strength of the evidence in each area. One of the key skills for psychology students is critical thinking and for this reason the tasks featured in this series focus upon developing this way of thinking. Thus, you are not expected simply to learn a set of facts and figures, but to think about the implications of what we know and how this might be applied in everyday life. Better assessment answers are the ones that take this critical approach.

It is also important to note that psychology is a theoretical subject: when answering any question about psychology do not only refer to the prevailing theories of the field but outline the development of them as well. It is also important to evaluate these theories and models either through comparison with other models and theories or through the use of studies that have assessed them and highlighted their strengths and weaknesses. It is essential to read widely – within each section of this book there are always directions to interesting and pertinent papers relating to the specific topic area. Find these papers, read these papers and make notes from these papers. But don't stop there. Let them lead you to other sources that may be important to the field. One thing that an examiner hates to see is the same old sources being cited all of the time: be innovative and, as well as reading the seminal works, find the more obscure and interesting sources as well – just make sure they're relevant to your answer!

Tips for exam success

Exams are one form of assessment that students often worry about the most. The key to exam success, as with many other types of assessment, lies in good preparation and self-organisation. One of the most important things is knowing what to expect – this does not necessarily mean knowing what the questions will be on the exam paper, but rather what the structure of the paper is, how many questions you are expected to answer, how long the exam will last and so on.

To pass an exam you need a good grasp of the course material and, obvious as it may seem, to turn up for the exam itself. It is important to remember that you aren't expected to know or remember everything in the course, but you should be able to show your understanding of what you have studied. Remember as well that examiners are interested in what you know, not what you don't know. They try to write exam questions that give you a good chance of passing – not ones to catch you out or trick you in any way. You may want to consider some of these top exam tips:

- Start your revision in plenty of time.
- Make a revision timetable and stick to it.
- Practice jotting down answers and making essay plans.
- Practise writing against the clock using past exam papers.
- Check that you have really answered the question and have not strayed off the point.
- Review a recent past paper and check the marking structure.
- Carefully select the topics you are going to revise.
- Use your lecture/study notes and refine them further, if possible, into lists or diagrams and transfer them onto index cards/Post-it notes. Mind maps are a good way of making links between topics and ideas;
- Practise your handwriting – make sure it's neat and legible;

One to two days before the exam

- Recheck times, dates and venue.
- Actively review your notes and key facts.
- Exercise, eat sensibly and get a few good nights' sleep.

On the day

- Get a good night's sleep.
- Have a good meal, two to three hours before the start time.
- Arrive in good time.
- Spend a few minutes calming and focusing.

In the exam room

- Keep calm.
- Take a few minutes to read each question carefully. Don't jump to conclusions – think calmly about what each question means and the area it is focused on.
- Start with the question you feel most confident about. This helps your morale.
- By the same token, don't expend all your efforts on that one question – if you are expected to answer three questions then don't just answer two.
- Keep to time and spread your effort evenly on all opportunities to score marks.
- Once you have chosen a question, jot down any salient facts or key points. Then take five minutes to plan your answer – a spider diagram or a few notes may be enough to focus your ideas. Try and think in terms of 'why and how', not just 'facts'.
- Keep reminding yourself of the question and try not to wander off the point.
- Remember that quality of argument is more important than quantity of facts.
- Take 30–60-second breaks whenever you find your focus slipping (typically every 20 minutes).

Some key pointers

- Can you answer the questions posed in this text satisfactorily?
- Have you read the additional material to make your answer stand out?
- Remember to criticise appropriately – based on evidence.
- Test your knowledge by using the material presented in this text or on the website: www.pearsoned.co.uk/psychologyexpress.

Glossary

accessibility debate The debate concerning whether it is possible to access (or identify and understand) latent constructs from observable characteristics.

additive assumption An assumption which suggests that heritability is determined by the relative strength of genetic and environmental factors, and that these factors will always account for 100% of the variance in behaviour.

additive genetic variance Variation in the phenotype which is the result of a combination of numerous genes.

admixture hypothesis Proposed by Page and Grandon, this suggests that the apparent birth-order effect on intelligence is an artefact of the fact that parents with lower IQ scores tend to have more children than parents with higher IQ scores.

aggregate data Data combined from several measurements.

anthropomorphism The attribution of human qualities (e.g. motivation) on to animals, natural phenomena or inanimate objects.

approach–approach conflict Proposed by Dollard and Miller, this refers to a situation whereby an individual is unable to satisfy a drive because they are presented with two equally desirable, yet incompatible goals.

approach–avoidance conflict Proposed by Dollard and Miller, this refers to a situation whereby an individual is unable to satisfy a drive because they have to choose between two equally undesirable goals.

aptitude The ability to process and react to novel problems/stimuli. Generally this refers to the potential for achievement.

aptitude tests Tests which are designed to assess a person's ability on a particular task, or set of tasks. Usually refers specifically to traditional notions of cognitive abilities.

archetypes Proposed by Jung, these refer to universal symbols that exert influence on our dreams, fantasies, relationships and behaviour.

assortive mating A process by which individuals choose to mate with individuals who are either like themselves (positive assortive mating) or unlike themselves (negative assortive mating).

attainment The ability to recall/ remember information that has been learnt (i.e. achievement).

automation The process by which responses become habitual in specific contexts (i.e. completed without conscious thought or reflection). See also **habitual responses**.

autonomic nervous system (ANS) A subdivision of the peripheral nervous system, which can be further subdivided into the sympathetic and parasympathetic nervous systems. The ANS is primarily responsible for involuntary bodily functions (e.g. heart rate, digestion).

avoidance–avoidance conflict Proposed by Dollard and Miller, this refers to a situation whereby an individual is unable to satisfy a drive because they cannot choose between two equally undesirable goals.

avoiding type A personality type proposed by Adler, which characterises individuals who, when faced with a problem, deny it exists or pretend that it is someone else's.

bandwidth In relation to traits, this refers to the 'breadth' and 'depth' of the characteristic in question. This distinguishes between specifically targeted, narrow traits and multidimensional composite, broad traits. The bandwidth of a trait is also used to decide what level in a hierarchy the trait will be placed at.

basic anxiety Proposed by Horney, this explains the psychological impact of poor parenting and is proposed as a factor that can lead to the development of defensive attitudes.

behavioural genetics A field of study which is concerned with quantifying the contribution of genetics to behaviour and identifying the specific genes, or gene clusters, which are associated with particular traits.

behavioural signature of personality A term coined by Mischel to explain the unique pattern of behavioural variability.

beliefs A psychological state that refers to when an individual holds a proposition to be true.

biologisation Refers to the growing western cultural trend of placing emphasis on biological and evolutionary theories of intelligence.

biopsychosocial models Multidisciplinary models which explore how biological, psychological, environmental and social factors combine to contribute to people's functioning.

brain asymmetry This can either refer to the functional asymmetry of the brain (i.e. the differences in the functions that each hemisphere of the brain is primarily responsible for), or the specific neuroanatomical differences between the right and left hemispheres.

broad heritability An estimate of the total genetic variance in a population, which contains both additive and non-additive genetic variance.

burnout A condition which can arise from exposure to prolonged and/or excessive stress, and is characterised by a state of emotional, mental and physical exhaustion.

cardinal traits Proposed by Allport, these refer to the single traits which greatly influence a person's personality and behaviour.

case studies A research design more commonly associated with the idiographic and hermeneutic approaches. They represent intensive analyses of an individual unit (which may be a person or event). Although case studies can provide rich data, it is difficult to generalise findings from them beyond the particular case studied.

central nervous system (CNS) Chiefly refers to the brain and spinal cord, and is responsible for integrating the information it receives from the body and co-ordinating activity (e.g. movement).

central traits Proposed by Allport, these refer to the 5–10 traits which best describe an individual's personality.

charismatic leadership A style of leadership which is highly visionary, innovative and motivational: charismatic leaders tend to be inspirational and have exceptional communication skills.

child-effects model Proposed by Reiss, this suggests that a parent and child share genes, which brings about similar behaviour in both. In this model the child's behaviour is seen as having an impact on the parent's behaviour, but this change does not impact on the child's behaviour.

circular causality Refers to the proposition that individual differences can influence the expression of physical factors, but physical factors can also influence the expression of individual differences.

circumplex A model, such as Wiggins' Circumplex, which comprises two orthogonal axes and specifies the nature of the relationship between the factors it identifies. Typically circumplex theories are conceptualised as circular in shape.

clinical outcomes The 'end result' following a medical intervention (e.g. survival).

Cognitive-Affective Personality System (CAPS) A cognitive-affective theory of personality proposed by Mischel and Shoda, which suggests that personality can be best understood by examining the interaction between 'person' and 'situation'.

cognitive elite A term coined by Herrnstein and Murray to refer to the highest class of a new class-system that they believed would evolve based upon IQ scores. Specifically, the cognitive elite are those individuals who fall in the top end of the normal distribution bell curve.

cognitive maps Proposed by Tolman, these are the mental models, or representations, which people create about the locations and attributes of phenomena in their everyday lives.

collective unconscious Proposed by Jung, this refers to the body of instincts, fears, images and archetypes (universal symbols) which we inherit from our ancestors and which unconsciously influence our thoughts, feelings and behaviour.

common personality traits Personality traits which are useful for classifying groups of individuals and for making comparisons between groups.

componential subtheory Part of Sternberg's triarchic theory of social intelligence, this refers to the mental mechanisms which underpin intelligent behaviour.

conditioned response A term developed by early behaviourists, such as Pavlov and Skinner, to refer to a response which has been learned following repeated pairings of a stimulus and a reinforcement.

conditioning A process by which behaviour is modified, through the association of a specific behaviour with some form of reward.

confession In Jungian therapy this represents the first stage of treatment, whereby an individual recognises there is an issue and seeks assistance from an analyst.

confluence model A model proposed by Zajonc to account for the apparent relationship between birth-order and IQ, which suggests that IQ may be affected by changes in the familial environment (e.g. resources).

conscious The aspect of the mind that contains all the thoughts, feelings and memories that we are actively aware of.

constructive alternativism Proposed by Kelly, this refers to the belief that everyone is capable of changing their present interpretation of events.

constructs (psychological) Complex psychological concepts which are usually hypothetical and latent in nature: that is, they are not directly observable.

contextual subtheory Part of Sternberg's triarchic theory of social intelligence, this refers to the interaction between mental mechanisms and the external world which produces intelligent behaviour.

continuity hypothesis The proposition that personality disorders (amongst other phenomena) should be viewed as dimensional, rather than categorical.

coping styles Cognitive strategies that are adopted in response to stressors.

corollaries In terms of Kelly's personal construct theory, these are the interpretative processes which allow us to develop personal constructs.

correlational designs A design which merely *measures* two or more variables, rather than manipulating them, to explore the relationship between them. Correlational designs are widely used within Individual Differences psychology, owing to the fact that it is not always possible, or ethical, to manipulate one or more of the variables of interest.

criterion bias Bias in a diagnostic tool which arises as a result of bias within the defining criteria for the disorder of interest.

Cronbach's alpha A statistical test used to determine the internal reliability of a scale.

crystallised intelligence Refers to all the skills and experience an individual accumulates across their life. For this reason it is culturally bound, whereas 'fluid intelligence' is said to be culture-free. Crystallised intelligence is evidenced by such things as a person's vocabulary and general knowledge.

death instinct (thanatos) One of the forces/drives proposed by Freud which creates psychic energy, and largely consists of the urge to harm or destroy.

decontextualisation Refers to the growing western cultural trend of placing value on abstract reasoning and the removal of context from decision making.

defence mechanisms According to Freud, these are the means by which conflicts are resolved or managed through protecting the individual from anxiety, or by distorting reality.

defensive attitudes According to Horney, these are a means of dealing with anxiety, pain or uncertainty.

denial A protective device against pain whereby an individual claims the upsetting event has not occurred.

depression A psychological and physiological state in which people experience loss of interest, pleasure and feelings of self-worth, amongst others.

deviation IQ The ratio of tested IQ scores against a standardised IQ, usually expressed as a quotient in terms of a standard deviation. Developed owing to the problems identified with the traditional IQ concept.

diathesis-stress models Also referred to as vulnerability-stress models, these propose that characteristics confer increased risk of developing disorders, which will be triggered upon experiencing a sufficient amount of stress.

differential gene reproduction The process of an organism's reproductive success relative to others.

differential psychology Often used interchangeably with 'Individual Differences' or Individual Differences psychology, but usually has a broader meaning. It refers to the field of psychology which aims to understand individual and group differences, both in humans and in animals.

disease-prone personality type Personality typologies which have been used to explain subsets of people who appear to be at greater risk of developing specific illnesses, diseases or disorders.

domain specificity A term associated with evolutionary theory, which refers to the situation in which an adaptation is viewed as solving a particular problem.

domains of knowledge Specialist areas that specify the boundaries of a researcher's knowledge, expertise and interests.

dominant genetic variance Refers to the fact that some genes will be expressed (dominant genes), but others will not (recessive genes).

double approach–avoidance conflict Proposed by Dollard and Miller, this refers to a situation whereby an individual is unable to satisfy a drive because they cannot choose between multiple desirable and undesirable goals.

dream analysis A therapeutic technique pioneered by psychoanalysts, such as Freud and Jung. It involves encouraging patients to talk about the content of their dreams, and the symbols contained therein are then interpreted.

drives Utilised by theorists working in a variety of fields in different ways, but usually refers to unconscious processes/ urges which influence a person's thoughts, feelings and behaviour (e.g. Freud's 'libido').

ecological validity The degree to which the behaviours, thoughts or feelings observed or recorded in a study reflect the behaviours, thoughts or feelings that would be observed in a naturally occurring environment or situation.

education In Jungian therapy this represents the third stage of therapy, whereby the patient identifies ways of managing the issue and developing their personality.

ego The part of the mind which undertakes reasoned thought, such as thinking, planning and organising activities, and attempts to balance the demands of the id with the demands of the superego.

elucidation In Jungian therapy this represents the second stage of therapy, whereby the patient comes to understand what the issues really are.

emics The psychological characteristics that are unique to a particular culture.

environmental factors Aspects or characteristics of the environment.

environmentality The estimate of the average variance in a specific behaviour across a population, which is accounted for by environmental factors (see also **heritability**).

epistatic genetic variance Refers to the fact that some genes act in combination and interact to effect the expression of other genes.

equal environments assumption The assumption that the environments experienced by twins are no more similar than the environments experienced by siblings.

etics The psychological characteristics which are common to all cultures.

eugenics The doctrine which states that humanity can be improved through selective breeding.

evolutionary personality theories A branch of personality psychology which is relatively new. These theories aim to explore personality as an evolved 'solution' to adaptive problems faced by humans (and our ancestors) over huge time periods. As such they are possibly more concerned with the origins of psychological, social and behavioural phenomena than with their content per se.

existential philosophy A branch of philosophy which is concerned with understanding how human beings live and make sense of their lives.

expectancies A concept important to early learning theory: expectancies are subjective cognitions about the probability of a behaviour bringing about a desired outcome. Strong expectancies mean that an individual is more confident that the behaviour will be 'successful'.

experiential subtheory Part of Sternberg's triarchic theory of social intelligence, this refers to the interaction between experience, and the internal and external world, which produces intelligent behaviour.

external locus of control When an individual believes that events or circumstances are beyond their control.

external validity The validity of generalised (usually causal) inferences from a study to the wider population from which the sample used was drawn (see also internal validity).

externalisation Proposed by Horney, this refers to the situation in which an individual projects their own thoughts and feelings onto other people.

extinction When a conditioned response becomes weaker and weaker, until it dies out altogether, because it is no longer being reinforced.

factor analysis A group of data reduction statistical analysis techniques, which allows for the identification of groups of terms which cluster together (factors) within a larger set of variables/items.

factor loadings Values which indicate the degree to which an item correlates with a factor. They also provide an indication of the amount of variance within an item which is accounted for by a factor.

feeling A term proposed by Jung which refers to the situation when we evaluate the desirability of what we are presented with.

fluid intelligence The capacity for abstract reasoning, free of cultural influences. It is evidenced by people's ability to acquire new information and make inferences about new patterns or relationships in stimuli.

Flynn effect The observed year-on-year population rise in IQ test scores, observed across a number of countries.

free association A therapeutic technique used in psychoanalysis and psychodynamic therapy, whereby a patient is encouraged to talk about anything that comes to their mind, in the belief that important memories may be revealed.

functional neuroimaging A branch of techniques which aim to measure some metric of brain activity.

functionalism Attempts to understand the functions which behaviour and experiences serve and is less concerned with trying to identify the organisation and structure of the mind (see also structuralism).

functionality In evolutionary theory, this is the premise that adaptations serve a practical function.

functionally equivalent class of situations Proposed by Mischel, Shoda and Wright to explain consistency of behaviour across situations, by suggesting that people perceive situations as similar and therefore behave in similar ways.

fundamental postulate One of the cornerstones of Kelly's personal construct theory, which suggests that a person's psychological processes are directed by the way in which they anticipate events. This suggests that the way we think, feel and behave is based on our subjective perceptions of the world around us.

General Intelligence ('g') First proposed by Spearman, this refers to the general factor of intelligence that underlies all cognitive ability.

generalised expectancy The process whereby people come to believe that reinforcements are controlled by their own behaviour, or by external forces.

genetic factors Primarily refers to all the information which is inherited by an offspring from their biological parents, through DNA.

genetic markers A specific gene, or genes, which is recognised as producing a specific trait.

genetic model In Freud's terminology this refers to the developmental factors (not genetic factors) which influence the development of personality: specifically, people must go through a series of developmental stages for personality to develop fully.

genotype An individual's genetic makeup.

getting type A personality type proposed by Adler, characterised by the use of other people to achieve goals and putting in as little effort as possible to achieve goals.

Gigantic Three model A neurophysiological model of personality proposed by Eysenck, which suggests that personality can be understood in terms of the following dimensions: extraversion, neuroticism and psychoticism. Also referred to as the PEN model and the tripartite model.

god archetype Proposed by Jung to account for the fact that at times of distress human beings sometimes turn to a higher power, regardless of whether a god exists or not. It is therefore a concept which resides within the collective unconscious.

grand theories Theories which aim to describe and explain all aspects of a given phenomenon, such as Freud's psychoanalytic theory of the development, stability and mechanisms underlying personality.

habits A term which refers to a learnt association between a stimulus and response.

habitual responses Automatic responses (such as behaviour) which occur in specific contexts, such as changing gear in a car without being explicitly aware that you are doing so.

hedonism Refers to the proposition that the pursuit of pleasure is the only true goal in life.

heritability The estimate of the average variance in a specific behaviour across a population, attributable to genetic factors.

hormonal differences Differences in specific chemicals released by glands in the body which have been proposed to explain differences in observed behaviour. For example, it has been suggested that observable sex differences in aggression may be attributable to hormones such as testosterone, rather than to such processes as socialisation.

human genome The total genetic information stored within a human being's chromosomes.

id Proposed by Freud, this refers to the part of the mind and personality which stores all the unacceptable drives and instincts.

identity crisis Proposed by Erikson, this refers to the result of the ego not fully developing, and preventing a true sense of self being developed and as a result preventing the attainment of goals.

idiographic approach Views personality and other individual differences variables as unique to each individual and impossible to explain or predict across people using the same terms.

implicit theories of intelligence Refers to 'popular culture' theories of intelligence, and those theories of intelligence which are held unconsciously by people.

individual differences The variables or characteristics which psychologists attempt to identify in order to describe and explain inter-individual and intra-individual variation.

Individual Differences psychology The field of psychology which aims to identify, describe and explain the ways in which people differ in terms of their thoughts, feelings and behaviour.

inferiority complex Proposed by Adler, this refers to the situation in which a person becomes fixated on their weakness and inferiorities.

instincts According to Freud, instincts are *innate forces*, the conflict between which ultimately produces psychic energy (the driving force behind all behaviour and actions).

intelligence There are many definitions of intelligence, but broadly this refers to the ability to solve mental problems and acquire new knowledge and skills.

intelligence quotient (IQ) Typically actually refers to deviation IQ. However, traditional IQ refers to the ratio of tested mental age to chronological age, usually expressed as a quotient multiplied by 100.

interactionism The approach which suggests that to understand people's behaviour it is necessary to explore how situational, environmental and person factors interact.

interests A tendency, or preference, to engage in a particular kind of task.

inter-individual variation The ways in which people differ from each other, in their patterns of thoughts, feelings and behaviour.

internal locus of control Refers to those situations in which an individual attributes the cause of an event to their own behaviour.

internal validity The extent to which a research design (typically a true experiment) allows you to make appropriate and accurate causal inferences between the variables under investigation. Internal validity is extremely important when you are considering making generalisations about causal relationships to the wider population from which the sample used in the research was drawn (see **external validity**).

inter-rater reliability Refers to the consistency in judgements between two (usually trained) observers.

intraclass correlations A statistical technique which can be used to explore how (for example) raters' judgements vary across observations, to provide a measure of the reliability and consistency of these judgements.

intra-individual variation The ways in which a person's own thoughts, feelings and behaviour may differ across situations, time or their lifespan.

intra-rater reliability The extent of consistency within *an individual's* ratings on a test or scale on two or more occasions (in those situations in which little variation is expected or desirable). Intra-rater reliability is usually assessed by means of correlation.

intuitive A jungian term which refers to the approach taken to understand the world around us by using premonitions or gut-instincts.

job analysis The process whereby characteristics of a job are recorded and the skills which are required to perform the job effectively are identified.

kappa A statistical technique which can be used to assess the degree of agreement between two raters.

knowledge acquisition components Part of Sternberg's triarchic theory of intelligence, these components are specifically involved in learning from experience.

latent constructs Constructs which are 'hidden' and not directly observable.

L-data (life record data) Measurements of behaviour which are taken from an individual's actual life, such as A-level results.

leadership style A relatively stable pattern of behaviour which a leader adopts and which impacts upon the way they relate to their group members and exert influence over them.

learning processes In Kolb's theory, these reflect the mechanisms by which people learn from experience and include such things as learning through involvement in new experiences, or learning through reflecting on your own experience. Preferences for different learning processes come together to produce **learning styles**.

learning styles In Kolb's theory, these reflect patterns in people's preferences for the mechanisms by which they learn, and are relatively stable. However, learning styles have been studied by many different theorists working in different fields, and each proposes different types of learning style.

lexical approach The approach to studying personality (and other characteristics) which involves firstly identifying the salient descriptors of that particular factor in a culture's language.

lexical hypothesis The proposition that all meaningful information about personality (and other characteristics) can be obtained from the language used within a culture to describe and discuss it. Specifically, the number and frequency of the descriptor use will reflect the importance of that concept within that culture.

life history A means of documenting the schedule of growth, survival and reproduction throughout an individual's life, developed by theorists such as Wilson.

life instinct (libido) One of the forces/drives proposed by Freud which creates psychic energy, and largely consists of sexual energy.

life-process energy A concept proposed by Jung as an extension of Freud's life and death instincts: it refers to a broader psychic energy force that arises as a result of conflicts between opposing forces within the psyche (personality as a whole).

locus of control Proposed by Rotter, this describes how people typically attribute their successes or failures to either internal or external factors.

longevity Typically refers to 'life expectancy'. Longevity is often used as a clinical outcome variable, following medical intervention, alongside survival and quality of life.

lumpers In terms of approaches to intelligence theory, lumpers are those models which propose a unitary, broad factor underlying intelligence. However, this term can also refer to a learning style proposed by Cohen.

masculine protest Proposed by Adler, this reflects an individual's decision to overcome inferiority by exaggerating a sense of superiority in front of others. However, it can also refer to the more specific decision to reject the stereotypical female role of weakness associated with femininity.

mental disorders Psychological disorders which impair normal functioning and can cause distress for the individual (and potentially those who interact with them).

mental representations Also referred to as cognitive maps, or mental models, these refer to the ways in which people create and store information about the locations and attributes of phenomena in their everyday lives.

metacomponents Part of Sternberg's triarchic theory of intelligence: these components are specifically involved in helping an individual to recognise a problem and mobilise resources to deal with it effectively.

method of amplification A process involved in dream analysis whereby the analyst and patient identify the significant symbols in a dream and focus on them in increasing depth to understand them.

micro-theories Theories which focus on specific and often narrow topics, such as studying 'shyness' exclusively.

modelling A term used by Bandura to refer to the process of social learning through imitation of a 'model'.

molecular-genetic theories One of the newest directions in behavioural genetics, this aims to identify the specific genes associated with personality traits.

moral anxiety One of the three major anxiety types which Freud proposed arise from an imbalance in the three structures of the mind. Specifically, moral anxiety occurs when there is a conflict between the ego and superego, and the demands of the superego are not met.

motivations These typically refer to the drives or forces (which may be conscious or unconscious) that direct our behaviour, and influence the way we think and feel. They are conceptualised in various different ways by theorists working in different fields (e.g. humanistic v. cognitive v. psychodynamic).

narrow heritability An estimate of the total genetic variance in a population, which contains only additive genetic variance.

natural selection A key concept in evolutionary theory which suggests that over time mutations arise which may better enable an organism to survive. If harmful mutations arise, then organisms may be less likely to survive. Over time beneficial mutations may spread across a population, and this is one of the processes by which evolution occurs.

negative assortive mating A process by which individuals choose to mate with individuals who are dissimilar to themselves.

negative eugenics A term coined by Galton to refer to finding methods of decreasing the fertility of 'undesirables' (individuals who demonstrated poor qualities in relation to intelligence, health and moral character).

negative reinforcement A process involved in operant conditioning whereby the consequences of an act discourage it from being repeated.

neo-Freudians The psychoanalysts who identified limitations of Freud's theories and developed their own approaches in new directions to account for this.

neurophysiological theories Theories which propose that the driving force behind individual differences are neurological or physiological variables (e.g. Eysenck's PEN model).

neurotic anxiety One of the three major anxiety types which Freud proposed arises from an imbalance in the three structures of the mind. Specifically, neurotic anxiety occurs when there is conflict between the id and the ego.

neurotic needs The ten neurotic needs proposed by Horney, which she suggested arose from defensive attitudes that were maladaptive in nature, but aimed to protect the individual from harm.

nomothetic approach Views personality, intelligence and other individual difference variables as describable and predictable in terms of predefined attributes.

non-genetic factors Primarily refers to environmental and social factors.

non-shared environmental influences Those aspects of the environment which are experienced differently by members of the same family living together (e.g. siblings or twins).

norm group A group used as a point of comparison for a test, or individual case. For example, a norm group allows you to assess the performance of an individual against a comparable population's scores.

norms Numbers, values, levels or ranges that are representative of a group, and which can be used as a basis for comparison with individual cases. This allows you to see where an individual's score falls in relation to the norm group (e.g. above or below average).

numerousness A term associated with evolutionary theory, which refers to the premise that organisms develop many adaptive mechanisms to solve the variety of issues they face.

objective anxiety One of the three major anxiety types which Freud proposed arise from an imbalance in the three structures of the mind. Specifically, objective anxiety occurs when a real threat to the person is perceived.

observational learning An alternative label given by Bandura to the concept of social learning. It refers to the fact that people do not need to have direct experiences of an event/situation to learn from them: they can observe the experiences of others and learn vicariously.

operant behaviour Proposed by Skinner, this refers to behaviour which has been learnt as a result of operant conditioning.

operant conditioning A process of associative learning whereby the evaluation of reinforcement is viewed as important. For example, desired behaviour is rewarded and undesirable behaviour is discouraged.

parasympathetic nervous system A subdivision of the autonomic nervous system, which is primarily concerned with 'rest and digest' activities.

parent-effects model A model proposed by Reiss which suggests that parents and child share genes, which brings about similar behaviour. In this model the child's behaviour impacts on the adults' behaviour, and this change in the adults' behaviour does have an impact on the child's behaviour.

partial reinforcement schedules A reinforcement schedule which occurs when the reward for a behaviour is not given every time the behaviour is performed, and can produce behaviour which is very resistant to change.

passive model One of the models proposed by Reiss as a possible explanation for how family environment influences the way genotypes form phenotypes. Specifically, the passive model suggests that personality is explained by the 50% overlap in genes between child and parents.

patient-centred outcomes Those outcomes which are important to the patient.

PEN model Eysenck's hierarchical personality taxonomy, also known as the Gigantic Three theory or tripartite model of personality. PEN refers to the three dimensions of psychoticism, extraversion and neuroticism, which Eysenck believed sufficient to describe and explain personality.

penis envy A term coined by Freud to refer to the stage when females become aware that they do not have a penis, which can lead to feelings of shame, jealousy and deficiency.

performance components Part of Sternberg's triarchic theory of intelligence: these components are specifically involved in problem solving (e.g. encoding, comparing and responding to information), and are directed by the metacomponents.

peripheral nervous system Refers to all the sensory and motor neurons and receptors, muscles and glands which connect the surface of the body with the nervous system.

persona archetype Proposed by Jung to refer to the different masks we wear when engaged in different roles (e.g. mother, student).

personal constructs Proposed by Kelly to refer to the criteria we use to perceive and interpret events.

person factors Refer to an individual's thoughts, feelings and biological variables which contribute to their inner state.

personal unconscious A term coined by Jung to refer to the unconscious part of the mind that contains all our socially unacceptable urges, which are unique to us (not inherited from our ancestors).

personality The set of psychological characteristics and mechanisms within an individual that are relatively enduring and are reflected by tendencies to think, feel and act in certain ways.

personality disorder Persistent and pervasive patterns of thinking, feeling and behaving which do not conform to cultural expectations, and can impair normal functioning and lead to distress (for the individual and those who interact with them).

personality psychology Often used to refer to the field of psychology which studies personality and individual differences. In this book, it is used to refer solely to the study of personality.

person–situation interaction approach Another name for the interactionist perspective, which posits that to understand behaviour person- and situation-factors must be examined together.

phenotype All your observable characteristics.

phylogenic inheritance The process through which genetic information contributes to phenotypic variance between people.

positive assortive mating A process by which individuals choose to mate with individuals who are like themselves.

positive eugenics A term coined by Galton to refer to finding methods of increasing the fertility of 'desirables'.

positive reinforcement A process involved in operant conditioning whereby the repetition of a desired act is encouraged.

pre-conscious The part of the mind which contains those thoughts which are currently unconscious to us, but which can be brought into the conscious mind if required.

pre-morbid characteristics Characteristics which predispose an individual to ill health or psychopathology.

primary drives Drives which are innate and are based on physiological needs that help us to survive (e.g. thirst, hunger).

primary factors A term used by Cattell to denote the 16 source traits that he identified using factor analysis, which he felt were required to provide a meaningful description of a person's personality.

primary mental abilities The independent cognitive abilities which Thurstone proposed as describing and explaining human intelligence.

primary process thinking A term proposed by Freud to denote the type of thinking undertaken by the id: thinking without basis in reality or without logical rules.

primary reinforcers The reinforcers which are required to satisfy primary (physiological) drives, such as eating food to satisfy hunger.

principle of entropy Proposed by Jung to refer to the drive to create balanced energies across our psyche.

principle of equivalence Proposed by Jung, this refers to the fact that activity in one part of the psyche will lead to decreased activity in another part of the psyche.

principle of opposites Proposed by Jung, this refers to the process whereby life-process energy is created within the psyche.

projection A defensive measure adopted whereby an individual externalises their unacceptable feelings and attributes them to others.

projective techniques A psychoanalytic therapeutic technique which involves presenting ambiguous stimuli (such as pictures) and asking a patient to interpret them. This process is repeated and any themes in the patient's responses noted, in the belief that this will help to reveal important issues which can be explored further by therapist and patient.

proportion of shared variance The extent to which parents and their child (or siblings) differ. An important concept in twin and adoption studies.

psyche A term proposed by Jung which refers to the totality of personality.

psychic determinism Freud's proposition that everything happens for a reason.

psychogenic models Models which propose that individual differences cause (or influence) physical factors.

psychometrics The field of psychology which involves designing, administering and interpreting quantitative measures of psychological variables, such as personality, intelligence and motivation. One of its core objectives, therefore, is to quantify psychological phenomena, through the process of scaling.

psychopathology Also referred to as abnormal psychology, this can denote the approach to studying the causes, treatment and consequences of psychological disorders and mental illness, or can be used to refer to the presence of psychological disorder/ mental illness.

psychosexual stages The developmental stages which Freud believed all people progress through, and through the successful competition of which one fully develops one's personality and superego.

psychosocial conflicts Crises which represent 'turning points' in people's development. They are socially directed, such as learning how to interact socially with others.

Q-data (also referred to as S-data) Refers to data collected via self-report personality/intelligence measures.

quality of life A term that is typically used to evaluate the general wellbeing of an individual.

quantification The act of determining or expressing the quantity of something.

quasi-experiments Experiments which exert control over confounding variables where possible, but which make use of naturally occurring groups (e.g. gender, patient treatment groups) as independent variables. This research design is often adopted because it would be impossible, or highly unethical, to use a true experimental design to explore the issues of interest.

random reinforcement schedule A schedule of reinforcement whereby rewards are given at random intervals in response to desired behaviour.

rational-emotive behaviour therapy A form of therapy proposed by Ellis, which aims to increase the rationality of people's thoughts, feelings and behaviour, to alleviate distress.

rationalisation A form of defence mechanism whereby an individual justifies an event after it has occurred, to hide the true motivation for the event.

reaction formation A defence mechanism which involves overcoming an unacceptable impulse by exaggerating the opposite tendency.

reality principle Refers to the situation whereby our thinking is based on what is occurring in the external world.

reciprocal determinism Bandura's proposition that cognitive and environmental factors interact to motivate behaviour.

reflective observation A process of learning through observing others, or by reflecting on our own practices.

regression A family of statistical techniques which allows you to examine the unique relationship between an outcome variable and one or more predictor variables. Regression also allows you to predict scores on an outcome variable, even if the values on the predictor variables that you are interested in are not contained within a dataset.

reinforcement value Our preference for specific types of reinforcement which are available to us.

reinforcements The consequences of a behavioural act (which can either encourage or discourage the repetition of the act).

relativist critique The perspectives which questions whether some Individual Differences theories, or even the concept of traits in general, are applicable outside specific western cultures (also referred to as the cultural-relativist critique).

repertory grid A therapeutic tool developed by Kelly to uncover people's personal constructs.

repression A defence mechanism which involves keeping material that is found to be unacceptable, in the unconscious mind.

resource dilution model A model proposed to explain the apparent relationship between IQ and birth order, which suggests that parent resources become 'stretched' when the number of children increases, thereby diluting the resources available to any one child (which will influence the development of intelligence).

respondent behaviour Behaviour which arises as a result of classical conditioning.

ruling type A personality type proposed by Adler, characterised by an intense desire for superiority and willingness to exploit others to achieve this. This stems from the individual not possessing the necessary social interest or courage to achieve superiority legitimately.

schizophrenia A complex mental disorder which is often long term in nature and is (typically) characterised by hallucinations, confused thinking and delusions, changes in behaviour, and distress.

secondary drives Drives which are learnt, initially to cope with the demands of our primary drives.

secondary process thinking A term coined by Freud to refer to the thinking which is undertaken by the ego, which involves strategising and problem-solving. It is thinking which is rational and reflects the actual situation that the individual is faced with in the external world.

secondary reinforcers The reinforcers which were originally neutral to the individual, but which have acquired a value because they have become associated with the satisfaction of primary drives.

secondary traits Proposed by Allport, these reflect the traits which are important to understanding people's preferences, but do not constitute a core aspect of their personality.

selective breeding Also known as artificial selection. Selective breeding involves breeding animals for desired qualities and is often used as an analogy for natural selection on a much smaller time scale.

selective combination Part of Sternberg's triarchic theory of social intelligence, this refers to a sub-process of the knowledge acquisition components, which is specifically involved in synthesising information.

selective comparison Part of Sternberg's triarchic theory of social intelligence, this refers to a sub-process of the knowledge acquisition components, which is specifically involved in the comparison of old and new information.

selective encoding Part of Sternberg's triarchic theory of social intelligence, this refers to a sub-process of the knowledge acquisition components, which is specifically involved in sifting out relevant from irrelevant information.

selective placement The potential practice of placing children with adoptive parents who are similar, which could present problems when attempting to establish environmentality.

self archetype Proposed by Jung to refer to the potential we all have to achieve balance within our psyche, and to accept ourselves and our own identity.

self-efficacy An individual's belief that they can effectively perform a behaviour, which will bring them a desired response.

self-reinforcing This occurs when an individual evaluates their own behaviour and chooses to continue or end it.

sensing A term proposed by Jung which refers to the situation when we experience a stimulus without evaluating it.

sexual selection The process by which some organisms appear to develop characteristics which are viewed as advantageous when competing for mates. Although these characteristics may provide benefits in terms of mating success, they may not provide *survival* advantages.

shaping The situation in which behaviour which *approximates* the desired behaviour is rewarded, to assist the learner to learn the correct behaviour.

shared environmental influences Those aspects of the environment which are experienced in the same way by members of the same family living together (e.g. siblings or twins).

Situationists Theorists, such as Mischel, who argue that behaviour cannot be understood in terms of person factors alone. Early situationists in particular suggested that situational factors were more important in determining behaviour than individual dispositional factors.

situationist challenge The argument proposed by theorists such as Mischel that behaviour cannot be understood in terms of person factors alone. The early situationist challenge proposed that situation factors had greater influence over behaviour than person factors. However, this position was later amended and became the foundations of the interactionist approach.

situationist debate See **situationist challenge**.

Skinner box Also referred to as an operant conditioning chamber. The Skinner box was a piece of experimental apparatus designed by Skinner, in which an animal (usually a pigeon or rat) was given food pellets for performing a particular behaviour (e.g. pressing a lever in the box).

social learning theories Also referred to as social-cognitive models. Social learning theories are those which propose that people learn new behaviour through observing and imitating other people's behaviour.

socially useful type A personality type proposed by Adler, to reflect a person who approaches life proactively and co-operates with others in order to achieve goals.

somatic nervous system One of the subdivisions of the peripheral nervous system, this is chiefly concerned with conducting signals from sensory receptors to the central nervous system, and signals from the central nervous system to skeletal muscles. It is therefore most associated with the control of body movements.

somatogenic models Models which suggest that physical factors cause (or influence) psychological differences in Individual Differences.

source traits A term used by Cattell to denote the 16 primary factors that he identified using factor analysis, which he felt were required to provide a meaningful description of a person's personality.

specific abilities ('S') First proposed by Spearman, these refer to abilities which relate to specific tasks and account for variations in performance on different tests.

splitters In terms of approaches to intelligence theory, splitters are those models which propose a set of distinct factors underlying intelligence. However, this term can also refer to a learning style proposed by Cohen.

standard deviation A measure of the variance of a set of scores.

states Transient phenomena, also referred to as moods, which typically reflect behaviour performed at that moment.

statistical approach In relation to the identification of traits, the statistical approach refers to the method of identifying traits pioneered by Spearman and Cattell, which was believed to be empirical.

stimulus–response relationships The bond between a stimulus and a response, viewed by many early behaviourists as the foundation of behaviour.

stress Typically refers to physical, psychological and social forces and pressures, which place demands upon an individual which they find difficult to meet.

structural equation modelling A family of statistical techniques which are chiefly used to explore whether theoretical models are plausible when compared to observed data.

structural model The model of the mind proposed by Freud which comprises the id, ego and superego.

structural neuroimaging A group of non-invasive techniques which allow the structure of the brain to be observed.

structuralism Attempts to understand how the organisation and structure of the mind relate to behaviour and experiences. Structuralism has largely been replaced by the notion of functionalism.

style of life Proposed by Adler, this refers to a person's approach to life.

subordinate personal construct Lower-order personal constructs in Kelly's personal construct theory.

superego Proposed by Freud, this refers to the part of the mind which contains the morals and values of society and represents a person's conscience.

superordinate personal construct Higher-order personal constructs in Kelly's personal construct theory.

survival A form of clinical outcome measure following a medical intervention.

sympathetic nervous system A subdivision of the autonomic nervous system, which is primarily concerned with 'fight or flight' activities.

tautology In psychometrics, tautology refers to the debate about whether tests (e.g. IQ tests) measure the constructs we *define*, or whether the constructs studied are merely products of the tests we create.

taxonomies An organisational system of traits, which are frequently hierarchical in nature.

T-data Data collected from standardised tests following procedures which make it difficult to fake or distort the results.

temperament Refers to Individual Differences in emotional and behavioural styles which are evident very early in life, and which are often taken as evidence for the biological basis of personality.

tests of maximal performance Tests which are designed to assess what we have learned and our capacity to learn new things.

tests of typical performance Tests which are designed to assess how we usually think, feel and behave.

theoretical approach In relation to the identification of traits, this refers to the method of identifying traits based on a prior theory: That is, the theory directs the theorist to those traits which should be important to study.

therapeutic alliance The relationship between a therapist/clinician/counsellor and patient/client.

thinking In Jungian terminology, 'thinking' refers to interpreting an experience using reason and logic.

topographic model The model of the mind proposed by Freud which comprises the pre-conscious, conscious and unconscious.

traits Internal dispositions to think, feel and behave in certain ways, which represent relatively stable patterns across situations and across time.

trait theory Theories which place the emphasis for determining behaviour on relatively stable, internal dispositions of an individual.

transactional leadership A style of leadership characterised by the leader's practice of contingent reward systems to control their followers' behaviour and exert influence.

transformation In Jungian therapy this represents the fourth stage, whereby the individual achieves equilibrium of the psyche's opposing forces.

transformational leadership A style of leadership characterised by the ability to inspire others to go beyond their own self-interests, for the good of their group or society.

triadic reciprocal causation A term coined by Bandura to refer to the mutual influence of person, environment and behaviour.

tripartite trait model Also referred to as the Gigantic Three model, and PEN model, of personality. A neurophysiological model of personality proposed by Eysenck, which suggests that personality can be understood in terms of the following dimensions: extraversion, neuroticism and psychoticism.

true experiments Experiments in which the researcher manipulates one or more independent variables and measures the impact on a dependent variable, whilst holding all other variables constant. In the social sciences, true experiments are rare (if not impossible) because of confounding variables which cannot be manipulated by the researcher (e.g. gender). As a result, many research designs in the social sciences are quasi-experimental.

types Often viewed as an alternative to traits, types are distinct categories which a subset of people belong to, which represent clusters of characteristics.

typologies An organisational system based upon types, rather than traits.

unconditioned response A naturally occurring and automatic response to a stimulus.

unconditioned stimulus A stimulus which reliably elicits an unconditioned response.

unconscious In many psychoanalytic theories, this is the part of the mind which contains thoughts, feelings, drives and urges which an individual is not consciously aware of. These thoughts, feelings and drives are often viewed as irrational and may not have any basis in reality.

validity Refers to the extent to which any measure, or construct, accurately assesses or represents the construct it is intended to. There are many subtypes of validity, each of which can be assessed in different ways.

variation Typically refers to the degree to which behaviours, thoughts and feelings differ between people (inter-individual variation) or within the same individual (intra-individual variation) across situations or time. However, variation is also an important concept in evolutionary psychology and may refer to variation in genes or environments.

vicarious reinforcement Reinforcement which occurs through observing the reinforcement experienced for a particular behaviour by another person.

vulnerability-stress models Also referred to as diathesis-stress models. These propose that characteristics confer increased risk of developing disorders, which will be triggered upon experiencing a sufficient amount of stress.

wish fulfilment Occurs when the id produces a mental representation or fantasy about an object, to produce temporary satisfaction, because the object of desire cannot be obtained in reality.

References

Abrahams, K. (1927). A short study on the development of the libido. In S. Freud (ed.). *Selected papers*. London: Hogarth Press.

Adler, A. (1927). *Understanding human nature*. New York: Greenberg.

Adler, A. (1964). *Social interest: A challenge to mankind*. New York: Capricorn Books.

Adler, A. (1973). *The practice and theory of individual psychology*. Totowa, NJ: Littlefield, Adams & Co.

Adler, A. (1979). Advantages and disadvantages of the inferiority feeling. In H. Ansbacher and R. Ansbacher (eds), *Superiority and social interest: A collection of Alfred Adler's later writings*. New York: Norton.

Ajzen, I. (2005). Attitudes, personality and behavior (2nd edn). Maidenhead: Open University Press

Alexander, F. (1939). Emotional factors in essential hypertension, *Psychosomatic Medicine, 1*, 175–9.

Alexander, F. (1950). *Psychosomatic medicine*. New York: Norton.

Allinson, C. & Hayes, J. (1996). The Cognitive Style Index: A measure of intuition-analysis for organizational research, *Journal of Management studies, 33*, 119–35.

Allix, N. (2000). The theory of multiple intelligences: A case of missing cognitive matter, *Australian Journal of Education, 44*, 272–88.

Allport, G. (1961). *Pattern and growth in personality*. New York: Rinehart and Winston.

Allport, G. & Odbert, H. (1936). Trait-names: a psycho-lexical study, *Psychological Monographs, 47*, i–171.

Allred, K. D. & Smith, T. W. (1989). The hardy personality: Cognitive and physiological responses to evaluative threat, *Journal of Personality and Social Psychology, 56*, 257–66.

Almagor, M., Tellegen, A. & Waller, N. (1995). The big seven model: A cross-cultural replication and further exploration of the basic dimensions of natural language trait descriptors, *Journal of Personality and Social Psychology, 69*, 300–7.

Alston, W. (1975). Traits, consistency and conceptual alternatives for personality theory, *Journal for the Theory of Social Behavior, 5*, 17–48.

Amelang, M. (1997). Using personality variables to predict cancer and heart disease, *European Journal of Personality, 11(5)*, 319–42.

American Psychiatric Association (2000). *Diagnostic and statistical manual of mental disorders*, 4th edn (DSM-IV). Washington, DC: American Psychiatric Association.

American Psychological Association (2003). *Guidelines for the use of animals in behavioural projects in schools*. Washington DC: American Psychological Association.

Andreassi, J. (2006). *Psychophysiology: Human behavior and physiological response* (5th edn). London: Psychology Press.

Anglina, D., Cohenab, P. & Chena, H. (2008). Duration of early maternal separation and prediction of schizotypal symptoms from early adolescence to midlife, *Schizophrenia Research, 103*, 143–50.

Ashton, M. & Lee, K. (2005). A defense of the lexical approach to the study of personality, *European Journal of Personality, 19*, 5–24.

Avolio, B. (1999). *Full leadership development: Building the vital forces in organizations*. Thousand Oaks, CA: Sage.

Balin, E. & Hirschi, A. (2010). Who seeks career counselling? A prospective study of personality and career variables among Swiss adolescents, *International Journal for Educational and Vocational Guidance, 10*, 161–76.

Bandura, A. (1962). Social learning through imitation. In M.R. Jones (ed.), *Nebraska symposium of motivation* (pp. 211–69). Lincoln: University of Nebraska Press.

Bandura, A. (1965). Influence of models' reinforcement contingencies on the acquisition of imitative responses, *Journal of Personality and Social Psychology, 1,* 589–95.

Bandura, A. (1971). Vicarious and self-reinforcement processes. In R. Glaser (ed.), *The nature of reinforcement* (pp. 228–78). New York: Academic Press.

Bandura, A. (1977). *Social learning theory.* Englewood Cliffs, NJ: Prentice Hall.

Bandura, A. (1982). Self efficacy mechanisms in human agency, *American Psychologist, 37,* 122–47.

Bandura, A. (1989). Human agency in social cognitive theory. *American Psychologist, 44,* 1175–84.

Bandura, A. (1994). Self-efficacy. In V. Ramachandran (ed.), *Encyclopaedia of human behavior.* New York: Academic Press.

Bandura, A. (1995). *Self-efficacy in changing societies.* Cambridge: Cambridge University Press.

Bandura, A. (1998). Personal and collective efficacy in human adaptation and change. In J. Adair, D. Belanger & K. Dion (eds), *Advances in psychological science* (Vol. 1: *Personal, social and cultural aspects*). Hove, UK: Psychology Press.

Bandura, A. (1999). Social cognitive theory of personality. In L. Pervin & O. John (eds), *Handbook of personality: Theory and research* (2nd edn, pp.154–96). New York: Guilford.

Bandura, A. & Cervone, D. (1983). Self evaluative and self-efficacy mechanisms governing the motivational effects of goal systems, *Journal of Personality and Social Psychology, 45,* 1017–28.

Bandura, A., Ross, D. & Ross, S. (1961). Transmission of aggression through imitation of aggressive models, *Journal of Abnormal and Social Psychology, 63,* 575–82.

Baran, S. & Davis, D. (2008). *Mass communication theory: Foundations, ferment and future* (5th edn). Boston, MA: Wadsworth.

Barbato, G., Monica, C., Costanzo, A. & Padova, V. (2012). Dopamine activation in neuroticism as measured by spontaneous eye blink rate, *Physiology & Behavior, 105,* 332–36.

Bargh, J. (2005). Bypassing the will: Toward demystifying the nonconscious control of social behaviour. In R. Hassin, J. Uleman & J. Bargh (eds), *The new unconscious* (pp. 37–60). New York: Oxford University Press.

Barrick, M., Mount, M. & Gupta, R. (2003). Meta-analysis of the relationship between the Five-Factor Model of personality and Holland's Occupational Types, *Personnel Psychology, 56,* 45–74.

Barton, K., Dielman, T. & Cattell, R. (1971). The prediction of school grades from personality and IQ measures, *Personality, 2,* 325–33.

Bartram, D. & Lindley, P. (2007). *Psychological testing: The BPS Occupational Test Administration Open Learning Programme.* Oxford: Wiley-Blackwell.

Bass, B. (1997). Does the transactional-transformational leadership paradigm transcend organizational and national boundaries? *American Psychologist, 52,* 130–9.

Bastone, L. & Wood, H. (1997). Individual differences in the ability to decode emotional facial expressions, *Psychology: A Journal of Human Behavior, 34,* 32–6.

Baxter, D., Motiuk, L. & Fortin, S. (1995). Intelligence and personality in criminal offenders. In D. Saklofske & M. Zeidner (eds), *International Handbook of Personality and Intelligence* (pp. 673–86). New York: Plenum.

Bell, J., Campbell, S., Erikson, M., Hogue, T., McLean, Z., Rust, S. & Taylor, R. (2003). An overview: DSPD programme concepts and progress, *Issues in Forensic Psychology, 4,* 11–23.

Belmont, L. & Marolla, F. (1973). Birth order, family size and intelligence, *Science, 182,* 1096–101.

Benet-Martínez, V. & Waller, N. G. (2002). From adorable to worthless: Implicit and self-report structure of highly evaluative personality descriptors, *European Journal of Personality, 16,* 1–41.

Benjamin, J., Li, L., Patterson, C., Greenberg, B., Murphy, D. & Hamer, D. (1996). Population and familial association between the D4 Dopamine receptor gene and measures of novelty seeking, *Nature Genetics, 12,* 81–4.

Benton, D. & Roberts, G. (1988). Effect of vitamin and mineral supplementation on intelligence of a sample of school children, *Lancet, 1,* 140–4.

Bergeman, C., Chipuer, H., Plomin, R., Pedersen, N., McClearn, G., Nesselroade, J., Costa, J. & McCrae, P. (1993). Genetic and environmental effects on openness to experience, agreeableness and conscientiousness: An adoption/twin study, *Journal of Personality, 61,* 159–79.

Binet, A. & Simon, T. (1905). New methods for the diagnosis of the intellectual level of subnormals. In H. H. Goddard (ed.), *Development of intelligence in children (the Binet–Simon Scale)* (E. S. Kite, trans., pp. 37–90). Baltimore, MD: Williams & Wilkins.

Bjerkedal, T., Kristensen, P., Skjeret, G. & Brevik, J. (2007). Intelligence test scores and birth order among young Norwegian men (conscripts) analyzed within and between families, *Intelligence, 35,* 503–14.

Blake, J. (1981). Family size and the quality of children, *Demography, 18,* 421–42.

Block, J. (1961). *The Q-sort methodology in personality assessment and psychiatric research.* Springfield, IL: Charles C. Thomas.

Boring, E. (1923). Intelligence as the tests test it, *New Republic, 35,* 35–7.

Borkenau, P., Riemann, R., Spinath, F. & Angleitner, A. (2006). Genetic and environmental influences on Person x Situation profiles, *Journal of Personality, 74,* 1451–80.

Bornstein, R. (2010). Psychoanalytic theory as a unifying framework for 21st century personality assessment, *Psychoanalytic Psychology, 27,* 133–52.

Bouchard, T. & Loehlin, J. (2001). Genes, evolution, and personality, *Behavior Genetics, 31,* 243–73.

Bouchard, T. & McGue, M. (1981). Family studies of intellignece: A review. *Science, 212,* 1055–9.

Bouchard, T. (1994). Genes, environment and personality, *Science, 264,* 1700–1.

Boyatzis, R. & Goleman, D. (2001). *The Emotional Competence Inventory: University edition.* Boston, MA: HayGroup.

Braden, J. (1995). Intelligence and personality in school and educational psychology. In D. Saklofske & M. Zeidner (eds), *International handbook of personality and intelligence* (pp. 621–50). New York: Plenum.

Braungart, J., Plomin, R., DeFries, J. & Fulker, D. (1992). Genetic influence on tester-rated infant temperament as assessed by Bayley's Infant Behavior Record: Nonadoptive and adoptive siblings and twins, *Developmental Psychology, 28,* 40–7.

British Psychological Society (2007). *Guidelines for psychologists working with animals.* Leicester: British Psychological Society.

Brody, N. (2006). Beyond 'g'. In K. Murphy (ed.) *A critique of emotional intelligence: What are the problems and how can they be fixed?* Mahwah, NJ: Erlbaum.

Bryman, A. & Cramer, D. (2011). *Quantitative data analysis with IBM SPSS 17, 18 &19: A guide for social scientists.* London: Routledge.

Buck, R. (1999). The biological affects: A typology, *Psychological Review, 106,* 301–36.

Burger, J. (2010). *Personality* (7th edn). Belmont, CA: Wadsworth.

Burns, J. (2003). *Transformational leadership.* New York: Scribner.

Buss, A. & Plomin, R. (1975). *A temperament theory of personality development.* New York: Wiley.

Buss, A. & Plomin, R. (1984). *Temperament: Early developing personality traits.* Hillsdale, NJ: Erlbaum.

Buss, D. (1988). From vigilands to violence: Tactics of mate retention in American undergraduates, *Ethology and Sociobiology, 9,* 291–317.

Buss, D. (1991). Evolutionary personality psychology, *Annual Review of Psychology, 42,* 459–91.

Buss, D. (1994). *The evolution of desire: Strategies of human mating.* New York: Basic Books.

Buss, D. (1995a). Evolutionary psychology: A new paradigm for psychological science, *Psychological Inquiry, 6,* 1–49.

Buss, D. (1995b). Psychological sex differences: Origins through sexual selection, *American Psychologist, 50*, 164–8.

Buss, D. & Barnes, M. (1986). Preferences in human mate selection, *Journal of Personality and Social Psychology, 50*, 559–70.

Buss, D. & Duntley, J. (2006). The evolution of aggression. In M. Schaller, D. Kenrick and J. Simpson (eds), *Evolution and social psychology* (pp. 263–86). New York: Psychology Press.

Buss, D. & Hawley, P. (eds) (2011). *The evolution of personality and individual differences.* New York: Oxford University Press.

Cahan, S. & Cohen, N. (1989). Age versus schooling effects on intelligence development, *Child Development, 60*, 1239–49.

Caprara, G. & Cervone, D. (2000). *Personality: Determinants, dynamics and potentials.* Cambridge: Cambridge University Press.

Caprara, G., Vecchione, M., Alessandri, G., Gerbino, M. & Barbaranelli, C. (2011). The contribution of personality traits and self-efficacy beliefs to academic achievement: A longitudinal study, *British Journal of Educational Psychology, 81*, 78–96.

Capron, C. & Duyme, M. (1989). Assessment of effects of socio-economic status on IQ in a full cross-fostering study, *Nature, 340(6234)*, 552–4.

Carlo, G., Okun, M., Knight, G. & de Guzman, M. (2005). The interplay of traits and motives on volunteering: Agreeableness, extraversion and prosocial value motivation, *Personality and Individual Differences, 38*, 1293–1305.

Carlyle, T. (1907). *On heroes, hero-worship, and the heroic in history.* Boston, MA: Houghton Mifflin.

Carragher, T., Carragher, D. & Schliemann, A. (1985). Mathematics in the streets and in schools, *British Journal of Developmental Psychology, 3*, 21–9.

Carroll, J. (1993). *Human cognitive abilities: A survey of factor-analytic studies.* New York: Press Syndicate of the University of Cambridge.

Carver, C. & Scheier, M. (1998). *On the self-regulation of behavior.* New York: Cambridge University Press.

Caspi, A. & Roberts, B. (2001). Personality development across the life course: The argument for change and continuity, *Psychological Inquiry, 12*, 49–66.

Caspi, A., Roberts, B. & Shiner, R. (2005). Personality development: Stability and change, *Annual Review of Psychology, 56*, 453–8.

Cattell, R. (1943). The description of personality: Basic traits resolved into clusters, *Journal of Abnormal and Social Psychology, 38*, 476–507.

Cattell, R. (1950). *Personality: A systematic, theoretical, and factual study.* New York: Wiley.

Cattell, R. (1957). *Personality and motivation: Structure and measurement.* New York: Harcourt, Brace & World.

Cattell, R. (1963). Theory of fluid and crystallized intelligence: A critical experiment. *Journal of Educational Psychology, 54*, 1–22.

Cattell, R. (1971). *Abilities, their structure, growth, and action measurement.* New York: Houghton Mifflin.

Cattell, R. (1977). *Handbook of modern personality theory.* Washington, DC: Hemisphere.

Cattell, R. (1987). *Intelligence: its structure, growth and action.* New York: Springer.

Cattell, R. & Kline, P. (1976). *The scientific analysis of personality and motivation.* New York: Academic Press.

Cattell, R., Eber, H. & Tatsuoka, M. (1970). *Handbook for the 16 PF.* Champaign, IL: Institute for Personality and Ability Testing.

Ceci, S. (1991). How much does schooling influence general intelligence and its cognitive components? A reassessment of the evidence, *Developmental Psychology, 24*, 703–22.

Chamorro-Premuzic, T. (2007). *Personality and Individual differences.* Oxford: BPS Blackwell.

Chamorro-Premuzic, T. (2011). *Personality and individual differences* (2nd edn). Chichester: BPS Blackwell.

Chamorro-Premuzic, T. & Furnham, A. (2003a). Personality predicts academic performance: Evidence from two longitudinal university samples, *Journal of Research in Personality, 17*, 319–38.

Chamorro-Premuzic, T. & Furnham, A. (2003b). Personality traits and academic examination performance, *European Journal of Personality, 17*, 237–50.

Chamorro-Premuzic, T. & Furnham, A. (2005). Intellectual competence, *The Psychologist*, *18*, 352–4.

Chamorro-Premuzic, T. & Furnham, A. (2006). Intellectual competence and the intelligent personality: A third way in differential psychology, *Review of General Psychology*, *10*, 251–67.

Chauhan, K. & Ahmad, H. (2007). Perception of parental attitude amongst socially withdrawn children. In R. Singh & R. Shyam (eds), *Psychology of wellbeing* (pp. 413–23). New Delhi: Global Vision Publishing House.

Chen, J. & Gardner, H. (2005). Assessment based on multiple-intelligence theory. In D. Flanagan and P. Harvison (eds), *Contemporary intellectual assessment: theories, tests and issues* (2nd ed.), New York: Guilford.

Christensen, A., Turner, C., Holman, J. & Gregory, M. (1991). Health locus of control and depression in end-stage renal disease, *Journal of Consulting and Clinical Psychology*, *59*, 419–24.

Cohen, R. A. (1967). Primary group structure, conceptual styles and school achievement. Unpublished Doctoral Dissertation: University of Pittsburg, PA.

Cohen, R. J. & Swerdlik, M. E. (2002). *Psychological testing and assessment: An introduction to tests and measurement* (5th edn). Boston, MA: McGraw Hill.

Cohen, J., Cohen, P., Chen, H., Kasen, S. & Brook, J. (2006). Parenting behaviours associated with risk for offspring personality disorder during adulthood, *Archives of General Psychiatry*, *63*, 579–87.

Conn, S. & Rieke, M. (1994). *The 16PF fifth edition technical manager*. Champaign, IL: Institute for Personality and Ability Testing.

Contrada, R. J., Cather, C. & O'Leary, A. (1999). Personality and health: Dispositions and processes in disease susceptibility and adaptation to illness. In L. A. Pervin and O. P. John (eds), *Handbook of personality: Theory and research* (2nd edn, pp. 576–604). New York: Guilford.

Cooper, R., Guo, X., Rotimi, C., Luke, A., Ward, R., Adeyemo, A. & Danilov, S. (2000). Heritability of angiotensin-converting enzyme and angiotensinogen: A comparison of US blacks and Nigerians, *Hypertension*, *35*, 1141–7.

Cooper, C. (2002). *Individual differences* (2nd edn). London: Hodder Arnold.

Costa, P. & McCrae, R. (1992). *Revised Neo Personality Inventory (NEP-PI-R) and NEO Five-Factor Inventory (NEO-FFI) professional manual*. Odessa, FL: Psychological Assessment Resources.

Costa, P., McCrae, R. & Arenberg, D. (1980). Enduring dispositions in adult males, *Journal of Personality and Social Psychology*, *38*, 793–800.

Court, J. (1983). Sex differences in performance on Raven's Progressive Matrices: A review, *Alberta Journal of Educational Research*, *29*, 54–74.

Cramer, P. (1991). *The development of defense mechanisms: Theory, research, and assessment*. New York: Springer.

Cronbach, L. (1970). *Essentials of psychological testing* (3rd edn). New York: Harper & Row.

Dabbs, J., Alford, E. & Fielden, J. (1998). Trial lawyers and testosterone: Blue-collar talent in a white-collar world, *Journal of Applied Social Psychology*, *28*, 84–94.

Dabbs, J., Strong, R. & Milun, R. (1997). Exploring the mind of testosterone: A beeper study, *Journal of Research in Personality*, *31*, 557–87.

Damasio, A. (1994). *Descartes' error: Emotion, reason, and the human brain*. New York: Putnam.

Davidson, R. (1993). The neuropsychology of emotion and affective style. In M. Lewis and J. Haviland (eds), *Handbook of emotions* (pp. 143–54). New York: Guilford Press.

Davidson, R. (2003). Affective neuroscience and psychophysiology: Toward a synthesis, *Psychophysiology*, *40*, 655–65.

Davidson, R., Ekman, P., Saron, C., Senulis, J. & Friesen, W. (1990). Approach/withdrawal and cerebral asymmetry: Emotional expression and brain physiology, *Journal of Personality and Social Psychology*, *58*, 330–41.

Dawis, R. & Lofquist, L. (1984). *A psychological theory of work adjustment*. Minneapolis, MN: University of Minnesota Press.

Deary, I., Spinath, F., & Bates, T. (2006). Genetics of intelligence, *European Journal of Human Genetics*, *14*, 690–700.

Deary, I., Whalley, L. & Starr, J. (2003). IQ at age 11 and longevity: Results from a follow-up of the Scottish Mental Survey 1932. In C. Finch, J. Robine & Y. Christen (eds), *Brain and longevity: Perspectives in longevity* (pp. 153–64). Berlin: Springer.

Deary, I., Whalley, L., Lemmon, H., Crawford, H. & Starr, J. (2000). The stability of individual differences in mental ability from childhood to old age: Follow-up of the 1932 Scottish Mental Survey, *Intelligence, 28*, 49–55.

Denollet, J. (2005). DS14: Standard assessment of negative affectivity, social inhibition, and Type D personality: A potential risk factor refined, *Journal of Psychosomatic Research, 49*, 255–66.

Department of Health (2000). *Reforming The Mental Health Act – summary.* London: The Stationery Office. Retrieved from http://www.dh.gov.uk/en/Publicationsandstatistics/Publications/PublicationsPoliceyAndGuidance/DH_4007591.

DeRoberts, E. (2006). Deriving a humanistic theory of child development from the works of Carl Rogers and Karen Horney, *The Humanistic Psychologist, 34(2)*, 172–99.

Devlin, B., Daniels, M. & Roeder, K. (1997). Heritability of IQ, *Nature, 388*, 468–71.

Dollard, J. & Miller, N. (1941). *Social learning and imitation.* New Haven, CT: Yale University Press.

Dollard, J. & Miller, N. (1950). *Personality and psychotherapy: An analysis in terms of learning, thinking, and culture.* New York: McGraw-Hill.

Downey, D. (2001). Number of siblings and intellectual development: The resource dilution explanation, *American Psychologist, 56*, 497–504.

Ellis, A. (1958a). Rational psychotherapy, *General Psychology, 59*, 35–49.

Ellis, A. (1958b). *Sex without guilt.* New York: Grove Press.

Ellis, A. (1978). Towards a theory of personality. In R. Corsini (ed.), *Readings in current personality theories.* Itasca, IL: Peacock.

Ellis, A. (1979). The theory of rational-emotive therapy. In A. Ellis and J. Whiteley (eds), *Theoretical and empirical foundations of rational-emotive therapy.* Monterey, CA: Brooks/Cole.

Engel, G. (1977). The need for a new medical model: A challenge for biomedicine, *Science, 196*, 129–36.

Engler, B. (2008). *Personality theories* (8th edn). Boston: Wadsworth.

Epstein, S. (1983). Aggregation and beyond: Some basic issues on the prediction of behavior, *Journal of Personality, 51*, 360–92.

Erikson, E. (1963). *Childhood and society* (2nd edn). New York: Norton.

Erikson, E. (1968). *Identity: Youth and crisis.* New York: Norton.

Erikson, E. (1975). *Life history and the historical moment.* New York: Norton.

Evans, S., Ferrando, S., Rabkin, J. & Fishman, B. (2000). Health locus of control, distress and utilization of protease inhibitors among HIV-positive men, *Journal of Psychosomatic Research, 49*, 157–62.

Exner, J. (1974). *The Rorschach: A comprehensive system*, vol. 1. New York: Wiley.

Eysenck, H. (1967). *The biological basis of personality.* Springfield, IL: Charles C. Thomas.

Eysenck, H. (1971). *Race, intelligence and education.* London: Maurice Temple Smith.

Eysenck, H. (2000). *Intelligence: A new look.* London: Transaction.

Eysenck, H. (2004). *Decline and fall of the Freudian Empire.* New Brunswick, NJ: Transaction.

Eysenck, H. & Eysenck, S. (1975). *Eysenck personality questionnaire manual.* San Diego, CA: Educational and Industrial Testing Service.

Eysenck, H., & Eysenck, S. (1976). *Psychoticism as a dimension of personality.* London: Hodder & Stoughton,

Eysenck, H. & Eysenck, S. (1982). Recent advances in cross-cultural study of personality. In C. Spielberger and J. Butcher (eds), *Advances in personality assessment.* Hillsdale, NJ: Erlbaum.

Eysenck, H. & Eysenck, M. (1985). *Personality and Individual Differences: A natural science approach.* New York: Plenum Press.

Eysenck, H. & Eysenck, S. (1991). *Manual for the EPQR-R.* Sevenoaks: Hodder & Stoughton.

Eysenck, H. & Wilson, G. (1976). *Know your personality*. Harmondsworth, Middlesex: Penguin.

Eysenck, S., Eysenck, H. & Barrett, P. (1985). A revised version of the psychoticism scale, *Personality and Individual Differences, 6*, 21–29.

Feist, G. (1998). A meta-analysis of the impact of personality on scientific and artistic creativity, *Personality and Social Psychological Review, 2*, 290–309.

Feist, G. (1999). The influence of personality on artistic and scientific creativity. In R. Sternberg (ed.), *Handbook of creativity* (pp. 273–96). New York: Cambridge University Press.

Fiedler, F. (1967). *A theory of leadership effectiveness*. New York: McGraw-Hill.

Fiske, S. (2007). Core social motivations: Views from the couch, consciousness, classroom, computers and collectives. In J. Shah & W. Gardner (eds), *Handbook of motivation science*, New York: Guilford Press.

Fiske, A., Kitayama, S., Markus, H. & Nisbett, R. (1998). The cultural matrix of social psychology. In D. Gilbert, S. Fiske & G. Lindzey (eds), *The handbook of social psychology* (pp. 915–81). Boston, MA: McGraw-Hill.

Flach, F. (1990). Disorders of the pathways involved in the creative process, *Creativity Research Journal, 3*, 138–65.

Flagel, S., Akil, H. & Robinson, T. (2009). Individual differences in the attribution of incentive salience to reward-related cues: Implications for addiction, *Neuropharmacology, 56(S1)*, 139–48.

Flanagan, D., McGrew, K. & Ortiz, S. (2000). *The Wechsler Intelligence Scales and Gf-Gc theory: A contemporary approach to interpretation*. Needham Heights, MA: Allyn & Bacon.

Fleeson, W. (2001). Toward a structure- and process-integrated view of personality: Traits as density distribution of states, *Journal of Personality and Social Psychology, 80*, 1011–27.

Fleeson, W. (2004). Moving personality beyond the person situation debate: The challenge and the opportunity of within person variability, *American Psychologist, 13*, 83–7.

Fleeson, W. & Gallagher, P. (2009). The implications of big-five standing for the distribution of trait manifestation in behavior: Fifteen experience-sampling studies and a meta-analysis, *Journal of Personality and Social Psychology, 97*, 1097–114.

Flynn, J. (1984). The mean IQ of Americans: Massive gains 1932 to 1978, *Psychological Bulletin, 95*, 29–51.

Flynn, J. (1987). Massive IQ gains in 14 nations: What IQ tests really measure, *Psychological Bulletin, 101*, 171–91.

Flynn, J. (1994). IQ gains over time. In R. Sternberg (ed.), *Encyclopedia of human intelligence* (pp. 617–23). New York: Macmillan.

Fox, N. & Davidson, R. (1987). Electroencephalogram asymmetry in response to the approach of a stranger and maternal separation, *Developmental Psychology, 23*, 233–40.

Franken, I. & Muris, P. (2005). BIS/BAS personality constructs and college students' substance use, *Personality and Individual Differences, 40*, 1497–1503.

Fransella, F., Bell, R. & Bannister, D. (2004). *A manual of Repertory Grid Technique* (2nd edn). Chichester: John Wiley.

Fraser, S. (1995) Introduction. In S. Fraser (ed.), *The bell curve wars: race intelligence, and the future of America*. New York: Basic Books.

Freud, S. (1950). *Totem and taboo*. London: Hogarth Press.

Frey, M. & Detterman, D. (2004). Scholastic assessment or g? The relationship between the Scholastic Assessment Test and general cognitive ability, *Psychological Science, 15*, 373–8.

Friedman, M. & Rosenman, R. (1957). Comparison of fat intake of American men and women: Possible relationship to incidence of clinical coronary artery disease, *Circulation, 16*, 339–47.

Friedman, M. & Rosenman, R. (1959). Association of specific overt behaviour pattern with blood and cardiovascular findings, *Journal of the American Medical Association, 169*, 1286–96.

Friedman, M. & Rosenman, R. (1974). *Type A behavior and your heart*. New York: Knopf.

References

Friedman, H., Kern, M. & Reynolds, C. (2010). Personality and health, subjective well-being, and longevity, *Journal of Personality, 78*, 179–216.

Funder, D. (2001). Personality, *Annual Review of Psychology, 52*, 197–221.

Funder, D. (2006). Towards a resolution of the personality triad: Persons, situations, and behaviors, *Journal of Research in Personality, 40*, 21–34.

Funder, D. (2009). Persons, behaviours and situations: An agenda for personality psychology in the postwar era, *Journal of Research in Personality, 43*, 120–6.

Funder, D. & Ozer, D. (1983). Behaviour as a function of situation, *Journal of Personality and Social Psychology, 44*, 107–12.

Gale, A. (1987). The psychophysiological context. In A. Gale and B. Christie (eds), *Psychophysiology and the electronic workplace* (pp. 17–32). Chichester: Wiley.

Gallup, G. & Suarez, S. (1985). Alternatives to the use of animals in psychological research, *American Psychologist, 40(10)*, 1104–11.

Galton, F. (1865). Hereditary talent and character, *Macmillan's Magazine, 12*, 157–166, 318–27.

Galton, F. (1869). *Hereditary genius: An inquiry into its laws and consequences.* London: Macmillan.

Galton, F. (1876). The history of twins as a criterion of the relative powers of nature and nurture, *Royal Anthropological Institute of Great Britain and Ireland Journal, 6*, 391–406.

Galton, F. (1884). Measurement of character, *Fortnightly Review, 36*, 179–85.

Galton, F. (1908). *Memories of my life.* London: Methuen.

Garb, H. (1997). Race bias, social bias, and gender bias in clinical judgement, *Clinical Psychology: Science and Practice, 4*, 99–120.

Gardner, H. (1983). *Frames of mind: The theory of multiple intelligences.* New York: Basic Books.

Gardner, H. (1993). *Multiple intelligences: The theory in practice.* New York: Basic Books.

Gardner, H. (1999). *Intelligence reframed.* New York: Basic Books.

Gardner, H. (2004). Audiences for the theory of multiple intelligences, *Teachers College Record, 106*, 212–20.

Gardner, R. & Moriarty, A. (1968). Dimensions of cognitive control at preadolescence. In R. Gardner (ed.), *Personality development at preadolescence* (pp. 108–18). Seattle: University of Washington Press.

Gardner, R. & Schoen, R. (1962). Differentiation and abstraction in concept formation, *Psychological Monographs, 76(41)*, 1–21.

Ge, X. & Conger, R. (1999). Early adolescent adjustment problems and emergence of late adolescent personality, *American Journal of Community Psychology, 27*, 429–259.

Geary, D. C. (1996). Sexual selection and sex differences in mathematical abilities, *Behavioral and Brain Sciences, 19*, 229–84.

Geary, D. C. (2007). Educating the evolved mind: Conceptual foundations for an evolutionary educational psychology. In J. S. Carlson & J. R. Levin (eds), *Educating the evolved mind* (pp. 1–99, Vol. 2, *Psychological perspectives on contemporary educational issues*). Greenwich, CT: Information Age.

Geen, R. (1984). Preferred stimulation levels in introverts and extroverts: Effects on arousal and performance, *Journal of Personality and Social Psychology, 46*, 1303–12.

Goldberg, L. (1990). An alternative 'description of personality': The Big Five factor structure, *Journal of Personality and Social Psychology, 59*, 1216–29.

Goldberg, L. & Saucier, G. (1995). So what do you propose we use instead? A reply to Block, *Psychological Bulletin, 117*, 221–5.

Goleman, D. (1995). Emotional intelligence: Why it can matter more than IQ. New York: Bantam.

Goleman, D. (2001). An EI-based theory of performance. In C. Chernis and D. Goleman (eds), *The emotionally intelligent workplace* (pp. 27–44). New York: Jossey-Bass.

Goleman D. & Boyatzis, R. (2005). *Emotional Competence Inventory* (ECI). Boston: Hay Resources Direct.

Goleman, D., Boyatzis, R. & McKee, A. (2002). *Primal leadership: Realizing the power of emotional intelligence.* Boston: Harvard Business School Press.

Goodwin, J. (2009). *Research In psychology: Methods and design.* Danvers, MA: John Wiley.

Gosling, S. (1998). Personality dimensions in spotted hyenas (Crocuta crocuta), *Journal of Comparative Psychology, 112,* 107–18.

Gosling, S. (2001). From mice to men: What can we learn about personality from animal research? *Psychological Bulletin, 127,* 45–86.

Gottfredson, L. (2004). Intelligence: Is it the epidemiologists' elusive 'fundamental cause' of social class inequalities in health? *Journal of Personality and Social Psychology, 86,* 174–99.

Gottfredson, L. & Deary, I. (2004). Intelligence predicts health and longevity, but why? *Current Directions in Psychological Science, 13,* 1–4.

Gould, S. (1995). Curveball. In. S. Fraser (ed.), *The bell curve wars: race, intelligence, and the future of America* (pp. 11–22). New York: Basic Books.

Gray, J. (1991). The neuropsychology of temperament. In J. Strelau and A. Angleitner (eds), *Explorations in temperament: International perspectives on theory and measurement* (pp. 105–28). New York: Plenum Press.

Gray, J. (1987b). Perspective on anxiety and impulsivity: A commentary, *Journal of Research in Personality, 21,* 493–509.

Green, M. & Jethwa, J. (2009). *Succeeding in the 2009 UK clinical aptitude test (UKCAT),* Nottingham: Apply2 Ltd.

Grigorenko, E. & Sternberg, R. (1995). Thinking styles. In D. Saklofske & M. Zeidner (eds), *International handbook of personality and intelligence* (pp. 205–29). New York: Plenum.

Guilford, J. (1967). *The nature of human intelligence,* New York: McGraw-Hill.

Guilford, J. (1975). Creativity: A quarter century of progress. In I. Taylor & J. Getzels (eds), *Perspectives in Creativity* (pp. 37–59). Chicago: Aldine.

Gustafsson, J. (1984). A unifying model for the structure of intellectual abilities. *Intelligence, 8(3),* 179–203.

Hakstian, R. & Cattell, R. (1978). Higher stratum ability structure on a basis of 20 primary abilities, *Journal of Educational Psychology, 70,* 657–9.

Halpern, D. (2000). *Sex differences in cognitive abilities* (3rd edn). Mahwah, NJ: Erlbaum.

Halpern, D. & LaMay, M. (2000). The smarter sex: A critical review of sex differences in intelligence, *Educational Psychology Review, 12,* 170–89.

Hamilton, W. (1964). The evolution of social behaviour, *Journal of Theoretical Biology, 7,* 1–52.

Hampson, S. (ed.) (2000). *Advances in personality psychology* (vol. 1). London: Psychology Press.

Hansen, P., Floderus, B., Frederiksen, K. & Johansen, C. (2005). Personality traits, health behavior, and risk for cancer, *Cancer, 103,* 1082–91.

Harris, R. (1995). Where is the child's environment? A group socialization theory of development, *Psychological Review, 102,* 458–89.

Hart, C., Taylor, M., Smith, G., Whalley, L., Starr, J., Hole, D., Wilson, V. & Deary, I. (2003). Childhood IQ, social class, deprivation, and their relationships with mortality and morbidity risk in later life: Prospective observational study linking the Scottish Mental Survey 1932 and the Midspan studies, *Psychosomatic Medicine, 65,* 877–83.

Hart, S. (2008). *Brain, attachment, personality: An introduction to neuroaffective development.* London: Karnac.

Hartshorne, H. & May, A. (1928). *Studies in the nature of character: vol. 1. Studies in deceit.* New York: Macmillan.

Harvey, O., Hunt, D. & Schroder, H. (1961). *Conceptual systems and personality organization.* Oxford: Wiley.

Haselgrove, M. & Hogarth, L. (2011). Introduction. In M. Haselgrove & L. Hogarth (eds), *Clinical applications of learning theory.* London: Psychology Press.

Haslam, N. (2007). *Introduction to personality and intelligence.* London: Sage.

Haslam, N. & Kim, H. (2002). Categories and continua: A review of taxometric research, *Genetic, Social, and General Psychology Monographs, 128,* 271–320.

Hebb, D. (1955). Drives and the CNS (conceptual nervous system), *Psychological Review, 62,* 243–54.

Hennig, K. & Walker, L. (2008). The darker side of accommodating others: Examining the interpersonal structure of maladaptive constructs, *Journal of Research in Personality, 42(1)*, 2–21.

Heppner, P., Wampold, B. & Kivlighan, D. (2007). *Research design in counseling.* Belmont, CA: Thomson.

Herrstein, R. & Murray, C. (1994). *The bell curve: Intelligence and class structure in American life.* New York: Free Press.

Holland, J. (1973). *Making vocational preferences inventory.* Palo Alto, CA: Consulting Psychologists Press.

Horn, J. & Cattell, R. (1966). Refinement of the theory of fluid and crystallised general intelligences, *Journal of Educational Psychology, 57*, 253–70.

Horney, K. (1945). *Our inner conflicts: A constructive theory of neurosis.* New York: Norton.

Horney, K. (1950). *Neurosis and human growth: The struggle toward self-realization.* New York: Norton.

Horney, K. (1977). *The neurotic personality of our time.* New York: Routledge and Kegan Paul.

Horney, K. (1993). *Feminine psychology.* New York: Norton.

Howe, M. (1988a). The hazard of using correlational evidence as a means of identifying the causes of individual ability differences: A rejoinder to Sternberg and a reply to Miles, *British Journal of Psychology, 79*, 539–45.

Howe, M. (1988b). Intelligence as explanation, *British Journal of Psychology, 79*, 349–60.

Howe, M. (1997). *IQ in question: The truth about intelligence.* London: Sage.

Howell, D. (2006). *Statistical methods for psychology* (6th edn). Belmont, CA: Thomson Wadsworth.

Ingram, R. & Loxton, D. (2005). Vulnerability-stress models. In B. Hankin & J. Abela (eds), *Development of Psychopathology: A vulnerability-stress perspective* (pp. 32–46). New York: Sage.

Irwing, P. & Lynn, R. (2005). Sex differences in means and variability on the progressive matrices in university students: A meta-analysis, *British Journal of Psychology, 96*, 505–24.

Jang, K., Livesley, W. & Vernon, P. (1996). Heritability of the big five personality dimensions and their facets: A twin study, *Journal of Personality, 64*, 577–91.

Jenkins, C., Ronsenman, R. & Friedman, M. (1968). Replicability of rating the coronary-prone behaviour pattern, *British Journal of Preventative & Social Medicine, 22*, 16–22.

Jensen, A. (1980). *Bias in mental testing.* New York: Free Press.

Jensen, A. (1998). *The g factor: The science of mental ability.* Westport, CT: Praeger.

Jorgensen, R., Blair, T., Kolodziej, M. & Schreer, G. (1996). Elevated blood pressure and personality: A meta-analytic review, *Psychological Bulletin, 2*, 293–320.

Jung, C. (1954). *The development of personality.* New York: Pantheon.

Jung, C. (1959). *The archetypes and the collective unconscious.* Princeton, NJ: Princeton University Press.

Jung, C. (1964). *Man and his symbols.* New York: Dell.

Jung, C. (1965). *Memories, dreams, reflections.* Princeton, NJ: Princeton University Press.

Jung, C. (1968). *Analytical psychology: Its theory and practice.* New York: Pantheon.

Juni, S. (1996). Review of the NEO Personality Inventory. In J. Conoley & J. Impara (eds), *Twelfth mental measurements yearbook* (pp. 863–8). Lincoln: University of Nebraska Press.

Kagan, J. (1966). Reflection-impulsivity: The generality and dynamics of conceptual tempo, *Journal of Abnormal Psychology, 71*, 17–24.

Kagan, J. (1999). The concept of behavioural inhibition. In L. Schmidt & J. Schulkin (eds), *Extreme fear, shyness, and social phobia: Origins, biological mechanisms, and clinical outcomes.* New York: Oxford University Press.

Kanfer, R., Ackerman, P., Murtha, T. & Goff, M. (1995). Personality and intelligence in industrial and organizational psychology. In D. H. Saklofske & M. Zeidner (eds), *International Handbook of Personality and Intelligence* (pp. 577–602). New York: Plenum.

Kaufman, A. & Lichtenberger, E. (2005). *Assessing adolescent and adult intelligence* (3rd edn). Boston: Allyn & Bacon.

Kelly, G. (1955). *The psychology of personal constructs* (vols 1 & 2). New York: Norton.

Kelly, G. (1963). *A theory of personality: The psychology of personal constructs.* New York: Norton.

Kenrick, D. & Funder, D. (1988). Profiting from controversy: Lessons from the person–situation debate, *American Psychologist, 43*, 23–34.

Kern, M. & Friedman, H. (2008). Do conscientious individuals live longer? A quantitative review, *Health Psychology, 27*, 505–12.

Keyes, C., Shmotkin, D. & Ryff, C. (2002). Optimizing well-being: The empirical encounter of two traditions, *Journal of Personality and Social Psychology, 82*, 1007–22.

Klein, G. (1953). Cognitive system-principles of leveling and sharpening: Individual differences in assimilation effects in visual time-error, *Journal of Psychology: Interdisciplinary and Applied, 37*, 105–22.

Klein, G. (1954). Need and regulation. In M. R. Jones (ed.), *Nebraska Symposium on Motivation.* Lincoln: University of Nebraska Press.

Klein, G. (1970). *Perceptions, motives and personality.* New York: Knopf.

Klein, G., Gardner, R. & Schlesinger, H. (1962). Tolerance for unrealistic experiences: A study of the generality of a cognitive control, *British Journal of Psychology, 53*, 41–55.

Kline, P. (1996). Intelligence: The Psychometric view, London: Routledge

Kline, P. (2000). *Handbook of psychological testing* (2nd edn). London: Routledge.

Knutson, B., Wolkowitz, O., Cole, S., Chan, T., Moore, E., Johnson, R., Terpstra, J., Turner, R. & Reus, V. (1998). Selective alteration of personality and social behavior by serotonergic intervention, *American Journal of Psychiatry, 155*, 373–8.

Kobasa, S. C. (1979). Stressful life events, personality, and health: an inquiry into hardiness, *Journal of Personality and Social Psychology, 37*, 1–11.

Kobasa-Ouellette, S. C. and Di Placido, J. (2001). Personality's role in the protection and enhancement of health: Where the research has been, where it is stuck, how it might move. In E. Baum, T. A. Revenson and J. E. Singer (eds), *Handbook of health psychology* (pp. 175–93). Mahwah, NJ: Erlbaum.

Kofman, S. (1985). *The enigma of woman: Woman in Freud's writings.* Ithaca, NY: Cornell University Press.

Kolb, D. (1976). *Cognitive styles in infancy and early childhood.* New York: Academic Press.

Kolb, D. (1981). *The learning style inventory.* Boston: McBer.

Kyllonen, P. & Shute, V. (1989). A taxonomy of learning skills. In P. Ackerman, R. Sternberg & R. Glaser (eds), *Learning and Individual Differences: Advances in theory and research* (pp. 117–63). New York: Freeman & Co.

Lachar, B. (1993). Coronary-prone behavior: Type A behavior revisited, *Texas Heart Institute Journal, 20(3)*, 143–51.

Larsen, R. & Buss, D. (2010). *Personality psychology: Domains of knowledge about human behaviour* (4th edn). New York: McGraw-Hill.

Lazarus, R. & Folkman, S. (1984). *Stress, appraisal and coping.* New York: Springer.

Lee, V., Brooks-Gunn, J., Schnur, E. & Liaw, F. (1990). Are Head Start effects sustained? A longitudinal follow-up comparison of disadvantaged children attending Head Start, no preschool, and other preschool programmes, *Child Development, 61*, 495–507.

Levine, S., Vasilyeva, M., Lourenco, S., Newcombe, N. & Huttenlocher, J. (2005). Socioeconomic status modifies the sex difference in spatial skill, *Psychological Science, 16*, 841–5.

Lewin, K., Dembo, T., Festinger, L. & Sears, P. (1944). Level of aspiration. In J. McV Hunt (ed.), *Personality and the behaviour disorders: A handbook on experimental and clinical research* (Vol. 1, pp. 333–78). New York: Ronald Press.

Leyens, J., Parke, R., Camino, L. & Berkowitz, L. (1975). Effects of movie violence on aggression in a field setting as a function of group dominance and cohesion, *Journal of Persoanlity and Social Psychology, 32*, 346–60.

Liebert, R. & Baron, R. (1972). Some immediate effects of televised violence on children's behavior, *Developmental Psychology*, *6*, 469–75.

Lillard, A. (1998). Ethnopsychologies: Cultural variations in theories in mind, *Psychological Bulletin*, *123*, 3–32.

Lindley, P. (2001). *Review of personality assessment instruments* (2nd edn). Leicester: BPS Books.

Lisney, M. (1989). *Psychology: Experiments, investigations and practicals*. Oxford: Blackwell.

Locke, E. & Latham, G. (1990). Work motivation and satisfaction: Light at the end of the tunnel, *Psychological Science*, *1*, 240–6.

Loehlin, J. (1992). *Genes and environment in personality development*. Newberry Park, CA: Sage.

Loehlin, J., Horn, J. & Willerman, L. (1990). Heredity, environment, and personality change: Evidence from the Texas Adoption Project, *Journal of Personality*, *58*, 221–43.

Loehlin, J., McCrae, R., Costa, P. & John, O. (1998). Heritabilities of common and measure-specific components of the Big Five personality factors, *Journal of Research in Personality*, *32*, 431–53.

Loehlin, J., Neiderhiser, J. & Reiss, D. (2003). The behavior genetics of personality and the NEAD Study, *Journal of Research in Personality*, *37*, 373–87.

Lohman, D. (2001). Issues in the definition and measurement of abilities. In J. Collis and S. Messick (eds), *Intelligence and personality: Bridging the gap in theory and measurement* (pp. 79–98). Mahwah, NJ: Erlbaum.

Lubinski, D. (2000). Scientific and social significance of assessing Individual Differences: 'Sinking shafts at a few critical points', *Annual Review of Psychology*, *51*, 405–44.

Lubinski, D. & Humphreys, L. (1990). A broadly based analysis of mathematical giftedness, *Intelligence*, *14*, 327–55.

Lynn, R. (1990). The role of nutrition in secular increase of intelligence, *Personality and Individual Differences*, *11*, 273–86.

Lynn, R. (1994a). Sex differences in brain size and intelligence: A paradox resolved, *Personality and Individual Differences*, *17*, 257–71.

Lynn, R. (1994b). Some reinterpretations of the Minnesota transracial adoption study, *Intelligence*, *19*, 21–28.

Lynn, R. & Irwing, P. (2004). Sex differences on the progressive matrices: A meta-analysis, *Intelligence*, *32*, 481–98.

Macaskill, N. & Macaskill, A. (1996). Rational-emotive therapy plus pharmacotherapy versus pharmacotherapy alone in the treatment of high cognitive dysfunction depression, *Cognitive Therapy and Research*, *20*, 575–92.

MacDonald, K. (1997). Life history theory and human reproductive behavior: Environmental/contextual influences and heritable variation, *Human Nature: An Interdisciplinary Biosocial Perspective*, *8*, 327–59.

Mackintosh, N. (1998). *IQ and human intelligence*. Oxford: Oxford University Press.

Macmillan, M. (2000). *Restoring Phineas Gage: A 150th retrospective*, *9*, 46–66.

Mahoney, B. (2011). *Critical Thinking in Psychology: Personality and Individual Differences*. Exeter: Learning Matters.

Maltby, J., Day, L. & Macaskill, A. (2010). *Personality, individual differences and intelligence* (2nd edn). Harlow: Pearson Education.

Markus, H. & Nurius, P (1986). Possible selves, *American Psychologist*, *41*, 954–69.

Maslow, A. (1987). *Motivation and personality*. New York: Harper and Row.

Mather, J. & Anderson, R. (1993). Personalities of octopuses (Octopus rubescens), *Journal of Comparative Psychology*, *107*, 336–40.

Matthews, G., Derryberry, D. & Siegle, G. (2000). Personality and emotion: Cognitive science perspectives. In S. Hampson (ed.), *Advances in Personality Psychology* (Vol. 1, pp. 199–237).

Matthews, G. & Gilliland, K. (1999). The personality theories of H. J. Eysenck and J. A. Gray: A comparative review. *Personality and Individual Differences*, *26*, 583–626.

Matthews, G., Deary, I. & Whiteman, M. (2003). *Personality traits*. Cambridge: Cambridge University Press.

Matthews, G., Deary, I. & Whiteman, M. (2009). *Personality traits* (3rd edn). Cambridge: Cambridge University Press.

Matthews, G., Zeidner, M. & Roberts, R. (2004). *Emotional intelligence: Science and myth*. London: MIT Press.

Mayr, E. (1982). *The growth of biological thought: Diversity, evolution, and inheritance*, Cambridge, MA: Harvard University Press.

McAdams, D. & Pals, J. (2006). A new Big Five fundamental principles for an integrative science of personality, *American Psychologist, 61*, 204–17.

McAdams, D. (1995). What do we know when we know a person? *Journal of Personality, 63*, 365–96.

McCrae, R. (1996). Social consequences of experiential openness, *Psychological Bulletin, 120*, 327–37.

McCrae, R. & Costa, P. (1994). The stability of personality: Observations and evaluations, *Current Directions in Psychological Science, 3*, 173–5.

McCrae, R. & Costa, P. (1997). Personality trait structure as a human universal, *American Psychologist, 52*, 509–516.

McCrae, R., Costa, P., del Pilar, G., Rolland, J. & Parker, W. (1998). Cross-cultural assessment of the five-factor model: The Revised NEO Personality Inventory, *Journal of Cross-Cultural Psychology, 29*, 171–88.

McCrae, R., Costa, P., Ostendorf, F., Angleitner, A., Hřebíčková, M., Avia, M., Sanz, J., Sánchez-Bernardos, M., Kusdil, E., Woodfield, R., Saunders, P. & Smith, P. (2000). Nature over nurture: Temperament, personality, and lifespan development, *Journal of Personality and Social Psychology, 78*, 173–86.

McCrae, R., Loeckenhoff, C. & Costa, P. (2005). A step toward DSM-V: Cataloguing personality-related problems in living, *European Journal of Personality, 19*, 269–86.

McGrew, K. (2005). The Cattell-Horn-Carroll theory of cognitive abilities. In D. Hanagan and P. Harrison (eds), contemporary intellectual assessment: theories, tests and issues (2nd ed.), New York: Guilford.

McGue, M., Bouchard, T., Iacono, W. & Lykken, D. (1993). Behavioral genetics of cognitive ability: A life-span perspective. In R. Plomin & G. McClearn (eds), *Nature, nurture, and psychology* (pp. 59–76). Washington, DC: American Psychological Association.

Messick, S. & Kogan, N. (1963). Differentiation and compartmentalization in object-sorting measure of categorizing style, *Perceptual and Motor Skills, 16*, 47–51.

Miller, J. G. & Schaberg, L. (2003). Cultural perspectives on personality and social psychology. In T. Millon & M. Lerner (eds), *Comprehensive handbook of psychology*: Vol. 5, *Personality and social psychology* (pp. 31–56). New York: John Wiley.

Miller, R. (1987). Empathic embarrassment: Situational and personal determinants of reactions to the embarrassment of another, *Journal of Personality and Social Psychology, 53*, 1061–9.

Miller, S. & Maner, J. (2009). Sex differences in response to sexual versus emotional infidelity: The moderating role of individual differences, *Personality and Individual Differences, 46*, 287–91.

Mischel, W. (1968) *Personality and assessment*. New York: Wiley.

Mischel, W. (1973). Toward a cognitive social learning reconceptualization of personality, *Psychological Review, 80*, 252–83.

Mischel, W. (1999). Personality coherence and dispositions in a cognitive-affective personality (CAPS) approach. In D. Cervone and Y. Shoda (eds), *The coherence of personality: Social-cognitive bases of consistency, variability, and organisation* (pp. 37–60). New York: Guilford.

Mischel, W. & Shoda, Y. (1995). A cognitive-affective system theory of personality: Reconceptualising situations, dispositions, dynamics, and invariance in personality structure. *Annual Review of Psychology, 49*, 229–58.

Monroe, S. & Simmons, A. (1991). Diathesis-stress theories in the context of life stress research: Implications for the depressive disorders, *Psychological Bulletin, 110*, 406–25.

Morey, L., Alexander, G. & Boggs, C. (2005). Gender in American Psychiatric Press Textbook of Personality Disorders. In J. Oldham, A. Skodal & D. Bender (eds), Washington DC: American Psychiatric Publishing, pp. 541–60.

Mortensen, E., Michaelsen, K., Sanders, D. & Reinisch, J. (2005). A dose-response relationship between maternal smoking during late pregnancy and adult intelligence in male offspring, *Paediatric & Perinatal Epidemiology, 19,* 4.

Mount, M., Barrick, M. & Murray, R. (1998). Five reasons why the 'Big Five' article has been frequently cited, *Personnel Psychology, 51,* 849–57.

Munafò, M. & Flint, J. (2011). Dissecting the genetic architecture of human personality, *Trends in Cognitive Sciences, 15,* 395–400.

Murray, H. (1938). *Explorations in personality.* New York: Oxford University Press.

Myers, I. B., McCaulley, M. H., Quenk, N. L. & Hammer, A. L. (1998/2003). *MBTI manual: A guide to the development and use of the Myers-Briggs Type Indicator* (3rd edn). Palo Alto, CA: Consulting Psychologists Press.

Neisser, U., Boodoo, O., Bouchard, T., Boykin, A., Brody, N., Ceci, S., Halpern, D., Loehlin, J., Perloff, R., Sternberg, R. & Urbina, S. (1996). Intelligence: Knowns and unknowns, *American Psychologist, 51,* 77–101.

Nettle, D. (2005). An evolutionary approach to the extraversion continuum, *Evolution and Human Behavior, 26,* 363–73.

Newcombe, T. (1929). *Consistency of certain extrovert–introvert behaviour patterns in 51 problem boys.* New York: Columbia University, Teachers College, Bureau of Publications.

Norman, W. (1963). Towards an adequate taxonomy of personality attributes: Replicated factor structure in peer nomination personality ratings, *Journal of Abnormal and Social Psychology, 66,* 574–83.

Norman, P., Bennett, P., Smith, C. & Murphy, S. (1997). Health locus of control and leisure-time exercise, *Personality and Individual Differences, 23,* 769–74.

O'Carroll, R. E., Smith, K. B., Grubb, N. R., Fox, K. A. A. & Masterson, G. (2001). Psychological factors associated with delay in attending hospital following a myocardial infarction, *Journal of Psychosomatic Research, 51,* 611–14.

Ozer, D. & Benet-Martinez, V. (2006). Personality and the prediction of consequential outcomes, *Annual Review of Psychology, 57,* 401–21.

Page, E. & Grandon, G. (1979). Family configuration and mental ability: Two theories contrasted with US data, *American Educational Research Journal, 16,* 257–72.

Paivio, A. (1971). Imagery and deep structure in the recall of English nominalizations, *Journal of Verbal Learning and Verbal Behavior, 10,* 1–12.

Paris, J. (2003). Personality disorders over time: Precursors, course and outcome, *Journal of Personality Disorders, 17,* 479–88.

Pask, G. & Scott, B. (1972). Learning strategies and individual competencies, *International Journal of Man-Machine Studies, 4,* 217–53.

Pask, G. (1976) Styles and strategies of learning, *British Journal of Educational Psychology, 46,* 128–48.

Patterson, G. (1977). Naturalistic observation in clinical assessment, *Abnormal Child Psychology, 5,* 309–22.

Patterson, T. & Joseph, S. (2007). Person-centered personality theory: Support from self-determination theory and positive psychology, *Journal of Humanistic Psychology, January, 47,* 117–39.

Pavlov, I. (1906). The scientific investigations of the psychical faculties or processes in the higher animals, *Science, 24,* 613–19.

Pavlov, I. (1927). *Conditioned reflexes.* London: Oxford.

Pavlov, I. (1928). *Lectures on conditioned reflexes.* New York: International Publishers.

Penke, L., Denissen, J. & Miller, G. (2007). The evolutionary genetics of personality, *European Journal of Personality, 22,* 3–30.

Perkins, D. & Bishopp, D. (2003). Dangerous and severe personality disorder and its relationship to sexual offending, *Issues in Forensic Psychology, 4,* 24–40.

Peterson, C. & Seligman, M. (2002). *Character strengths and virtues: A handbook and classifcation.* New York: Oxford University Press & American Psychological Association.

Petrie, A. (1967). *Individuality in pain and suffering.* Chicago: University of Chicago Press.

Phares, E. & Rotter, J. (1956). An effect of the situation on psychological testing, *Journal of Consulting Psychology, 20,* 291–3.

Piaget, J. (1952). *The origins of intelligence in children*. New York: International Universities Press.

Plomin, R. (1986). *Development, genetics and psychology*. Mahwah, NJ: Erlbaum.

Plomin, R. (2004). *Nature and nurture: An introduction to human behavioral genetics*. London: Wadsworth.

Plomin, R. & Caspi, A. (1999). Behavioral genetics and personality. In L. Pervin & O. John (eds), *Handbook of personality: Theory and research* (2nd edn, pp. 251–76). New York: Guilford Press.

Plomin, R. & Spinath, F. (2004). Intelligence: Genetics, genes, and genomics, *Journal of Personality and Social Psychology, 86*, 112–29.

Plomin, R., Caspi, A., Corley, R., Fulker, D. W. & DeFries, J. (1998). Adoption results for self-reported personality: Evidence for nonadditive genetic effects? *Journal of Personality and Social Psychology, 75*, 211–18.

Plomin, R., Chipuer, H. & Loehlin, J. (1990). Behavioral genetics and personality. In L. Pervin (ed.), *Handbook of personality: Theory and research* (pp. 225–43). New York: Guilford.

Plomin, R, Chipuer, H. & Neiderhiser, J. (1994). Behavioural genetic evidence for the importance of nonshared environment. In E. Hetherington, D. Reiss & R. Plomin (eds), *Separate social worlds of siblings: The impact of non-shared environment on development* (pp. 1–31). Hillsdale, NJ: Erlbaum.

Plomin, R., DeFries, J., McClearn, G. & McGuffin, P. (2008). *Behavioral genetics*. New York: Worth Publishers.

Plucker, J. (1996). Secondary science and mathematics teachers and gender equity: Attitudes and attempted interventions, *Journal of Research in Science Teaching, 33*, 737–51.

Polanyi, M. (1966). *The tacit dimension*. New York: Doubleday.

Polanyi, M. (1976). Tacit knowledge. In M. Marx & F. Goodson (eds), *Theories in contemporary psychology* (pp. 330–44). New York: Macmillan.

Powell, R., Symbaluk, D. & Honey, L. (2008). *Introduction to learning and behaviour* (3rd edn). Belmont, CA: Wadsworth.

Prediger, D. & Johnson, R. (1979). *Alternatives to sex-restrictive vocational interest assessment* (ACT Research Report No. 79). Iowa City, IA: ACT.

QAA (2010) *Quality Assurance Agency benchmark for psychology*. London: Quality Assurance Agency.

Ramey, C. T. & Ramey, S. L. (2004). Early educational interventions and intelligence: Implications for Head Start. In E. Zigler & S. Styfco (eds), *The Head Start debates* (pp. 3–17). Baltimore, MD: Paul H. Brookes.

Ree, M. & Earles, J. (1992). Intelligence is the best predictor of job performance, *Current Directions in Psychological Science, 1*, 86–9.

Reevy, G., Ozer, Y. & Ito, Y. (2010). *Encylopedia of emotion*, Vol. 1. Santa Barbara, CA: ABC-CLIO.

Regan, P. & Atkins, L. (2006). Sex differences and similarities in frequency and intensity of sexual desire, *Social Behavior and Personality, 34*, 95–102.

Reiss, D. (1997). Mechanisms linking genetic and social influences in adolescent development: Beginning a collaborative search, *Current Directions in Psychological Science, 6*, 100–5.

Rettew, D., Zanarini, M., Yen, S., Grilo, C., Skodol, A., Shea, M., McGlashan, T., Morey, L., Culhane, M. & Gunderson, J. (2003). Childhood antecedents of avoidant personality disorder: A retrospective study. *J.Am. Adad. Child Adolesc. Psychiatry, 42*, 1122–30.

Richards, G. (2009). *Psychology: The key concepts*. London: Routledge.

Richardson, K. (1991). *Understanding Intelligence*. Philadelphia: Open University Press.

Riding, R. & Raynor, S. (1998). *Cognitive styles and learning strategies*. London: David Fulton.

Ridley, M. (1999). *Genome: The autobiography of a species in 23 chapters*. London: Fourth Estate.

Riemann, R., Angleitner, A. & Strelau, J. (1997). Genetic and environmental influences on personality: A study of twins reared together using the self- and peer report NEO-FFI scales, *Journal of Personality, 65*, 449–75.

Riemann, R., Grubich, C., Hempel, S., Mergl, S. & Richter, M. (1993). Personality and attitudes towards current political topics, *Personality and Individual Differences, 15,* 313–21.

Ritchhart, R. (2001). From IQ to IC: A dispositional view of intelligence, *Roeper Review, 23,* 143–50.

Roberts, B. (1997). Plaster or plasticity: are adult work experiences associated with personality change in women? *Journal of Personality, 65,* 205–32.

Roberts, B. & Jackson, J. (2008). Sociogenomic personality psychology, *Journal of Personality, 76,* 1523–4.

Robins, R., Fraley, C. & Krueger, R. (2007). *Handbook of research methods in personality psychology.* New York: Guilford Press.

Rodgers, J. (2001). What causes birth order–intelligence patterns? The admixture hypothesis, revived, *American Psychologist, 56,* 599–612.

Rodgers, J., Harrington, C., van der Oord, E. and Rowe, D. (2000). Resolving the debate over birth order, family size, and intelligence, *American Psychologist, 55,* 599–612.

Rogers, C. (1961). *On becoming a person.* Boston, MA: Houghton Mifflin.

Rosenman, R., Brand, R., Jenkins, C., Friedman, M., Straus, R. & Wurm, M. (1975). Coronary heart disease in the Western Collaborative Group Study: Final follow-up experiences of 81/2 years, *JAMA, 233,* 872–7.

Rosenthal, R. (1990). How are we doing in soft psychology? *American Psychologist, 45,* 775–7.

Rosenthal, R. & Rosnow, R. (1991). *Essentials of behavioral research: Methodology and data analysis* (2nd edn). New York: McGraw-Hill.

Rotter, J. (1966). Generalized expectancies for internal versus external control of reinforcement, *Psychological Monographs: General and Applied, 80,* 1–28.

Rotter, J. (1982). *The development and application of social learning theory.* New York: Praeger.

Runco, M. (2004). Creativity, *Annual Review of Psychology, 55,* 657–87.

Rushton, J. (1985). Differential K theory: The sociobiology of individual and group differences, *Personality and Individual Differences, 6,* 441–52.

Rushton, J. & Ankney, C. (1996). Brain size and cognitive ability: Correlations with age, sex, social class, and race, *Psychonomic Bulletin and Review, 3,* 21–36.

Rychlak, J. (1988). *The psychology of rigorous humanism* (2nd edn). New York: New York University Press.

Salovey, P. & Mayer, J. (1990). Emotional intelligence, *Imagination, Cognition and Personality, 9,* 185–211.

Saucier, G. (1994). Mini-Markers: A brief version of Goldberg's Unipolar Big-Five Markers, *Journal of Personality Assessment, 63,* 506–16.

Saucier, G. & Goldberg, L. (1996). The language of personality: Lexical perspectives on the five-factor model. In J. Wiggins, (ed.), *The Five-Factor Model of Personality* (pp. 21–50). New York: Guilford Press.

Saucier, G. & Goldberg, L. (2001). Lexical studies of indigenous personality factors: Premises, products and prospects, *Journal of Personality, 69,* 847–79.

Saulsman, L. & Page, A. (2004). The five-factor model and personality disorder empirical literature: A meta-analytic review, *Clinical Psychology Review, 23,* 1055–85.

Scarr, S. (1981). *Race, social class and individual differences in IQ.* Mahwah, NJ: Erlbaum.

Scarr, S. (1992). Developmental theories for the 1990s: Development and individual differences, *Child Development, 63,* 1–19.

Schneider, B. (1992). Multidimensional health locus of control as partial predictor of serum phosphorus in chronic hemodialysis, *Psychological Reports, 70,* 1171–4.

Schnoll, R., Martinez, E., Tatum, K., Glass, M., Bernath, A., Ferris, D. & Reynolds, P. (2011). Increased self-efficacy to quit and perceived control over withdrawal symptoms predict smoking cessation following nicotine dependence treatment, *Addictive Behaviours, 36(1–2),* 144–7.

Schützwohl, A. & Koch, S. (2004). Sex differences in jealousy: The recall of cues to sexual and emotional infidelity in personally more and less threatening context conditions, *Evolution and Human Behavior*, *25*, 249–57.

Schwartz, C., Wright, C., Shin, L., Kagan, J. & Rauch, S. (2003). Inhibited and uninhibited children 'grown up': Amygdalar responses to novelty, *Science*, *300(5627)*, 1952–3.

Schwartz, S. (1992). Universals in the content and structure of values: Theoretical advances and empirical tests in 20 countries. In M. Zanna (ed.), *Advances in experimental social psychology*, Vol. 25 (pp. 1–65). New York: Academic Press.

Schwartz, S. (1994). Are there universal aspects in the structure and contents of human values? *Journal of Social Issues*, *50*, 19–45.

Segal, N. (1997). Same-age unrelated siblings: A unique test of within-family environmental influences on IQ similarity, *Journal of Educational Psychology*, *89*, 381–90.

Serpell, R. (2001). Intelligence and culture. In R. Sternberg (ed.), *Handbook of intelligence* (pp. 549–77). Cambridge: Cambridge University Press.

Shekelle, R., Gale, M. & Norusis, M. (1985). Type A score (Jenkins Activity Survey) and risk of recurrent coronary heart disease in the Aspirin Myocardial Infarction Study, *American Journal of Cardiology*, *56*, 221–5.

Sherman, R., Nave, C. & Funder, D. (2010). Situational similarity and personality predict behavioral consistency, *Journal of Personality and Social Psychology*, *99*, 330–43.

Shoda, Y., Mischel, W. & Wright, J. (1993). The role of situational demands and cognitive competencies in behaviour organization and personality coherence, *Journal of Personality and Social Psychology*, *65*, 1023–35.

Shoda, Y., Mischel, W. & Wright, J. (1994). Intraindividual stability in the organization and patterning of behavior: Incorporating psychological situations into idiographic analysis of personality, *Journal of Personality and Social Psychology*, *67*, 674–87.

Shontz, F. (1975). *The psychological aspects of physical illness and disability*. New York: Macmillan.

Shouksmith, G. (1973). *Intelligence, creativity, and cognitive style*. London: Angus & Robertson.

Shute, V. & Glaser, R. (1990). A large-scale evaluation of an intelligence discovery world: Smithtown, *Interactive Learning Environments*, *1*, 51–77.

Shweder, R. & Sullivan, M. (1993). Cultural psychology: Who needs it?, *Annual Review of Psychology*, *44*, 497–523.

Siever, L. & Davis, K. (1991). The pathogenesis of mood disorders. In K. Davis and H. Klar (eds), *Foundations of psychiatry* (pp. 254–62). Philadelphia: Saunders.

Sizkmund, W. & Babin, B. (2005). *Exploring market research* (9th edn). Mason, OH: Thomson.

Skinner, B. (1938). *The behavior of organisms*. New York: Appleton-Century-Crofts.

Skinner, B. (1948). *Walden Two*. New York: Macmillan.

Skinner, B. (1953). *Science and human behavior,* New York: Macmillan.

Skinner, B. (1971). *Beyond freedom and dignity*. New York: Knopf.

Skinner, B. (1972). *Cumulative record: A selection of papers* (3rd edn). New York: Appleton-Century-Crofts.

Skinner, B. (1976). *About behaviorism*. New York: Vintage.

Smillie, L. D., Cooper, A., Proitsi, P., Powell, J. F. & Pickering, A. (2010). Variation in DRD2 dopamine gene predicts extraverted personality, *Neuroscience Letters*, *468*, 234–7.

Smith, D., Durkin, M., Hinton, V., Bellinger, D. & Kuhn, L. (2003). Influence of breastfeeding on cognitive outcomes at age 6–8 years: Follow-up of very low birth weight infants, *American Journal of Epidemiology*, *158*, 1075–82.

Spearman, C. (1904) 'General Intelligence', objectively determined and measured, *American Journal of Psychology*, *15*, 201–92.

Spearman, C. (1927). *The abilities of man: Their nature and measurement*. New York: Macmillan.

Stankov, L., Boyle, G. & Cattell, R. (1995). Models and paradigms in personality and intelligence research. In D. Saklofske & M. Zeidner (eds), *International handbook of personality and intelligence: Perspectives on individual differences* (pp. 15–43). New York: Plenum Press.

Stelmack, R. (1990). Biological basis of extraversion: Psychophysiological evidence, *Journal of Personality, 58*, 293–311.

Steptoe, A. & Wardle, J. (2001). Locus of control and health behaviour revisited: A multivariate analysis of young adults from 18 countries, *British Journal of Psychology, 92*, 659–72.

Stern, W. (1912). *Die Psychologische Methoden der Intelligenz-Prüfung.* Barth: Leipzig.

Sternberg, R. (1985). *Beyond IQ: A triarchic theory of human intelligence.* New York: Cambridge University Press.

Sternberg, R. (1988). A triarchic theory of intellectual giftedness. In R. Sternberg & J. E. Davidson (eds), *Conceptions of giftedness.* Cambridge: Cambridge University Press.

Sternberg, R. (1993). Sternberg Triarchic Abilities Test (STAT), unpublished test.

Sternberg, R. (1994). Thinking styles. In. R. Sternberg & P. Ruzigis (eds), *Personality and intelligence.* Cambridge: Cambridge University Press.

Sternberg, R. (1997a). *Successful intelligence*, New York: Plume.

Sternberg, R. (1997b). The concept of intelligence and its role in lifelong learning and success, *American Psychologist, 52*, 1030–7.

Sternberg, R. & O'Hara, L. (2000). Intelligence and creativity. In. R. Sternberg (ed.), *Handbook of intelligence* (pp. 611–30). New York: Cambridge University Press.

Sternberg, R., Castejón, J., Prieto, M., Hautamäki, J. & Grigorenko, E. (2001). Confirmatory factor analysis of the Sternberg Triarchic Abilities Test in three international samples: An empirical test of the triarchic theory of intelligence, *European Journal of Psychological Assessment, 17*, 1–16.

Sternberg, R., Forsythe, G., Hedlund, J., Horvath, J., Wagner, R., Williams, W., Snook, S. & Grigorenko, E. (2000). *Practical intelligence in everyday life.* Cambridge: Cambridge University Press.

Stuart, K., Borland, R. & McMurray, N. (1994). Self-efficacy, health locus of control, and smoking cessation, *Addictive Behaviors, 19*, 1–12.

Tenenbaum, G. & Bar-Eli, M. (2007). Personality and intellectual abilities in sport psychology. In D. Smith & M. Bar-Eli (eds), *Essential readings in sport and exercise psychology.* Leeds: Human Kinetics.

Thurstone, L. (1934). The vectors of mind, *Psychological Review, 41*, 1–32.

Thurstone, L. (1935). *The vectors of the mind: Multiple-factor analysis for the isolation of primary traits.* Chicago: University of Chicago Press.

Thurstone, L. (1938). Primary mental abilities, *Psychometric Monographs, 1*, ix–121.

Tolman, E. (1948). Cognitive maps in rats and men, *Psychological Review, 55*, 189–208.

Torgersen, S., Lygren, S., Oien, P., Skre, L., Onstad, S., Edvardsen, J. et al. (2000). A twin study of personality disorders, *Comprehensive Psychiatry, 41*, 416–25.

Trapnell, P. (1996). Openness versus intellect: A lexical left turn, *European Journal of Personality, 8*, 273–90.

Triandis, H. (1997). Cross-cultural perspectives on personality. In R. Hogan, A. Johnson & S. Briggs (eds), *Handbook of personality psychology* (pp. 439–65). London: Academic Press.

Turkheimer, E. & Waldron, M. C. (2000). Nonshared environment: A theoretical, methodological and quantitative review, *Psychological Bulletin, 126*, 78–108.

Tyrer, P., Duggan, C., Cooper, S., Craword, M., Seivewright, H., Rutter, D., Maden, T., Byford, S. & Barrett, B. (2010). The successes and failures of the DSPD experiment: The assessment and management of severe personality disorder, *Medicine, Science and the Law, 50*, 95–9.

Van Hiel, A. & Mervielde, I. (1996). The Five-Factor Model personality dimensions and current political beliefs: An empirical update in a non-student sample. Unpublished manuscript.

Vernon, P. E. (1950). *The structure of human abilities.* London: Methuen.

Vernon, P. (1961). *The structure of human abilities* (2nd edn), London: Methuen.

Vernon, P. E. (1979). *Intelligence: Heredity and environment.* San Francisco: W. H. Freeman & Co.

Verona, E., Patrick, C. & Joiner, T. (2001). Psychopathy, antisocial personality, and suicide risk, *Journal of Abnormal Psychology*, *110*, 462–70.

Vig, S. (2009). Classification versus labelling. In J. Jacobson, R. Foxx & J. Mulick (eds), *Controversial therapies for developmental disabilities: fad, fashion, and science in professional practice*. Mahwah, NJ: Erlbaum.

Wagner, R. K. & Sternberg, R. J. (1989). Tacit knowledge inventory for sales: Written. Unpublished test.

Waller, N. (1999). Evaluating the structure of personality. In C. Cloninger (ed.), *Personality and psychopathology* (pp. 155–97). Washington, DC: American Psychiatric Association.

Wallston, K. & Wallston, B. (1982). Who is responsible for your health: The construct of health locus of control. In G. Sanders & J. Suls (eds), *Social psychology of health and illness* (pp. 65–95). Hillsdale, NJ: Erlbaum.

Walton, D. & Roberts, B. (2004). On the relationship between substance use and personality traits: Abstainers are not maladjusted, *Journal of Research in Personality*, *38*, 515–35.

Watson, J. (1913). Psychology as the behaviorists view it, *Psychological Review*, *20*, 158–77.

Watson, J. (1927). *Behaviourism*. New Jersey: Transaction.

Watson, J. & Rayner, R. (1920). Conditioned emotional reactions, *Journal of Experimental Psychology*, *3*, 1–14.

Wechsler, D. (2008). Wechsler Adult Intelligence Scale: Technical and interpretive manual (4th edn), San Antonio, TX: Pearson.

Weiner, I. & Craighead, W. (2010). *The Corsini encyclopedia of psychology*, vol. 2, Hoboken, NJ: John Wiley.

Weller, H., Repman, J., Lan, W. & Rooze, G. (1995). Improving the effectiveness of learning through hypermedia-based instruction: The importance of learner characteristics, Special Issue: Hypermedia: Theory, research, and application, *Computers in Human Behavior*, *11*, 451–65.

Westen, D. (1997). Divergences between clinical and research methods for assessing personality disorders: Implications for research and the evolution of Axis II, *American Journal of Psychiatry*, *154*, 895–903.

Westen, D. (1998). The scientific legacy of Sigmund Freud: Toward a psychodynamically informed psychological science, *Psychological Bulletin*, *124*, 333–71.

Westen, D., Novotny, C. & Thompson-Brenner, H. (2004). The empirical status of empirically supported psychotherapies: Assumptions, findings, and reporting in controlled clinical trials, *Psychological Bulletin*, *130*, 631–63.

Westman, M. (1990). The relationships between stress and performance: The moderating effects of hardiness, *Human Performance*, *3*, 141–55.

Widiger, T. & Samuel, D. (2005). Evidence-based assessment of personality disorders, *Psychological Assessment*, *17*, 278–87.

Wiebe, R. (2004). Delinquent behavior and the Five-Factor Model: Hiding in the adaptive landscape? *Individual Differences Research*, *2*, 38–62.

Wiggins, J. (1979). A psychological taxonomy of trait-descriptive terms: I. The interpersonal domain, *Journal of Personality and Social Psychology*, *37*, 395–412.

Willerman, L. (1979). Effects of families on intellectual development, *American Psychologist*, *34*, 923–9.

Wilson, G. (1975). *Manual for the Wilson–Patterson Attitude Inventory*. Windsor: NFER.

Witkin, H. (1964). Origins of cognitive style. In C. Sheerer (ed.), *Cognition: Theory, research, promise*. New York: Harper and Row.

Witkin, H. (1977). Role of the field-dependent and field-independent cognitive styles in academic evolution: A longitudinal study, *Journal of Educational Psychology*, *69*, 197–211.

Witkin, H., & Goodenough, D. (1977). Field dependence and interpersonal behavior, *Psychological Bulletin*, *84*, 661–89.

Witkin, H., Lewis, H., Hertzman, M., Machover, K., Meissner, P. & Wapner, S. (1954). *Personality through perception: An experimental and clinical study*, New York: Harper.

Witkin, H., Moore, C., Oltman, P., Goodenough, D., Friedman, F., Owen, D. & Raskin, E. (1977). Role of the field-dependent and field-independent cognitive styles in academic evolution: A longitudinal study, *Journal of Educational Psychology, 69*, 197–211.

Witkin, H. A., Oltman, P. K., Raskin, E. & Karp, S. A. (1971). *A manual for the embedded figures tests*. Palo Alto, CA: Consulting Psychologists Press.

World Health Organization (2011). *The ICD-10 classification of mental and behavioural disorders*. Geneva: World Health Organization Press.

Zajonc, R. (1976). Family configuration and intelligence: Variations in scholastic aptitude scores parallel trends in family size and the spacing of children, *Science, 192*, 227–36.

Zajonc, R. (2001). The family dynamics of intellectual development, *American Psychologist, 56*, 490–6.

Zajonc, R. & Markus, H. (1975). Birth order and intellectual development, *Psychological Review, 82*, 74–88.

Zanarini, M. & Frankenberg, F. (1997). Pathways to the development of borderline personality disorder, *Journal of Personality Disorders, 14*, 18–25.

Zimmerman, M. & Coryell, W. (1989). The reliability of personality disorder diagnoses in a non-patient sample, *Journal of Personality Disorders, 3*, 53–7.

Zuckerman, M. (2006). Biosocial bases of sensation seeking. In T. Canli (ed.), *Biology of personality and individual differences* (pp. 37–59). New York: Guilford Press.

Index

Terms in **bold** refer to glossary entries